JOHN WESLEY'S TEACHINGS

Also by Thomas C. Oden

John Wesley's Teachings, Volume 1

John Wesley's Teachings, Volume 2

John Wesley's Teachings, Volume 3

John Wesley's Teachings, Volume 4

VOLUME 2

CHRIST AND SALVATION

JOHN WESLEY'S TEACHINGS

THOMAS C. ODEN

ZONDERVAN.com/
AUTHORTRACKER
follow your favorite authors

ZONDERVAN

John Wesley's Teachings, Volume 2

This title is also available as a Zondervan ebook. Visit www.zondervan.com/ebooks.

Requests for information should be addressed to:

Zondervan, *Grand Rapids, Michigan 49530*

Library of Congress Cataloging-in-Publication Data

Oden, Thomas C.
John Wesley's teachings / Thomas C. Oden.
v. cm.
Rev. ed. of: John Wesley's scriptural Christianity. c1994.
Includes bibliographical references and indexes.
Contents: v. 1. God and providence— v. 2. Christ and salvation— v. 3. The practice of pastoral care— v. 4. Issues of ethics and society.
ISBN 978-0-310-49267-2 (softcover)
1. Wesley, John, 1703-1791. 2. Theology, Doctrinal. 3. Methodist Church—Doctrines. 4. Theology, Doctrinal—History—18th century. 5. Methodist Church—Doctrines—History—18th century. I. Oden, Thomas C. John Wesley's scriptural Christianity. II. Title.
BX8331.3.O35 2012
230'.7092—dc23 2012001655

Cover design: John Hamilton Design
Cover image: Corbis® Images
Interior design: Beth Shagene
Edited by Katya Covrett and Laura Dodge Weller

Printed in the United States of America

---

14 15 16 17 18 19 /DCI/ 24 23 22 21 20 19 18 17 16 15 14 13 12 11 10 9 8 7 6 5 4 3 2

With immense gratitude for my closest colleagues:

Christopher A. Hall, Michael Glerup, and Joel C. Elowsky—
fellow editors for over twenty years in envisioning,
writing, and producing together these fifty volumes:

The Ancient Christian Commentary on Scripture Series

The Ancient Christian Doctrine Series

The Ancient Christian Texts Series

The Early African Christianity Series

Contents

Preface

This is a reader's guide to John Wesley's teaching on Christology and soteriology. This second volume introduces his thought on the basic tenets of Christian teaching on Christ and salvation, justification, faith, the Holy Spirit, grace, predestination, regeneration, sanctification, sin in believers, divine judgment, and new creation.

It follows arguments set forth in volume 1, *God and Providence*. It will be followed by studies on the practice of pastoral care and ethics.

These expositions present a plain account of Wesley's works, with constant citation from Wesley's own texts. My goal is to convey the core argument of all major and most minor texts of John Wesley in the most concise way.

Wesley left behind an enormous corpus of literature. This vast body includes 151 teaching homilies; six decades of journals (1735 – 91); manuscript diaries (now published); and eight volumes of letters, essays, doctrinal tracts, occasional writings, and prefaces. The untold numbers of hymns were mostly written by John's brother Charles but edited by John. In this volume, I seek to deliver to the nonprofessional reader the gist of Wesley's patrimony on Christology and soteriology. While it cannot claim to be comprehensive, it seeks to include core insights from all of these varied genres of literature.

In 1994 Zondervan published my earlier study of Wesley's doctrine under the title *John Wesley's Scriptural Christianity: A Plain Exposition of His Teaching on Christian Doctrine* (*JWSC*). In this present edition, much of the content of that single volume is now expanded and extensively revised, quadrupling the content of the earlier single volume.

Tracking References to the Major Editions

The preferred scholarly edition for Wesley is the Oxford/Abingdon Bicentennial edition, *The Works of John Wesley* (Oxford: 1975 – 83; Nashville: 1984 –), signified by B.[1]

The most frequently reproduced edition, often still the only one appearing on library and pastoral bookshelves, is the Thomas Jackson edition, first published in

[1] In rare cases where Sugden's edition of the Standard Sermons (see Abbreviations: *SS*) is quoted, the reader's attention is directed especially to his annotations.

1829 – 31, signified by J for Jackson. Thus, whenever B or J appears in the footnotes, the reader is being directed to either the Bicentennial edition (B) or the Jackson edition (J). This is necessary, because the reader may have access to one but not both editions. Many more copies of the Jackson edition have been distributed than the Bicentennial edition.

Here are the key guidelines for the scholarly apparatus:

- Volume references in Arabic numerals refer to the Bicentennial edition. Volume references in uppercase Roman numerals refer to the Jackson edition.
- Both the Bicentennial edition (B) and the Jackson edition (J) are available in searchable CD-ROMs or online. In the case of B, the current disk is still incomplete, awaiting print publication of many volumes.
- Distinguishing a B reference from a J reference is easy: If the first digit is an Arabic numeral, the reference is to B. If the first digit is an uppercase Roman numeral, the reference is to J. A reference to B 4:133 indicates the Bicentennial edition, volume 4, page 133. But a reference to J IV:133 indicates the Jackson edition, volume 4 (IV), page 133.
- In cases where a new homily is being introduced in order to be discussed more fully, I have referenced in parentheses the Bicentennial edition (B) in this conventional order: the homily number, the date of the homily, and the volume and page references in the Bicentennial edition. Where the Jackson edition (J) is referenced, I have listed the homily number and the volume and page references in Jackson.
- At times the homily numbers appear in a different order and number in the Bicentennial than in the Jackson edition.[2]

My purpose is to assist those who wish to access handily the proper text in the available edition. Readers will more frequently be working out of either J or B but ordinarily not both. For convenience, I cite both editions. An appendix titled Alphabetical Correlation of the Sermons in the Jackson and Bicentennial Editions can be found at the back of all volumes. Those who are doing scholarly research work are advised to work with the Bicentennial edition whenever possible.

[2] "The Trouble and Rest of Good Men" appears as Sermon 109 in the Bicentennial edition (#109) and as Sermon 127 in the Jackson edition (J #127). The numbering is often the same but in some instances different.

Abbreviations

ACCS	*The Ancient Christian Commentary on Scripture.* Edited by Thomas C. Oden. 29 volumes. Downers Grove, IL: InterVarsity, 1997–2010.
AHR	*American Historical Review.*
AM	*Arminian Magazine.*
art.	article.
AS	*Asbury Seminarian.*
B	Bicentennial edition of *The Works of John Wesley.* Edited by Frank Baker and Richard Heitzenrater. Oxford: Clarendon, and New York: Oxford University Press, 1975–83; Nashville: Abingdon, 1984–; in print: volumes 1, 2, 3, 4, 7, 18, 19, 20, 21, 22, 23, 24.
BCP	Book of Common Prayer.
BETS	*Bulletin of the Evangelical Theological Society.*
Bull.	Bulletin.
CC	Thomas C. Oden. *Classic Christianity: A Systematic Theology.* San Francisco: HarperOne, 2009.
CCD	"A Clear and Concise Demonstration of the Divine Inspiration of Holy Scripture," J XI: 484.
CH	*A Collection of Hymns for the Use of the People Called Methodists*, vol. 7 of the Bicentennial edition.
Chr.	Christian.
ChrCent	*Christian Century.*
CL	Christian Library.
COC	John Leith. *Creeds of the Churches.* Atlanta: John Knox, 1982.
Confes.	1962 Confession of the Evangelical United Brethren.
CWT	Robert W. Burtner and Robert E. Chiles. *A Compend of Wesley's Theology*. Nashville: Abingdon, 1954.
Diss.	Dissertation.
Div.	Divinity.

DOS *The Doctrine of Original Sin.*

DPF "Dialogue between a Predestinarian and His Friend."

DSF "The Doctrine of Salvation, Faith and Good Works" (extracted from the Edwardian Homilies).

DSWT Thomas C. Oden. *Doctrinal Standards in the Wesleyan Tradition.* Grand Rapids: Zondervan, 1988.

EA "An Earnest Appeal to Men of Reason and Religion."

ENNT *Explanatory Notes upon the New Testament.*

ENOT *Explanatory Notes upon the Old Testament.*

EQ *Evangelical Quarterly.*

ETS Evangelical Theological Society.

Ev. Evangelical.

EWT Paul Mickey. *Essentials of Wesleyan Theology*. Grand Rapids: Zondervan, 1980.

FA "A Farther Appeal to Men of Reason and Religion."

FAP Francis Asbury Press, Zondervan.

FB Howard Slaate. *Fire in the Brand.* New York: Exposition, 1963.

FW Kenneth Collins. *A Faithful Witness: John Wesley's Homiletical Theology*. Wilmore, KY: Wesleyan Heritage, 1993.

FWAT Mildred Bangs Wynkoop. *Foundations of Wesleyan-Arminian Theology*. Kansas City: Beacon Hill, 1967.

HSP Charles Wesley and John Wesley. *Hymns and Sacred Poems.*

Institutes John Calvin. *Institutes of the Christian Religion.* Philadelphia: John Knox, 1962.

Int *Interpretation — Journal of Bible and Theology.*

J Jackson edition of Wesley's Works. Edited by Thomas Jackson, 1829 – 32. 1872 edition reprinted in many 14-volume American editions (Eerdmans, Zondervan, Christian Book Distributors, et al.); digitally available on Wesley.nnu.edu.

JBR *Journal of Bible and Religion.*

JJW *The Journal of John Wesley*. Edited by N. Curnock. 8 vols. London: Epworth, 1916.

Jnl. Journal.

JTS *Journal of Theological Studies.*

JWO *John Wesley*. Edited by Albert C. Outler. Library of Protestant Theology. New York: Oxford University Press, 1964.

JWPH Robert Monk. *John Wesley: His Puritan Heritage*. Nashville: Abingdon, 1966.

JWSC Thomas C. Oden. *John Wesley's Scriptural Christianity: A Plain Exposition of His Teaching on Christian Doctrine*. Grand Rapids: Zondervan, 1994.

JWTT Colin Williams. *John Wesley's Theology Today*. Nashville: Abingdon, 1960.

KJV King James Version.

LCM "Letter to the Rev. Dr. Conyers Middleton."

LJW *Letters of John Wesley*. Edited by John Telford. 8 vols. London: Epworth, 1931.

LLBL "A Letter to the Right Reverend Lord Bishop of London."

LPC "Letter on Preaching Christ" (same as "Letter to an Evangelical Layman," December 20, 1751).

LQHR *London Quarterly and Holborn Review.*

LS Thomas C. Oden. *Life in the Spirit*. San Francisco: HarperSanFrancisco, 1992.

Mag. Magazine.

Meth. Methodist.

MH *Methodist History.*

Minutes "Minutes of Some Late Conversations between the Rev. Mr. Wesley and Others."

MLS *Martin Luther: Selections from his Writings*. Edited by John Dillenberger. New York: Doubleday, 1961.

MM *Methodist Magazine.*

MOB William M. Arnett. "John Wesley: Man of One Book." PhD dissertation. Drew University, 1954.

MPL *Patrologia Latina*. Edited by J. P. Migne. Patrologiae Cursus Completus. Paris: Series Graeca, 1857 – 66; Series Latina, 1878 – 90.

MQR *Methodist Quarterly Review.*

MR *Methodist Review.*

NDM Reinhold Niebuhr. *The Nature and Destiny of Man*. 2 vols. New York: Scribner, 1941, 1943.

NRSV New Revised Standard Version.

NT New Testament.

OED *Oxford English Dictionary.*

OT Old Testament.

PACP *A Plain Account of Christian Perfection.*

PCC "Predestination Calmly Considered."

PM *Preacher's Magazine.*

Pref. Preface.

Publ. Publishing, Publishers.

PW *Poetical Works of Charles Wesley and John Wesley*. Edited by George Osborn. 13 vols. London: Wesleyan Methodist Conference, 1868 – 72.

PWHS *Proceedings of the Wesleyan Historical Society.*

Q Question.

QR *Quarterly Review.*

RC Roman Catholic.

RE Henry Rack. *Reasonable Enthusiast.* London: Epworth, 1989.

RJW George Croft Cell. *The Rediscovery of John Wesley*. New York: Henry Holt, 1935.

RL *Religion in Life.*

SDC *Sources of Christian Dogma* (Enchiridion Symbolorum). Edited by Henry Denzinger. Translated by R. Deferrari. New York: Herder, 1954.

SS *The Standard Sermons of John Wesley*. Edited by E. H. Sugden. 2 vols. London: Epworth, 1921; 3rd ed., 1951.

SSM *Sunday Service of the Methodists of the United States of America* (1784). Edited by Edward C. Hobbs. Nashville: Methodist Student Movement, 1956.

TCNT Twentieth Century New Testament.

Theo. Theological.

TIRC "Thoughts on the Imputation of the Righteousness of Christ."

TJW William R. Cannon. *Theology of John Wesley: With Special Reference to the Doctrine of Justification*. New York: Abingdon, 1946.

TSF "Thoughts on Salvation by Faith."

TUN "Thoughts upon Necessity."

UMC United Methodist Church.

unpubl. Unpublished.

WC John Deschner. *Wesley's Christology*. Grand Rapids: Zondervan, 1989.

WHS Lycurgus M. Starkey. *The Work of the Holy Spirit*. Nashville: Abingdon, 1962.

WL Thomas C. Oden. *The Word of Life.* Systematic Theology. Vol. 2. San Francisco: HarperSanFrancisco, 1988.

WMM *Wesleyan Methodist Magazine.*

WQ Donald Thorsen. *The Wesleyan Quadrilateral.* Grand Rapids: Zondervan, 1990.

WQR *Wesleyan Quarterly Review*

WRE John W. Prince. *Wesley on Religious Education*. New York: Methodist Book Concern, 1926.

WS Harald G. A. Lindström. *Wesley and Sanctification*. Nashville: Abingdon, 1946.

WTH Albert C. Outler. *The Wesleyan Theological Heritage: Essays*. Edited by Thomas C. Oden and Leicester Longden. Grand Rapids: Zondervan, 1991.

WTJ *Wesleyan Theological Journal*.

XXV Twenty-Five Articles. Adapted from the Sunday Service of 1784.

XXXIX Anglican Thirty-Nine Articles of Religion.

Introduction

A. The Teaching Homily as Christian Doctrine

In his address to readers of his collected works of 1771, Wesley made a preliminary attempt at a rough sequential organization of his instructional homilies: "I wanted to methodize these tracts, *to [ar]range them under proper heads*, placing those together which were on similar subjects, and in such order that one might illustrate another.... There is *scarce any subject of importance, either in practical or controversial divinity, which is not treated* of more or less, either professedly or occasionally."[1] Wesley's own careful ordering of his work is the systematic design we will build on.

1. The Scope of Wesley's Teaching

No major Christian doctrine is neglected in Wesley's teaching. Key classic teaching topics are treated with remarkable internal consistency. My objective is to set forth the implicit inner cohesion of these diverse points of Wesley's teaching.

There is an intuitive sense of order in this wide range of homilies and essays. My task is to organize Wesley's teaching in a sequence natural to his own design and consistent with the classic Christian tradition to which he appealed. Wesley did not invent this systematic sequence. He was the grateful inheritor of the well-known order of salvation in ancient Christian teaching. This order can be seen implicitly in the Council of Nicaea and in the consensus-bearing texts of Cyril of Jerusalem, John of Damascus, Thomas Aquinas, and John Calvin. Among Anglican divines, it is prominent in Thomas Cranmer, John Jewel, and John Pearson.

I will show that the whole range of classic loci (points of theology) appears in Wesley's large body of writings, but they are not easily recognized as a systematic whole because of the nature of the teaching homily, which focused on a single text of sacred Scripture. Only in a few of these loci, notably original sin and the way of salvation, are these dealt with at great length historically and systematically.

Wesley's intent was not to write a comprehensive ecclesial theology such as that

[1]"Preface to the Third Edition," J I:3, in a brief address "To the Reader" in the thirty-two duodecima volumes of 1774, italics added.

of Richard Hooker or a commentary on the creed, such as John Pearson before him, but to speak plainly to his connection[2] of spiritual formation on all major themes of Christian teaching.

2. The Teaching Homily

Wesley taught his connection by published homilies. The earliest of these were collected and frequently published as his Standard Sermons (in various editions numbering forty-eight, fifty-two, and fifty-three).

The way Christian doctrine was taught by eighteenth-century Anglican divines was through published teaching sermons, not rococo tomes on specific doctrines. Wesley was born and bred in this Anglican centrist tradition of homiletic instruction.

The notion of an established, reliably transmitted book of homilies was a familiar pattern of the English church tradition (following Thomas Cranmer, Lancelot Andrewes, John Jewel, and Matthew Parker), where it referred to a collection of prepared thematic teaching sermons designed to instruct congregations on received Christian doctrine.[3] Wesley followed this two-hundred-year Anglican tradition by modestly offering his own tutorial homilies to those in his direct connection of spiritual formation.[4]

3. The Whole Compass of Divinity

We do not have from Wesley's hand, as from Calvin or Suarez or Melanchthon, a definitive systematic theology in the sense of a comprehensive and sequential organization of the topics of theology. With Wesley what we have are occasional instructional homilies, many preached numerous times on his lengthy journeys through England, Scotland, and Ireland. Though not organized as systematic theology, they were designed for standard doctrinal instruction, published for future reference, and clearly intended to inform the entire curriculum of evangelical studies on the "whole compass of divinity."[5]

Among the charges made against Wesley in his lifetime,[6] which he answered in detail, was the indictment by Roland Hill, who thought that he remained "absolutely

---

[2]The British archaic spelling, *connexion*, is dear to astute insiders. It is rarely in use except among traditional British Methodists. Because it appears awkward to modern readers, we will not insist on the archaic form.

[3]*LJW* 1:305, 312; 3:382; 4:125 – 26, 379 – 81; JWO 119 – 33, 204 – 6, 417; FA, B 11:175, cf. 279. See also John Cosin and Jeremy Taylor.

[4]The root word of *homily* is *homos*, the same root from which our terms *homogeneity*, *homogenize*, and *homoousian* come. A *homilios* is an assembly, and a *homilia* is an intentional, reflective, deliberate, considered instruction to gathered hearers. Since so many have a distasteful aversion to the very word *sermon*, tarred by a long history of browbeating, legalistic emotivism, I prefer the more descriptive term "teaching homily" as a contemporary dynamic equivalent. Cf. Collins, *FW* 11 – 14.

[5]*LJW* 4:181; 5:326.

[6]Among other complaints, he was charged with contradictions and inconsistencies, B 9:56, 375; evasions, B 9:374 – 75; and hypocrisy, B 9:304.

unsettled with regard to every fundamental doctrine of the gospel," and that "no two disputants in the Schools can be more opposite to each other than he is to himself."[7] Wesley wrote detailed and amusing responses to critics Roland Hill, Conyers Middleton, and George Lavington to demonstrate the consistency of his teaching over his long life. He defended himself against charges of internal incongruities. He took pains to demonstrate that the supposed discrepancies that others thought they had identified were based on the eighteenth-century reader's hasty misstatement or failure to grasp his intent.[8]

Neither Wesley nor his successors ever issued an edition of his published works deliberately sequenced in the order of standard points of classic systematic theology.[9] Our task is to show the systematic cohesion and range of his homilies and essays. If this task had been undertaken sooner, Wesley might have been earlier acknowledged as a major Protestant thinker rather than as his stereotype of pragmatic organizer so characteristic of nineteenth-century interpreters.

To those who imagine that Wesley lacked a systematic mind,[10] I will show that every major point of classic Christian teaching is addressed in his instructional homilies, supplemented by his essays, journals, prefaces, and letters, with minimal lapses and incongruities.[11] Within the scope of his fifty plus years of writing, Wesley covered virtually every pivotal issue of Christian theology, Christology, soteriology, ecclesiology, pastoral care, and ethics. It is difficult to find any major question of Christian doctrine that he grossly disregarded.

Though there is nothing in Wesley or most other Anglican sources that has the structural appearance of the ponderous dogmatic style of the seventeenth-century Lutheran or Reformed orthodox dogmatics, still no essential article of faith is left unattended, as we will see.[12]

---

[7]Some Remarks of Mr. Hill's "Review of All the Doctrines Taught by Mr. John Wesley," J X:377, quoting Roland Hill.

[8]Some Remarks of Mr. Hill's "Review of All the Doctrines Taught by Mr. John Wesley," J X:381. In response to Hill, Wesley patiently refuted 101 specific arguments arranged under twenty-four heads. As an experienced former teacher of logic, he did not lack confidence that he could "unravel truth and falsehood, although artfully twisted together."

[9]With the swollen footage of Wesley studies in history archives, it is surprising that no previous writer has attempted the task set before us here in this series: a plain exposition of the core arguments of his teaching, explicated text by text in his own words, with an attempt to cover his major writings.

[10]John Deschner, who has written the definitive work on Wesley's Christology, maintains that "Wesley's theology is not a settled system of doctrine, as Calvin's or Schleiermacher's theologies are. It is rather the effort of an energetic mind to organize for popular use the principal element of a message" (*WC* 14). Cf. Albert C. Outler, "John Wesley: Folk-Theologian," *Theology Today* 34 (1977): 150 – 66. The most eminent interpreters of Wesley — G. Cell, A. Outler, T. Langford, J. Deschner, R. Heitzenrater, D. Thorsen — are all uncomfortable with the claim that Wesley was a systematic theologian. They tend to regard it as a stretch of the imagination to view Wesley under the rubric of dogmatician or systematic theological teacher or exacting catechist. My purpose is to show that this is more plausible than usually thought.

[11]*LJW* 5:326.

[12]For doctrinal summaries, see JWO 183 – 85, 386ff.

B. Wesley's Evangelical Connection of Spiritual Formation

1. The Connection

To stand "in Wesley's connection" traditionally has meant that one looks to him for spiritual formation. Hundreds of thousands of believers in the eighteenth and nineteenth centuries stood faithfully within this connection, some with greater or lesser distance. The entire early Methodist movement was voluntarily and personally mentored by this remarkable pastoral guide. He gave himself unreservedly to the pastoral care of thousands in countless English, Irish, Welsh, and Scottish villages, traveling incessantly to serve the interests of their spiritual maturation.

Many today remain obliquely in Wesley's evangelical connection or remnants of it, though more distanced by time and history. Some who remain committed to the churches resulting from his ministry are now asking how they might again be formed by his wisdom, the truth of his message, and the joyful integrity of his outlook. Others not in the Wesleyan family of evangelical churches can benefit by seeing in Wesley a godly leader of special spiritual power.

It is remarkable that persons thoroughly immersed in modern consciousness still seek to reappropriate Wesley's counsel, not only by means of the text of his writings and sermons, but also by attending to the roots from which he drew strength — especially the patristic, Anglican, holy living, and Reformed traditions. Untold numbers of people over the globe have been personally formed by his spirit, even when unaware of it.

2. The Scope of the Wesleyan Connection Today

The family of churches Wesley's ministry spawned is vast and worldwide. It includes not only the eight-million-member United Methodist Church (larger than combined Lutheran and Episcopalian bodies in the United States), but also a conspicuous assortment of worldwide church bodies that have spun off from Methodist and holiness revival preaching.

Chief among these are the Wesleyan Church, the Free Methodist Church, the Church of the Nazarene, the Salvation Army, the African Methodist Episcopal, the AME Zion traditions, and the British Methodists. Even more numerous worldwide are many forms of charismatic and Pentecostal communities that preach entire sanctification, assurance, and holy living. Notably, the African-Instituted Churches Movement in Africa has profuse echoes of Wesley's teaching. Wesley's teaching is among the major prototypes of modern global evangelical theology. No serious account of the history of world evangelical thought could omit Wesley.

C. My Purpose

1. Why I Write on Wesley: A Note on Vocation

A personal vocational memorandum may help some readers to get in touch with my motivation for doing this study.

My vocation since 1970 has been centered on the recovery of classic Christian teaching, especially in its early phases in the patristic period. Over many years, a significant part of that vocation has been teaching candidates for ordination in this tradition. This has extended into providing scholarly resources for the larger Wesleyan family of churches, and evangelicals generally, especially those seeking to recover their vital historic roots.

This is why I write. It is not merely an incidental part of my vocation, nor disrelated to that aspect of my vocation that has focused in recent years on postmodern orthodoxy and classical consensual Christianity.[13]

In the 1980s and early 1990s, I worked steadily on a systematic theology that was grounded in classic, historic Christian teaching. That three-volume work has now been thoroughly revised in a one-volume edition titled *Classic Christianity: A Systematic Theology* (San Francisco: HarperCollins, 2009). Since 1979 I have earnestly pledged to my readers that I intend to propose nothing original as if it might be some improvement on apostolic teaching and its early exegesis.

After seventeen years of editing the *Ancient Christian Commentary on Scripture,* focused on patristic texts,[14] I turn again to the same tree of classic Christianity in its eighteenth-century evangelical form. Its modern expression is the community of faith into which I was born, baptized, and ordained. Many years after I was ordained, I was reborn into this faith.

I want to show how a particular branch of that patristic tradition, Wesleyan theology, has grown out of the same root of ancient ecumenical teaching. Wesley's eighteenth-century movement corresponds closely with classic fourth-century consensus Christian teaching. Wesley's teaching springs out of what he called, in lowercase, the catholic spirit.[15]

I do not see these two tasks — patristic exegesis and Wesleyan preaching — as conflicted, but complementary. Both projects are close to the center of my vocation:

[13]As one who grew up on the prairie with the dust of the Oklahoma plains still my most familiar environment, I have for three and a half decades been teaching in the New York area. Working in the shadow of the prototype international cosmopolis, I find myself located by ordination in the heart of Protestantism's second-largest denomination, teaching in one of its leading academic institutions. Inwardly this feels to me to be some sort of hidden providence beyond mere human artifice, placing on me a weighty challenge. It is both an opportunity and a challenge to remain faithful both to Wesley and to Wesley's current organizational elites.

[14]*Ancient Christian Commentary on Scripture,* ed. Thomas C. Oden, 29 vols. (Downers Grove, IL: InterVarsity, 1993 – 2010).

[15]I promised my readers in my systematic theology that I would not foist off Arminian or Wesleyan or even Protestant thinking. I pledge nothing new that would pretend to override the wisdom of classic Christianity. In these volumes I continue that pledge.

the rediscovery of ancient ecumenical theology, and the recovery of classical Christianity within my own evolving Wesleyan tradition.[16] This correlation has been neglected in the secondary literature. Many of Wesley's ultramodern interpreters are focused on accommodating Wesley in ways congenial to contemporary audiences. Some have entirely recast Wesley in terms of liberation theology or process theology or gender studies in a way that leaves Wesley himself only vaguely recognizable. My mission is to let him speak for himself in his own language to modern believers.

2. Clear Exposition

Rather than squeezing the thought of the texts into a preconceived systematic order of theological points, I am here asking what order the texts themselves demand. This way of ordering the sequence of the texts is more inductive than deductive. I begin with the texts and ask how they fall into a sequence natural to themselves. The sequence is determined far more by Wesley's own guidelines in his teaching homilies and in his own reasoning and language than by a set of predisposing topics imposed on the texts.

Two reference points are constantly correlated in what follows: the text itself, written for an eighteenth-century audience, and our contemporary language situation to which I believe the text still speaks. My aim is to offer a present-day interpretation and exposition of Wesley's teaching in contemporary language, deliberately seeking to be expressly accountable to his own text.

If the method is inductively expository, its inherent order is instinctively systematic. My modest task is merely to arrange and explicate Wesley's texts in the prevailing classic order of the ancient Christian writers, but with the special imprint of Wesley's own priorities, colloquialisms, idioms, and predilections.[17] By "classic order" I mean the chain of theological reasoning generally found in the tradition from Irenaeus and Cyril of Jerusalem through John of Damascus and Thomas Aquinas to John Calvin and John Pearson.[18]

3. Adhering to Primary Sources

I have deliberately focused on primary sources in this study, leaving it to others, especially those with more historical than systematic interests, to pursue developmental questions concerning Wesley's theological and biographical transforma-

[16]I do not want my readers to draw the unintended conclusion that I have abandoned my longstanding consensual patristic classical effort as I at long last refocus on my own Wesleyan tradition as a modern expression of ancient ecumenical teaching.

[17]There is surprisingly little repetition in Wesley when the sequence is viewed economically in this traditional order. As writer and editor, he was a stickler for economy of style.

[18]The expository method has not been comprehensively applied to Wesley's writings. The leading recent interpreters of Wesley, Albert Outler, Frank Baker, and Richard Heitzenrater have wisely sought to place him in historical context. They have left open the field for simple exposition. Of those who have tried to provide a general account of Wesley's theology, see Further Reading at the end of this section.

[19]Other scholars are currently making significant inquiries into Wesley's theology, notably Randy Maddox, Kenneth Collins, Theodore Runyon, and William Abraham. They are skilled in and intent on

tions in their social contexts.[19] However intriguing the psychological, social, and historical-critical approaches may be to me, they have a track record of not yielding profound theological insights. These insights require tested methods of exegesis according to the analogy of faith, as Wesley insisted. They apply the criteria of internal coherence, unity, and continuity of apostolic and canonical testimony, and a conciliatory will. The hermeneutical method of this study is to work more with the intratextual theological truth of the primary text itself than with the history of its development.[20]

This method exists in tension to some extent with some Reformed evangelicals who, without a thorough reading of Wesley's own writings, may tend to caricature him (against his explicit wish) as Pelagian or lacking a sound doctrine of grace. Some Lutherans cannot imagine that Wesley grasped justification by grace through faith. Some Anglicans remember only one thing about Wesley, and that is that he caused the separation of Methodism from the Church of England. They are forgetting that he himself remained Anglican all his life and resisted precisely that separation with all his might. Most of all, Wesley's own texts resist those Wesleyans who so sentimentalize and idealize his pragmatic skills that he is not taken seriously as an independent thinker.

D. History and Doctrine

1. The Chief Mentor of Wesley Studies

These volumes stand in a singular relation of appreciation to the work of my incomparable mentor, Albert C. Outler — complementary, sympathetic, and grateful. I have spent most of my professional life as a systematic theologian with avid interests in early Christianity. Outler spent his as a historical theologian with avid interests in ecumenical teaching, ancient and modern. My method is primarily systematic; Outler's was primarily historical. These are complementary methods.

The theological method underlying this study weighs in more heavily on divine revelation as a premise of a wholesome historical inquiry, since the meaning of universal history is the overarching subject of the discipline of theology. Outler's method has weighed in more heavily on historical inquiry without neglecting theological implications. This is why I remain grateful for Outler's enormous contribution but still remain less bound to jump the hoops of critical historians who commonly have a constricted view of evidence. In all my writings since the 1970s, I have sought to expand the range of evidence to include "revelation as history"

entering into the vast arena of secondary literature on Wesley, to assess its adequacy, a worthy task that I do not here attempt.

[20]Though I commend the work of colleagues who prefer to engage the secondary literature, the more I read it, the more I come to see that it has put upon itself the limitations of hyper-historicism. A complementary emphasis is now needed: empathic exposition of theological themes in Wesley draw directly from his own text rather than from contemporary historians. Here the focus is deliberately on the primary texts themselves.

(Pannenberg). This is a method that is consistent with Wesley's teachings, although I did not fully grasp it until reading Cyril the Great.

The following attempt seeks to order Wesley's thought cohesively, comprehensively, and systematically. This is a task that my beloved teacher Albert Outler never aspired to do, and in fact may have looked upon somewhat disdainfully.

Outler's vocation was to provide an exhaustive placement of Wesley in his historical context, showing his sources and accurately describing his thought in its historical-autobiographical development, which he did in an exemplary way. My modest attempt stands on his shoulders. It presupposes his work and the work of other historians in this recent period that he described as the "Third Phase" of Wesley studies, a phase whose methods have been dominated by historians — brilliant, but who have not wished to enter into the plausibility of Wesley's exposition of the plain sense of sacred Scripture.[21]

2. Whether Wesley Was a Systematic Theologian

I have never aspired to being a historian in the sense that Élie Halévy, V. H. H. Green, and Richard Heitzenrater are primarily historians. I am unapologetically an orthodox scholar with respect to classic texts, with lifelong interests in historical wisdom. I work unashamedly according to the methods of classic Christian exegesis, which form the foundation of all that we today call a theology of revelation.[22] If historians sometimes assume that such a task is implausible or even impossible, my purpose is to show its viability in a particular arena: Wesley's teaching.[23] Albert Outler made Wesley accessible to Wesleyans as a folk theologian. I seek to make Wesley accessible to non-Wesleyans as a wise teacher of classic Christianity.

Without denying or ignoring the intriguing question of how Wesley's theology

[21]I am restless both with those historians who cannot take Wesley seriously as a theologian and with those theologians who refuse to see Wesley in his historical-intellectual context.

[22]If some may misinterpret my intent as claiming too much for Wesley as systematician, let me refine the point more modestly: Wesley was an evangelical preacher whose intellectual temperament exhibited a steady concern for cohesion and consistency grounded in a wide data base. On this score, I think Wesley is not so overtly systematic as Thomas Aquinas or Calvin or Barth, but more so than Luther or Newman, and equally so as Cranmer and Edwards.

[23]The method of this study resists a strong tendency among some recent historians to restrict historical knowledge to scientific and empirical evidences in a way that dismisses all talk of revelation. Wesley was tutored by Oxford historians who did not narrow historical evidences in this way. Some historians today are prone to caricature orthodox Christian teachers as always prematurely jumping to conclusions, overleaping piles of evidence, missing developmental complexities, and overlooking contextual influences. Orthodox Christian teachers have a wider data base than do modern historians, since they do not narrow historical knowledge to empirical and scientific models of knowing. Orthodox method sometimes portrays modern historians as fixated on picking up ephemeral pieces of evidence but never grasping the larger picture, always too hesitant to make any judgments about how the changing views of a living person cohere through their mutations. Some are so fixated on the specifics of the context that the wisdom that motivated them to take a historical figure seriously has become diffused and lost. In Wesley studies I admire the excellent work of rigorous historians such as Albert Outler, Frank Baker, Richard Heitzenrater, Alan K. Walz, and my esteemed colleagues at Drew — Kenneth E. Rowe and Charles Yrigoyen. I think their splendid work still yearns for a larger presentation of evidence that can be based only on the premises most dear to Wesley — divine revelation and the authority of apostolic teaching for understanding universal history.

developed and changed over time, my question is fashioned differently: To what degree, if any, does the gist of the whole of Wesley's theological contribution admit of consistent cohesion, with viable, organic conception and design?[24]

Those who begin by insisting that the percentage is zero will have to be convinced by the Wesley texts themselves. If the percentage is anything above zero, then the burden of proof rests on the expositor to show textually that there indeed is in the primary text a solid core of cohesive teaching.[25] That is my assignment.

Wesley has been prematurely dismissed as unsystematic on the ground that his writings were largely occasional and not ordered in a methodical, systematic manner.[26] My objective is to show that all of his occasional writings indeed had a cohesive and implicitly systematic core. That core is textually available to anyone who cares to examine it fairly.

Wesley is a special sort of systematic theologian — his interrelated reflections emerge directly out of his wide range of active pastoral relationships. This is especially noticeable in his letters, where pastoral and moral advice and spiritual admonition abound yet integrate into a connected pattern of deliberate reflection. Readers who look for a systematic theologian strongly grounded in pastoral care will find it more in Wesley than in Friedrich Schleiermacher or Karl Barth, who ostensibly might otherwise appear to be "more systematic." The remainder of this series in fact will be devoted to the *pastoral* and *moral* aspects of Wesley's teaching.

One further whimsical note: Though Wesley is often imagined to be unduly sober and humorless, I have found many engaging passages where he radiates brilliant sparks of wit and comic perception.[27] Rather than merge them into a separate section on humor, I have decided to let them lie quietly in the text, awaiting the reader's unanticipated discovery. There is no other motive greater in my mind than proactively sharing with you the steady joy I have found in reading Wesley, which centers in taking pleasure in the good news of God's own coming.

---

[24]The most systematically ignored aspect of the secondary literature on Wesley's teaching is the triune frame of his theology, embracing his ordering of discipline, sacrament, pastoral practice, and moral reasoning. In the section on the Trinity in this volume (pp. 72–74), I will show how important this is to him and how triune reasoning permeates the entire enterprise with his doctrines of God the Father, God the Son, and God the Holy Spirit.

[25]Focal questions to be pursued are: Does Wesley's teaching illumine the evangelical pastoral task today? How fully developed are his doctrines of creation, providence, the triune God, theological method, sin and grace, justification and sanctification, Word and sacraments, and eschatology? It is commonly acknowledged that Wesley gave explicit attention to selected areas of theology such as soteriology and ecclesiology, and the work of the Holy Spirit, but to what extent did Wesley attend sufficiently to the wider range of theological questions so as to be rightly regarded as a reliable guide to Christian doctrine as a whole? Is it possible to sort out Wesley's essays, sermons, and occasional writings in terms of the categories of classical doctrines of systematic theology and survey them generally in a brief scope?

[26]It need not count against the cohesive thought of a writer that he is capable of occasional writings in which specific challenges are answered, provided those occasional writings are consistent with the larger literary whole. The attempt to explain this cohesion through various theories of Wesley's development have often resulted in an unnecessary fragmentation of that wholeness.

[27]If typographers could insert a smiley face in the margins each time one of these sparks flies, the margins would be well furnished.

3. How to Make Practical Use of This Study

It is customary in an introduction to sketch the ways in which the work has practical utility or moral relevance. This series, for example, may be practically used for devotional reading, for moral reflection, or even for topical sermon preparation. Even more so, it serves as a reference work for identifying the range of Wesley's ideas and opinions. The indexes and Further Reading sections serve as a guide for the reader who is particularly interested in a topic such as ecological recovery, moral relativism, enthusiasm, catholicity, experience, paradise, final justification, providence, or any of countless others. These may intrigue the curious, inspire the devout, or give courage to those weary in well-doing.

Wesley's teaching awaits being fruitfully applied to numerous pressing issues of contemporary society, such as addictive behaviors, poverty, and nihilism. Instead, I prefer to alert you to what is most likely to be enjoyed from these pages: Wesley's good sense, practical wisdom, and nonspeculative earthy realism. Since there is so much to be relished and enjoyed in Wesley, it seems deadly to think of this endeavor only in terms of what one ought to do in relation to it.

Further Reading on Wesley's Theology

Overviews of Wesley's Theology

Baker, Frank. "The Doctrines in the Discipline." In *From Wesley to Asbury: Studies in Early American Methodism*, edited by Frank Baker, 162–82. Durham, NC: Duke University Press, 1976.

Burwash, Nathaniel. *Wesley's Doctrinal Standards.* Introduction. Toronto: William Briggs, 1881; reprint, Salem, OH: Schmul, 1967.

Campbell, Ted A. *Methodist Doctrine: The Essentials.* Nashville: Abingdon, 1999.

Cannon, William R. *Theology of John Wesley: With Special Reference to the Doctrine of Justification.* Nashville: Abingdon, 1946.

Cell, G. C. *The Rediscovery of John Wesley.* New York: Henry Holt, 1935.

Coke, Thomas, and Francis Asbury. *The Doctrines and Discipline of the Methodist Episcopal Church in America.* Philadelphia: Henry Tuckniss, 1798.

Collins, Kenneth J. *Faithful Witness.* Wilmore, KY: Wesleyan Heritage, 1993.

———. *The Theology of John Wesley: Holy Love and the Shape of Grace.* Nashville: Abingdon, 2007.

———. *Wesley on Salvation.* Grand Rapids: Zondervan, 1989.

Harper, Steve. *John Wesley's Message for Today.* Grand Rapids: Zondervan, 1983.

Lee, Umphrey. *John Wesley and Modern Religion.* Nashville: Cokesbury, 1936.

Mickey, Paul. *Essentials of Wesleyan Theology.* Grand Rapids: Zondervan, 1980.

Norwood, Frederick A. *The Story of American Methodism.* Chap. 3, "Roots and Structure of Wesley's Theology." Nashville: Abingdon, 1974.

Outler, Albert C. "John Wesley as Theologian: Then and Now." *MH* 12, no. 4 (1974): 64 – 82.

———. "Toward a Reappraisal of John Wesley as Theologian." *Perkins School of Theology Journal* 14, no. 2 (1961): 5 – 14.

———, ed. *John Wesley.* Introduction, 3 – 33. Library of Protestant Theology. New York: Oxford University Press, 1964.

Pope, William Burt. *A Compendium of Christian Theology.* 3 vols. London: Wesleyan Methodist Book-Room, 1880.

Ralston, Thomas N. *Elements of Divinity.* New York: Abingdon, 1924.

Slatte, Howard A. *Fire in the Brand: Introduction to the Creative Work and Theology of John Wesley.* New York: Exposition, 1963.

Sugden, Edward H. *Wesley's Standard Sermons.* London: Epworth, 1921. See introduction and annotations.

Summers, Thomas O. *Systematic Theology.* 2 vols. Edited by J. J. Tigert. Nashville: Methodist Publishing House South, 1888.

Watson, Philip. *The Message of the Wesleys.* New York: Macmillan, 1964.

Watson, Richard. *Theological Institutes.* 2 vols. New York: Mason and Lane, 1836, 1840; edited by John M'Clintock, New York: Carlton & Porter, 1850.

Williams, Colin W. *John Wesley's Theology Today.* Nashville: Abingdon, 1960.

Systematic Theologies Largely Based on Wesley's Theology

Banks, John S. *A Manual of Christian Doctrine.* 1st American edition. Edited by J. J. Tigert. Nashville: Lamar & Barton, 1924.

Binney, Amos, with Daniel Steele. *Theological Compend Improved.* New York: Phillips and Hunt, 1875.

Burwash, Nathaniel. *Manual of Christian Theology.* 2 vols. London: Horace Marshall, 1900.

Gamertsfelder, S. *Systematic Theology.* Harrisburg: Evangelical Publishing House, 1952.

Merrill, Stephen M. *Aspects of Christian Experience.* New York: Walden and Stone, 1882.

Miley, John. *Systematic Theology.* Reprint, Peabody, MA: Hendrickson, 1989.

Miner, Raymond. *Systematic Theology.* 2 vols. Cincinnati: Hitchcock and Walden, 1877 – 79.

Outler, Albert C. *Theology in the Wesleyan Spirit.* Nashville: Tidings, 1975.

Pope, William Burt. *A Compendium of Christian Theology.* 3 vols. London: Wesleyan Methodist Book-Room, 1880.

Ralston, Thomas N. *Elements of Divinity.* New York: Abingdon, 1924.

Summers, Thomas O. *Systematic Theology.* 2 vols. Edited by J. J. Tigert. Nashville: Methodist Publishing House South, 1888.

Tillett, Wilbur. *Personal Salvation.* Nashville: Barbee and Smith, 1902.

Watson, Richard. *Theological Institutes.* 2 vols. New York: Mason and Lane, 1836, 1840; edited by John M'Clintock, New York: Carlton & Porter, 1850.

Weaver, Jonathan. *Christian Theology.* Dayton: United Brethren Publishing House, 1900.

Wynkoop, Mildred Bangs. *Foundations of Wesleyan-Arminian Theology.* Kansas City: Beacon Hill, 1967.

The Relation of Wesley's Theology to His Biography

Clarke, Adam. *Memoirs of the Wesley Family.* London: J. & T. Clarke, 1823.

Coke, Thomas, and Henry Moore. *The Life of the Rev. John Wesley, A.M.* London: G. Paramore, 1792.

Gambold, John. "The Character of Mr. John Wesley." *MM* 21, 1798.

Green, Vivian H. H. *The Young Mr. Wesley.* London: Edward Arnold, 1961.

Heitzenrater, Richard P. *The Elusive Mr. Wesley.* 2 vols. Abingdon, 1984.

———. *Mirror and Memory: Reflections on Early Methodism.* Nashville: Abingdon, 1989.

Schmidt, Martin. *John Wesley: A Theological Biography.* 2 vols. in 3. Nashville: Abingdon, 1963 – 73.

Tuttle, Robert. *John Wesley: His Life and Theology.* Grand Rapids: Zondervan, 1978.

Tyerman, Luke. *The Life and Times of the Rev. John Wesley.* 3 vols. New York: Harper, 1872.

Bibliographical Resources

Baker, Frank, comp. *A Union Catalogue of the Publications of John and Charles Wesley.* Durham, NC: Duke University, 1966.

———. "Unfolding John Wesley: A Survey of Twenty Years' Study in Wesley's Thought." *QR* 1, no. 1 (1980).

Bassett, Paul M. "Finding the Real John Wesley." *Christianity Today* 28, no. 16 (1984).

Green, Richard. *The Works of John and Charles Wesley: A Bibliography.* 2nd ed. New York: AMS, 1976.

Jarboe, Betty M. *John and Charles Wesley: A Bibliography.* Metuchen, NJ: Scarecrow, 1987.

Jones, Arthur E. *A Union Checklist of Editions of the Publications of John and Charles Wesley: Based upon the "Works of John and Charles Wesley: A Bibliography"* by Richard Green. Madison, NJ: Drew University Press, 1960.

Rowe, Kenneth E. *Methodist Union Catalogue.* Metuchen, NJ: Scarecrow, 1975ff.

Humor in Wesley

Crawford, Robert C. "John Wesley's Humour." *MM* 157 (1934): 313 – 15.

Foster, Henry J. "Wesley's Humour." *WMM* 126 (1903): 446 – 49.

Page, W. Scott. "Wesley and the Sense of Humour." *MR*, 1906, 13.

Perkins, J. P. "The Humour of John Wesley." *WMM* 143 (1920): 697 – 98.

VOLUME TWO

CHRIST AND SALVATION

JOHN WESLEY'S TEACHINGS

CHAPTER 1

Jesus Christ

A. The Incarnate Crucified Lord

Wesley prayed that the people in his connection of spiritual formation might be saved from supposed "improvements" on the apostolic testimony or presumed christological innovations.[1] Wesley at no point hinted that there is a needed purification, progression, or remodeling of ancient ecumenical christological definitions.[2] There is very little of that in magisterial Protestantism. The Reformers gladly accepted ancient ecumenical definitions of the apostolic church, and Wesley followed in their steps.

The study of the doctrine of Christ (Christology) has two parts: The person of Christ as God-man (*theantropos*) and the work of Christ as mediator of salvation to humanity.

1. The Person of Christ

In Wesley's view, it is precisely in the text of the New Testament that we meet the "inmost mystery of the Christian faith," where "all the inventions of men ought now to be kept at the utmost distance" to allow Scripture to speak of the one mediator who has "become the guarantor of a better covenant" (Heb. 7:22 NIV).[3]

Wesley summarized his thinking: "I do not know how any one can be a Christian believer ... till God the Holy Ghost witnesses that God the Father has accepted him through the merits of God the Son; and having this witness, he honors the Son, and the blessed Spirit, 'even as he honors the Father.'"[4]

a. Two Natures: Truly God, Truly Human

The foundation of the doctrine of Jesus Christ is found in Scripture: truly God, truly human. Wesley confidently employed the language of the Council of

[1]Wesley was distrustful of novelty in theology generally but most of all respecting Christology; see B 2:181, 550; 3:106–9, 193, 235, 524–25; 4:183, 394.

[2]*LJW* 5:334.

[3]Letter to William Law, 2.3, *LJW* 3:354–55, in reference to Anna Maria van Schurmann; cf. B 2:379–85, 421.

[4]"On the Trinity," B 2:385, sec. 17; John 5:23.

Chalcedon in phrases like "real God, as real man,"[5] "perfect, as God and as man,"[6] and "the Son of God and the Son of Man," whereby one phrase is "taken from his divine, and the other from his human nature."[7]

The Son's unity with the Father is a unity of divine essence, nature, substance, and glory. All the attributes of God the Father are manifested in God the Son. Wesley paraphrased Jesus, saying, "I am one with the Father in essence, in speaking, and in acting."[8] The Father is Jesus' Father "in a singular and incommunicable manner; and ours, through Him, in such a kind as a creature is capable of."[9] To say these divine attributes are "incommunicable" means that the Son's unique nature as eternal Son is not in itself transferable in its fullness to finite beings, but that persons through faith participate in his sonship "in such a kind as a creature is capable of."[10]

Though inseparably united with the Father, the Son is a distinguishable voice from the Father as a person yet always understood emphatically within their unity of essence.[11] The Son is worthy of worship since "Christ is God."[12]

b. Arguments Concerning the Divinity of Christ

Wesley often called Jesus simply "God,"[13] or ὁ ὤν, the one who is spoken of in Romans 9:5. There the classic view of the two natures of Christ is clear: "'He that existeth, over all, God blessed for ever': the supreme, the eternal, 'equal with the Father as touching his Godhead, though yielding to the Father as touching his manhood.'"[14]

In the Sermon on the Mount, Jesus speaks as "ὁ ὤν," the one who *incomparably is*, "the being of beings, Jehovah, the self-existent, the supreme, the God who is over all."[15] He speaks in the first person, and thus claims the divine name, "I AM," of Exodus 3:14 (John 8:24, 27 – 28, 58). His eternal generation distinguishes him from all creatures. "He has all the natural, essential attributes of his Father ... the entire Divine Nature."[16]

The ascription of all divine attributes of the Father to the eternal Son is taken for granted as the faith of the ancient church. To the Son are ascribed "all the attributes and all the works of God. So that we need not scruple to pronounce him God of God, Light of Light, very God of very God, in glory equal with the Father, in majesty coeternal."[17]

[5]*ENNT* on Phil. 2:6; "On Knowing Christ after the Flesh," B 4:98 – 101.

[6]*ENNT* on Heb. 2:10.

[7]*ENNT* on Luke 22:70, italics added; cf. *WC* 15; 3:90 – 95; 4:97 – 106.

[8]*ENNT* on John 14:10.

[9]*ENNT* on John 20:21.

[10]*ENNT* on John 1.

[11]*ENNT* on John 1:1; 8:16 – 19.

[12]*ENNT* on 1 Cor. 1:2; 1 Thess. 3:11; 5:27; Rev. 20:6.

[13]*ENNT*, passim, cf. John 12:41; Col. 1:17; Rev. 1:4.

[14]"The Lord Our Righteousness," B 1:452, sec. 1.1; cf. "Upon Our Lord's Sermon on the Mount, I," intro., 9; Athanasian Creed, BCP.

[15]"Upon Our Lord's Sermon on the Mount, I," B 1:474, proem 9; cf. B 4:61; *CH*, B 7:121 – 26, 403 – 4.

[16]*Compend of Natural Philosophy*, J V:215, italics added; *LJW* 1:118; 2:67; cf. *CH*, B 7:313, 316, 382, 386, 391.

[17]"Spiritual Worship," B 3:91, sec. 1.1.

The incarnation reveals the harmony of God's attributes, especially the subtle interfacing of God's justice, which must discipline the sinner, and God's mercy, which reconciles the sinner—a reconciliation that occurs out of divine love as an event in history on the cross.[18] Through incarnation and atonement, we learn "that not sovereignty alone, but justice, mercy, and truth hold the reins."[19]

c. Arguments Concerning the Humanity of Christ

"In the fullness of time He was made man, another common Head of mankind, a second general Parent and Representative of the whole human race."[20] In becoming "flesh," God becomes fully human, not simply body but all that pertains to humanity.[21]

He is a "real man, like other men," even "a common man, without any peculiar excellence or comeliness," who becomes weary, who weeps, who is tempted as we are yet without sin, who increases in wisdom "as to his human nature," who passes through stages of development like other human beings, who as man lives within limitations of time, finitude, and the restrictions of contextual knowing.[22]

Wesley commented freely on the temperament of Jesus, his psychological dynamics, interpersonal relationships, and courage, yet without displacing the premise that he is truly human, truly God, not one without the other.

In all this there is no hint of a docetic (flesh-repudiating) tendency in Christology.[23] Above all his humanity is seen in his death and burial. "He did not use His power to quit His body as soon as it was fastened to the cross, leaving only an insensible corpse to the cruelty of His murderers; but continued His abode in it, with a steady resolution."[24] In the bodily ascension, God "exalted Him in his human nature."[25]

d. The Assumption of Human Nature by the Son in the Virgin Birth

"I believe that he was made man, joining the human nature with the divine in one person, being conceived by the singular operation of the Holy Ghost and born of the Blessed Virgin Mary."[26] "Christ, the Second Person, had a being before he was born of a virgin,"[27] but it was the being of the *preexistent Son*,[28] not a preexistent human flesh—an idea that Wesley considered "exceeding dangerous" since it tended to compromise the Son's coequality and coeternality with the Father.[29]

---

[18]*ENNT* on 1 John 4:8; Rom. 3:25–26; see also B 1:186; 2:479; *CH*, B 7:235, 534, 707.

[19]PCC J X:235; *ENNT* on Rom. 9:21 and Mark 3:13.

[20]"Justification by Faith," B 1:185–86, sec. 1.7.

[21]*ENNT* on John 1:14; cf. 3:201–2.

[22]*ENNT* on Mark 6:6; Luke 2:40, 43, 52; John 4:6; Phil. 2:7–8; Heb. 2:17; cf. B 1:337; 3:273; *LJW* 8:89–90.

[23]*ENNT* on Gospels, passim; cf. *WC* 27, 28.

[24]*ENNT* on Matt. 27:50; cf. *WC* 32.

[25]*ENNT* on Eph. 1:20; Luke 24:51.

[26]Letter to a Roman Catholic, JWO 494, sec. 7.

[27]*Compend of Natural Philosophy*, B 5:215.

[28]*CH*, B 7:505.

[29]"The End of Christ's Coming," B 2:478–79, sec. 2.2. Wesley found this tendency in Isaac Watts, who pleaded with God not to be displeased because he "[could] not believe him to be coequal and

In the *virginal conception*, "the power of God was put forth by the Holy Ghost, as the immediate divine agent in this work."[30] "As Christ was to be born of a pure virgin, so the wisdom of God ordered it to be of one espoused; that, to prevent reproach, He might have a reputed father according to the flesh."[31]

Mary who was "as well after as before she brought him forth, continues a pure and unspotted virgin."[32] The nativity hymns of Charles Wesley splendidly attest the virgin conception and Christmas theology.

Yet the angelic salutation "gives *no room for any pretense of paying adoration* to the virgin."[33] "[Mary] rejoiced in hope of salvation through faith in Him, which is a blessing common to all true believers, more than in being His mother after the flesh, which was an honor peculiar to her.... In like manner he has regarded our low estate; and vouchsafed to come and save her and us."[34]

e. The Mystery of the Personal Union

Insofar as the mediator between God and humankind shares our humanity, he does not need to know the time of the day of judgment, for "*as man*," that is insofar as Jesus was flesh and blood in finite time, he was a palpable human being. How could he be if he dwelt in finite time? But according to his divine nature, "He knows all the circumstances of it."[35]

All that belongs to the divine nature appears in the human nature. All that appears in the human nature belongs to the divine nature. In this way, Wesley explicitly affirmed the classic doctrine of communication of properties or *perichoresis*.[36] This is "the communication of properties between the divine and human nature: whereby what is proper to the divine nature is spoken concerning the human; and what is proper to the human is, as here [John 3:13], spoken of the divine."[37]

Wesley speaks, for example, of "the blood of the only-begotten Son of God." The assumption is that the human properties of the man Jesus have been shared participatively with the one person of the God-man, Jesus Christ,[38] in an "amazing union."[39] It is this union that David Lerch, in *Heil und Heiligung bei John Wesley*, regards as the christological key to Wesley.[40] This perichoresis is what places Wesley so close to ancient Christian orthodoxy.

The personal union of one who is truly God and truly human *theanthropos*

---

coeternal with the Father." See Isaac Watts, *A Solemn Address to the Great and Ever Blessed God* (1745); cf. *WC* 29.

[30]*ENNT* 203 on Luke 1:35.

[31]*ENNT* 202 on Luke 1:27.

[32]Letter to a Roman Catholic, J X:81, sec. 7; JWO 495; *ENNT* 18 on Matt. 1:25.

[33]*ENNT* 203 on Luke 1:28.

[34]*ENNT* 204 on Luke 1:47.

[35]*ENNT* on Mark 13:32; "Christian Perfection," B 2:103, sec. 1.6.

[36]Lat. *communicatio idiomatorum*.

[37]*ENNT* 312.

[38]*ENNT* 479 on Acts 20:28.

[39]*ENNT* 330 on John 6:57.

[40]David Lerch, *Heil und Heiligung bei John Wesley* (Zürich: Christliche Vereinsbuchhandlung, 1941), 70. A similar point is made by Franz Hildebrandt, *From Luther to Wesley*, London: Lutterworth, 1951, 40.

— "the God-man"[41] — is at once "man and Mediator." God is "His *Father*, primarily, with respect to His divine nature, as his only-begotten Son; and, secondarily, with respect to His human nature, as that is personally united to the divine."[42] Echoing the ancient councils, the Son is "*without father*, as to His human nature; *without mother*, as to His divine."[43] The Son is obedient to the Father as seen in the New Testament. But the Son is not thereby inferior in nature with the Father.

As fully human, he "bids His disciples also to pray" to his Father, "but never forbids their praying to Himself" as eternal Son.[44]

B. The Christology of the Articles of Religion

1. God and Humanity in Personal Union

The primary doctrinal text that best reveals Wesley's Christology is article 2 of the Articles of Religion on the Son of God. Its two clauses distinguish the *person* from the *work* of Christ.

In one spare sentence, we have the summary teaching of the Son as the Word of God, preexistent Logos with the Father, the address of the Father, sent by the Father, truly God, of one substance with the Father, truly eternal who becomes incarnate assuming human nature, born of the blessed Virgin, one person with two natures, truly human and truly divine, undivided. The Son is the Word of the Father, not less God than the Father, of one substance (*homoousios*) with the Father.

God took human nature in the womb of Mary so that in the Son two whole and perfect natures, God and humanity, became one person. In this one person, we have not half God or half man, not an Arian-like almost God, not part God, but according to the teaching of the ancient christological tradition, Godhead and humanity joined together in one hypostatic union of two natures in one person never to be viewed as separable.[45]

2. The Work of Christ

a. The Work He Came to Do

If this is *who* Christ is, *what* did this unique person do that evidences his divine Sonship, and *why?* This theandric mediator did something for each one of us

[41]*ENNT* 435 on Acts 10:36.

[42]*ENNT* 702 on Eph. 1:3.

[43]*ENNT* 827 on Heb. 7:3, which Deschner regards as a "mis-exegesis," since elsewhere Wesley teaches that "God is also father of Jesus Christ in his human nature," *WC* 42. Yet Wesley is correct to regard Christ as "*without father*, as to His human nature," consistent with the ancient ecumenical tradition (cf. *WL* 109 – 10), and especially the Eleventh Council of Toledo, where it is confessed that "He was begotten from the Father without a mother before all ages, and in the end of the ages He was generated from a mother without a father" (Jacques Dupuis, ed., *The Christian Faith: In the Doctrinal Documents of the Catholic Church* [New York: Alba House, 1982], 170; cf. SCD para. 282 – 86, 110 – 11).

[44]Letter to Samuel Sparrow, October 9, 1773, *LJW* 6:46.

[45]Council of Chalcedon, *COC* 35 – 36; XXV, art. 2; "Spiritual Worship," B 3:90 – 95, sec. 1.

sinners. His work is consummated in his atoning action in which he *suffered for us, was crucified for us, died for us,* and *was buried* (XXV, art. 2).

This descent theme points to the length to which God goes to show his love for us by sharing our humanity, and by his death and resurrection, to bridge the alienation between the holiness of God and fallen humanity.

b. His Atoning Death Reconciles God and Humanity

The work of Christ's life is consummated in the atoning deed of his death, to be a sacrifice not only covering and redeeming our primordial guilt inherited from the history of sin, but also the actual sin resulting from our own free decisions and collusions.[46] Why? *To reconcile his Father to us.*[47] The focus is neither on reconciling us to the Father nor to one another, as if that could occur apart from the Son's reconciling his Father to us. Reconciling the wrath of God and the sin of man is his work. His work is what he does, as distinguished from "who he is."

c. He Suffered unto Death for Our Sins

He who is truly God became truly human and truly suffered. Patripassianism is thereby rejected, for the Father did not suffer, but the Son suffered as incarnate Lord, was crucified for us, died, and was buried.[48] This is a shorthand way of speaking about salvation from sin for all who repent and believe.

This pardon covers all sin: inherited and acquired, social and personal, primordial and historical. No individual act of natural freedom can excise itself from this distorted, despairing human condition. All who are born enter a history burdened by sin. In addition to that inherited burden, each of us has made our actual personal self-determined additions to that history of sin.

The Son's atonement is addressed to and sufficient for every individual sinner who shares in the heartrending history of sin. For those who reach the age of responsibility, it is effective for their salvation when they repent and believe. For those who have not reached the age of accountability or who are unable to take responsibility for themselves, sufficient grace works preveniently to draw them toward the means of grace that would enable their salvation, provided they use the available means of grace (prayer, Scripture, and common worship) when they are able. Though this grace is always sufficient, our self-determining wills may be deficient by our own choice.

d. He Rose Again from the Dead — The Resurrection

The third article confesses the resurrection as the decisive event that makes sense out of Christ's death: "Christ did truly rise from the dead and took again his body with all things appertaining to the perfection of man's nature, wherewith he ascended into heaven and there sitteth until he returns to judge at the last day" (XXV, art. 3).

---

[46]Nicene Creed, BCP.

[47]In its sparseness, the Nicene christological article mentions nothing at all about Jesus' baptism, earthly ministry, preaching, teaching, prophetic work, or miracles.

[48]*LJW* 3:353–54.

The first clause attests the central truth of the history of our salvation, that Christ indeed rose from the dead in a real body, a glorified body that experienced all the common things that pertain to human nature. It is Christ who represents sinners in the presence of the Father. Having ascended into heaven, he sits in session at the right hand of the Father and intercedes on our behalf and will return on the last day.[49] This is the central salvation occurrence that vindicates the whole work of Jesus in his earthly ministry and on the cross.[50]

e. The Descent to the Nether World

Despite the absence of the phrase "descent into hell" in Wesley's Sunday Service, there is strongly evident elsewhere in Wesley's Christology a large-scale descent[51] theme:

> from eternal Logos of the Father to incarnation to death,
> from death to burial,
> from burial to the *descent to the nether world.*

And only then is there a *mighty reversal in the resurrection*:

> Christ raised from the dead,
> ascended to heaven, sitting at the right hand of God the Father,
> and promised to come again with glory to judge the quick and the dead, whose kingdom shall have no end.

To understand each of these phases of descent and ascent is to grasp the essence of Wesley's Christology. The step that most requires explanation is the descent to the nether world.

(1) The Descent to Hell

(a) Why Omitted in the "Sunday Service"? That Christ descended into hell was omitted in the 1784 Sunday Service that Wesley sent to the churches in America. Among the Thirty-Nine Articles is article 3, "On the Going Down of Christ into Hell": "As Christ died for us and was buried, so also is it to be believed that he went down into hell."

Wesley excised that article in his liturgical advice to American Methodists. All he did was strike the phrase from the service, offering no detailed explanation of this omission or its motives or implications.

It is likely that the main reason Wesley did not include the descent of Christ into the netherworld is not that it lacked biblical support, but that it was even in his time regarded as a controversial hypothesis among scholars. In narrowing the thirty-nine to twenty-four articles, he was trying to make a plain and spare statement, as consensual as possible, of necessary affirmations of faith.

[49]*CH*, B 7:155, 696; cf. 1:121.

[50]B 4:102 – 3.

[51]On the divine *kenosis*, see B 3:201 – 2; *CH*, B 7:315 – 16, 323.

(b) The Debate: But we cannot conclude from that omission that Wesley disregarded the Scripture texts that arguably attest the descent into hell. Yet he was also aware of the nest of exegetical problems embedded in them. He did not want these to become a burden to his shortened form of evangelical confession.

On Acts 2:27 Wesley noted that "it does not appear that ever our Lord went into hell. His soul, when it was separated from the body, did not go thither, but to paradise (Luke 23:43)."[52] "His body was then laid in the grave and his soul went to the place of separate spirits."[53]

Deschner argues that *his motive* was that he was "loath to teach anything suggesting a second chance for those who resisted repentance in this life."[54] So the "descent to hell" theme, unobtrusively stricken, without any divisive attempt to controvert it, has remained largely absent from the Wesleyan tradition of worship until recent years.

In the 1989 hymnal published by the United Methodist Church, the phrase reappeared in transmuted form as "He descended to the dead" rather than "went down into hell."[55]

f. Ascension, Session, and Intercession

The Son descended to us to share our common human life. Having completed his atoning mission on the cross, he ascended to the Father as our Advocate. Wesley taught that these three crucial points of confession bring the work of Christ to a proper conclusion:

He ascended to the heavenly presence of the Father.
He sits at the right hand of the Father.
He intercedes for us.

The purpose of ascension is intercession and the due reception of legitimate authority in the emerging governance of God. The reign of God is already inaugurated, to be completed on the last day. The worshiping community expects the return of Christ on the last day to judge all acts of human freedom.

(1) Ascension

The ascension is attested in all four Gospels. It is preached in Acts, in Paul, and the General Epistles. Accordingly, his body rose from the finite world of space, time, and matter into the heavenly sphere to enter into the presence of the Father as intercessor for the faithful.[56]

This event signaled that he had returned exalted to the Father to intercede and

[52]*ENNT* 399.

[53]Letter to a Roman Catholic, JWO 495, sec. 8. For a more explicit discussion of the exegetical issues surrounding the descent into the netherworld, see *CC*.

[54]*WC* 51. It should be noted, however, that one of the key texts Deschner relied on, Homily #141 J, "On the Holy Spirit," is now known to be not Wesley's but John Gambold's; cf. B 4:547.

[55]United Methodist Publishing House, *United Methodist Hymnal* (Nashville: Abingdon, 1989), 7; cf. B 4:189.

[56]See Wesley's *ENNT* commentary on Heb. 1:3; 4:14; 9:24; 1 Peter 3:18 – 22; Rev. 12:5; 19:11.

to establish and consummate his divine governance. His earthly mission is complete, his heavenly ministry begun.

(2) Session

To sit at the right hand of the Father means to participate fully in God's majesty.[57] Christ governs in the kingdom of power, grace, and glory to reign eternally, having dominion over all things. Jesus is given that name above every name, that at his name every knee should bow and every tongue confess that he is Lord.[58] "When this priest had offered for all time one sacrifice for sins, he sat down at the right hand of God. Since that time he waits for his enemies to be made his footstool, because by one sacrifice he has made perfect forever those who are being made holy."[59]

(3) Intercession

Christ enters into an intercessory ministry for humanity in the presence of the Father as the Advocate for sinners. In him "we have one who speaks to the Father in our defense."[60] The faithful take comfort in this eternal access to the Father, that their prayers may be heard, that they will be kept from evil,[61] knowing that Christ's sacrifice is sufficient.[62]

We are commanded and permitted to offer our prayers in his name (John 14:13 – 14). The essential pattern of Christ's intercessory ministry is already anticipated in the high-priestly prayer of John 17. Jesus prayed that the faithful may "be with me where I am" (John 17:24).

g. The Articles of Religion on Atonement

The Articles of Religion remain a doctrinal standard in the American Wesleyan connection,[63] unamendable constitutionally save by a highly unlikely process of amendment of the constitution itself.[64] The homilies yet to be discussed deal more explicitly with the relevance of Christ's work for personal salvation, fully explicating the themes of justification, assurance, new birth, and sanctification.

(1) Article 20 on Atonement

If sin has become a kind of second nature to us, and we are far fallen from our original righteousness, what has God done that has the effect of saving us?

57*ENNT* on Matt. 24:30; 25:31; Luke 22:69; Heb. 1:3.

58*ENNT* on Phil. 2:6 – 11.

59*ENNT* on Heb. 10:12 – 14.

60*ENNT* on 1 John 2:1.

61*ENNT* on John 17:15.

62*ENNT* on Heb. 9:23 – 24.

63With a few exceptions, see *DSWT* 81 – 173.

64The Evangelical United Brethren Confession similarly combines all key affirmations of Wesley's Christology: "We believe in Jesus Christ, truly God and truly man, in whom the divine and human natures are perfectly and inseparably united. He is the eternal Word made flesh, the only begotten Son of the Father, born of the Virgin Mary by the power of the Holy Spirit. As ministering Servant he lived, suffered and died on the cross. He was buried, rose from the dead and ascended into heaven to be with the Father, from whence he shall return. He is eternal Savior and Mediator, who intercedes for us, and by him all men will be judged."

The answer is found most concisely in article 20[65] titled "Of the One Oblation of Christ Finished upon the Cross." Christianity speaks of an "offering of Christ, once made," for which no other satisfaction is either possible or necessary. What happened on the cross is not the death of a good man only, but the death of God the Son who comes to us in mission to reconcile the Father to us.[66]

Only one who was truly human could become the representative of humanity before God the Father. Only one who was truly God could offer a fitting sacrifice for the sins of all humanity.[67]

From the self-offering of this unique theandric (God-man) Person comes "the perfect redemption, propitiation and satisfaction." It is entirely adequate to save from sin. It is a perfect and complete sacrifice, a wholly sufficient conciliation of the divine rejection of sin and satisfaction of divine justice.[68]

(2) The Once-for-All Sacrifice for Sins

We are mercifully clothed in the Son's own righteousness by grace through faith. God's holiness at the heavenly throne is met by God's love on the cross so that sinners can be reconciled to God by the holy love of God. Those who are intent upon looking for the language of liberation in the Articles of Religion will find it embedded in article 20, for in the cross we have redemption of humanity from bondage to sin.[69] The atoning act is already fully accomplished "for all the sins of the whole world,"[70] though not all accept its conditions by responding in faith active in love.

This once-for-allness is contrasted with the medieval teaching of repeated sacrifice. When this Anglican article was written, the sixteenth-century Anglican tradition was trying to set itself apart from deteriorating aspects of the scholastic sacramental teaching in which the sacrifice of Christ was presumed to be offered repeatedly in the Mass. What was being protested was the notion that the very operation of the Mass was regarded as a renewal of the sacrifice of Christ, a view rejected by the Augsburg Confession and Anglican Articles. "Wherefore the sacrifice of masses in which it is commonly said that the priest doth offer Christ for the quick and the dead, to have remission of pain or guilt, is a blasphemous fable and dangerous deceit."

It may seem anachronistic to Protestants in a modern ecumenical age that this same article contains a strong polemic against the abuses of medieval Catholic sacramentalism and the Council of Trent. Thus we find a helpful ecumenical clarification of the intent of the Articles in the United Methodist *Discipline* following 1968, that in the present time these articles are to be read in the light of their historic

[65]Cf. art. 31 of the Thirty-Nine Anglican Articles, Of the One Oblation of Christ Finished upon the Cross.

[66]*LJW* 2:320.

[67]"The End of Christ's Coming," B 2:478 – 80, sec. 2.

[68]"On Working Out Our Own Salvation," B 3:199 – 202, proem; Letter to William Law, January 6, 1756, *LJW* 3:353.

[69]Cf. *LJW* 6:89, 94.

[70]XXV, art. 20.

context and biases, and in relation to current ecumenical realities.[71] This does not suggest that this is a dismissible argument, but that it is best viewed in historical context.

h. Wesley's Celebration of Nicene Christology

The Wesleyan tradition, like the Anglican and the ancient ecumenical tradition, has relied liturgically on the Nicene-Constantinopolitan Creed as a prototype of classic christological teaching.[72]

Wesley recited and revered the creed regularly as an Anglican priest in his daily offices. For this reason, it cannot be regarded as a diversion of Wesleyan studies if we make reference to the major loci of the creed, which confesses faith in one Lord Jesus Christ, the only Son of God, eternally begotten of the Father. Not a creature, the Son is eternally the Son of the Father, Light from Light, True God from True God, begotten not made, of one being with the Father, through whom all things were made. For us and our salvation he came down from heaven (the descent/humiliation motif), was incarnate of the Holy Spirit by the Virgin Mary, and became truly human.

We are not speaking of a demigod who never quite became a part of our human nature but of a fully human person who does not cease being God, true God, who for our sakes was crucified under Pontius Pilate, suffered death, and was buried and on the third day arose again in accordance with the Scripture. He ascended into heaven and is seated at the right hand of the Father, and he will come again in glory to judge the living and the dead, and his kingdom will have no end.[73] Each phrase of the creed was again and again confirmed in the homilies of Wesley.

C. The Christology of the Eucharistic Liturgy

1. The 1784 Order for the Administration of the Lord's Supper

a. The Questions Placed before the Communicant

There is no shorter route to the core of Wesley's Christology than an examination of Wesley's Order for the Administration of the Lord's Supper in the 1784 service, the Wesleyan eucharistic liturgy as a concentrated statement of christological reasoning. The basic questions are clear-cut and straightforward:

To whom is the call to Communion addressed?
To whom is the confession addressed?
Who is forgiven?
How am I to be assured of its truth?
How does Christ's death substitute for my sin?
Is it sufficient for my salvation?

[71]A Resolution of Intent of the General Conference of 1970, General Conference *Journal*, 254–55; cf. Book of Resolutions, United Methodist General Conference, 1968, 65–72.

[72]B 2:256n.; 3:91n., 460–61; 4:33, 63, 199; cf. *CH*, B 7:387n., 661n.

[73]BCP; *CH*, B 7:155, 584, 696.

What is the sole condition for receiving it?
What voluntary obligation does it place on me?
How do I participate in the divine nature through bread and wine?
Who is the Mediator who was acting on my behalf?
What has God the Son done for me?
Why did God suffer and die for me?

The Wesleyan form of Eucharist follows the Book of Common Prayer and modifies it only marginally. It begins with an invitation to all those who truly and earnestly repent of their sins.

b. The Call to Communion and Act of Confession

The *call to Communion* is not to the unserious or those who have only superficially examined their lives, or to the impenitent, but precisely to those who through repentance are already bringing themselves to a point of spiritual readiness and contrite expectation of the presence of Christ.[74]

Holy Communion is offered to those who, repenting, are seeking to live in love and charity with their neighbors, "intending to lead a new life, following the commandments of God, walking from henceforth in his holy ways." Such are they who are called to draw near with faith and take this sacrament to their comfort, making their confession to God meekly kneeling upon their knees.[75]

The *confession* is addressed to almighty God, recalling that our minds have misconceived our true good, our mouths misspoken the truth, our deeds and hands worked mischief.[76] These sins are beheld in relation to the holy God, for they are committed not merely against our better selves or the offended neighbor, but "against thy divine majesty."[77]

c. Forgiveness and Assurance

Christ's *forgiveness* is addressed to all, but those prepared to receive that forgiveness must be attentive to those penitential disciplines that take forgiveness seriously. The gospel gives "*assurance* of pardon to the penitent, but to no one else."[78] Those who come thirsting to the Lord's Table come with contrite hearts, asking God to have mercy, praying for forgiveness of all that is past, seeking grace that we may ever hereafter serve and please God in newness of life.

With that confession, we are readied by grace for the *petition for pardon* — to ask forgiveness for all them that with hearty repentance and true faith are turning to God, who pardons and delivers sinners from sins and strengthens the penitent in all goodness.[79]

[74]*SSM* 131.
[75]Ibid.
[76]*LJW* 3:327.
[77]*SSM* 132.
[78]Letter to His Mother, February 28, 1730, *LJW* 1:48, italics added.
[79]*SSM* 131 – 35.

The act of *absolution* occurs in the comfortable words of Scripture announcing the forgiveness of God, whose reliable word is conveyed through the ordained elder: "If anyone sins, we have an advocate with the Father, Jesus Christ the righteous," the expiation on behalf of our sins. In this *substitution* metaphor, one life is being given for another.

The *reception of forgiveness is conditional* upon faith: "If we confess our sins, he is faithful and just and will forgive us our sins and purify us from all unrighteousness" (1 John 1:9 NIV).[80]

d. Holy Communion

The *prayer of humble access* moves us one step closer to the moment of lively communion with the resurrected Lord. Think of this as an eschatological banquet table in which the risen Lord is present in the life of the church and we are invited personally to his table.

We do not presume to come to this feast trusting in our own righteousness, but in God's manifold and great mercies. We are of ourselves not worthy to gather up the crumbs under that table. But it belongs to God's character always to have mercy. Each believer is called to walk in newness of life and evermore dwell in him. This is a serious act of trust. If neglected, the approach to communion is incomplete.

To commune with Christ is to *receive his shed blood and share in his broken body*. Our sincere self-offering occurs in response to God's offering to us.[81] It is not merely a memorial of his death. It is an offering to share in Christ's suffering and death. It rehearses the promise made to us in baptism: to participate in Christ's cross and resurrection in our ordinary lives.

e. The Prayer of Consecration

From this follows a prayer of *consecration* that gives thanks for the tender mercy of God the Father who offers his only Son in complete giving, suffering on the cross for our redemption.[82] It is this mighty salvation event that he offered in instituting the Supper, and he commanded us to continue a perpetual memory of his costly death until his coming again. We celebrate this self-offering as a sufficient sacrifice for our sins and for the sins of the whole world.[83]

In Holy Communion we pray for the grace to share as partakers of the divine nature through him, holding fast to the recollection of his passion, death, and resurrection for us. But Holy Communion is not merely an act of remembrance of his life, death, and resurrection. More so it is a participation in his divine nature, insofar as finitude permits.[84] Bread and wine are consecrated as the body and blood of Christ, given for us, as testimony to the new covenant.[85]

---

[80]*SSM* 132–33.
[81]*SSM* 135.
[82]*CH*, B 7:107–11, 113, 228–29, 269–70, 337–38.
[83]*SSM* 136.
[84]B 1:56, 73, 75, 99, 150, 398–99, 498.
[85]*SSM* 136–37.

This 1784 service of Communion brings us as close to Wesley's Christology as anything he set before his connection of spiritual formation. He commended that it be received by us *as often as possible*. It has been celebrated the world over with scant revision by those who have stood in Wesley's connection.

2. The Crux of Wesley's View of the Work of Christ

a. The Work of Christ as Prophet, Priest, and King

In his Letter to a Roman Catholic, Wesley summarized the classic threefold teaching of the work of the messianic Savior as prophet, priest, and king:

> I believe that Jesus of Nazareth was the Saviour of the world, the Messiah so long foretold; that being anointed with the Holy Ghost,
> - he was a *prophet*, revealing to us the whole will of God;
> - that he was a *priest*, who gave himself a sacrifice for sin, and still makes intercession for transgressors;
> - that he is a *king*, who has all power in heaven and earth, and will reign till he has subdued all things to himself.[86]

b. Questions for Self-Examination in Receiving Life in Christ

It is useful here to recall the searching questions about Jesus Christ embedded in the homily "The Catholic Spirit":[87]

- Having absolutely disclaimed all thy own works, thy own righteousness, hast thou "submitted thyself unto the righteousness of God," "which is by faith in Christ Jesus"?
- Art thou "found in him, not having thy own righteousness, but the righteousness which is by faith"?
- And art thou, through him, "fighting the good fight of faith, and laying hold of eternal life"?
- Dost thou believe in the Lord Jesus Christ, "God over all, blessed for ever"?
- Is he "revealed in" thy soul?
- Dost thou "know Jesus Christ and him crucified"?
- Does he "dwell in thee, and thou in him"?
- Is he "formed in thy heart by faith"?

Intensely personal questions, they cannot be answered carelessly. These questions were intentionally framed so as to be seriously asked and answered. To answer them affirmatively constitutes the prevailing assumption of joining hands in Christian koinonia.

3. The Priestly Work of Christ: Atonement

Christ's work is understood as the payment of ransom, or satisfaction. All sinners are up to their necks in debts that can never be paid. Christ's work pays all the

---

[86]Letter to a Roman Catholic, JWO 494, sec. 7; cf. 1:121; 2:37 – 38, 161; 4:433, bullets added.
[87]"Catholic Spirit," B 2:87, sec. 1.13, bullets added.

debts. He suffered for all humanity, bore our punishment, paid the price of our sins for us. We thus have nothing to offer God but the merits of Christ.

This follows the Anglican "Homily of Salvation" in which the work of the Son atones to satisfy God's justice, following the Latin idea of atonement found in Tertullian, Cyprian, and more fully developed by Anselm of Canterbury.[88] This same substitutionary Christology can also be viewed from another angle as Christ's victory over the powers of evil, for in the atonement he binds up the power of the strong man, sin.[89]

Both the humanity and divinity of Christ are necessary for Christ's atoning work. Christ is "our great High-priest, 'taken from among men, and ordained for men in things pertaining to God': as such, 'reconciling us to God by his blood,' and 'ever living to make intercession for us.' "[90]

The actor in the atonement is "one Christ, very God and very man."[91] The Crucified One is the theandric mediator, seen especially "from the perspective of His divine nature, but provided with a human nature as a necessary instrument for His atoning work, which consists primarily in His death."[92] Wesley paraphrased John 14:19: "Because I am the Living One in My divine nature, and shall rise again in My human nature, and live for ever in heaven: therefore, ye shall live the life of faith and love on earth, and hereafter the life of glory."[93]

4. God's Love to Fallen Man

The text of the homily "God's Love to Fallen Man" is Romans 5:15: "Not as the transgression, so is the free gift" (Wesley's translation) [Homily #59 (1782), B 2:422–35; J #59, V:231–49].

a. A Felicitous Fall (Felix Culpa)

If God foresaw the consequences of Adam's fall, why would it not have been wiser of God to have prevented that fall altogether? We are tempted to imagine in our pride that God blundered and that "even I could have done better."

But would it have been a better universe if human history had been entirely and absolutely prevented from falling? Wesley answered emphatically that God, foreknowing the fall, also knew that the good that would come out of the redemption following the fall would be greater than the evil to be suffered. Looking backward, we can now see that it is only through the history of fallenness that another history, that of redeeming grace, becomes meaningful.[94]

---

[88] *WC* 56–70.

[89] "The Spirit of Bondage and of Adoption"; cf. Gustaf Aulen, *Christus Victor* (New York: Macmillan, 1940), 20–24.

[90] "The Law Established through Faith, II," B 2:37, sec. 1.6; Heb. 5:1; Rom. 5:9–10; Heb. 7:25; *CH*, B 7:114–15, 364, 529–31.

[91] XXV, art. 2; *ENNT* on Phil. 2:8.

[92] *WC* 167.

[93] *ENNT* 366.

[94] "God's Love to Fallen Man," B 2:423–24, proem.

Wesley followed that view of creation and atonement that asserts that the fall was ironically *a felicitous fall*, a *felix culpa, a happy fault*, a blessed disaster, when seen in the light of its resolution in redemption.[95] For out of its misery came a redemption not possible without the absurd history of humanity turning its back on God's goodness and grace.

It was formally within the power of God to prevent human disobedience. But God did not choose the simple way of an absolute divine decree, which would have circumvented human freedom. God knew that it was best to allow estranged freedom to play itself out in disobedience, which God did not prefer or will but permitted, knowing that he could redeem whatever consequences would emerge. God permitted the fall in order that something more advantageous would come from it — the redemption of humanity.[96]

b. God's Foreknowledge of the Fall Adds Value to the Advantage We Derive from the Fall

The foreknowing God knew that "the evil resulting" from the fall was "not worthy to be compared with ... the good resulting from salvation." So "to permit the fall of the first man was far best for mankind in general." In this way "by the fall of Adam, mankind in general have gained a capacity ... of attaining more holiness and happiness on earth than it would have been possible for them to attain if Adam had not fallen."[97]

Without the premise of the fallenness of human freedom, there would have been "no occasion" for redemption and no need for "such 'an Advocate with the Father' as 'Jesus Christ the righteous.'" There would have been no need for the Son's "obedience unto death" and "no such thing as faith in God thus loving the world," hence no justification, no redemption.[98] Without Adam's fall, we "might have loved the Author of our being ... as our Creator and Preserver.... But we could not have loved him as 'bearing our sins in his own body on the tree.'"[99]

"We see, then, what unspeakable *advantage we derive from the fall*." The imperative "If God *so* loved us, how ought we to love one another!" would have been "totally wanting if Adam had not fallen."[100]

5. How God Brings Good from Evil

a. Affliction as the Foundation of Passive Graces Such as Patience

"How much good does [God] continually bring out of this evil! How much holi-

[95]The ancient Latin Easter hymn celebrated *O felix culpa quaetantum ac talem meruit habere redemptorem*; cf. *WL* 115 (see *CC*).

[96]B 2:424 – 35; 4:26.

[97]"God's Love to Fallen Man," B 2:424, proem.

[98]"God's Love to Fallen Man," B 2:425 – 26, sec. 1.1, 2; cf. 3:201 – 2.

[99]"God's Love to Fallen Man," B 2:427, sec. 1.3; 1 Peter 2:24; cf. Samuel Hoard, "God's Love to Fallen Mankind," 1633, extracted in the *Arminian Magazine*, 1778, vol. 1.

[100]"God's Love to Fallen Man," B 2:428, sec. 1.5, italics added; cf. *CH*, B 7:517 – 18, 530 – 31.

ness and happiness out of pain!"[101] "What are termed afflictions in the language of men are in the language of God styled blessings." "Had there been no pain, [Christianity] could have had no being. Upon this foundation ... all our passive graces are built.... What room could there be for trust in God if there was no such things as pain or danger?" The "passive graces" are those virtues that come not from our actions, but from our enduring the actions of others.

"Had there been neither natural nor moral evil in the world, what must have become of patience, meekness, gentleness, longsuffering?... The more they are exercised, the more all our graces are strengthened."[102]

"As God's permission of Adam's fall gave all his posterity a thousand opportunities of *suffering*, and thereby of exercising all those passive graces which increase both their holiness and happiness; so it gives them opportunities of *doing good* in numberless instances.... And what exertions of benevolence, of compassion, of godlike mercy, had then been totally prevented!"[103]

"Unless in Adam all had died, every child of man must have personally answered for himself to God.... Now who would not rather be on the footing he is now? Under a covenant of mercy?"[104]

b. The Universality of Sin through Adam's Fall and Grace through Christ's Salvation

The universality of grace is correlated in Romans 5 with the universal consequences of Adam's fall. Lacking a universal human predicament, there would have been no need for a universal divine-human remedy. Had Adam not fallen, Christ would have been unnecessary. If the wrongdoing of one brought death upon all, that is happily exceeded by the grace of God in the one man Jesus Christ. That God primordially wills the salvation of all from the beginning does not imply that God prevents our freedom from being tempted. Election is universal in the primordial sense that God is willing that all be saved; but all are not saved by virtue of the voluntary sin that pervades human history, for which we humans are corporately responsible. "And none ever was or can be a loser but by his own choice."[105]

Wesley explained the scriptural distinction between present justification and final justification on the last day: "Justification sometimes means our acquittal at the last day. But ... that justification where our Articles and Homilies speak [means] present pardon and acceptance with God; who therein declares His righteousness and mercy, by or for the remission of the sins that are past."[106] Thus, "the justification

[101]"God's Love to Fallen Man," B 2:428, sec. 1.5, 6.
[102]"God's Love to Fallen Man," B 2:429–30, sec. 1.7, 8.
[103]"God's Love to Fallen Man," B 2:430, sec. 1.9.
[104]"God's Love to Fallen Man," B 2:432–33, sec. 2.12.
[105]"God's Love to Fallen Man," B 2:434, sec. 2.15.
[106]Letter to Thomas Church, February 2, 1745, *LJW* 2:186; B 1:121; 2:156.

whereof St. Paul and our Articles speak, is one only.... Yet I do not deny that there is another justification (of which our Lord speaks) at the last day."[107]

Further Reading on the Person and Work of Jesus Christ

Christology

Collins, Kenneth J. *The Scripture Way of Salvation: The Heart of John Wesley's Theology.* Nashville, Tennessee: Abingdon, 1997.

Deschner, John. *Wesley's Christology.* Dallas: SMU Press, 1960; reprint with foreword, Grand Rapids: Zondervan, 1988.

Harper, Steve. *John Wesley's Theology Today.* Chap. 4 on converting grace. Grand Rapids: Zondervan, 1983.

Hildebrandt, Franz. *Christianity according to the Wesleys.* London: Epworth, 1956.

———."Wesley's Christology." *PWHS* 33 (1962): 122–24.

Kirkpatrick, Dow, ed. *The Finality of Christ.* Nashville: Abingdon, 1966.

Lerch, David. *Heil und Heiligung bei John Wesley.* Zürich: Christliche Vereinsbuch-handlung, 1941.

Mason, C. E. "John Wesley's Doctrine of Salvation." Master's thesis, Union Theological Seminary, 1950.

McIntosh, Lawrence. "The Nature and Design of Christianity in John Wesley's Early Theology." PhD diss. Drew University, 1966.

Outler, Albert C. "Offering Christ: The Gist of the Gospel." In *Theology in the Wesleyan Spirit*, 35–65. Nashville: Discipleship Resources, 1975.

Rack, Henry. "Aldersgate and Revival." In *Reasonable Enthusiast*, 137–81. London: Epworth, 1989.

Rattenbury, J. E. *The Evangelical Doctrines of Charles Wesley's Hymns.* London: Epworth, 1941.

Schilling, Paul. "John Wesley's Theology of Salvation." In *Methodism and Society in Theological Perspective*, 44–64. Nashville: Abingdon, 1960.

Scott, Percy. *John Wesleys Lehre von der Heiligung vergleichen mit einem Luther-isch-pietistischen Beispel.* Berlin: Alfred Topelmann, 1939.

Verhalen, Philippo A. *The Proclamation of the Word in the Writings of John Wesley.* Rome: Pontificia Universitas Gregoriana, 1969.

Wilson, Charles R. "John Wesley's Christology." In *A Contemporary Wesleyan Theology*, edited by C. W. Carter, 342–50. Grand Rapids: Zondervan, 1983.

[107]Some remarks on Mr. Hill's "Farrago Double-Distilled," J X:430; on final justification, see *LJW* 3:244, 250. "No good works can be done before justification. Yet I believe (and that without the least self-contradiction) that final salvation is 'by works as a condition,' in the sense of good works flowing out of faith, works meet for repentance: 'Whatever you did for one of the least of these brothers of mine, you did for me!'" (Matt. 25:40; J X:432).

Wesley's Christological Antecedents and Developments

Cushman, Robert Earl. "Salvation for All: John Wesley and Calvinism." In *Methodism*, edited by W. K. Anderson, 103 – 15. New York: Methodist Publishing House, 1947.

Green, Vivian Hubert Howard. *The Young Mr. Wesley.* New York: St. Martin's, 1961.

Heitzenrater, R. P. "John Wesley's Early Sermons." *PWHS* 31 (1970): 110 – 28; also in R. P. Heitzenrater, *Mirror and Memory*, 150 – 62. Nashville: Kingswood, 1989.

Hildebrandt, Franz. *From Luther to Wesley.* London: Lutterworth, 1951.

Knox, Ronald. *Enthusiasm.* New York: Oxford, 1950.

Outler, Albert C., ed. *John Wesley*. Library of Protestant Theology. New York: Oxford University Press, 1964.

Sermons and Homilies Appointed to be Read in Church in the Time of Queen Elizabeth of Famous Memory (1547 – 71). Oxford: Clarendon, 1802.

Wood, A. Skevington. *The Burning Heart: John Wesley, Evangelist.* Exeter: Paternoster, 1967.

CHAPTER 2

The Scripture Way of Salvation

A. Salvation by Faith

The Standard Sermons, titled *Sermons on Several Occasions* (first four volumes of the original series), are Wesley's key teaching homilies. The first of all these homilies is "Salvation by Faith." The text is Ephesians 2:8: "By grace you are saved through faith" (Wesley's translation) [Homily #1 (1738), B 1:117 – 30; J #I, V:7 – 17].

Preached at St. Mary's Church in Oxford, it was written only eighteen days after Wesley's life-changing experience of pardon at Aldersgate. Deeply affected by the power of that breakthrough, he stated its essence: "Grace is the source, faith the condition of salvation."[1] All else in all the standard sermons turns on this pivot: Salvation is a free, unmerited divine gift, rightly received by trusting the forgiving act of God the Son.

1. Defining Faith Negatively by What It Is Not

Saving faith is best characterized by distinguishing it from what faith is not. Saving faith is:

different from the general faith of natural humanity,
different from despairing demonic recognition of Christ's lordship,[2] and
different from that form of rational faith found in empirical and historical inquiry.[3]

a. Saving Faith Is Not General Faith of Moral Virtue in Natural Humanity

Wesley distinguished saving faith from the general form of faith present in natural human moral consciousness. The faith that saves from sin is not the same as the faith that arises in ordinary experiences of trust in the world. There is a form of faith that is evidenced by the sincere and conscientious practice of moral virtue in

[1]"Salvation by Faith," B 1:118, prologue 3.

[2]This is the convicted despair felt by the demonic powers upon recognizing that the Messiah would end their power — the closest the demonic can get to faith, a kind of convicted but despairing persuasion of the truth.

[3]"Salvation by Faith," B 1:118, prologue 3.

natural humanity. That faith in itself does not bring divine pardon. In eighteenth-century terms, this was sometimes called "the faith of the heathen." Not necessarily a demeaning term in the eighteenth century, the word *heathen* was commonly employed in the Hebrew sense of *goi*[4] (Gentiles) and the Greek sense of *ethnos* (people, the nations). It referred to those who do not worship the God of Israel or of Jesus Christ but may have access to rational knowledge of the being and attributes of God and a hope of future judgment. They may show behavioral evidences of justice, love, and mercy. These evidences of natural trust and human hope amid fallen human freedom may anticipate saving faith in a preliminary way. But they fall short of that saving faith that is enabled by divine grace that trusts in the atoning work and pardoning power of God the Son.[5]

b. Saving Faith Is Not the "Faith of the Devils" Who Recognize Christ but Do Not Assent to His Lordship

Nor is saving faith the despairing demonic recognition of Christ's lordship described by theologians as "the faith of the devils," who not only know what the heathen know of God, but also unbelievingly know that "Jesus Christ is the Son of God, the Christ, the Saviour."[6]

In the New Testament, the demonic powers rightly identify Christ but do not assent to his lordship. They know intensely and desperately that Jesus is the Christ. That is precisely why they are afraid of the revelation he bears: it will undermine their false life. When the demons come upon Christ, they distinguish him immediately and scatter, knowing that the Son of God has appeared. They are cast into swine who bolt abruptly into the sea.[7] They recognize that Christ is Lord but do not trust in his promise. Rather, they flee from him in panic. The "faith" of the devils is not saving faith.

In saving faith, Christ is welcomed as Lord. He calls on each person in range of his voice to trust in him in order to prepare them for life in the kingdom of God. Seekers are called to cast their whole lot on the truth of his Word and trust in this incomparably trustable one.[8] This is the faith that saves from sin.

The recognition of Christ by the demonic powers does not cause them to renounce all other false gods. Simple recognition that Jesus is the Christ, even by the demonic powers, is hardly the same as the renouncing of all other gods and turning to him in faith.[9]

---

[4]"On Faith (Heb. 11:6)," B 3:493 – 95, sec. 1.

[5]"The Almost Christian," B 1:131 – 32, sec. 1.1 – 3.

[6]"Salvation by Faith," B 1:119, sec. 1.2; "The Way to the Kingdom," sec. 1.6.

[7]Mark 5:12 – 17; cf. Sören Kierkegaard, *The Concept of Anxiety* (Princeton: Princeton University Press, 1981).

[8]"Even the devils believe that Christ was born of a virgin, that He wrought all kinds of miracles, that for our sakes He suffered a most painful death to redeem us from death everlasting . . . and yet for all this faith, they be but devils." Letter to Thomas Church, June 1746, *LJW* 2:269.

[9]"Salvation by Faith," B 1:119, sec. 1.2.

c. Saving Faith Is Not Faith Based on Speculative Rational or Empirical Inquiry

Saving faith is not the same as *that form of confidence that results from natural human observation of facts.* By scientific methods people can come to trust in the reliability of natural laws and processes, the relation of cause to effect, and in the rational order of creation. But that is not the faith that saves from sin and death. Saving faith is not "barely a speculative rational thing, a cold, lifeless assent, a train of ideas in the head, but also a disposition of the heart."[10]

To receive that disposition of the heart, believers are attentive to the correct observation of facts, but the leading observation that brings them toward the porch of saving faith is that they repent and come to personal trust in the Savior.[11] Some disciples had left all to follow him and were preaching the coming kingdom and healing diseases, but they had not yet thoroughly experienced saving faith. The doubt of Thomas, the ambivalence of Peter, and the betrayal of Judas show this point. Their embryonic faith became saving faith only when they met the resurrected Lord and believed.

2. What Then Is Saving Faith?

Grace is not enabled by faith. Faith is enabled by grace. To imagine that grace comes from faith turns the order of salvation on its head. Rather, grace makes faith possible. Faith is *the disposition of the whole heart, mind, strength, and will to receive grace joyfully.* In the apostolic preaching, faith is the sole condition of salvation. Those who have faith are saved.[12]

"Christian faith is then not only an assent to the whole gospel of Christ, but also a full reliance on the blood of Christ, a *trust* in the merits of his life, death, and resurrection; a recumbency on him as our atonement and our life, as *given for us* and *living in us.*"[13]

Saving faith is a "*sure confidence* which a man hath in God, that through the merits of Christ *his* sins are forgiven, and *he* is reconciled to the favour of God; and, in consequence hereof, a closing with him and cleaving to him as our 'wisdom, righteousness, sanctification, and redemption,' or, in one word, our salvation."[14]

Saving faith is this total trust, casting one's whole life on the truth manifested in the resurrected Christ. It is a disposition of the heart to embrace and hold fast the merit of the Son dying on the cross. We are saved by grace through this active reliance and recumbency.[15]

---

[10]"Salvation by Faith," B 1:120, sec. 1.4.
[11]"The Scripture Way of Salvation," B 2:156 – 63, sec. 2.3.
[12]"On Faith (Heb. 11:6)," B 3:497 – 98, sec. 1.10 – 13.
[13]"Salvation by Faith," B 1:121, sec. 1.5, italics added.
[14]"Salvation by Faith," B 1:121, sec. 1.5; cf. "An Earnest Appeal," B 11:68 – 69, sec. 59.
[15]"Salvation by Faith," B 1:121 – 22, secs. 1.5 – 2.2.

3. The Three Tenses of Turning Away from the Death of Sin and toward the Life of Faith

Saving faith renovates our relation with time. There are three tenses of time: present, past, and future. All tenses are transformed by saving faith. Faith saves

from the *power of present sin,*
from the *guilt of past sin,* and
from *fear of future punishment.*

Faith saves *from all sin.*[16]

a. Faith Saves in the Present Tense from Habitual Sin, Willful Sin, and Sins Resulting from Infirmities

God's pardoning act saves the believer now *from the present power of sin.*[17] This applies to all sins in the present tense, whether they are

habitual,
willful, or
due to our finiteness.

Saving faith transforms the believer's relation with *time present.* It saves from *habitual sin,* which no longer reigns in the believer, though it may remain; or second, from *willful sin,* insofar as the will while abiding in faith is "utterly set against all sin, and abhorreth it as deadly poison," or *the compulsive desire to sin,* for grace is undermining the emergence of unholy desire in us. Thus, one born of God is being freed not to sin habitually or by compulsive desire or even by *sins resulting from human infirmities.*[18] Lacking concurrence of the will, infirmities and evidences due to our created finitude "are not properly sins." We are presently saved from the reign of sin even though the remnants of sin remain in a history of sin that has continuing fallout.[19]

b. Faith Saves in the Past Tense from the Guilt of All Past Sin

Saving faith saves *from the guilt of past sin.* For Christ has "blotted out the handwriting that was against us" — the verdict, the sentence of death, "nailing it to the cross." The accusations against us are by faith blotted out from the record.

Forgiven, we enter into a new relation with our past, having no need to carry it around as a burden of guilt.[20]

c. Faith Saves from Fear of Future Punishment

Saving faith saves *from the fear of future punishment,* from all anxiety about God's holy justice on the last day. The future is taken up into the shelter of faith. So

[16]"Salvation by Faith," B 1:121 – 25, sec. 2; cf. B 1:383; 3:179; 4:26.
[17]"Salvation by Faith," B 1:121; cf. 2:156.
[18]"Salvation by Faith," B 1:124, sec. 1.6.
[19]"Salvation by Faith," B 1:121 – 23, sec. 1.5 – 7.
[20]"Salvation by Faith," B 1:121 – 22, sec. 1.1 – 3.

long as belief is sustained, the believer does not constantly fear God's future judgment of his sin. That is already overcome. Dread has been conquered. The future has been brought safely under the wing of ongoing participation of life in Christ.

Saving faith stands in a different relation to the Father than fear. It is no longer preoccupied by the terror of God's anger against the corruption of the goodness of creation. That terror has been left at the foot of the cross.

Those who walk by faith are not paralyzed by fear of the final sentence of divine judgment. They behold God as a Father who brings a reconciling peace from which nothing can separate them.[21] "They are also saved from the fear, though not from the possibility, of falling away from the grace of God."[22]

4. Sin Loses Its Power

a. Those Born of God Do Not Sin (1 John 5:18)

On the basis of these promises, John wrote, "We know that those who are born of God do not sin" (1 John 5:18 NRSV), insofar as their new birth is sustained by grace through faith. By that faith "God protects them, and the evil one does not touch them" (1 John 5:18 NRSV).

Justification overcomes sin. Sin has no power over those who walk daily in faith. Believers cannot say, "I have never sinned." But insofar as they stand within saving faith, they can trust that God pardons them.[23]

Now is the only moment in which it is imperative not to sin. All future moments are left entirely to the pardon of grace if accompanied by faith.

Salvation is not just a theory. It is an experienced deliverance from all sorts of sin. Saving grace is actually sufficient to change our lives now and into the future. This is a radical understanding of the extent of God's saving work in us. Justification denotes "a deliverance from guilt and punishment, by the atonement of Christ actually applied to the soul of the sinner now believing on him, and a deliverance from the power of sin, through Christ 'formed in his heart.'"[24]

b. Salvation for Life in Christ

Born again of the Spirit into a new life "hidden with Christ in God" (cf. Col. 3:3 NIV), the believer gladly receives "the sincere milk of the word ... [and] grow[s] thereby" (cf. 1 Peter 2:2), growing from faith to faith, from grace to grace, until at length he comes to receive the inheritance of full salvation — he comes "unto a perfect man, unto the measure of the stature of the fulness of Christ" (Rom. 1:17; cf. Eph. 4:13).[25]

From this new birth, one may grow in faith by grace toward perfect love, receiving strength from God by being fed by the Word. God's saving activity intends to

[21]"Salvation by Faith," B 1:122, sec. 1.4.
[22]PCC, sec. 74; "On Perfection," prologue; cf. *LJW* 3:100 – 101.
[23]"Salvation by Faith," B 1:124, sec. 2.6.
[24]"Salvation by Faith," B 1:124, sec. 2.7; *CH*, B 7:290 – 92.
[25]"Salvation by Faith," B 1:124, sec. 1.7.

transform the whole self from willful sinning, sinful desiring, and habitual sinning toward wholly trusting in God, so as to reshape the whole life of the believer. The heart is bent away from the idolatry of the world and toward the reception of the gifts God gives.[26]

5. The Doctrinal Minutes: Salvation Begun, Continued, and Completed

The sum of salvation is stated in the Doctrinal Minutes: "In asserting salvation by faith, we mean this: 1. That pardon (salvation begun) is received by faith producing works; 2. That holiness (salvation continued) is faith working by love; 3. That heaven (salvation finished) is the reward of this faith."[27]

The Doctrinal Minutes constitute the earliest constitutional core of the later Doctrinal Standards of the Wesleyan traditions. They were hammered out "in conference" by Wesley and the preachers in the early days of the revival.

6. The Preface to the Hymns on Salvation

In the preface to the 1740 *Hymns and Sacred Poems*, the Wesleys distinguished salvation *from* and salvation *for* — salvation *from fear*, knowing the believer has peace with God; *from doubt*, aware of the Spirit's witness of assurance; and *from sin*, so as to become servants of righteousness, according to the promise "that the true child of God does not sin; he is in the charge of God's own Son and the evil one must keep his distance" (1 John 5:18 Phillips).

Freed from self-will, they desire nothing but the will of God. Free from evil thoughts, there is "no room for this in a soul which is full of God." Free from "that great root of sin and bitterness, pride," they "feel that all their sufficiency is from God."

"Not that they have 'already attained' all they shall attain, either 'are already,' in this sense, 'perfect.' But they daily go on 'from strength to strength: Beholding now as in a glass the glory of the Lord, they are changed into the same image, from glory to glory.'"[28]

7. Antinomian Dangers to Be Avoided

a. Whether Salvation by Faith Stimulates License

Everything not of faith, since unresponsive to God, lives under the shadow of sin and death. The gifts of God are ignored.

God wishes us to come to him by the way he has illumined. God wishes us to trust his own costly plan of salvation, not invent another imagined to be better.[29]

The sinner who at heart remains corrupt cannot atone for his own sinfulness through his own works. There is no merit in any work when considered apart from

---

[26]"Salvation by Faith," B 1:125 – 30, sec. 3; cf. "Spiritual Worship," J VI:430, sec. 2.5, 6.
[27]Minutes, 1746, May 13, Q3, JWO 159.
[28]*HSP* (1740), pref. 4 – 7, J XIV:323 – 25.
[29]"Salvation by Faith," B 1:125 – 30, sec. 3.

grace. "All who preach not faith do manifestly make void the law....'We establish the law,' both by showing its full extent and spiritual meaning; and by calling all to that living way, whereby 'the righteousness of the law' may be fulfilled in them."[30]

b. Law and Gospel

We cannot rightly fulfill any part of the law without trusting what God has done for us on the cross. Justifying faith does not void but fulfills the law, so that the law becomes rightly established through faith.[31]

Some who have this faith may be tempted to continue in sin that grace may abound, yet God's grace when rightly understood leads to repentance and deeds of mercy, not license.[32] When faith becomes the occasion for resting easy or refusing to do good works, it ceases to be faith.[33]

True faith always produces good works fitting to its circumstances. The thief on the cross, whose faith brought a promise of paradise, had no further opportunity to express his faith in good works. He did all the works of mercy that were possible for him hanging on a cross. Anyone grounded in faith will be manifesting good works, living an accountable and useful life. Law and gospel are to be preached together. Faith does not reduce the gospel to license.[34]

c. Whether Salvation by Faith Induces Pride and Despair

Even the best of human motivations are tempted to pride. Saving faith constantly seeks to become active in love. It is a tonic against pride and against any boasting in ourselves. Justifying faith glories in the gracious gift that has the transforming power to change our pride.[35] We come always to the Lord's Table humbly, and if not humbly, not truly or efficaciously.[36]

Repentance in one sense may bring us temporarily to despair over our own adequacies with the purpose of shaping our behavior toward further growth in faith. We have no natural ability to save ourselves. This leads us more fully to trust in God's saving work. "For none can trust in the merits of Christ till he has utterly renounced his own."[37] There is thus a redeeming aspect in this constructive kind of despair that points toward deeper faith.[38] No one is prepared to trust in God's righteousness until he has come to despair of his own.[39]

---

[30]"Salvation by Faith," B 1:125, sec. 3.2; cf. *LJW* 6:122.

[31]"The Original, Nature, Property, and Use of the Law," B 2:16, sec. 4.23.

[32]"Dialogue between an Antinomian and His Friend," J X:266–84.

[33]"Salvation by Faith," B 1:126–27, sec. 3.4.

[34]Minutes, 1745, August 2, J VIII:284–85. As Luther ("that champion of the Lord of hosts") discovered; "Salvation by Faith," B 1:129, sec. 3.9. Only eighteen days before, Wesley had "felt his heart strangely warmed" while listening to the reading of the introduction to Luther's commentary on Romans. Later, in 1749, Wesley published a life of Luther.

[35]"Walking by Sight and Walking by Faith," B 4:56–58, secs.16–19.

[36]"Salvation by Faith," B 1:126, sec. 3.3.

[37]"Salvation by Faith," B 1:127, sec. 3.5.

[38]"A Call to Backsliders," B 3:210–26.

[39]"Salvation by Faith," B 1:127–28, sec. 3.5, 6.

Some worry that justification is a humiliating, uncomfortable, even masochistic doctrine, lowering self-esteem. Saving faith is better understood as a reversal of low self-esteem. It at last offers a firm basis for genuine self-affirmation and the recovery of self-worth. For we are being actively loved by the one most able to love and most worthy of being loved. It is profoundly comforting inasmuch as it is primarily a doctrine about God's mercy and forgiveness to sinners.[40]

But should such a volatile and dangerous teaching be preached indiscriminately to all? Wesley answered that it must be preached precisely to sinners, namely, to "every creature," and especially to the poor who "have a peculiar right to have the gospel preached unto them."[41] "Never was the maintaining of this doctrine more seasonable than it is at this day.... It is endless to attack, one by one, all the errors" of the church, "but salvation by faith strikes at the root."[42] "For this reason the adversary so rages whenever 'salvation by faith' is declared."[43]

B. The Scripture Way of Salvation

The text of the homily "The Scripture Way of Salvation" is Ephesians 2:8: "By grace are ye saved through faith" [Homily #43 (1765), B 2:153–69; J #43, V:43–54].

1. The Means, Faith; the End, Salvation

Christianity is that plain and simple religion that teaches that the sublime goal of human life, salvation, can be obtained only by the *means*, faith.[44] "The *end* is, in one word, salvation; the means to attain it, faith."[45] By this end and means, "we see the *spiritual world*, which is all round about us, and yet no more discerned by our natural faculties than if it had no being."[46] "It is by this faith ... that we *receive Christ* ... in all His offices, as our Prophet, Priest, and King."[47]

"Faith necessarily implies an assurance," a recognition of evidence within, that I am a child of this Abba. "A man cannot have a childlike *confidence* in God till he knows he *is* a child of God."[48]

"By this faith we are saved, justified, and sanctified."[49] Faith is "the only condition of justification,"[50] which is God's verdict demonstrating willingness to pardon sinners. "We are sanctified as well as justified by faith."[51]

"Both repentance, and fruits meet for repentance, are, in some sense, necessary

[40]XXXIX, art. 11.
[41]"Salvation by Faith," B 1:128, sec. 3.7.
[42]"Salvation by Faith," B 1:128–29, sec. 3.8.
[43]"Salvation by Faith," B 1:129, sec. 3.9.
[44]B 1:120–21, 138–39; 3:497–98.
[45]"The Scripture Way of Salvation," B 2:156, proem 1, italics added.
[46]"The Scripture Way of Salvation," B 2:160–61, sec. 2.1.
[47]"The Scripture Way of Salvation," B 2:161, sec. 2.2; *CH*, B 7:314–15, italics added.
[48]"The Scripture Way of Salvation," B 2:161–62, sec. 2.3.
[49]"The Scripture Way of Salvation," B 2:162, sec. 2.4.
[50]"The Scripture Way of Salvation," B 2:163, sec. 3.2.
[51]"The Scripture Way of Salvation," B 2:163, sec. 3.3.

to justification. But they are not necessary in the *same sense* with faith, nor in the *same degree*. Not in the *same degree*; for those fruits are only necessary *conditionally*; if there be time and opportunity for them.... Not in the *same sense*; for this repentance and these fruits are only *remotely* necessary, necessary in order to the continuance of his faith, as well as the increase of it; whereas faith is *immediately and directly* necessary to sanctification" as it is to justification.[52]

2. Expect It Now!

Justifying faith "may be *gradually* wrought in some." In this case, the believer is likely to go through a growing process leading toward fuller responsiveness to grace, and may not experience a "particular moment wherein sin ceases to be." "But it is infinitely desirable," wrote Wesley, "that it should be done *instantaneously* ... in a moment, in the twinkling of an eye."[53] This in fact often did occur in the context of the revival. It was repeatedly attested by those who experienced it.

"By this token you may surely know whether you seek [salvation] by faith or by works. If by works you want something to be done *first, before* you are sanctified." But if you seek it by faith, you may expect it *as you are*."[54] It is not difficult to know whether you are ready for saving grace. If you are ready, expect it now.

The line is drawn sharply between a false salvation by works and a true salvation by faith. If works, you imagine you must act first before grace enters. If by faith, you come as you are, expecting grace to work precisely in your condition as a sinner.

"There is an inseparable connection between these three points, — expect it *by faith*, expect it *as you are*, and expect it *now*!"[55]

3. Relating the Pardon of the Son to the Power of the Spirit

a. The Moment of Justification Begins the Gradual Work of Sanctification

A work of sanctification is taking place that enables the believer to put to death the deeds of the sinful nature. Grace seeks full responsiveness. It aims at entire sanctification, full salvation, the perfection of love that so fills the heart that there is no more room for sin.[56]

We will deal more fully with sanctification in a later chapter, but for now, the basic relation is clearly stated: "At the same time that we are justified, yea, in that very moment, sanctification *begins*."[57] To say it begins does not mean that it is complete.

Wesley makes a crucial distinction between what God does for us and what God

[52]"The Scripture Way of Salvation," B 2:163, 167, sec. 3.2, 13, italics added.
[53]"The Scripture Way of Salvation," B 2:168 – 69, sec. 3.18, italics added.
[54]"The Scripture Way of Salvation," B 2:169, sec. 3.18.
[55]Ibid.
[56]"The Scripture Way of Salvation," B 2:162 – 69, sec. 3.
[57]"The Scripture Way of Salvation," B 2:158, sec. 1.4, italics added.

does in us. *Justification* refers to *a relational change* whereby God accepts us into a new relation of sonship and daughterhood; *sanctification* refers to *a real change* whereby we are "inwardly renewed by the power of God."[58] God's pardon changes our relation with God. God's Spirit works within our spirits to elicit a real change in our behavior that we may more fully refract the image of God in us.

"From the time of our being born again, the gradual work of sanctification takes place. We are enabled 'by the Spirit' to 'mortify the deeds of the body,' of our evil nature; and as we are more and more dead to sin, we are more and more alive to God. We go on from grace to grace."[59]

Justifying grace gives birth to a new life of holy living. From that moment on, sanctifying grace is at work to complete the work of the Spirit in the believer's heart.

"No man is sanctified till he believes; every man when he believes is sanctified."[60] To the extent that he unreservedly believes, though subject to lapses, he is made the temple of God by grace.

b. The Power of Sin Stunned, Not Dead

Sin is not unequivocally destroyed in the new birth, but its power is broken. Its effects are "suspended." "Temptations return, and sin revives, showing it was but stunned before, not dead. They now feel two principles in themselves, plainly contrary to each other: the flesh lusting against the spirit, [fallen] nature opposing the grace of God."[61]

Meanwhile, the witness of the Spirit attests that the believer is a child of God. Wesley knew that Macarius of the Desert Fathers "fourteen hundred years ago" understood that neophytes in faith may "presently imagine they have no more sin." But the more experienced and prudent in faith realize that even after concupiscence may have "withered quite away ... for five or six years ... yet after all, when they thought themselves freed entirely from it, the corruption that lurked within, was stirred up anew."[62] The Spirit does not leave us in our backslidden state but continues to shepherd us toward full responsiveness to grace.

c. Sin Remains but Does Not Reign

For this reason there is a repentance that follows justification for sins remaining in justified believers. We will discuss this further in chapter 10, "On Remaining Sin after Justification." Wesley wrote: "There is a repentance consequent upon, as well as a repentance previous to, justification ... the repentance consequent upon justification [being] widely different from that which is antecedent to it." The repentance that follows justification is "a conviction wrought by the Holy Ghost, of

[58]Ibid.
[59]"The Scripture Way of Salvation," B 2:160, sec. 1.8.
[60]"The Scripture Way of Salvation," B 2:164, sec. 3.3.
[61]"The Scripture Way of Salvation," B 2:159, sec. 1.6; Gal. 5:17.
[62]Ibid.; see 159n., from *The Spiritual Homilies of Macarius the Egyptian* (1721); translation "by a presbyter of the Church of England."

the *sin* which still *remains* in our heart; of the *phronema sarkos, the carnal mind,* which 'does still remain,' (as our Church speaks,) even in them that are regenerate, although it does no longer *reign*; it has not now dominion over them."[63]

Sin may *remain* in the life of faith, but it does not *reign*. It has lost its power to hold sway over the believer. The faith by which "we are sanctified, saved from sin, and perfected in love" is a divine evidence and conviction that God has promised this new life in Scripture. What God has promised he is able to perform, and he is willing to do now. Indeed, he "doeth it."[64]

"Of all the written sermons, this one had the most extensive history of oral preaching behind it," according to Outler, and remains "the most successful summary of the Wesleyan vision of the *ordo salutis.*"[65]

[63]"The Scripture Way of Salvation," B 2:165, sec. 3.6, italics added.
[64]"The Scripture Way of Salvation," B 2:166 – 68, sec. 3.13 – 17.
[65]"Order of Salvation," JWO, intro.; "The Scripture Way of Salvation," B 2:154.

CHAPTER 3

Justification

A. Justification by Faith

The text of the leading homily on "Justification by Faith" is Romans 4:5: "To him that worketh not, but believeth on him that justifieth the ungodly, his faith is counted for righteousness" [Homily #5 (1746), B 1:181 – 99; J #5, V:53 – 64].

More than any other Wesley homilies, this one sets forth the core classic Pauline and Reformation teaching of justification. It deals with the verdict expressed in God the Son's self-sacrificing action on the cross. Justification is first viewed in relation to the history of sin leading to the cross, then in relation to sanctification, its recipients, and its sole condition.[1]

1. The Salvation History Setting: Creation, Fall, and the Promise of Redemption

a. Creation and Fall

Our *original* condition is not alienation from God, but receptive trust, divine-human encounter, personal dialogue, and unsullied reflection of the divine goodness.[2] Human history was made in the image of God: holy, dwelling in love, as God is love, knowing no evil. To uncorrupted humanity (Adam and Eve before the fall), God gave a perfect law requiring simple obedience. There was no leeway for falling short. For the first man and woman were "altogether equal to the task assigned and thoroughly furnished for every good word and work."[3]

From that first primitive condition, freedom has gone awry in a sordid story of disobedience and *fallenness* into a history of sin in which the whole of human history has become estranged from God. Sin, guilt, and death have come to pervade this fallen human condition.[4]

This shameful history sets the context, the "general ground," for the teaching of

[1]On justification, see *LJW* 1:248; 2:107; B 1:182 – 99, 320 – 21; *CH*, B 7:11, 80, 142; cf. *LJW* 5:96; 6:296; *JJW* 5:194.

[2]"The Image of God." Salvation is the restoration of the image of God; "Salvation by Faith," para. 1; "Original Sin," sec. 3.5.

[3]"Justification by Faith," B 1:184, sec. 1.1 – 3.

[4]"God's Approbation of His Works," B 2:397 – 98, sec. 2.1.

justification. Without sin there is no reason for the grace of justification. Sin has a disastrous history.[5]

b. Christ's Once-for-All Atoning Sacrifice for My Sins

Into this fallen human condition, God sends his Son as a once-for-all sacrifice for the sins of the world. God the Son on the cross embodies the incomparable word of divine pardon apart from any act or merit of our own. He invites us to be reconciled again to the Father and brought back into our original condition of holiness and happiness.

This reconciling act of God is our justification, our being uprighted in the presence of God, not by anything we have done on our own but by what God has done for us on the cross. If one "does a piece of work, his wages are not 'counted' as a favour; they are paid as debt. But if without any work to his credit he simply puts his faith in him who acquits the guilty, then his faith is indeed 'counted as righteousness'" (Rom. 4:4–5 NEB). The Son's righteousness is credited to my account.

c. Justification Completed on the Cross by Atoning Grace

The sinner is uprighted by atoning grace declared on the cross, by God's own righteousness, which is the work of Christ for us, a juridical act — an act of the divine Judge alone — that occurs through an event, the cross.

As in Adam, "the common father and representative of us all," death passed upon all humanity, "even so, by the sacrifice for sin made by the second Adam, as the representative of us all, God is so far reconciled to the world, that He hath given them a new covenant."[6] The cross reconciles God to the world, and only by his gracious mercy reconciles the world to God.

Justification is already completed on the cross and not something for me to complete by any action but faith. Saving faith is our trusting response to this divine deed of justification in which we are counted righteous. God the Spirit works in the heart to transform our behavior so that it bears fruit.[7] This is the doctrine that places Wesleyan teaching close to the heart of the magisterial Reformation — Luther, Calvin, Reformed, and contemporary evangelical teaching.

2. What God Does for Us through the Son Is Related to What God Works in Us by the Spirit

a. The Difference between Justification and Sanctification

Justification is "what God *does for us* through his Son." Sanctification is what God "*works in us* by his Spirit."[8] This is one of the most crucial distinctions in Wesley's teaching. It is not meant to separate the Son and Spirit but to show the

[5]"Justification by Faith," B 1:184–87, sec. 1.1–9.

[6]"Justification by Faith," B 1:185–87, sec. 1.5–9; *CH*, B 7:120, 210.

[7]"Justification by Faith," B 1:186–87, sec. 1.7–9; cf. B 1:642.

[8]See "The New Birth," B 2:187, sec. 1, italics added; "The Great Privilege of Those That Are Born of God," sec. 1.1.

difference between the work of God the Son and God the Spirit in the one Holy Trinity. The Son is born, crucified, buried, and resurrected. The Spirit penetrates the believer's heart so that the work of the Son may be inwardly received.

God's work for us through the Son prepares the ground for God's work in us through the Spirit, the new birth of receiving justifying grace. Having been born anew in Christ's love, we are freed to grow further in faith by sanctifying grace.[9]

b. God's Justifying Act Comes as a Verdict Credited to Our Favor through Faith

Justification is a forensic declaration, a *verdict* credited in our favor, God's act for us. That does not instantly make the hearer behaviorally righteous — that is, measured directly by behavioral change. That behavioral change is the work of the Holy Spirit who works to perfect in time what is given in justification. The Spirit's work in us seeks the complete and mature embodiment of the life of faith.[10]

c. Through Sanctification the Spirit Inwardly and Outwardly Bears Fruit from God's Justifying Verdict in the Son

Sanctification is the "immediate *fruit* of justification." It remains "a distinct gift of God." It is distinguished from justification just as growth is related to but distinguishable from birth. Wesley knew that Scripture used the term *justification* in a generic sense "so as to include sanctification also, yet in general use they are sufficiently distinguished from each other both by St. Paul and the other inspired writers."[11] At the instant of conversion, the believer experiences the "immediate fruit of justification."

Justification is the objective ground of regeneration, the beginning of a new birth that culminates in a growing process. If justification enables a new birth, sanctification enables a steadily growing process. Nobody grows until he or she is born. Nobody enters into this process of sanctification except by being born by justifying grace.[12]

d. The Triune Premise of Salvation Teaching

The triune voice of the one God underlies this whole process of personal salvation. It is a pivotal Wesleyan teaching: justification is the work of the Son, while sanctification is the work of the Spirit. They are integrally joined since God is one, and inseparable, because "the Lord ... is the Spirit" (2 Cor. 3:17). Yet they are distinguishable in voice because the mission of the Spirit is to bring to full expression the ministry of the Son who is truly human, truly God.

Justification does not undermine conscience. It does not argue with the just address of the moral law. It transforms by divine grace the person's relation to the law.

---

[9]"Justification by Faith," B 1:187, sec. 2.1.
[10]JWO 201 – 2.
[11]"Justification by Faith," B 1:187, sec. 2.1.
[12]"Justification by Faith," B 1:187 – 90, sec. 2.

"Least of all does justification imply that God is deceived in those whom he justifies" or that God pretends that sinners are what they are not.[13]

"The plain scriptural notion of justification is pardon, forgiveness of sins. It is that act of God the Father whereby, for the sake of the propitiation made by the blood of his Son, he 'showeth forth his righteousness (or mercy) by the remission of the sins that are past.' "[14] To those justified by faith "God 'will not impute sin' to his condemnation" (Rom. 4:7 – 8, B 1:189n). The legal definition of *impute* is to attach to a person responsibility for injuries due to a relationship, such as Christ has taken responsibility for our sins. For Protestant theology, *impute* means to render a verdict of pardon. The sinner under the blessing of divine pardon is not condemned.

All his past sins "in thought, word, and deed, 'are covered,' are blotted out; shall not be remembered or mentioned against him, any more than if they had not been. God will not inflict on that sinner what he deserved to suffer, because the Son of his love hath suffered for him."[15] Justification is the inclusive (plenary) act covering the whole range of the believer's sin, in thought, word, and deed.

3. Whether Only Sinners Are Justified

a. Only Sinners Need Pardon

To whom is this justifying grace addressed? Precisely to the ungodly! Only sinners have the need or occasion for pardon.[16] The shepherd responds urgently to seek and save the one who is lost, who in repentance knows his lostness.[17] The physician comes to heal not those already healthy but those struggling mightily with the sickness of the history of sin.[18]

This has consequences for the way we order theological reflection: justification makes way for sanctification, just as the work of the Son on the cross makes way for the mighty work of the Spirit.

This ordering must not be turned on its head, so as first to require sanctification, as if only the perfected saints are justified. It is not that one must first become holy so as to be worthy of being justified.[19] That in fact was what Wesley, in his Georgia period, might have seemed close to believing, that one had best seek to be holy to ready oneself for justifying grace.[20] It remains disputed whether he did in

[13]"Justification by Faith," B 1:188, sec. 2.4.

[14]See Rom. 3:25; cf. B 1:189n. In a letter to John Newton, May 14, 1765, Wesley wrote: "I think on justification just as I have done any time these seven and twenty years — and just as Mr. Calvin does. In this respect I do not differ from him a hair's breadth." Calvin, however, as Outler notes, asserts that "in justification, faith is merely passive" (*Institutes of the Christian Religion*, 3.20.5), whereas "Wesley understood justifying faith as 'active' " (B 1:189n.).

[15]"Justification by Faith," B 1:189 – 90, sec. 2.5.

[16]"Justification by Faith," B 1:190, sec. 3.1.

[17]"Justification by Faith," B 1:191, sec. 3.3.

[18]"Justification by Faith," B 1:191 – 92, sec. 3.3, 4.

[19]"Justification by Faith," B 1:191, sec. 3.2.

[20]The holy living tradition of Jeremy Taylor had stressed that "works meet for repentance" (Acts 26:20 KJV) were ordinarily required as evidences of readiness for justification, especially when understood as final justification on the last day. See Taylor, *Unum Necessarium Deus justificatus*, chap. ix, "Works" (London: Brown, Green, and Longmans, 1850), 2:598 – 99.

fact. But by the time he preaches this sermon, it is apparent that this order is made clear: justification is the premise of any work of sanctification and any response to sanctifying grace.[21]

William Law, Wesley's earlier mentor, had viewed religion primarily as sanctification, conformity to the life of Christ, bearing the cross, mortification as the essence of piety, and the necessary condition of justification.[22] Writing to Law in May of 1738, Wesley recognized that Law's way was a deadly capitulation to legalism, and that faith in Christ's work of atonement was the only necessary condition of justification. Sanctification is "not the cause, but the effect" of justification.[23]

b. Only by Faith Is God's Pardon Received

What is the sole condition of receiving this justification? Only one word can express it: faith. Faith is understood as trust (Gk. *pistis*). The believer trusts in the truthfulness of God's word addressed on the cross. Faith is the divine evidence or conviction of the truth of things not seen by our bodily eyes.[24]

Justifying faith hinges not merely on the conceptual conviction that God was in Christ, but more so on the sure personal trust that Christ died *for me*.[25] The *pro me* theme so prominent in Luther is reappropriated here. The surprising awareness that this gift is truly "for me" is written decisively into the language of the Aldersgate narrative — even to me! A small room on Aldersgate Street was the setting for Wesley's heart being "strangely warmed." There he received this divine evidence.

Faith is "the sole condition of justification,"[26] and in fact "the *only necessary* condition" of justification.[27] Without faith one is still under the curse of the law. Faith is counted to the believer as righteousness.[28]

4. The Terms on Which Saving Grace Is Received

a. Simply Repent and Believe

"The terms of acceptance for fallen man are repentance and faith. 'Repent and believe the gospel.' "[29] Repent and believe. Repentance turns away from sin, while faith turns toward grace, so as to view this as a single turning.

What about infants who cannot sapiently believe? Wesley answers cautiously:

> Infants indeed our Church supposes to be justified in baptism, although they cannot then either *believe* or *repent*. But she ["our Church"] *expressly requires*

---

[21]XXXIX, art. 12; "The Doctrine of Salvation, Faith and Good Works," sec. 2.6.

[22]William Law, *Serious Call to the Devout and Holy Life* (London: J. M. Dent, 1728), 112 – 13, 165, 219; *WS* 56.

[23]*HSP* (1739), J XIV:320, pref. 2. For further comments on William Law, see B 1:34 – 35, 476 – 77; 3:328 – 30, 504 – 7; *LJW* 1:161; 3:215, 332, 370.

[24]"Justification by Faith," B 1:191, sec. 3.2.

[25]"Justification by Faith," B 1:194, sec. 4.2.

[26]"Justification by Faith," B 1:197, sec. 4.6. Elsewhere he conjoins with faith repentance: "The Repentance of Believers," sec. 2.6; Minutes, 1745; "Principles of a Methodist Farther Explained," 6.4.

[27]"Justification by Faith," B 1:195 – 96, sec. 4.4, 5, italics added.

[28]"The Scripture Way of Salvation," B 2:153 – 69.

[29]Letter to James Hervey, *LJW* 3:375.

> *both repentance and faith in those who come to be baptized when they are of riper years.* As earnestly therefore as our Church inculcates justification by faith alone, she nevertheless supposes repentance to be previous to faith, and "fruits meet for repentance"; yea, and universal holiness to be previous to final [eschatological] justification.[30]

b. Under God's Justifying Verdict the Believer Is Counted as If Upright, Clothed in Christ's Righteousness

Righteousness is given at the moment of faith, when the sinner casts himself upon the mercy of God in an act of trust that occurs only by grace. Who can doubt in such a complete yielding that the believer is completely forgiven at that moment?

Justification is a legal metaphor by which it is said we are counted as if upright in the presence of God due to the act of the Son on the cross to take upon himself the sins of the world. It is intended for all even though not all receive it voluntarily. This judicial act of justification grants full pardon,[31] a complete release from the penalty of sin to all who believe in Jesus Christ and receive him as Lord.[32]

God chose faith to combat pride so that we cannot come before God claiming our goodness, but only come ready to mirror God's own goodness.[33] Sinners are urged not to try to plead their own righteousness lest they destroy their own souls, but rather to look solely to the cross, which takes away sin.

"Thou ungodly one, who hearest or readest these words! thou vile, helpless, miserable sinner! I charge thee before God the Judge of all, go straight unto Him, with all thy ungodliness. Take heed thou destroy not thy own soul by pleading thy righteousness, more or less. Go as altogether ungodly, guilty, lost, destroyed.... Thou art the man! I want thee for my Lord! I challenge *thee* for a child of God by faith!"[34]

B. The Doctrinal Minutes on Justification

1. Justification Defined

Now we come to the crux of Wesley's teaching of salvation. It is found textually in a condensed five-page document that anyone can read in five minutes.[35]

a. The Doctrinal Importance of the Minutes of 1744

Wesley established a yearly conference, the first of which was held in 1744, where Methodist leaders were brought together for decisive conversation on doctrine and discipline. The definitions of official Wesleyan doctrine were hammered out in dialogue with his frontline advocates. The outcome of this conversational

[30]FA, pt. 1, 2.4; B 11:111, italics added.
[31]*LJW* 3:371; B 1:189, 585–87; 2:157–58; JWO 197, 202, 273.
[32]See the Articles of Religion on the Holy Spirit and soteriology.
[33]"The New Birth," B 2:190, sec. 1.4.
[34]"Justification by Faith," B 1:198–99, sec. 4.9.
[35]JWO 136–49.

process is seen in the Larger Minutes, often called the Doctrinal Minutes, of the first three years of annual conferences, 1744 – 47.

The record of those conversations became key reference points for doctrinal preaching among all early Methodist preachers, the core of what was later to be known as "our doctrines" in subsequent *Disciplines.* These were published under the title "Minutes of Some Late Conversations between the Rev. Mr. Wesley and Others."[36]

Their intent was to clarify key points of doctrine and practice in the emerging revival movement, especially justification, assurance, and sanctification. The minutes were recorded in the form of questions asked and consensually answered.

b. The First Question of Methodist Doctrine: What Is It to Be Justified?

The most crucial stage of definition of the doctrine of justification was at the very beginning of the formation of the minutes of the first conference that ultimately led to the Discipline.[37] It was question 1 on Wesley's agenda.

On June 25, 1744, Wesley met with close associates to set forth precise language on the doctrine of justification. These minutes "constitute the most important single exhibition of the manner and the substance of Wesley's theologizing."[38] The purpose was to gather key advisers and ask (1) what we teach, (2) how to teach it, and (3) "what to do to regulate our doctrine, discipline and practice."

The first conference focused on basic doctrine, as if "in the immediate presence of God, that we may meet with a single eye and as little children who have everything to learn, that every point may be examined from the foundation," that it might be settled surely and "bolted to the bran."[39] To "bolt to the bran" means to refine and purify, to examine thoroughly, so as to separate or discover everything important, to sift or separate the coarser from the finer particles of something, as bran from flour.

The first question was of highest importance: "What is it to be justified?" It is highly significant that the leading question for Methodist doctrine was from the outset "justification." This focuses the light on the essential beginning point for all Wesleyan teaching.[40]

---

[36]J VIII:275 – 98.

[37]However important, this document is not easy to locate. It is most conveniently found in its full version in Albert Outler's *John Wesley* (New York: Oxford University Press, 1964) and in a slightly edited version in the Jackson edition, VIII:275 – 78. Unfortunately, in the Bicentennial edition, to date, it is almost buried with little fanfare and with minimal help from either the text (B 9:20, where it should have been more fully developed as the lead doctrine of classic Methodist teaching) or in the scholarly apparatus and indexes of volume 9 where it is almost entirely overlooked. It is regrettable that so little rigorous attention has been paid in contemporary secondary literature to the precedent-setting importance of the Minutes of that day, June 25, 1744, from which all subsequent official Methodist doctrine and discipline emerged and became enlarged. It is puzzling that the Bicentennial edition, which is otherwise edited in such an exemplary way, should so neglect these earliest decisive Minutes that it is hard to find reference to them at all, either at some convenient point in the edition's design, or in the text or in the scholarly apparatus and indexes. A full text of these five pages with full commentary would have served the edition better. This may suggest a troubling neglect of justification teaching in modern Methodism.

[38]JWO 135.

[39]JWO 136

[40]Q1, JWO 136 – 37.

c. Justification Defined as Divine Pardon

Justification is "to be pardoned and received into God's favour." A pardon is a verdict of noncondemnation. The act of pardoning is accomplished by God. The recipient of pardon is received into God's favor or grace.

This once-for-all pardon is given so certainly by God that "if we continue therein, we shall be finally saved."[41] After thorough discussion with full consent, as recorded by Wesley's own hand, this definition was consensually confirmed.

Divine pardon invites and requires acceptance of that pardon. Those who continue in the reception of that verdict of pardon are saved from condemnation.[42]

Faith is the sole "condition of justification."[43] Those who believe in God's promise as fulfilled on the cross are justified and not condemned.

d. How Repentance Precedes Faith

Repentance must precede faith. For who can be ready to receive divine pardon but one who is truly contrite? Hence repentance must "go before faith."

By repentance the person comes before the holy God with a profound and heartfelt "conviction of sin." That conviction must be evidenced by an intention toward "obeying God as far as we can." "As far as we can" implies that the initial work of justifying grace assumes serious intent, not a cavalier or superficial resolve.

Wesley calls repentance "a low [or anticipative or preliminary] species of faith, i.e., a supernatural sense of an offended God. Justifying faith is a supernatural inward sense or sight of God in Christ reconciling the world unto himself."[44]

The work of sanctification is just beginning, but the sincere intent to obey God in faith is the operational beginning. "Works meet for repentance" imply obeying God, forgiving others, doing good, attending upon the ordinances of God, and "using his ordinances according to the power we have received."[45] These ordinances include praying, reading Scripture, and attending common worship, leading toward faithful baptism and the ongoing reception of Holy Communion (Q3).

2. Faith Defined

a. The Evidence or Manifestation of Things Not Seen

"What is faith?" (Q4): "*Faith*, in general, is a divine supernatural *elenchus*" – an "evidence or manifestation of things not seen, i.e., of past, future, or spiritual things. 'Tis a spiritual sight of God and the things of God."[46]

What is meant by "things not seen"? Living in the present, we cannot see the past. It is accessed only by memory. Within time we cannot see what is in the future. It is accessed by imagination, possibility, and conjecture, but we do not see it. Liv-

[41]Minutes, 1744, June 25, Q1, JWO 137.
[42]Q2, JWO 137.
[43]Minutes, 1744, June 25, Q2, JWO 137.
[44]Minutes, 1744, June 25, Q4, JWO 137, brackets inserted.
[45]Minutes, 1744, June 25, Q3, JWO 137.
[46]JWO 137.

ing within present time and space, we cannot without grace awaken the spiritual senses. The Spirit moves invisibly, without empirical recognition, without corporeal substance, such as that expected in a laboratory. This evidence of "things not seen" is a gift of God, not of fallen nature as such. By this "spiritual sight" enabled by our "spiritual senses," faith sees "the things of God."[47] "The things of God" refer to grace, divine pardon, faith, and all that pertains to life in God.

What is being recognized or "seen" in receiving God's pardon? "Justifying faith is a supernatural inward sense or sight of God in Christ reconciling the world unto himself. First, a sinner is convinced by the faith by which he is justified, or pardoned, the moment he receives it. Immediately the Spirit bears witness." This pardon received is "saving faith, whereby the love of God is shed abroad in his heart."[48]

b. How the Spirit's Witness Makes the Knowledge of Pardon Clear

In the same document we find question 5: "May not a man be justified and not know it?"

Answer: "No man can be justified and not know it," since *the Spirit bears witness within.* This is experienced as clearly as "ease after pain, rest after toil, light after darkness."[49]

The fruits of justifying faith are "peace, joy, love, power over all outward sin and power to keep down all inward sin." This spiritual sense is "the very essence of faith, love and obedience, the inseparable properties of it."[50]

c. How Willful Sin Is Inconsistent with Justifying Faith

For those justified, no willful sin is "consistent with justifying faith." "If a believer *wilfully sins,* he thereby *forfeits* his pardon," requiring a new repentance.[51] But there is no necessity that a believer needs ever again to come into condemnation. Ordinarily he will not "unless by ignorance and unfaithfulness." "Yet it is true that the first joy does seldom last long, that it is commonly followed by doubts and fears, and that God usually permits very great heaviness before any large manifestation of himself."[52]

3. How Faith Becomes Active in Love

Since faith becomes active in love, the works of love follow after faith. Faith is lost only through disobedience, not through the "want of works" as such. Faith is made perfect by the works of love. "The more we exert our faith, the more 'tis increased" (Q13).

But "St. Paul says Abraham was not justified by works; St. James, he was justified by works. Do they not then contradict each other?" No. Paul "speaks of that

[47]Ibid.
[48]Ibid., italics added.
[49]Ibid., italics added.
[50]JWO 138.
[51]Q9, JWO 138.
[52]Q10, JWO 138.

justification which was when Abraham was seventy-five years old" (before Isaac was born); James, "of that justification which was when he offered up Isaac on the altar.... St. Paul speaks of works that precede faith, St. James of works that spring from faith" (Q14).

4. The Joyful Awareness of Pardon

Wesley's letters confirm that justification is the gracious act of God by which he grants full pardon of all guilt and complete release from the penalty of sins committed, so that penitent sinners are accepted as righteous.[53]

"Pardon and acceptance, though they may be distinguished, cannot be divided."[54] All who believe in Jesus Christ and receive him as Lord and Savior are saved. Sincerity of intention toward God is a necessary but not sufficient condition for salvation. The sole sufficient condition for justification is clear: penitent faith. Thus, repent and believe. Repentance consists of conviction of sin, and faith in the conviction that God showed his love by dying for me, the premise of all holiness and good works.[55]

Consciousness of pardon is central to the whole evangelical revival ethos. This represented a shift of consciousness from the discipline-focused, pre-Aldersgate Holy Club of Oxford to the grace-saturated revival movement after 1738. At Oxford there was a strong resolution and total commitment to the holy life. But what was missing was a sweeping appropriation of justification by grace through faith, which only after 1738 became fully grasped. This does not mean that justification teaching was absent altogether before Aldersgate, but it did not yet have the personal experiential force and emotive power that it was soon to have. The joyful awareness of pardon would become the central energy of the revival. "Wherein does our doctrine now differ from that we preached when at Oxford? Chiefly in these two points: We then knew nothing of the righteousness of faith in justification, nor of the nature of faith itself as implying consciousness of pardon."[56]

5. Article 9 on Justification

God was in Christ reconciling the world to himself. The ninth article of the Twenty-Five Articles of Religion is on justification. It confesses that "we are *accounted righteous* before God, only for the merit of our Lord and Saviour Jesus Christ, *by faith*, and not for our own works or deservings. Wherefore, that we are justified by faith only is a most wholesome doctrine, and very full of comfort."[57] We are "uprighted" in the presence of the Father by the merit of the Son on the cross.

[53]In his "Conversation with the Bishop of Bristol," 1739, Wesley concisely defined "justifying faith" as "a conviction wrought in a man by the Holy Ghost, that Christ hath loved him, and given himself for him; and that, through Christ, his sins are forgiven." J XIII:499.

[54]Letter to James Hervey, *LJW* 3:377.

[55]Minutes, 1744, June 25, Q4–7, JWO 137–38.

[56]Minutes, 1746, May 13, Q4, JWO 160.

[57]XXV, art. 9, italics added.

The favor of the Father is received only for the merit of the Son. Justification is by grace through faith.

We learn how tainted by self-interest is our best work. But we are freed to celebrate the unmerited goodness of God in coming to us in the flesh on the cross. The gospel teaches us to despair over our own attempts to fulfill the law apart from grace. It trusts only in God's own fulfilling of the law for us.

The privilege of every believer is freedom from bondage to the law, freedom from guilt and anxiety, from all sin when it is contritely confessed and bears fruits meet for repentance. The righteousness of Christ is imputed to all humanity. All are cleared juridically from the guilt of Adam's sin, awaiting de facto repentance and faith.

This is a "most wholesome doctrine," edifying and strengthening the penitent, enabling spiritual health, as opposed to the heavy legalism that hammers people down with the law. After 1738 Wesley strongly advocated classic Reformation teaching of *sola fide, sola gratia*, and *sola scriptura*. These themes are found abundantly in Luther, Calvin, and Cranmer.[58]

6. Imputed Righteousness through Christ's Obedience and Death

a. Imputed Righteousness

Through the obedience and death of Christ for us, we are "made partakers of the divine nature," being "reunited to God." Adam's sin is imputed to all humanity in the sense that in Adam all die. "By the merits of Christ all men are cleared from the guilt of Adam's actual sin," and through "the obedience and death of Christ ... believers are reunited to God and made partakers of the divine nature."[59]

Thus "faith is imputed unto us for righteousness." Paul provides the text: "As by one man's disobedience many were made sinners, so by the obedience of one shall many be made righteous" (Rom. 5:19).[60]

b. The Dangers of Antinomianism

Does this imputation lean toward antinomianism ("the doctrine that makes void the law through faith")? This false inference must be avoided. Antinomians teach that "Christ abolished the moral law; that Christians therefore are not obliged to observe [common worship]; that one branch of Christian liberty is liberty from obeying the commandments of God; that it is bondage to do a thing because it is commanded ... that a believer is not obliged to use the ordinances of God or to do good works; that a preacher ought not to exhort to good works."[61]

Paul wrote to the Galatians in response to the challenge of those who were

[58]"Principles of a Methodist," J VIII:361–63, secs. 2–7.
[59]Minutes, 1744, June 25, Q16, JWO 139; *LJW* 3:379.
[60]Rom. 5:19; Minutes, Q16.
[61]Minutes, Q17–20.

preaching that "except ye be circumcised and keep the whole law of Moses, ye cannot be saved." Paul clarified that "no man can be justified or saved by the works of the law, either moral or ritual," and "that every believer is justified by faith in Christ without the works of the law," but he is referring here to "all works that do not spring from faith in Christ."[62] What Christ has abolished is the "ritual law of Moses," not the moral law underlying it.

c. Reward Not for the Sake of Our Works

Wesley held that there is "no merit, taking the word strictly, but in the blood of Christ ... salvation is not by the merit of works," yet following Christ's own teaching, "we are rewarded *according to* our works ... this differs from *for the sake of our* works."

"Words in all languages ... may be taken either in a proper or improper sense. When I say, 'I do not grant that works are meritorious, even when accompanied by faith,' I take that word in a proper sense. But others take it in an improper, as nearly equivalent with rewardable.' "[63]

C. The Righteousness of Faith

The sixth of Wesley's standard teaching homilies is on "The Righteousness of Faith."[64] It is textually focused on Romans 10:5 – 8, which contrasts the righteousness that is by the law with the righteousness that is by faith.[65] The text is "The word is nigh thee, even in thy mouth, and in thy heart: that is, the word of faith, which we preach" [Homily #6 (1746), B 1:200 – 216; J #6, V:65 – 76].

1. The Despair That Arises from Trusting in the Righteousness That Is of the Law

The law is a harsh taskmaster. Wesley is relentless in describing the requirement of the law as such. The law makes radical demands, with no allowance for falling short.[66] If we decide we are going to live our lives under God's command only, not by the mercy of God, we have to do it consistently and completely or be judged by the rigors of the law.

The covenant of works requires that everyone fulfill every manner of righteousness, not only in perfect degree but without interruption.[67] Anything less brings a conscience permeated with offense. The law required the clear-cut alternative:

[62]Ibid.

[63]"Some Remarks on Mr. Hill's 'Farrago Double-Distilled,' " J X:434.

[64]In preaching on this text from his father's tombstone in Epworth, "several dropped down as dead; and among the rest such a cry was heard of sinners groaning for the righteousness of faith as almost drowned my voice." *JJW*, June 12, 1742.

[65]B 1:127, 196, 201 – 16, 592; 2:28 – 29; cf. *LJW* 3:82, 375; 5:222 – 23, 263.

[66]*LJW* 3:82, 375; 5:222 – 23, 263.

[67]The covenant of law too self-assuredly tends to assume that a statically perfected perfection is theoretically possible for fallen humanity, but this assumption is transmitted by justifying and sanctifying grace. "The Law Established through Faith, I," sec. 2.3, 4.

"Obey or die. It required no man to obey and die too. If any man had perfectly obeyed, he would not have died."[68]

The law brings us to despair over our own righteousness and gives us readiness to trust in God's righteousness. We cannot possibly fulfill the law. Why preach it then? Because the rigors of the law move us toward hearing the gospel. They indirectly teach us not to trust in our own righteousness but in God's.

Wesley admitted in *A Farther Appeal* that "it is my endeavour to drive all I can into what you [critics] may term another species of 'madness' ... which I term 'repentance' or 'conviction'" as preparatory to saving grace.[69] Yet Wesley looked with disfavor upon deliberate efforts to manipulate persons toward despair in order to bring them to faith.[70]

Wesley, like Luther, argued that those who attempt to live by the law with utter seriousness live always on the edge of despair, always aware of radical inadequacies. It is folly to live that way, when God offers us forgiveness through his Son.[71]

2. The Wisdom of Anchoring Oneself in the Righteousness of Faith

If that is folly, what is wisdom? Wisdom is to live by faith in God's own righteousness declared. It is receiving the assistance of the Spirit, who by grace calls us into trusting Christ's righteousness for us.[72] The covenant of grace requires no work prior to justification, but only that one believe in God's work done for us on the cross. The moment one believes in Jesus as Lord, one is saved from condemnation, guilt, and punishment for prior sin, and is given the power to serve God in true holiness from that time forward.

Faith is the condition by which humanity may recover the favor and image of God, receive the life of God in the soul, and be restored to the knowledge and love of God.[73]

The covenant of grace presupposes that fallen humanity lives in despair as if dead to God's righteousness, unholy and unhappy.[74] This is contrasted with the unblemished condition of humanity prior to the fall. Only grace illumines the folly of trusting in the righteousness that is of the law, which fundamentally misconceives the current human condition as if unfallen.[75] The only way to recover the favor and image of God, once lost, is through trusting the gift of the revealed righteousness that comes by faith.[76]

---

[68]Letter to James Hervey, *LJW* 3:277.

[69]FA, pt. 1, 7.12, B 11:196.

[70]"On Faith (Heb. 11:6)"; cf. B 11:196–99, sec. 1.11, 12.

[71]*SS* 1:131–34; 2:65.

[72]*SS* 1:138–39.

[73]"Salvation by Faith."

[74]Never lacking, however, the preparatory grace that underlies conscience. "On Working Out Our Own Salvation," J VI:508, sec. 3.4.

[75]"On the Wedding Garment," sec. 19; Minutes, May 13, 1746; *ENNT* on Heb. 8:8.

[76]"The New Birth," sec. 3.1.

"By 'the righteousness which is of faith,' is meant that condition of justification (and in consequence of present and final salvation, if we endure therein unto the end), which was given by God to *fallen man* through the merits and mediation of his only begotten Son. This was in part revealed to Adam soon after his fall, being contained in the original promise made to him and his seed concerning the seed of the woman, who would 'bruise the serpent's head.'"[77]

3. False Starts through Legal Obedience

Those who desire to be reconciled to the favor of God do not say in their hearts, "I must *first do this.* I must *first* conquer every sin, break off every evil word and work, and do all good to all men; or I must *first* go to Church, receive the Lord's Supper, hear more sermons, and say more prayers." For to do so would be to remain insensible to the righteousness of God, still "'seeking to establish thy own righteousness' as the ground of thy reconciliation. Knowest thou not that thou canst do nothing but sin till thou art reconciled to God? Wherefore then dost thou say, I must do this and *this first,* and then I shall believe? Nay, but *first believe.*"[78]

It is absurd to insist, "I can't be accepted yet because I am not *good enough.*" No one is good enough to merit God's atoning love. It is equally ruinous to say, "I must *do* something more before I come to Christ," or "wait for *more sincerity,*" for "if there be anything good in *sincerity,* why dost thou expect it *before* thou hast faith? — seeing that faith itself is the only root of whatever is really good and holy."[79]

D. Extractions from the Edwardian/Elizabethan Homilies

1. The Doctrine of Salvation, Faith, and Good Works (Extracted from the Edwardian Homilies)

Having recently returned from Georgia, on February 1, 1738, Wesley set about to publish an extract from the Anglican Homilies (variously called Cranmerian or Edwardian or Elizabethan Homilies),[80] which were the official teaching of the Church of England during the period of Edward VI, largely written by Thomas Cranmer (except for one by John Harpsfield and another by Edmund Bonner), to which twenty-one further homilies (by John Jewel and others) were added in the period of Queen Elizabeth.[81]

Wesley abridged these homilies for teaching purposes for his connection of spiritual formation. According to prevailing protocols of eighteenth-century editors

[77]"The Righteousness of Faith," B 1:205, sec. 1.7, italics added. Here Wesley is assuming a "double justification" received first by faith in the atoning work on the cross and finally confirmed in final justification on the last day. "Justification by Faith," sec. 2.5; Letter to Thomas Church, February 2, 1745.

[78]"The Righteousness of Faith," B 1:214, sec. 3.1.

[79]"The Righteousness of Faith," B 1:214 – 16, sec. 3.2 – 5. Cf. "The Almost Christian," sec. 1.9.

[80]*Certain Sermons or Homilies Appointed to be Read in Churches in the Time of the Late Queen Elizabeth*, 1603; repr., Oxford, 1840.

[81]*CC* 230 – 65; *Certain Sermons . . .*; cf. B 1:139, 193n.; 11:443 – 44, 451 – 53; *JJW* 2:101, 275.

(contrary to twentieth-century assumptions) he edited texts functionally in relation to his purpose of informing and instructing his connection.

This edited series of homilies became widely read in the eighteenth century and reprinted by the Wesleyan connection through nineteen editions. He himself appealed to these homilies commonly in his preaching, pastoral care, and irenics. He insisted that his own teaching of salvation, justification, faith, and good works was not different from the ancient ecumenical consensual teaching upheld by the Church of England. He did not want his detractors to imagine that he was inventing some cleverly fashioned new doctrine of justification.

2. Of the Salvation of Humanity

The premise of justifying faith is Christ's atoning work on the cross, to which we are enabled to respond by grace in lively faith. There is a triune premise in this sequence: God the Father is gracious toward us; God the Son manifests that grace on the cross; God the Holy Spirit enables our reception of that gracious work for us by faith.[82]

The faithful are not justified by repentance, nor by their good works.[83] It is not my seizing justification by my act of faith that justifies me. It is God's mercy through the atoning work of Christ that justifies me, and faith is my reception of that justification.

To embrace the promise of God's personally addressed Word does not mean that simply by intellectually assenting to God's promises we are saved, or by accepting a set of propositions.[84] Rather, it means personally meeting and trusting the word of this Incomparable One, the word of forgiveness spoken to us on the cross, that it is a true word and not a deception.[85]

3. Of True Christian Faith: The Complementary Teachings of James and Paul

Already we have seen in the 1744 Minutes that Paul and James are not contradictory. Wesley appeals to the Elizabethan Homilies to develop this point: "Having dealt with justification, these homilies turn to the relation of faith and works, correlating Paul's doctrine of justification through grace by faith alone and James's doctrine that faith without works is dead."

Wesley remained determined to hold these tightly together. The Homilies gave him the clearest statement of their intimate correlation. Without good works, faith is not true and vital faith.[86] Those who are living the life of faith are going to be actively engaged in the love of the neighbor, manifesting the love of God by loving

[82]DSF, secs. 1 – 5, JWO 124 – 25; cf. B 4:24; 1:349 – 50.
[83]DSF, secs. 6 – 9, JWO 125 – 27.
[84]DSF, sec. 14, JWO 128.
[85]DSF, secs. 7 – 14, JWO 126 – 29.
[86]*LJW* 7:302; *JJW* 2:354 – 56; B 1:689, 695; 2:164 – 66; 3:400 – 405; 9:94 – 99, 318 – 19, 325 – 28, 357 – 58.

one's neighbor, living out their faith through their actions.[87] Justification, whose sole condition is penitent faith, is never lacking in fruits of faith, by which believers are assured that the Spirit is working within.[88]

Wesley is meticulous in showing that Paul and James do not contradict each other. Without faith there is no good work that can be performed.[89] Those who "shine in good works without faith are like dead men who have goodly and precious tombs."[90] We do not do the work of faith prior to faith. Good works are the fruit and outgrowth of faith. Among good works that faith brings forth are obedience to God's commandments, right reading of the Word, giving oneself totally to God, loving God in all things, loving all persons in relation to the love of God, and obeying duly constituted authority.[91]

The "whole tenor" of the Anglican liturgy, articles, and homilies was concisely summarized by Wesley: "(1) That no good work, properly so called, can go *before* justification; (2) that *no degree* of true sanctification can be previous to it; (3) that as the *meritorious cause* of justification is the life and death of Christ, so the *condition* of it is faith, faith alone; and (4) that both inward and outward holiness are consequent on this faith and are the ordinary, stated conditions of final justification."[92]

E. The Lord Our Righteousness

This homily focuses on Jeremiah 23:6: "This is his name whereby he shall be called, THE LORD OUR RIGHTEOUSNESS" [Homily #20 (1765), B 1:444–65; J #20, V:234–46].

1. Christ's Active and Passive Obedience

Jesus' obedience implied not only an incomparably good *doing* (active obedience), but also an incomparably patient *suffering for others* (passive obedience). Jesus is attested in Scripture as "suffering the whole will of God from the time he came into the world till 'he bore our sins in his own body upon the tree.'"

Christ's work required an active obedience by which he actively fulfilled the law and a passive obedience by which he suffered death for sinners in order to enable their fulfillment of the law. But these forms of obedience must never be separated, though they may be distinguished. He acted for the good; he passively submitted to death.[93] "As the active and passive righteousness of Christ were never in fact separated from each other, so we never need separate them at all, either in speak-

[87]DSF, sec. 8, JWO 131.

[88]B 11:456–57.

[89]DSF, sec. 9, JWO 132.

[90]DSF, sec. 11, JWO 132.

[91]DSF, sec. 12, 13, JWO 133, 272–73, 362, 365, 373–74.

[92]FA, pt. 1, B 11:115, sec. 2.8, on the *sola fide* theme, cf. *LJW* 3:321 in response to Lavington, and 3:351, quoting Anna Marie van Schurrman's *Journal* in response to William Law. On the distinction between the formal and meritorious causes of justification, see FA, B 11:112–15; cf. 11:447–48; 1:78, 80–83, 382–83, 455–60; 2:157–58.

[93]See *WC*, passim.

ing or even in thinking," and this is what we mean when we speak of "the Lord our righteousness."[94] To participate in his life and death is to share his obedience both actively as doing and passively as suffering.

2. Believers Clothed in a Righteousness Not Their Own

In receiving God's justifying grace, we are receiving an imputed gift. It is offered freely on our behalf through grace alone.

Imputation is a juridical metaphor, and as such not yet more than the embryo of a behavior-reconstructing process. If the judge says in a courtroom, "You are free," and strikes the gavel, that is an imputation whereby one is declared free from offense to the law. But that declaration does not in itself determine that the behavior that follows will be responsible.

That Christ's righteousness is imputed means that "all believers are forgiven and accepted, not for the sake of anything in them, or of anything that ever was, that is, or ever can be done by them, but wholly and solely for the sake of what Christ hath done and suffered for them."[95] "This is the doctrine which I have constantly believed and taught for near eight and twenty years. This I published to all the world in the year 1738, and ten or twelve times since."[96] It is not that our self-initiated faith as such is imputed for righteousness. Rather, it is that "faith in the righteousness of Christ" is so imputed that the believer is clothed in a righteousness not his own, a glorious dress that enables and calls him to "put off the filthy rags" of his own righteousness.[97]

Christ's righteousness is imputed to us when we believe, and as soon as we believe, so that "faith and the righteousness of Christ are inseparable.[98] Believers may vary greatly in their ways of expressing this act of pardon while still remaining unified in their sharing experientially in Christ's righteousness.[99]

3. Distinguishing Christ's Divine and Human Righteousness

a. Christ's Righteousness: Divine/Human; Internal/External; Active/Passive

John Deschner provided this systematic outline-analysis of "The Lord Our Righteousness":[100]

---

[94]"The Lord Our Righteousness," B 1:452–53, sec. 1.1–4.

[95]"The Lord Our Righteousness," B 1:455, sec. 2.5; cf. *LJW* 3:248–49, 373, 385; 5:5; *JJW* 4:103; 6:173; B 2:153.

[96]See his abridgment of the Anglican Homilies, "The Doctrine of Salvation," "Faith and Good Works," sec. 1.5; "Justification by Faith," sec. 1.8; and his abridgment of John Goodwin's *Treatise on Justification*; cf. B 9:406, 410.

[97]"The Lord Our Righteousness," B 1:458, sec. 2.11.

[98]"The Lord Our Righteousness," sec. 2.1; cf. B 1:567–71; 4:219.

[99]"It is safest to trust in the merits of Christ," even for Bellarmine; and Wesley added, "Who would argue that 'notwithstanding his wrong opinions, he had no share' in Christ's righteousness?" "The Lord Our Righteousness," B 1:452–53, sec. 1.1–4.

[100]*WC* 157–58.

Christ's righteousness consists of two parts:
- His divine righteousness [God's essential righteousness].
- His human righteousness: this is imputed as a whole to man.

Christ's human righteousness consists of two parts:
- Internal human righteousness: Christ's human image of God.
- External human righteousness: Christ's obedience.

Christ's obedience in turn consists of two parts:
- Active obedience: what Christ did. Two aspects can also be distinguished here:
  - Negative active obedience: he did not sin.
  - Positive active obedience: he did God's will perfectly.
- Passive obedience: what Christ suffered.

b. The Righteousness Manifested in the Mediator

Accordingly, Christ's divine righteousness is identical with the essential righteousness of God, since the Father and Son are one. Christ's human *imago* is portrayed as a prototype or original transcript of Christ's own divine righteousness. It is a model for the progressive conformity of humanity to God's righteousness.[101]

> When Christ's sacrifice reestablishes the law, it is *this* representation of the law, i.e., Christ's humanity, which, crucified and risen, stands as the decisive definition of all law. The new commandment is not only love in the abstract, but that love which is defined by Christ's suffering humanity.... In Christ the law itself, as Christ's human *imago*, dies and rises again.... [Hence] the law, i.e., Christ's risen humanity, confronts believers as the consequence and promise, not the condition, of justification.... The oral law turns its promissory face to man, so to speak, in the risen humanity of Christ, imputed to believers in the form of participation in Christ's corporate Body.[102]

The righteousness belonging to the mediator may be viewed either as an *internal* righteousness (the image of God stamped on every power and faculty of his soul, without any defect or admixture of unholiness) or an *external righteousness* (knowing no outward sin, viewed negatively, and doing all things well, viewed positively).[103]

4. How Imputed Righteousness Becomes Implanted Righteousness

Wesley was especially interested in the implanting process that manifests itself behaviorally following the received imputation.[104] "I believe that God implants righteousness in everyone to whom He has imputed it."[105] Implanting is a vital, organic,

[101] "The Lord Our Righteousness," B 1:452, sec. 1.2; cf. *WC* 158–59.

[102] *WC* 159–60.

[103] "The Lord Our Righteousness," B 1:452–53, sec. 1.1–4.

[104] In 1765 Wesley published an extract of John Goodwin's *Treatise on Justification, Imputatio Fidei* (1642), which he found especially edifying; see *LJW* 4:274, 279–80, 287; B 1:83n.; 4:7n.

[105] "The Lord Our Righteousness," sec. 2.12; on imputed righteousness, see B 1:63, 294, 445, 452–63; 4:142–43.

horticultural metaphor. This is very different from a declarative, juridical metaphor.[106] It requires daily nurturing, not a simple bang of a gavel. It is the fruit of our acceptance by God, not the ground of it.[107]

To speak of the imputation of Christ's righteousness is not to argue that his divine nature as immutable holiness is directly imputed to us. Rather, it is the righteousness that belongs to him as the Son of God, yet truly man (*theanthropos).* He is the unique mediator between God and man who credits righteousness to us and works in us to manifest it. This in classical dogmatics is sometimes called the human righteousness of the theandric Son, to distinguish it from that righteousness that belongs to the divine nature in itself.[108]

In this way, through the atonement, God's own righteousness becomes God's righteousness *in us* as a gift by which humanity is made righteous (Rom. 1:17).[109]

Those to whom the righteousness of Christ is imputed are by the work of the Spirit being made righteous not in theory only. By grace their behavior is being actually uprighted. They are being renewed in the image of God in a lifelong process that seeks to manifest God's own holy love in our actions, both inwardly in a regenerated attitude and outwardly in the works of love.[110]

Holiness of heart and life is "not the cause, but the effect" of justification. "The sole cause of our acceptance with God ... is the righteousness and the death of Christ, who fulfilled God's law, and died in our stead."[111]

5. Caveat on the Excessive Use of the Imputation Metaphor

Some who are "otherwise well-meaning ... have been deluded and hardened, at least for the present, chiefly, if not merely, by the *too frequent* and improper use of the phrase *imputed righteousness*."[112] Those who overstress God's imputed righteousness with the particular spin that it has minimal implication for my personal behavior change, may tend toward antinomianism.[113] The imputed righteousness of Christ must not be used as an excuse or "a cover for ... unrighteousness."[114]

Some in Wesley's day became uneasy if anyone began to mention good works.

[106]See also the metaphor of imparted righteousness, B 1:63, 80, 643; 4:144; JWO 217 – 18, 274, 348.

[107]Neither do I deny *imputed righteousness* ("The Lord Our Righteousness," B 1:458, sec. 2.14). In this respect, Wesley distinguishes his view from that of Robert Barclay and the Quakers (B 1:460, sec. 2.16), but who suggested that all who are unclear in their opinions about imputed righteousness "are void of all Christian experience" (sec. 2.16)? On matters of opinion regarding the use of language, it is best to "think and let think" (B 1:464, sec. 2.20). Cf. "The Way to the Kingdom" (B 1:217 – 18, sec. 1.6).

[108]"On Working Out Our Own Salvation," sec. 4. In response to Roland Hill's criticism, he acknowledged that "by Christ's human righteousness," he meant "that mediatorial righteousness which was wrought by God in the human nature." "Some Remarks of Mr. Hill's 'Review of All the Doctrines Taught by Mr. John Wesley,' " J X:384.

[109]*ENNT* on Rom. 1:17; Phil. 3:9.

[110]It is this implanting and growth process that Wesley called by the name of "inherent righteousness."

[111]*HSP* (1739), pref. 2, J XIV:320.

[112]Letter to John Newton, February 28, 1766, *LJW* 5:5.

[113]JWO 301 – 2, 377 – 78; *LJW* 3:248 – 49, 373, 385; 5:5; *JJW* 4:103; 6:173; B 2:153.

[114]"The Lord Our Righteousness," B 1:462, sec. 2.19.

They feared that good works might be thought to precede justifying faith.[115] Wesley agreed with them on their concern that good works flow from faith and do not precede it. But if the focus of preaching turns toward the Son's saving action on the cross *so as to neglect the work of the Spirit in our hearts* and behavior processes, the balance of Scripture metaphors has been put off-center.[116]

F. On the Imputed Righteousness of Christ

To further clarify the imputed righteousness of Christ, Wesley wrote "Thoughts on the Imputed Righteousness of Christ" (J X:312 – 16) and a Letter to James Hervey, October 15, 1756 (*LJW* 3:371 – 88).[117]

1. How Imputed Righteousness May Become Exaggerated toward Antinomianism

In the gospel "the righteousness of God is revealed" (Rom. 1:17 NIV). "God made him who had no sin to be sin for us, so that in him we might become the righteousness of God" (2 Cor. 5:21 NIV). "The righteousness of God" in these cases refers to God's way of justifying sinners.[118]

However, Wesley did not find in Scripture the specific phrase "imputed righteousness of Christ." Hence "I dare not insist upon, neither require any one to use [it]. . . . I am myself the more sparing in the use of it, because it has been so frequently and so dreadfully abused; and because the Antinomians use it at this day to justify the grossest abominations."[119]

To illustrate the problem: "Is temperance imputed only to him that is a drunkard still: or chastity, to her that goes on in whoredom?" In this perverse way, according to Zinzendorf, obedience becomes "a proof of unbelief, and disobedience a proof of faith." Rather, "Nay, but a believer is really chaste and temperate. And if so, he is thus far holy" inwardly.[120]

Wesley thought that the "particular phrase" — the imputed righteousness of Christ — was subject to misinterpretation. In the hands of some it had become a ruse to avoid any effort actually to walk in the way of holiness, and hence had inadvertently "done immense hurt."[121] This particular "*mode of expression*," when used as

---

[115]This sermon (#20) served as a response to his former student James Hervey, whose *Theron and Aspasio* set forth the differences between Arminians and Calvinists, for whom the imputed righteousness of Christ was the central feature of justification. Outler recognizes this as a "landmark sermon" in which Wesley, fending off charges of Jesuitism and Bellarminism, draws careful lines between the nuances of the Synod of Dort and Arminian soteriology.

[116]See "The Original, Nature, Property, and Use of the Law" and "The Law Established through Faith, I and II."

[117]This letter is included in the preface to John Goodwin's *Treatise on Justification*, J X:316 – 46.

[118]"Thoughts on the Imputed Righteousness of Christ," J X:313.

[119]"Thoughts on the Imputed Righteousness of Christ," J X:315.

[120]"An Extract from A Short View of the Difference between the Moravian Brethren (so Called,) and the Rev. Mr. John and Charles Wesley," J X:203.

[121]*LJW* 3:371 – 72.

an excuse to idleness, "is always dangerous, often fatal."[122] "O how deep an aversion to inward holiness does this scheme naturally create!"[123]

Wesley affirmed that Christ is "our substitute as to penal sufferings" but not as a substitute for our responsive acts of love and obedience.[124] That we are "complete in him" refers also to our sanctification by cooperating grace, not merely justification by grace operating. "God, through [Christ], first accounts, and then makes us righteous."[125] Hence we had best not tout a thoughtless game of imputation without taking seriously the process of behavioral sanctification.

Christ tasted death for every man, but Wesley thought it "vain philosophy" to so stretch the point that the righteousness that justifies us is already in every sense behaviorally "carried on, completed ... wrought out," so that "the nice, metaphysical doctrine of imputed righteousness leads not to repentance, but to licentiousness."[126] Rather, the righteousness of God "signifies God's method of justifying sinners,"[127] while remembering that "he alone is truly righteous, whose faith worketh by love."[128]

2. Christ Does Not Repent for Us or Enact Our Belief without Us

The sole condition of our reception of justifying grace is "repent and believe." But Christ does not repent for us or enact our belief without us. Those who speak loosely this way invite lawlessness to "come in with a full tide."[129]

When Hervey contended that believers could remain "notorious transgressors in themselves," yet at the same time "have a sinless obedience in Christ," Wesley mused: "O syren [*sic*] song! Pleasing sound to James Wheatley, Thomas Williams, James Relly!" (leading antinomian defectors from Methodism).[130] "We swarm with Antinomians on every side. Why are you at such pains to increase their number!"[131] "The very quintessence of Antinomianism" is the easy premise that Christ has behaviorally and ethically "satisfied the demand of the law for me,"[132] without pairing that with the work of grace in me. It is a return straight to Zinzendorf's "Antinomianism without a mask" to say that all the claims of the law are done for us without eliciting a response of faith active in love.[133]

[122]Letter to James Hervey, *LJW* 3:381.
[123]Letter to James Hervey, *LJW* 3:384.
[124]*LJW* 3:373.
[125]Letter to James Hervey, *LJW* 3:384.
[126]*LJW* 3:373.
[127]Letter to James Hervey, *LJW* 3:382.
[128]*LJW* 3:375.
[129]Letter to James Hervey, *LJW* 3:379.
[130]*LJW* 3:379; cf. JWO 235, 377–78.
[131]Letter to James Hervey, *LJW* 3:385.
[132]Letter to James Hervey, *LJW* 3:386.
[133]Hervey argued that "our present blessedness does not consist in being free from sin." Wesley replied, "I really think it does," on the basis of the apostolic teaching that "you have been set free from sin and become slaves of righteousness" (Rom. 6:18) (*LJW* 3:380).

G. The End of Christ's Coming

The text of this homily is 1 John 3:8: "For this purpose was the Son of God manifested, that he might destroy the works of the devil" [Homily #62 (1781), B 2:471 – 84; J #62, V:267 – 77].

For the dilemma of sin, natural philosophy can offer only "broken reeds, bubbles, smoke!" "Nature points out the disease; but nature shows us no remedy."[134]

1. He Came to Destroy the Works of the Devil

Humanity is created in the moral image of God originally capable of righteousness and holiness,[135] and in the natural image of God capable of free self-determination.[136] Humanity in its created condition was "capable of mistaking, of being deceived, although not necessitated to it."[137] Now full of sin, unholy and unhappy, humanity has come near to losing the moral image of God.

The final end of Christ's coming is to destroy "sin and the fruits of sin," and all of the works of the adversary.[138] By making of himself a full, perfect, and sufficient sacrifice and satisfaction for the sins of the whole world, the incarnate Son has already begun to bind the power of evil.[139] The Spirit is enabling faith to become active in love, and thereby restore the moral image of God in holiness and righteousness.[140]

2. Full Salvation: Restoration of the Image of God

The saving activity of the triune God goes beyond simply a juridical declaring of freedom from guilt and punishment of sin. It also includes the *promise of freedom* from the "power and root of sin," by the offer of sanctifying grace, which looks toward a process of behavioral reflection and embodiment of the way of holiness. The steps by which this renewal occurs are familiar to gospel preaching. Faith trusts that God was in Christ reconciling the world to himself. This strikes at the root of pride and self-will, enabling repentance and faith.[141]

But this is not a simplistic argument for the complete and easy renovation of humanity from all sin immediately or the destruction of evil without a struggle. The combat between flesh and spirit remains in all the faithful. The Son "does not destroy the whole work of the devil in man, as long as he remains in this life. He does not yet destroy bodily weakness, sickness, pain, and a thousand infirmities incident to flesh and blood. He does not destroy all that weakness of understanding, which is the natural consequence of the soul's dwelling in a corruptible body," all of which are destroyed in death, which itself is overcome in the resurrection.[142]

[134]"The End of Christ's Coming," B 2:473, proem 3.
[135]"The End of Christ's Coming," B 2:475 – 76, sec. 1.7 – 9.
[136]"The End of Christ's Coming," B 2:474 – 75, sec. 1.3 – 6.
[137]"The End of Christ's Coming," B 2:474, sec. 1.3.
[138]"The End of Christ's Coming," B 2:478, sec. 2.1; *CH*, B 7:410, 443 – 44; *LJW* 4:122.
[139]"The End of Christ's Coming," B 2:478 – 79, sec. 2.1 – 5.
[140]"The End of Christ's Coming," B 2:480, sec. 2.6, 7.
[141]"The End of Christ's Coming," B 2:480 – 84, sec. 3.
[142]"The End of Christ's Coming," B 2:482, sec. 3.3.

The great advantage of faithful dying is the destruction of the remnants of sin due to human finitude.

"Real religion" is "a restoration, not only to the *favour*, but likewise to the *image* of God, implying not barely deliverance from sin, but the being filled with the fulness of God." Yet how little this is in "this enlightened age, wherein it is taken for granted, the world is wiser than ever it was from the beginning.... Among all our discoveries, who has discovered this?" It is best rediscovered by viewing Scripture "in one connected chain. And the agreement of every part of it, with every other," namely, by means of the analogy of faith that works by love toward "all inward and outward holiness."[143]

God is able and willing to destroy all sin in all that believe. Sin is not intrinsic to humanity as created by God, but a malformation, a disease of humanity that God is in the process of correcting.

Further Reading on Atonement and Justification

Atonement

Clifford, Alan C. *Atonement and Justification. English Evangelical Theology, 1640–1790: An Evaluation.* Oxford: Clarendon, 1990.

Deschner, John. *Wesley's Christology: An Interpretation.* Dallas: Southern Methodist University Press, 1985. Reprint of 1960 edition with a new foreword by the author.

Lindström, Harald G. *Wesley and Sanctification*, 105ff.; atonement, justification, 55ff.; the law, 75ff.; justification and sanctification, 83ff. Nashville: Abingdon, 1946.

Justification

Bolster, George R. "Wesley's Doctrine of Justification." *EQ* 24 (1952): 144–55.

Brockwell, Charles W., Jr. "John Wesley's Doctrine of Justification." *WTJ* 18, no. 2 (1983): 18–32.

Cannon, William R. *The Theology of John Wesley: With Special Reference to the Doctrine of Justification.* New York: Abingdon, 1946.

Collins, Kenneth J. "The Doctrine of Justification: Historic Wesleyan and Contemporary Understandings." In *Justification: What's at Stake in the Current Debate*, edited by Mark Husbands and Daniel J. Treier. Downers Grove, IL: InterVarsity, 2004.

———. "Justification by Faith." In *Wesley on Salvation.* Grand Rapids: Zondervan, 1989.

Cushman, R. E. "Salvation for All." In *Faith Seeking Understanding.* Durham, NC: Duke University Press, 1981, 63–74.

Gunter, W. Steven. *The Limits of Divine Love: John Wesley's Response to Antinomianism and Enthusiasm.* Chap. 4, "Via Salutis: Wesley's Early Steps"; chap. 6, "Faith Alone," and chap. 7, "Faith Alone Misunderstood." Nashville: Abingdon, Kingswood, 1989.

Hildebrandt, Franz. *From Luther to Wesley.* London: Lutterworth, 1951.

[143]"The End of Christ's Coming," B 2:482–84, sec. 3.5–6, italics added; cf. B 1:118, 495–96.

Monk, Robert. "Justification by Faith." In *John Wesley: His Puritan Heritage*, 75ff. Nashville: Abingdon, 1966.

Prince, J. W. "Repentance" and "Justification by Faith and Regeneration." In *Wesley on Religious Education*, 44ff. New York: Methodist Book Concern, 1926.

Rees, A. H. *The Doctrine of Justification in the Anglican Reformers.* London, 1939.

Smith, Harmon L. "Wesley's Doctrine of Justification: Beginning and Process." *LQHR* 189 (1964): 120 – 28. Also *Duke Divinity School Bulletin* 28 (1963): 88 – 98.

Starkey, Lycurgus M. "Order of Redemption" and "Justification and Faith." In *The Work of the Holy Spirit.* Nashville: Abingdon, 1962.

Tavard, George. *Justification.* New York: Paulist, 1983.

Wynkoop, Mildred Bangs. "The Function of Faith" In *Foundations of Wesleyan-Arminian Theology*, 222ff. Kansas City: Beacon Hill, 1967.

Conversion

Abraham, William J. *Aldersgate and Athens: John Wesley and the Foundations of Christian Belief.* Waco, TX: Baylor University Press, 2009.

Collins, Kenneth J. "The Conversion of John Wesley: A Transformation to Power," in *Conversion.* Edited by John S. Hong. Bucheon City, Kyungki-Do, South Korea: Seoul Theological University, 1993. Published in Korean.

———. *A Real Christian: The Life of John Wesley.* Nashville: Abingdon, 1999.

———. *Wesley on Salvation.* Chap. 2, "Convincing Grace and Initial Repentance." Grand Rapids: Zondervan, 1989.

Koerber, Carolo. *The Theology of Conversion according to John Wesley.* Rome: Neo-Eboraci, 1967.

H. Countering Christological Distortions

1. On Knowing Christ after the Flesh

The text of this homily is 2 Corinthians 5:16: "Henceforth know we no man after the flesh: yea, though we did know Christ after the flesh, yet now henceforth know we him no more" [Homily #123 (1789), B 4:97 – 106; J #107, VII:291 – 97].

Finding few definitive treatments on this important theme, Wesley felt that this text had been grossly misconstrued by some forms of pietism. His own translation of the preceding passage is "He died for all, that they who live might not henceforth live unto themselves [seek their own honor, or profit, or pleasure] but unto him. So that we from this time [we that know him by faith] know no one after the flesh." The NIV reads, "So from now on we regard no one from a worldly point of view" — in a merely human fashion, based on their outward lives by worldly standards. "Though we once regarded Christ in this way, we do so no longer. Therefore, if anyone is in Christ, the new creation has come!" (vv. 16b – 17). Wesley commented: "This uncommon expression ... seems to mean: We regard no man according to his former state, — his country, riches, power, or wisdom. We consider all men only in their spiritual state." If we merely behold Christ "after the flesh ... loving him as a man, with a natural affection, we miss his divinity, for Christ is God."[144]

The heretical prototypes of knowing Christ after the flesh are the Arians who viewed "Christ as inferior to the Father," and the Socinians who denied the atonement and did "not allow him to be the supreme God." This tendency is seen in the unitarian John Taylor, who indirectly demeaned Jesus by treating him "with great civility" as a "very worthy personage" while denying his divinity. Especially odious to Wesley was a sentimentalist hymnody that tended to deal with Christ in an overly familiar way by neglecting his deity.[145] Wesley urged the avoidance of "every fondling expression" and especially the impertinent use of the word *dear* as addressed to God, which is "one particular word, which I never use myself either in verse or prose, in praying or preaching.... I have sometimes almost scrupled singing (even in the midst of my brother's excellent hymn), 'That dear disfigured face,' or that glowing expression, 'Drop thy warm blood upon my heart.' "[146]

Christ's lordship is debased when treated with excessive fervor or emotive display, by "loud shouting, horrid, unnatural screaming, repeating the same words twenty or thirty times, jumping two or three feet high, and throwing about the arms or legs, both of men and women, in a manner shocking not only to religion, but to common decency!"[147] One wonders just what these people were doing. Wesley thought it showed "improper familiarity with God."

Since Wesley presupposed the patristic teaching of *perichoresis*, the interpenetrating of the two natures in one person, he found the pietistic sentimentality and overfamiliarity one-sided. The antidote to all this is a rigorous traditional Christology whereby we " 'honor the Son even as we honor the Father.' We are to pay him the same worship as we pay to the Father. We are to love him with all our heart and soul; and to consecrate all we have and are, all we think, speak, and do, to the THREE-ONE GOD, Father, Son, and Spirit."[148]

2. On Preaching Christ

a. Countering Antinomianism in the Preaching of the Righteousness of Faith

The "Letter to an Evangelical Layman, Dec. 20, 1751" (B 26:482–89)[149] appears in Albert Outler's Library of Protestant Theology collection of 1964 as a "Letter on Preaching Christ." The law-gospel correlation is central to this letter.

Those who have read Dietrich Bonhoeffer on "cheap grace" will understand

[144]"On Knowing Christ after the Flesh," B 4:98–99, secs. 1–3.

[145]"On Knowing Christ after the Flesh," B 4:100–101, secs. 4–7; Wesley found this tendency in the Moravian hymnody and even in Isaac Watts's *Horae Lyricae*.

[146]"On Knowing Christ after the Flesh," B 4:101–3, secs. 8–10.

[147]"On Knowing Christ after the Flesh," B 4:103, sec. 11.

[148]"On Knowing Christ after the Flesh," B 4:106, sec. 16.

[149]This is the same document as that which appears in Jackson's and Outler's editions under the title "Letter on Preaching Christ," JWO 232–37; J XI:486–92, written to an anonymous individual who had denounced Wesley as a legalist.

instantly the bent of antinomianism against which Wesley struggled. Some were preaching Christ without a cross, the gospel without any consequent requirement, forgiveness without response, pardon without perseverance, the mercy of God without ever mentioning human accountability in response to pardon.[150]

b. A Dialogue between an Antinomian and His Friend

In "A Dialogue between an Antinomian and His Friend" (J X:266–76), Wesley recognized the dangers of such antinomianism and considered them undermining of faith itself.[151] Those who preach the gospel must counter the false imagination that we are thereby being called to relax morally or flaunt the law or duties to God, self, and neighbor. There are great dangers in turning preaching into "soft words," so they "vitiate their taste, so that they cannot relish sound doctrine; and spoil their appetite, so that they cannot turn it into nourishment; they, as it were, feed them with sweetmeats, till the genuine wine of the kingdom seems quite insipid to them."[152]

c. Gospel and Law Correlated in Every Evangelical Testimony

Law and gospel are instead to be preached as intertwined, with the requirement of God clarified in the context of the gospel.[153] "Some think, preaching the law only, others, preaching the gospel only. I think, neither the one nor the other; but duly mixing both, in every place, if not in every sermon."[154] "The first and great command" is "Believe on the Lord Jesus Christ."[155]

This was the preaching of all the Methodists until James Wheatley, who began congratulating himself that he preached "only Christ," but did so by neglecting the close interface between law and gospel. This did incalculable harm, in Wesley's view, causing preachers to leave the ministry, and demoralizing society membership, as at Newcastle. But in the societies of Yorkshire where the gospel and law relation was held fast, Wesley found members "alive, strong, vigorous of soul, believing, loving, and praising God their Saviour." They had grasped the indicative-imperative: "Christ died for you; therefore die to sin." "The law thus preached both enlightens and strengthens the soul ... both nourishes and teaches ... is the guide, 'food, medicine, and stay' of the believing soul."[156]

To preach the *gospel* is to declare God's love to sinners.[157] To preach the *law* means to make clear God's requirement resulting from the gospel.[158] This Word of

[150]"A Dialogue between an Antinomian and His Friend," J X:266–76.

[151]B 9:370–72.

[152]LPC, sec. 9, "Letter on Preaching Christ," J XI:491, is identical with "To an Evangelical Layman," B 26:487.

[153]B 1:304–5, 551–55; 2:20–43; JWO 232–37.

[154]LPC, sec. 7, J XI:486; B 26:483.

[155]LPC, sec. 18, J XI:489; B 26:483; cf. Acts 16:31.

[156]LPC, sec. 18, J XI:489; B 26:485.

[157]*LJW* 1:158; 5:259, 292; B 1:229, 347–50.

[158]*LJW* 3:82.

God is heard prototypically, first in the Decalogue, and most fully in the Sermon on the Mount. Those who would preach the commands and not the gospel fall into the grip of legalism. Those who would preach the gospel without the divine requirement implicit in it risk falling down the slippery slope of antinomianism.[159]

Wesley, like Luther, was trying to protect the laity from both distortions. Preaching reassurances of God's pardon too hastily may result in only a slight healing of the wound of sin. It is chiefly in personal, one-on-one counsel with a "thoroughly convinced sinner that one should be preaching nothing but the gospel."[160]

Rightly understood in the light of the gospel, the law of the Lord converts the soul, makes us wise, rejoices the heart, and opens our eyes morally (Ps. 19:7 – 9). A proper balance of law and gospel was the basis for edifying the hearer. When the gospel is preached with proper linkage with the divine requirement, there follows a deeper expression of faith active in love, a greater sense of disciplined intentionality in the community.[161] He thought that this was being empirically validated through the very communities he himself was responsible for guiding.[162]

3. We Preach Christ Crucified

The text for the homily "We Preach Christ Crucified" is 1 Corinthians 1:23 – 24: "But we preach Christ crucified, unto the Jews a stumblingblock, and unto the Greeks foolishness; but unto them which are called, both Jews and Greeks, Christ the power of God, and the wisdom of God" (attributed to Wesley as transcribed by Mr. Williamson, on the opening of a new preaching house at Wakefield [1774], B 4:519 – 24 [appendix]). The theme is the close relation of God the Son's pardoning action with God the Spirit's indwelling.

a. The Close Relation of God's Pardon to the Spirit's Indwelling

To preach Christ crucified is to preach in the closest connection "*justification* by faith in his blood," whereby "faith is counted for righteousness," with *sanctification*, whereby one being born again from above finds that "as great a change must pass upon us as when we were born at first."

All our nature must be changed by "the operation of the Holy Ghost and then be made alive, receive a new life (which is hid with Christ in God), and so, being born again ... go on from grace to grace, till we appear at last before him."[163]

To those who imagine themselves reasonable, it is foolishness. But to those called, it is the power and wisdom of God.

b. Why Is God's Pardon a Stumbling Block to Self-Righteousness?

To the self-righteous, the gospel appears as a stumbling block. They think they

[159] B 1:347, 554 – 55; 2:125; 4:220.
[160] LPC, sec. 9, J XI:487; B 26:483.
[161] Letter to Ebenezer Blackwell, December 20, 1752, B 3:79 – 85.
[162] LPC, B 26:482 – 88; J XI:489 – 92.
[163] "We Preach Christ Crucified," B 4:521.

have sufficient righteousness of their own to justify themselves, desiring to be justified by their own works. There are always an abundance of works-righteousness advocates "in every Christian country."[164] The self-righteous have little conviction of sin, hence have no need for divine pardon.

To the antinomian, the opposite temptation is to "have an outside righteousness and on that account despise others." Faith appears without love.

c. Why Does the Gift of Divine Pardon Seem Incredibly Foolish to the Smartest People?

Second, to those who imagine themselves reasonable, this seems foolishness. Such preaching of justification and sanctification in closest connection is disregarded by those who "pride themselves in their own wisdom" and who attempt to "understand everything by their own reason," even when they cannot begin to explain the body-soul linkage or the deeper ground of moral accountability.

Talk to anatomist William Hunter or Unitarian John Taylor about such things and see how these teachings are regarded as foolishness. Taylor will tell you, "In process of time, I will mend," and Hunter will say, "a man can never be justified by the righteousness of another."[165] If preaching Christ crucified is a stumbling block to the moralists, it is foolish to those who imagine their own powers of intellect and action as wholly sufficient without God. In Paul's writings, they are called "the Greeks."

d. How Does the Wisdom of God Triumph over Human Wisdom?

To those effectively called, however, the preaching of God's pardon and the Spirit's guidance holds law and gospel together. This sense of balance is experienced as the *wisdom of God.* The triumph of the wisdom of God over human wisdom lies in the very character of God, who gives faith the power to mortify the limitations of the body. There "all his attributes and perfections harmonize: justice and mercy meet together."

Such preaching is also experienced as the "*power of God* with regard to sanctification." Grace overcomes sin. "You then found that sin had no more dominion over you. Then, my brethren, this was the moment of your sanctification."[166] "Moment" refers to a point in time when the recognition of God's power to overcome sin is grasped. That moment is experienced. Any experience must have a beginning in time.

"Then you were endowed with power from on high, and from that time you had power to mortify the deeds of the body and subdue all love to the world. Then the kingdom of heaven was like a grain of mustard seed," looking to grow toward the time when "nothing may dwell in your hearts but love alone."[167]

---

[164]Ibid.

[165]"We Preach Christ Crucified," B 4:522.

[166]"We Preach Christ Crucified," B 4:523.

[167]"We Preach Christ Crucified," B 4:523–24.

e. How the Faithful Are Called Outwardly, Inwardly, and Effectually

Anyone who has experienced any "remarkable turn of providence, either in prosperity or adversity" is thereby being "*outwardly called*" to forsake sin and turn to God. Those who have experienced "a wish that you may die the death of the righteous" are in this way being *inwardly called* to the life of grace. Anyone who is being given the present opportunity to receive the forgiveness of sins is thereby being *effectually* called by God's grace.[168] With this calling — outward, inward, and effectual — the believer experiences the power to live the holy life with the help of grace. This is a good and happy life.

4. Challenging Mystics' Speculations on the Atonement

This is the point to introduce a long and significant "Letter to William Law," written on January 6, 1756 (*LJW* 3:332 – 70; J IV:466 – 509).

a. Refuting the Denial of the Necessity of Christ's Death

Atonement, according to William Law in his later phase, was in Wesley's view merely a subjective event bordering on narcissism. William Law, whom Wesley had previously followed and revered, had fallen into the subjective comfort of ephemeral inner illumination. This implied a christological omission: it appears as if "the only work of Christ as your redeemer is to raise into life the smothered spark of heaven in you."[169] Wesley viewed this as sheer subjectivism.

Lacking any premise of the capacity of God for disciplining his children, there could be for Law "no scriptural doctrine of justification."

Wesley thought that William Law had no plausible answer to the question: "If the Son of God did not die to atone for our sins, what did He die for?"[170] In advancing the penal satisfaction view of atonement, Wesley argued that Christ's death is necessary to the whole fabric of faith. By this time, Wesley thought that Law seemed "not even to know what the term 'justification' means."

b. Anna Maria van Schurmann Commended as an Antidote to Law's Misunderstanding of Christ's Death

As a remedy, Wesley commended the plain account of the atonement by Anna Maria van Schurmann (1607 – 78). Her reflections appear in her *Journal*[171]and in *Eukleria*.[172]

Anna Maria van Schurmann was a woman of many talents, including art, linguistics, philosophy, and in her later years, French Reformed theology. She was born

[168]"We Preach Christ Crucified," B 4:523.

[169]Letter to William Law, sec. 2.3, *LJW* 3:351.

[170]Letter to William Law, sec. 2.2, 3, *LJW* 3:345 – 57.

[171]Anna Maria van Schurmann, *Journal*, 1:435d; see Anna Maria van Schurman and Fridericus Spanhemius, *Nobilis, Virginis Annae Maria à Schurman: Opuscula, Hebraca, Graeca, Latina, Gallica* (1648 Latin ed.).

[172]Anna Maria van Schurmann, *Eukleria*, pt. 11:118; see her autobiography, *Euclera seu melioris partis electio* (autobiography), 2 vols., 1673. Cf. Wesley's Letter to William Law, sec. 2.3, *LJW* 3:353 – 56.

in Cologne of a German mother and a Dutch father. Educated by her father, who died at an early age, she left Germany with her mother for Utrecht in the Netherlands, where she was instrumental in the founding of the University of Utrecht in 1636 and was permitted to attend classes sheltered behind a curtain. She left Utrecht to follow Jean Labadie, a French Reformed Church preacher. After Labadie's death, she entered the circle of leadership of another Dutch theologian, Gisbert Voetius (1589 – 1676). She wrote extensively in numerous languages. In her reflections on the atonement, she argued a brilliant series of points crucial to Wesley, which he used in his critique of William Law. Here is Wesley's summary:

1. Christ has acquired for us a right to eternal life "by His satisfaction and merits alone. Neither our repentance nor amendment can be any satisfaction for sin." It is only "through His blood that we have redemption" (see Eph. 1:7). He "sent His Son to be the propitiation for our sins" (see 1 John 4:9 – 10). The Lord is "OUR RIGHTEOUSNESS" (Jer. 23:6), who "gave himself a ransom for all" (1 Tim. 2:6). It was impossible for the sinner to satisfy God "by a partial and imperfect obedience. Neither could he merit anything from Him to whom he owed all things. There was need, therefore, of a Mediator who could repair the immense wrong he had done to the Divine Majesty … suffer in the place of His people, and merit for them pardon, holiness and glory."[173]

2. The imitation of Christ lies primarily in faith in Christ crucified, who "leaving you an example, that you should follow in his steps" (1 Peter 2:21 NIV), "died for us" that we might be "justified by his blood" (Rom. 5:8 – 9).[174]

3. "The origin and cause of our redemption is the ineffable love of God the Father, who willed to redeem us by the blood of His own Son; the grace of the Son, who freely took our curse upon Him, and imparts His blessing and merits to us; and the Holy Spirit who communicates the love of the Father and the grace of the Son to our hearts."[175]

4. Just here we stand at the "inmost mystery of the Christian faith," where "all the inventions of men ought now to be kept at the utmost distance" to allow Scripture to speak of the one Mediator who has "become the guarantor of a better covenant" (Heb. 7:22 NIV).

> He took up our pain and bore our suffering.… He was pierced for our transgressions, he was crushed for our iniquities; the punishment that brought us peace was on him, and by his wounds we are healed.… The LORD has laid on him the iniquity of us all.… He was led like a lamb to the slaughter.… He was cut off from the land of the living; for the transgression of my people he was punished. He was assigned a grave with the wicked … though he had done no violence. (Isa. 53:4 – 9 NIV)

---

[173]Anna Maria van Schurmann, quoted by Wesley in a letter to William Law, sec. 2.3, *LJW* 3:335; cf. FA, B 11:108; B 1:608 – 9.

[174]Anna Maria van Schurmann, quoted by Wesley in a letter to William Law, sec. 2.3, *LJW* 3:354.

[175]Ibid.

5. Yet all this "was only the prelude of a glorious victory" where through his resurrection he raised us up with him, and having born "the sin of many ... made intercession for the transgressors."[176]

6. Christ is not only a pattern, but principally the "surety of the new covenant, yea a sacrifice and a victim for the sins of his people."[177] "God presented Christ as a sacrifice of atonement, through the shedding of his blood ... so as to be just and the one who justifies those who have faith in Jesus" (Rom. 3:25 – 26 NIV). "We have been made holy through the sacrifice of the body of Jesus Christ once for all.... For by one sacrifice he has made perfect forever those who are being made holy" (Heb. 10:10 – 14 NIV). "In all the ancient types and figures, 'without shedding of blood there was no remission': which was intended to show there never could be any without the blood of the great Antitype, without that grand propitiatory sacrifice which (like the figure of it) was to be offered 'without the gate.'"[178]

7. In this way, the suffering Messiah atones for the sins of the people and restores them to God's favor. "Christ redeemed us from the curse of the law by becoming a curse for us" (Gal. 3:13). "He himself bore our sins in his body on the cross, so that we might die to sins and live for righteousness" (1 Peter 2:24). This is just what is denied by the Socinians who "rob Christ of the principal part of His priestly office, and leave Him only that of interceding for us by prayer."[179] In a similar way, Law's Christology had dwindled into "the very essence of Deism."[180]

Wesley drew from a brilliant woman of the Calvinist tradition to answer William Law's elusive atonement mysticism. Anna Maria van Schurmann was clear and scriptural. Law was vague and speculative.

c. Resisting Mystical Misunderstandings of the New Birth, Baptism, and Faith

Law had diminished regeneration to "nothing else but the regaining of our first angelic spirit and body," and faith to merely "a desire of coming to God," echoing the mystical longing for union with God.

Wesley pounced on the term "desire": "I know the contrary from experience. I had this desire many years before I even knew what saving faith was."[181] Faith is rather "an *elenchos*, an 'evidence,' or 'conviction' (which is totally different from a desire) 'of things not seen,' a supernatural, a divine evidence and conviction of the things which God hath revealed in His Word ... that the Son of God hath loved me and given Himself for me. Whosoever hath this faith is born of God."[182]

It is precisely such a subjectivist and mystical alteration of faith that led to Law's

---

[176]Ibid., sec. 2.3, *LJW* 3:354 – 55; cf. *CH*, B 7:290 – 92.
[177]Ibid.
[178]Ibid., sec. 2.3, *LJW* 3:356.
[179]Ibid.; *CH*, B 7:441 – 42.
[180]Letter to William Law, sec. 2.3, *LJW* 3:357.
[181]Letter to William Law, sec. 2.4, *LJW* 3:359; cf. *RJW* 94 – 129.
[182]Letter to William Law, sec. 2.4, *LJW* 3:359.

curious views on fervor and coldness in prayer, by which the soul seeks highest union with God *through* "fervor," and then paradoxically seeks a still higher union through coldness. While Law contended that "coldness in one's spiritual journey can be beneficial," Wesley maintained that such spiritual coldness puts the believers "at the peril of their souls."[183]

5. Countering Mystical Universalism and the Denial of the Means of Grace

a. Whether "Christ-in-Everyone" Universalism Induces Spiritual Inertia

Reflecting the mystical tradition, William Law had argued ambiguously for the presence of Christ in every human spirit, "lying there in a state of insensibility and death." Wesley wondered how Christ could be both alive, "knocking at the door of the heart," and yet be dead.

This led Law to a soft universalism (the idea of "Christ in everyman")[184] so as to make people at ease "who never believed at all." Wesley resisted this atonement universalism. This is not what is meant by "Christ died for all." Its outcome is that "Jews, Mohametans, Deists, Heathens, are all members of the Church of Christ! Should we not add devils too?" A false "catholicity" now magnanimously "takes in all the world."

"There can hardly be any doctrine under heaven more agreeable to flesh and blood; nor any which more directly tends to prevent the very dawn of conviction" than to say to the one asleep in sin: Christ is already in your heart; you have now the inspiration of the Spirit. "As soon as you have sewed this pillow to his soul, he sinks back into the sleep of death."[185]

b. Whether the Outward Means of Grace Are Inconsequential

The deeper problem of William Law was a romantic, self-sufficient view of the individual believer which Wesley perceived as a danger to faith. Wesley recognized clearly that Law had offered too simplistic a way of salvation, "a way so plain that they who follow it need no Bible, no human teaching, no outward means whatever, being everyone able to stand alone, everyone sufficient for himself."

Wesley needled Law for his "easy way to salvation." It comes "by the mere turning of your mind," as if "easily and immediately." All of this was "liable to ten thousand delusions."[186] Especially wrongheaded was Law's advice to "stop all self-activity; be retired, silent, passive, and humbly attentive to the inward light." Such a mixture of works-righteousness and quietism would be spiritually incendiary.[187]

183Letter to William Law, sec. 2.4, *LJW* 3:359–61.
184Letter to William Law, sec. 2.5, *LJW* 3:361.
185Letter to William Law, sec. 2.5, *LJW* 3:361–64.
186J IV:502.
187Letter to William Law, sec. 2.6, *LJW* 3:364–68; cf. B 1:376.

If Law is correct that we always have embedded within natural human consciousness "a Priest, a church, and an altar," then there is no need for the church: "no other supper, worship, priest, or altar." On the contrary, "there is but one scriptural way wherein we receive inward grace, through the outward means which God hath appointed."[188]

Against Law's tendency to place Christ and Scripture in flat opposition to each other, Wesley affirmed the classical Protestant view that the revealed and written Word work concurrently: "Both by the Bible and by experience we know that his Word and his Spirit act in connexion with each other."[189]

[188]Letter to William Law, sec. 2.6, *LJW* 3:367.
[189]Ibid.; J IV:505.

CHAPTER 4

The Holy Spirit

A. Person and Work of the Holy Spirit

1. How God the Spirit Acts within Us

All major points of Wesley's teaching of the Holy Spirit are summarized in one single wise sentence that appears in "A Letter to a Roman Catholic."[1] There Wesley astutely condensed his credo on the person and work of the Holy Spirit. It is stated in the form of a personal confession that begins, "I believe."

It contains only fifteen brief phrases, the first group on the *person*, the second group on the *work* of the Holy Spirit. We will examine each phrase:

a. The Person of the Holy Spirit: Who Is God the Spirit?

What language can we borrow to speak fitly of this incomparable Spirit who accomplishes God's work of saving grace? Who is the Holy One who does this work? Here is the first half of the sentence: "I believe the infinite and eternal Spirit of God, equal with the Father and the Son, to be not only perfectly holy in himself, but the immediate cause of all holiness in us." There are seven defining phrases in this avowal of belief:

1. The confession of God the Spirit begins with "I." It is a personal act of magnificent scope. It reveals that sincere faith that comes inwardly from the heart. Only some definite person with some name — a particular "I" — can pronounce this confession. But "I" do not stand alone. As a believer, I stand within a community of faith that has confessed this same faith from apostolic times, as attested in Scripture.
2. God the Spirit is beyond finite description. God the Spirit is infinite. God the Spirit cannot be measured as finite things can be measured.
3. God the Spirit is before, within, and after time. God the Spirit is eternal. God the Spirit transcends the whole temporal order.
4. Who is this one? Who is acting when the Holy Spirit acts? None other than the true God. God the Spirit possesses all the attributes of God.
5. Through God the Spirit, God the Father makes known his saving mercy

[1]Sec. 8, JWO 495.

through God the Son. God the Spirit is eternally in triune communion with the fullness of God. The Spirit is equal in deity with the Father and Son.
6. God the Spirit is perfectly holy in himself. The believer's holiness is cast within the limits of human finitude. God's own holiness transcends all those limits. The Spirit's holiness is unbounded, surpassing all human conceptions of holiness.
7. God the Spirit is the "immediate cause of all holiness in us." God the Spirit is not a remote cause, but an immediately causal actor and cooperative power residing in our hearts, intimately and instantly present to the believer.

This is *who* God the Spirit *is*. When we respond to the Holy Spirit, we are responding to this one. Though beyond our descriptive powers, it is fitting to make these ascriptions. But this is only the first half of the credo. It continues with a summary of *what* God the Spirit is *doing* in us, acting within our hearts.

b. The Work of the Holy Spirit

What sort of work is the Spirit doing? Every step along the way the Spirit is:

enlightening our *understandings*,
rectifying our *wills* and *affections*,
renewing our *natures*,
uniting our persons to Christ,
assuring us of our adoption as *sons* and *daughters*,
leading us in our actions,
purifying and sanctifying our souls and bodies to a full and eternal *enjoyment* of God.[2]

There are nine vital phrases in the second half of this confession on the work of the Spirit:

1. At the closest quarters within us, God the Spirit is helping us *understand*. Through the Spirit we see the light of God's grace.
2. Without coercing our *wills*, God the Spirit is drawing us ever closer to God's will, hedging the way, outlasting any resistances we may have. The twisted will is made straight.
3. By the Spirit's power, our *affections* are reversed from guilt to pardon, from sin to obedience, from alienation to reconciliation with God. We experience and feel this reversal. The affections of the heart are transformed. God the Spirit "acts on the wills and affections of men; withdrawing them from evil, inclining them to good, inspiring (breathing, as it were) good thoughts into them."[3]
4. By the Spirit, through faith, our *natures* are renewed. Our original nature, created in the image of God, is reborn. Our old fallen nature, which has caused so much unhappiness, is put away.
5. By the Spirit we share in personal communion with Christ. Our lives are hid in Christ. Since our nature is *united* with Christ, our personal life is lived out in him.

[2]Letter to a Roman Catholic, sec. 8, JWO 495, line breaks added.
[3]FA, pt. 1, B 11:108, sec. 1.6.

6. The Spirit witnesses within our spirits that we are children of God. We are fully *assured* of citizenship in heaven and our belonging to God's family in this life.
7. The Spirit takes domicile within our hearts. With redeemed affections, the Spirit *guides* our behaviors.
8. The Spirit intends to reclaim us fully to a complete life of full responsiveness to God. The Holy One draws us into his *holiness* unsparingly, insofar as we cooperate. Our bodies and souls are drenched in holy living.
9. We enjoy life with God — not only now but forever. We experience the happiness of living in the presence of God's holiness. This happiness in this life is a glimpse of the full measure of *blessedness* that we will experience with God in eternity.

B. Scriptural Christianity

Among Wesley's most quoted homilies is "Scriptural Christianity," fourth in the usual order of the Standard Sermons. The text points to the reality of the vast revival beginning at that time. It was Acts 2:4: "And they were all filled with the Holy Ghost" [Homily #4 (August 24, 1744),[4] B 2:159 – 80; J #4, V:37 – 52]. The focus is on how the Spirit fills our lives.

The context of this sermon is required to get its full force from the ornate high pulpit of Oxford's oldest church.

1. Filled with the Spirit

a. The Occasion

This homily comes at a heartrending moment of Wesley's life. It gives expression to a major vocational decision. It involved a redefinition of his relation to his colleagues at Oxford.

"Scriptural Christianity" was the last sermon Wesley preached at Oxford. All who read it know why. He knew his audience well. He had been among Oxford students and faculty for many years. He had studied with them and taught many of them. He had an ongoing appointment as fellow of Lincoln College. He was destined to become its most famous son. But at this point, that outcome could hardly be predicted.

Poignantly he later would write about this moment: "I preached, I suppose the last time, at St. Mary's. Be it so. I am now clear of the blood of these men. I have fully delivered my own soul."[5]

The University Church of St. Mary the Virgin on High Street at the center of Oxford is the parish church of Oxford University, built originally in the thirteenth

[4]This was the date of the festival of Saint Bartholomew, on which occurred the Massacre of Paris (1572), and the Great Ejectment of the Nonconformists in England (1662), in which both of Wesley's grandfathers had suffered rejection.

[5]"Short History of the People Called Methodist," sec. 30; *JJW* 1:470, August 24, 1744.

century, having functioned as a church since Anglo-Saxon times. The tower dates to 1280. It has seen many historic events, including the trial of the Oxford Martyrs in 1550 for their Protestant beliefs. Here Thomas Cranmer denounced the pope. Here John Wesley preached his memorable sermon on "The Almost Christian" in 1741. Three years later, it was here that Wesley denounced the laxity of senior university members. After this sermon he was never invited back.

b. Wesley's Vexation with Hypocrisy at Oxford Requiring a Prophetic Word

You can hear the exasperation in Wesley's voice, disheartened that Oxford had not proved the arena where his vision of Christian community could come alive.

He was washing his hands of Oxford. This was his moment to declare it.

When he preached this sermon, he did not intend it for publication. But in order to counter "false and scurrilous accounts," a printed version was produced.

As Ezekiel was called "to warn the people, then if anyone hears the trumpet but does not take warning and the sword comes and takes their life, their blood will be on their own head" (Ezek. 33:3 – 4 NIV), so Wesley felt called to warn his Oxford colleagues of their folly.

c. The Sweeping Vocational Decision Underlying the Last Oxford Sermon

At this point in his life, Wesley was making an irreversible vocational decision no longer to be an Oxford don, but instead to enter into the work of an itinerant evangelist. Despite his success as a young teacher, he was experiencing an entirely different calling. His word of warning to the gathered university is "Scriptural Christianity."

He described the reality of the early church as being filled with the Spirit. But the university is filled with itself. He especially wanted to report to them something of what was then happening in the evangelical revival. In contrast, as he looked about at his Oxford colleagues, he was compelled to say they had the form but not the power of godliness.

The homily begins in a gracious mood. It awaits the last section to deliver a cascade of questions that call to question the common assumptions about Christian life at Oxford.

2. The Fullness of the Spirit

The context of Acts 4:31 portrays the disciples immediately after Pentecost when the Spirit came upon them. They were "all filled with the Holy Spirit and spoke the word of God boldly" (NIV; cf. 2:4). Wesley too felt called to speak boldly.

a. The Gifts of Pentecost: The Faithful Are Filled with the Spirit

The gifts given with Pentecost are given for all and are "essential to all Christians in all ages." These gifts are the mind of Christ, the fruits of the Spirit, the life Christ lived. It is typical for the life of the believer to be filled with the Holy Spirit.[6] That is scriptural Christianity in all ages.[7]

Wherever scriptural Christianity is coming alive, the church is being filled with the Spirit. Where the mind of Christ is bearing the fruits of the Spirit and people are actually walking in the way of faith, there is scriptural Christianity.[8] This life begins with individuals and spreads by testimony and example through persecution, so as to cover the earth, looking finally toward the consummate victory of the sovereign God in and beyond history.[9]

b. The Ordinary Gifts of Spirit-Filled Believers

Make no mistake: The filling of the faithful with the Spirit was not to manifest *extraordinary* gifts. It was simply for bestowing the mind of Christ upon all so as to elicit the *ordinary* fruits of the Spirit in all (Gal. 5:22–24).

What happened at Pentecost is a model for what always happens when the Spirit fills the lives of believers. This filling is not extraordinary for the faithful. It is a gift given *ordinarily* within the faithful community. Wesley urged his hearers to proceed "without busying ourselves, then, in curious, needless inquiries, touching those extraordinary gifts," and focus instead on ordinary gifts constantly being given to faith.[10]

It is thus characteristic for ordinary believers to be "filled with the Holy Spirit." Wesley argued that the gifts of the Spirit are still being distributed to the church, and the work of the Spirit is still capable of transforming the community of faith in ways analogous to the experiences reported in Acts.

3. Scriptural Christianity in Its Rise

a. It Begins with Individuals

All who responded in faith to the good news of Peter's preaching on the day of Pentecost were emboldened to attest the witness of the Spirit within, having faith, love of God and humanity, victory over temptation, and zeal for good works.

The self-offering of the Holy Spirit is for the "more excellent purpose" of offering to sinners the mind of Christ, that by inward renewal they might by grace be enabled to "fulfill all outward righteousness," so that from new birth there would be integral and comprehensive behavioral transformation inwardly.[11] The love of God is shed abroad in our hearts by the Holy Spirit given to us (Rom. 5:5).[12]

Those who receive God's love, love each other in word, deed, and truth. They

[6]"Scriptural Christianity," B 1:160, proem 3.

[7]LCM (January 4, 1749) *LJW* 2:312 ff.

[8]"The Witness of the Spirit, I," B 1:283, sec. 2.12; *CH*, B 7:508–9.

[9]"Scriptural Christianity," B 1:161, proem 5.

[10]"Scriptural Christianity," B 1:160, proem 5; see J #89 "The More Excellent Way," sec. 2; cf. B 3:263–66; 9:353–54.

[11]"Scriptural Christianity," B 1:161–62, sec. 1.1–2.

[12]"Scriptural Christianity," B 1:163, sec. 1.4, 5.

are not puffed up.[13] They are meek and long-suffering. With this love shaping their lives, they would knowingly harm no one. One who receives this Spirit knows that it is not enough merely to abstain from doing evil, but one must do good continually.[14]

It is the ordinary work of the Spirit to awaken individuals to God's pardon and power. This happens through a social process, within a community, yet one by one to individuals within that community.

b. One by One

This Word comes to us one by one. The Spirit works patiently by personal testimony. This does not imply that this one-by-one meeting lacks community consequences. But the consequences for communities of worship and for society will occur only if there is deep inward transformation of the individual.

Wesley was neither an individualistic evangelist who neglected the worshiping community and its context, nor a political philosopher who started with ideas about social structures being transformed. All transformation comes from the heart.

The method of social change in scriptural Christianity moves steadily from individual conversion to its social implications. It does not presume to change the world by rationalistically setting up a theoretical strategy for social change.

This points to a decisive historical difference between the French Enlightenment and the evangelical revival tradition: The French Revolution was a heady, rationalistic, idea-oriented uprising, in which the revolutionaries were trying first to get the right notion of an ideal society. The British and American evangelical revivals proceeded not so much by means of a deductive revolutionary idealism, but with a historically formed, organic, incremental, personal understanding of human transformation. Wesley understood historical change from this more incremental, organic, one-by-one model that he found in the preaching of the Acts of the Apostles.[15]

c. The Transforming Power of Grace

The beginning place for the Holy Spirit is in the heart, with personal conversion enabled by divine grace. This grace comes before any self-initiated human decision. This grace elicits conviction of sin and repentance, and prepares for the receiving of the good news of God. The Spirit enables trust in the Word of God spoken in Christ. In due time, this brings the newly born believer into the family of God.

This process amounts to a new birth, a regeneration of spiritual life that places one's feet on the way toward holiness and happiness. The Spirit of adoption into this family of God leads toward an assurance of the forgiveness of sins and love of neighbor; temperance; guilelessness; vital community in the body of Christ, holding all things in common; union with Christ (Gal. 2:20); and peace with God.[16]

---

[13]"Scriptural Christianity," B 1:163, sec. 1.6.
[14]"Scriptural Christianity," B 1:164, sec. 1.9.
[15]"Scriptural Christianity," B 1:161 – 64, sec. 2.1 – 9.
[16]"Scriptural Christianity," B 1:162, sec. 1.2.

This is how Christianity appeared in its inception. "Such was Christianity on its rise," with persons suddenly and immediately being filled with the Spirit, lifting up their voices boldly in one accord, with one heart and mind, crucified to the world, feeding upon apostolic teaching, breaking bread, praying, sharing, and lacking nothing.[17]

4. Scriptural Christianity in Its Spread

a. The Spread of Scriptural Christianity from One to Another

Those persons effectively transformed by this good news felt called upon to attest it.[18] This good news spread from one to another, heart to heart. All were exhorted to believe, to live out their belief in love, and thereby to attest the ground of their belief. Love took the form of testimony. Each sought to awaken those spiritually asleep, attend those awakened, and nurture all who enter the family of faith. They thundered to the unawakened. They preached reconciliation to the convicted, reasoned with nonbelievers, encouraged believers, and patiently engaged in works of mercy.

Their labors were effective. They grew. They nurtured each person individually as each had special needs.[19]

b. Scriptural Christianity in Its Social Effects

The believers became salt, light, and leaven within the world. This is scriptural Christianity. Rightly taught, it elicits transformed lives in mission who manifest the compassion of God amid the misery of the world. The numbers were increasing of those who were beginning to turn the world upside down. Their labor was not in vain, since accompanied by the Spirit.[20]

By scriptural Christianity, Wesley referred not simply to the proclamation of the gospel but the living out of the life of the gospel concretely. When he spoke of scriptural holiness, he was talking about that transformed life that is lived in obedience to this good news. It is the life of those filled with the Holy Spirit, whose transformation becomes contagious from person to person, meeting persecution and trouble and persevering through suffering, and finally covering the earth.[21]

c. The Offense of the Gospel to the Self-Satisfied

But the world was offended. Those whose lives were inordinately attached to pleasure, reputation, acquisitive trade, and bigoted opinions were resistant. Especially offended were men of religion (in the sense of self-satisfied worldly religionists who were seeking to use religion for their own purposes).

[17]"Scriptural Christianity," B 1:165, sec. 1.10.
[18]"Scriptural Christianity," B 1:165, sec. 2.1.
[19]"Scriptural Christianity," B 1:165–67, sec. 2.1–4.
[20]"Scriptural Christianity," B 1:167, sec. 2.5.
[21]*CH*, B 7:476–87.

Christianity spread in world history. Yet "how soon did the tares appear"[22] wherever the wheat was sown. How soon did the mystery of iniquity work even alongside the mystery of godliness. How soon did the arch-deceiver find a seat even in the temple of God. Yet despite corruptions, the reign of God spread.[23]

Wherever the church proceeds in mission, it causes offense proportional to its triumphs. As scriptural Christianity grew, so did the persecution of believers. But by their fidelity the kingdom was spread ever more widely, for "their sufferings spake to all the world." Wesley himself had only recently been through a period of persecution, with the Wednesbury riots in the back of his mind. As their labor grew mightily and prevailed, "so much the more did the offenses prevail also."[24]

5. The Mission of Scriptural Christianity: To the Ends of the Earth

Scriptural Christianity first begins with individuals, spreads in committed, disciplined communities, and reaches out to the whole suffering world. Individuals come together into intentional communities as intensive change agents, and soon they in turn are quietly affecting society.

Greater things than what we have seen have been promised. The kingdom of God stands in prospect. Where God reigns, he subdues all things to himself, causing every heart to overflow with love and every mouth with praise.

This mission looks forward to the time when this testimony will cover the earth,[25] when the biblical hopes will be fulfilled (Isa. 2:1 – 4; 11:6 – 12). The prospect is for peace, an end to poverty and oppression, and a fulfillment of righteousness and final justice.

In this way, salvation is coming to the Gentiles — to all the nations.[26] There is no insurmountable obstacle or intrinsic reason why all cannot hear it. No absolute necessity prevents its universal spread. All the obstacles that the history of sin provides can be overcome by grace that elicits faith active in love.

The promised future is a transformed creation, where all are blessed, where mercy accompanies justice, where there is no evil speaking.[27] "Their 'love is without dissimulation'; their words are always the just expression of their thoughts, opening a window into their breast, that whosoever desires may look into their hearts and see that only love and God are there."[28] This future was already being lived out in the faithful, as seen in the revival. The mission of the church is to spread scriptural Christianity the world over.[29] They are happy who have the Lord for their God (Ps. 144:15).[30]

[22]"Scriptural Christianity," B 1:169, sec. 2.9.
[23]"Scriptural Christianity," B 1:167 – 68, sec. 2.5 – 7.
[24]"Scriptural Christianity," B 1:167 – 68, sec. 2.57.
[25]"Scriptural Christianity," B 1:168; J V:45, sec. 3.1.
[26]"Scriptural Christianity," B 1:169, sec. 3.2.
[27]"Scriptural Christianity," B 1:171, sec. 3.5.
[28]Ibid.; cf. "An Israelite Indeed," sec. 2.10; "On Dissimulation."
[29]"Scriptural Christianity," B 1:169 – 71, sec. 3.1 – 5.
[30]"Scriptural Christianity," B 1:172, sec. 3.6.

6. The Change of Tone

a. The Turn toward Encounter

Thus far the homily is unobjectionable and thoroughly scriptural. It is in touch with the best of Oxford manners. It is incredibly positive and hopeful. There is as yet no tone of ill-temper. Nothing yet has troubled the waters. Who would have imagined at this point that the remainder of this sermon would be remembered at Oxford as an eruption of indignation?

Wesley had laid the groundwork, but he was not through. He had not yet applied this text to this audience. He was a man of conscience. He could not take to the pulpit and ignore his duty to preach. He considered it spineless to come to a point of rare opportunity and let it go by with pleasantries. In the light of this text — "They were all filled with the Holy Ghost" — he could not leave his audience feeling at ease, smug, and full of themselves.

b. A Plain, Confrontative Application

So at the end of this sermon, he asks of those listening a simple question: Does scriptural Christianity exist at Oxford? Here at Oxford, he said to his university audience, where you might expect to find the best of Christian culture's expression, Christianity does not exist.[31]

Plain talk was required to break through. Just as Kierkegaard would later ask: Does Christianity exist in Denmark — where everyone was already baptized, where each one could produce a baptismal certificate, but where no one really knew what it meant? Modern readers are reminded of the spirit of Kierkegaard's *Attack on Christendom,* in which he said that Luther had his Ninety-Five Theses, but he had only one: to introduce Christianity to Christendom.

Wesley was convinced that there were few evidences of genuine repentance and faith and of the filling of the Spirit in the audience he was addressing. He said that even in the most educated, even in the most pious, even among clergy, there appeared slim evidence of living faith.[32] The sermon thus intentionally ended on a combative note. He ended his Oxford days on a strong note of earnest confrontation.

c. A Barrage of Questions

Wesley then fired a barrage of challenging questions to his stunned audience:[33]

Is this a community filled with the Holy Spirit?

You who are called and authorized to form the tender minds and consciences of youth, are you filled with the Spirit?[34]

Are those called to ministry serving as an earnest moral pattern to others in charity, spirit, faith, purity (1 Tim. 4:12)?

---

[31]"Scriptural Christianity," B 1:172 – 74, sec. 4.1 – 4.

[32]"Scriptural Christianity," B 1:175 – 76, sec. 4.6.

[33]"Scriptural Christianity," B 1:175, sec. 4.5.

[34]"Scriptural Christianity," B 1:175, sec. 6. Cf. *JJW*, February 8, 1736, conversation with Spangenberg.

Are candidates for ordination being taught of God, that they may be able to teach?[35]
Are they prepared to give themselves unreservedly to their ministry?
Are students teachable, willing to enter into a discipline of learning that would lead them to new life?
Do university students have either the form or power of godliness?
Do they give evidences of being on their way to perfect love?
Is that commitment being encouraged by daily prayer and good works?[36]
Or do we have a "generation of triflers, triflers with God, with one another, and with your own souls?"[37]

The time given for repentance may be short. There is not an infinite amount of time given for finite persons to repent.

d. God's Intent to Restore Scriptural Christianity

How can scriptural Christianity be restored? We have a right to look to ordained leadership, Wesley argued. But lacking that, it may fall that Christianity will be "restored by young, unknown, inconsiderable men."[38] Wesley was convinced that Oxford would not be ready for the alternative that the Holy Spirit had prepared.

Regardless of what happened at Oxford, the renewal of scriptural Christianity was happening in the world. It was a work of God through instruments and means of God's own choosing. Establishment religiosity would be surprised at what God did and the means God chose.

Who can restore scriptural Christianity? Only God. If we grieve the Spirit, the change may come through cultural crisis, famine, or pestilence. Better now to bend our knees to the living God.[39] So ends the sermon on scriptural Christianity.

e. Scriptural Christianity in the Emerging Revival

This section of this book is on Wesley's teaching on the work of the Spirit. The homily above is of the highest importance in grasping Wesley's vision of how the Spirit works. He was seeing this vision as already being embodied in the evangelical revival. The preaching is positive, intentional, earnestly scriptural, filled with the Spirit, and straightforward without mincing words.

In this series we are examining how Wesley worked carefully through all key points of the Christian teaching of salvation. This homily is placed in this crucial location in the sequence of topics because it focuses on the work of the Spirit in redeeming humanity one by one to its largest extension. It points to the fervency of belief in the Spirit's intent to transform both individuals and their broken society. This includes the willingness to challenge a complacent audience who might easily have accepted the body of the sermon but not its application.

[35]"Scriptural Christianity," B 1:177, sec. 4.8; BCP, Ordering of Priests.
[36]"Scriptural Christianity," B 1:178, sec. 4.9; cf. B 4:389 – 407; J #150 "Hypocrisy in Oxford."
[37]"Scriptural Christianity," B 1:179, sec. 4.10.
[38]"Scriptural Christianity," B 1:179, sec. 4.11.
[39]"Scriptural Christianity," B 1:179 – 80, sec. 4.11.

Next we turn to the more formal doctrinal statement of the teaching of the Holy Spirit contained in the Articles of Religion and the foundational Doctrinal Minutes.

C. The Doctrinal Standards on Pneumatology

Wesley's teaching on the Holy Spirit is formally and definitively set forth in the Articles and earliest Doctrinal Minutes. The Articles became enshrined in the Constitution of the American Methodist Church. The Minutes formed the core of classic Methodist doctrinal instruction on the Holy Spirit.

1. The Holy Spirit in Wesley's Rescension of the Articles of Religion, Article 4[40]

a. The Ancient Consensual Language of Article 4 on the Holy Ghost

Wesley's Article 4 confesses with the ancient church: "The Holy Ghost, proceeding from the Father, and the Son, is of one substance, majesty, and glory with the Father and the Son, very and eternal God." The doctrine of the Person of the Holy Spirit is in this way reflective of ancient ecumenical Christianity.

The Holy Spirit proceeds and is one in being with the Father and the Son. This aligns Methodist teaching with the Western view of the procession of the Spirit. Though Wesley valued highly the Eastern tradition, and commended it to his connection, he did not venture to enter into any exegetical differences on the procession of the Spirit today.

The majesty of the Father is the majesty of the Spirit. The glory of the Father is the glory of the Spirit. The Spirit is the eternal God.

The majesty of God the Son is the majesty of God the Spirit. The glory of God the Son is the glory of the Spirit. God the Spirit is none other than truly God, or in ancient language, "very God."[41]

So when we pray to the Spirit, we pray to God. God the Spirit, like God the Son, is nothing less than the eternal, all-wise, incomparably good giver of life. The Holy Spirit proceeds from and is one in being with the Father and the Son. The Spirit is of one substance with the Father and of one substance (consubstantial) with the Son.

This places Methodist doctrine entirely out of the range of Arianism and the other pneumatological heresies of early Christianity. Arianism refused to acknowledge that the Holy Spirit is of one substance with God. These definitions hark back to the ecumenical councils of the first five centuries. Wesley affirmed the deity of the Holy Spirit and in doing so confirmed classic Christian teaching.

[40] These two articles, except for minor grammatical emendations, are identical with the Articles of Religion of the Church of England. They were commended to the American Methodists in their Founding Conference of Christmas 1784. They have remained constitutionally established standards of doctrine not only for United Methodists, but in substance in many other worldwide Wesleyan bodies. See *DSWT*, chap. 7, 127–73, for a thorough review of these articles.

[41] *CH*, B 7:279–80, 502–3, 532–36, 623–25, 708–9.

b. The Work of the Spirit That Follows from Article 4

Although the Anglican-Methodist Article 4 does not in itself speak in detail of the work of the Spirit, we can reasonably derive implications from this article that pertain to scriptural passages that report and interpret the activities of this same Spirit, as in the book of Acts and letters of Paul.

The work of the Spirit is that of applying the ministry and mission of the Son to our hearts. The Holy Spirit is addressing us within the citadel of our consciousness to make clear to us what God has done for us in the Son. The Spirit is given to fulfill and consummate the work of the Son, which is offered on the cross as a perfect and completed work, but still requires a process in time for humans to receive it and grow thereby. This is where the Spirit remains steadily at work in time. The Holy Spirit is the holy God coming into us at close quarters to transform our lives.[42]

2. The Holy Spirit in Wesley's Rescension of the Articles of Religion, Article 5

a. The Ancient Consensual Language of Article 5 on the Holy Spirit in Scripture Affirmed

The article "The Sufficiency of the Holy Scripture for Salvation" declares five linked points:

1. "The Holy Scripture containeth all things necessary to salvation."
2. "Whatever is not read therein, nor may be proved thereby, is not to be required of any man." Advocates who seek to require some idea or interpretation not found in Scripture have already dismissed themselves from the conversation about truth in the Methodist connection, for such is not necessary to salvation.
3. Nothing absent from Scripture "should be believed as an article of faith."
4. If so, anything absent from Scripture should not "be thought requisite or necessary in salvation."
5. By the term *Holy Scriptures* we understand "those canonical books of the Old and New Testament of whose authority was never any doubt in the Church." Though modern historians may dispute the canon, there can be no doubt that the historic church has consensually received it even as we receive it.

b. The Spirit's Work in the Inspiration and Reading of Sacred Scripture

Since the Holy Spirit inspires Scripture, these five points pertain by inference to the work of the Spirit in engendering faith. Although not explicitly developed in this article, we have seen previously that the Spirit is an active participant in the inspiration, transmission, and interpretation of Scripture.

God the Spirit works to elicit the apostolic testimony to the Son and the Father. The same Spirit awakens responses of faith to the apostolic testimony. Even before the written phase of apostolic writing, the Spirit is found already eliciting the oral

[42]B 1:75–76; 2:191; 4:284.

phase of apostolic preaching, since preaching is "by the Spirit." Furthermore, the Spirit is crucial in the transmission of oral to written testimony, which then has become consensually received as normative for all Christian teaching.

It is by the Spirit that the apostles were guided to testify, and they were empowered by the Spirit to attest accurately. The Holy Spirit in this way guarantees the transmission and present efficacy of the written Word.

The guarantee of the truthfulness of the written Word is less an affirmation about reliable human investigation or historical criteria than it is an affirmation about the work of the Spirit. Believers trust the Scriptures because they trust God the Spirit to deliver them in a way sufficient for our salvation. If the Spirit is truly God, the Spirit-led written Word is surely the Word of God.

That Scripture is sufficient for salvation is not a conclusion that can be derived from historical arguments. It has the logical status of an a priori argument. The prior assumption is that God the Spirit is capable of witnessing sufficiently to salvation.

c. The Spirit Summons into Being the Written Word

The premise is that whatever is said of the Spirit will be consistent with Scripture, interpreted according to the analogy of faith in the community of faith. Scripture is nothing less than the Word of God written under the inspiration of the Spirit.

Lacking scriptural grounding, the cleverest hypothesis lacks authority for preaching. That is not to neglect reason, experience, or tradition, but to recognize that each of these sources of knowing are derivative and exist in relation to the primacy of the divine self-disclosure as attested in Scripture, which is the central norm of Christian doctrine.[43]

God the Spirit summons into being the written Word and attends it through a concrete history of consensual reception and transgenerational transmission. The whole notion of the authority of canon and canonization is the Spirit's own work on behalf of the truth and clarity of faith. It needed to be written to be preserved. It needed to be preserved to be transmitted. So the efficacy of the written Word belongs in theological systems under the heading of the work of the Spirit as much as under a statement of method establishing the authority of Scripture.[44]

The question of the authority of Scripture asks how the Holy Spirit enables the written Word to be accurately transmitted through the hazards of history. It is only God's own Spirit who can guarantee the authenticity of the canon, since in the economy of the Trinity, the Spirit is the one who attests its truth in our hearts.

How can we be sure we received a reliable canon? How do we know that it is not deeply flawed? We know because we trust that the Spirit of God who raised Jesus from the dead would not deliver to us a defective written Word. The reliability of the canon cannot be answered without the premise of the tending work of the Spirit,

[43]"Of the Church," B 3:45 – 57.

[44]Reformed confessions often have placed the doctrine of Scripture as the first heading of the loci of doctrines. Anglican and Methodist articles normally place the doctrine of the Holy Spirit prior to that of sacred Scripture. This is reflected in Wesley's espousal and rescension of the Anglican articles.

shepherding the written Word through time. What we have is a trustworthy and sufficient testimony. We count on God the Spirit to make plain the truth of God's coming.[45]

3. The Spirit's Work in Human Transformation

The Spirit works not only to elicit the Scripture as rule and guide for faith and practice, but also to summon into being the life and mission of the interpreting community.

Prior to Pentecost the church existed as promise of the Spirit. Following Pentecost the Spirit engenders the church in a fulfilled way. This work continues through the recurring proclamation of the Word and the administration of the sacraments, offering the means by which the living body of Christ is sustained. Every feature of the concept of authority is derivative from the grace of the Holy Spirit. We are now in the heartland of Wesleyan spiritual formation.

Those who look for the core of the Christian teaching of the personal and social empowerment of the laity will find it here in the work of the Holy Spirit, in the convicting, guiding, comforting, sustaining, and persevering activity of the Spirit. The Spirit first brings us to a conviction of our sin, helping us to stand seriously under the law, under judgment, and in due time to an awareness of the gospel. The Spirit is guiding us through a path that leads us to a community of faith, requiring and enabling full responsiveness to the good news of the Son.[46] The Spirit sustains and empowers the faithful and guides them into all truth.[47]

D. Assurance of Salvation

The Minutes of 1744 define not only core doctrines of justification and the indwelling work of the Spirit, but also the doctrine of assurance of salvation, a central feature of Wesley's teaching.

1. The Doctrinal Minutes on the Assuring Work of the Spirit

The Minutes of the early Methodist preachers' conferences ("Minutes of Several Conversations between the Rev. Mr. Wesley and Others, from the Year 1744 to 1789") attest the centrality of the witness of the Spirit.[48] They teach that the moment a person exercises faith, trusting God's reconciling Word, he or she is justified by the Son, with the Spirit bearing assuring witness within. The Spirit is inwardly attesting the power of grace to cleanse from all sin, so as wholly to refashion broken lives.

---

[45]Letter to "John Smith," March 25, 1747, *LJW* 2:90.

[46]B 2:53 – 58; 4:288 – 89, 357; FA, B 11:258 – 59; 9:199 – 200.

[47]Those who come into Wesley's connection of spiritual formation stand under a restriction on their capacity to change, revise, or supposedly "improve" the received doctrine of the Holy Spirit. The Restrictive Rules limit subsequent legislative bodies from amending the articles.

[48]*LJW* 3:136 – 37; 5:170, 202, 262; J VIII:275 – 339.

The Methodist revival lived out of the awareness of the Spirit's power to assure the believer of the active presence of justifying and sanctifying grace. All seekers can examine their own life to see if the evidences of the new life are present in the fruits of faith active in love.

First, the "sinner is convinced by the Holy Ghost, 'Christ loved me, and gave himself for me.'" Second, "immediately the same Spirit bears witness, 'Thou art pardoned; thou hast redemption in his blood.'"[49] It is the Spirit who assuredly attests this pardon, so powerfully that no one can experience it without knowing it.[50] Third, the Spirit works in eliciting the fruits of faith. "The immediate fruits of justifying faith" are "peace, joy, love, power over all outward sin and power to keep down all inward sin."[51]

All three movements from sin to faith are inwardly guided and coaxed by God the Spirit.

2. The Gift of the Spirit Is the Ordinary Privilege of Believers

Against those who hold that it is not the ordinary privilege of all believers, Wesley taught that the gift of the Spirit is the common entitlement of all who have faith, all who are adopted into the family of God. The Scriptures were written "that you may believe that Jesus is the Messiah, the Son of God, and that by believing you may have life in his name" (John 20:31 NIV). Those who remain deeply ambivalent about whether they have received this witness of the Spirit, even though they may have good tempers and lead a decent moral life, may still be struggling to receive the preparatory grace by which the Spirit intends to move the penitent toward justifying grace.

To sin willfully and impenitently subsequent to this new birth is voluntarily to throw away faith's benefits. Believers may enter a period of doubt without the loss of faith, but faith as such is not lost except by the lack of trust in God's righteousness, and then it may be regained by repentance, using the means of grace, eliciting a lively new reception of grace that elicits works of love.

This is the core doctrinal text of Methodist teaching on the assurance of salvation. What follows is the homiletical clarification of what this means practically to believers.

E. The Witness of the Spirit with Our Spirits

A central feature of Wesley's teaching of the Holy Spirit is the constant inner testimony of the Spirit in our hearts.[52] "The doctrine which it defends formed part of almost every sermon of Wesley's in these early years."[53]

[49]Minutes, 1744, June 25, Q4, JWO 137; cf. *CH*, B 7:195–96; B 1:274–75, 405.
[50]Minutes, 1744, June 25, Q5, JWO 137.
[51]Minutes, 1744, June 25, Q7, JWO 138.
[52]*CH*, B 7:196–97, 502.
[53]*SS* 1:199.

It is found in most concentrated form in the Standard Sermons, especially in Discourses I and II on "The Witness of the Spirit," and a sequel discourse on "The Witness of Our Own Spirit." (Note that two of the sermons relating to the Holy Spirit in the Jackson edition have been erroneously attributed to Wesley: "On Grieving the Holy Spirit" by William Tilly[54] and "On the Holy Spirit" by John Gambold.)[55]

1. The Witness of the Spirit, Discourse I

The text of the homily "The Witness of the Spirit, I," is Romans 8:16: "The Spirit itself beareth witness within our spirit, that we are the children of God" [Homily #10 (1746), B 1:267–84; J #10, V:111–23].

The consequences of the work of the witnessing Spirit are evidenced in the new birth, assurance, fruits of the Spirit, and radical yieldedness to God.[56] These are ordered not in chronological sequence but in spiritual affinity.

a. The First Misstep: Private Revelation and "Enthusiasm"

By 1746 Wesley had seen enough revivalist excesses to realize that some who claim to have received the Spirit of God have only egoistic delusions of their own spirits. Lacking discernment, the enthusiast uncritically identifies as God's Spirit that which is merely welling up within as a nativistic expression of earthly hopes and despairs. The familiar "New" Age flakiness that we today call channeling, imaging, and psychic intuition are tired reruns of what Wesley dubbed "enthusiasm."[57]

Enthusiasts may be deluded into a false assurance of saving grace by mistakenly identifying their own private spirit with God's own eternal Spirit. Worse, they may mistake a demonic spirit for the Spirit of God. They take the energies of their own spirit and project them upon God as if divine, an anticipation of Freud. They prematurely assume they possess the Spirit, and so miss beholding and experiencing the full reach of the Spirit of God witnessing within the human spirit.

"Enthusiasts" in Wesley's day were prone to claim the Spirit as a private inspiration apart from the history of the Spirit's disclosure. They defined the Spirit too emotively and privately. The work of the Spirit was not even recognized by some as actively present in the ordinary grace of divine worship: common prayer, Scripture reading, and sacramental life. In its egocentrism, enthusiasm tended to forget the mighty work of God in nature, history, and providence.[58]

b. The Opposite Nonstarter: Rationalistic Skepticism

In the opposite corner are rationalist skeptics who doubt that anyone can adequately know God and question whether reconciliation with the Father is even conceivable. They imagine that such matters are not subject to knowledge but only to

[54]B 4:531; *CH*, B 7:485–92.
[55]B 4:524; *CH*, VII:508–20.
[56]B 1:194, 267–99; 2:160–61, 206.
[57]"The Nature of Enthusiasm," B 2:44–60.
[58]"The Witness of the Spirit, I," B 1:269, proem 1.

rash speculation. If the skeptics are right, then even if God has saved humanity, no finite beholder could dependably perceive it, since such claims are intrinsically undemonstrable, hence unknowable.

Because they try to see without "the spiritual senses," rationalistic reductionists are often not ready to credit God's Spirit with any palpable activity, thereby reducing their range of observation and empirical experience. They are not ready to hear evidences of pardon, assurance, faith, and the fruits of faith. Some are all too quick to reduce the fruits of the Spirit to naturalistic, psychological, sociological, political, or physical causes.

c. The Spirit Provides the Middle Way

Wesley sought to weave a fine path between these two hazards that still remain with us today—inordinate emphasis either on our own individualistic personal experiences or on reductionist rationalism. The emotive reductionists oppositely tended to assume that my private experience is finally God talking to me regardless of what is said in the Scripture text, the historic tradition, or the worshiping community. The natural reductionists tended to assume that all knowledge can be ruled out that does not conform to a laboratory empiricist model.

Wesley did not try to reconcile two bad models. Rather, he resisted both the extreme skeptical rationalists who cannot imagine that the Spirit addresses us personally at the most inward levels of experience and those "enthusiasts" who speak too confidently of personal revelation without understanding the actual history of revelation.[59]

2. God's Spirit Bearing Witness with Our Spirits

a. Our Own Spirits Respond to God's Spirit

How do we know that we are children of God? First by the witness of our own spirit. "You undoubtedly know in your own breast, if, by the grace of God, [the witness of the Spirit] belongs to you. Your conscience informs you from day to day."[60] "Superadded to, and conjoined with" this inward witness is God's own witness that we are reconciled as children in the family of God. In Romans 8, Paul deliberately set forth the way God the Spirit makes known our salvation by himself witnessing in our hearts. There is a concurrence between what God whispers to us by his Spirit directly witnessing within us and what our own hearts say to us as a consequence. The Spirit of God works within our own spirit without denying either the finitude of our own perceptions or the transcendence of God's own Spirit.[61]

At what school do we learn that we have been adopted into this family, so that we can live this new life, and enjoy this liberty? Answer: Within the community of faith, nurtured by the means of grace. It is not simply my spirit desperately trying to

[59]"The Witness of the Spirit, I," B 1:270, proem 2.
[60]"The Witness of the Spirit, I," B 1:270–76, sec. 1.1–9.
[61]"The Witness of the Spirit, I," B 1:275–76, sec. 1.7–9.

persuade myself of this truth. Nor is it simply God decreeing this as if to circumvent my rational and emotive responsiveness. Both sides are held in creative tension and mutuality.[62]

Romans 8:16 requires a distinguishing of voices, so as to discern what one's own spirit is saying and what God is saying through revelation in history. Scripture informs the dialogue of the Spirit with the human spirit. At the core of the Wesleyan teaching of assurance is the question, do these jointly confirm each other? Do they elicit a reliable inward impression on the soul that I am a child of God?[63]

b. The Two Witnesses Work Together

God's Spirit always comes before the testimony of our own spirit but permits and enables the reverberation of our own testimony to confirm it. God witnesses in our hearts, and then we confirm this attestation. These two witnesses work together so that we can know that we are children of God, so much so that one "can no more doubt the reality of his sonship than he can doubt of the shining of the sun."[64]

"Faith is one thing; the full assurance of faith another.... Some Christians have only the first of these; they have faith, but mixed with doubts and fears. Some have also the full assurance of faith, a full conviction of present pardon; and yet not the full assurance of hope; not a full conviction of their future perseverance."[65] "The faith which we preach" as necessary to all Christians, is the full conviction of present pardon. "There may be faith without full assurance. And these lower degrees of faith do not exclude doubts.... This *plerophory,* or full assurance, is doubtless wrought in us by the Holy Ghost. But so is every degree of true faith."[66]

3. Testing Whether the Spirit's Work Is Discernible

This inner dialogue lies at the heart of the meaning of assurance. Apart from the Spirit's assuring work, there is no way to invent a credible or durable feeling of assurance. But the Spirit attests and offers assurance as a gift. God's own self-giving *is* the gift.[67] The Spirit attests the gift which the Father offers through the Son.[68]

a. Toward Self-Examination of the Spirit's Witness

A unique sort of spiritual reasoning occurs in God's assuring work. It happens by the honest examination of the witness of one's own spirit, accurately stated and articulated publicly through personal testimony.

[62]Letter to "John Smith," March 25, 1747, *LJW* 2:100 – 103.

[63]B 2:153 – 54, 161 – 62; 9:374 – 76; *CH*, B 7:58; FA, B 11:132 – 37, 398 – 99.

[64]"The Witness of the Spirit, I," B 1:276, sec. 1.12.

[65]Second Letter to Bishop Lavington, B 11:398, sec. 20; J IX:32; cf. JWO 50 – 52, 159 – 60, 165 – 66, 188 – 89, 363 – 64.

[66]Letter to Richard Tompson, February 5, 1756, *LJW* 3:161. On the distinction between the fullness of pardon and degrees of reception of full pardon, cf. *LJW* 3:374. On full assurance of faith, see B 2:153 – 54, 161 – 62. Letter to Dr. Rutherforth, B 9:374 – 76; *CH*, B 7:58; FA, B 11:132 – 37, 398 – 99; 9:61, 100, 376; *JJW* 2:49.

[67]B 1:149 – 55; 2:268, 410; 3:263 – 66; *CH*, B 7:583.

[68]"The Witness of the Spirit, I," B 1:271 – 72, sec. 1.2 – 4.

The Spirit's address through the written word of Scripture is at work to help correct private exaggerations. The Spirit illumines what is happening within subjective experience. We learn about our own spirit by self-examination, by honest listening to conscience, and by talking with others whom we have learned are trustworthy.[69]

How do we know it is not some fantasy or demonic power working within? By testing the competing spirits in the community of faith on the basis of Scripture, tradition, reason, and experience.

We are not without an ecclesial laboratory for testing the spirits. "God's way of working," as discussed in volume 1 on theological method, is here being put practically to work.[70] The "quadrilateral" points of reference constitute a practical guide for the testing of the spiritual senses.

This happens in a worshiping community. Each partner in dialogue is checking out attestations of the witness of the Spirit in terms of these criteria, all of which appear prominently in this homily.[71]

b. Attesting the Witness: Methodist "Testimony"

In the community of faith, each one is given opportunity to attest both the witness of one's own spirit and the apostolic memory of God's self-attestation. Within this community of praise and reflection and disclosure, one may come steadily and assuredly to know that one is a child of God, reclaimed into the family of God.

Wesley was confident that the Spirit would not disappoint when a believer follows these conditions and trusts these promises. This is not strictly speaking a natural or physical test, but rather a dialogical, conversational test in which we are asked to discern the Spirit in the context of a community of faith and common prayer, using Scripture as a guide and our own rational capacity as a hedge against inordinate egoism. Wesley was concerned that these points not be exaggerated so that egocentric adrenaline might claim to possess the Spirit unilaterally.[72]

On this premise, we can then disclose this truth mutually with other members of the gathered, confessing, worshiping community.[73] We can use our own reasoning to try to discern the truth of Scripture and the truth of the testimony of friends and of one's own heart. This testimony is highly experiential. But the experience is under the authority of Scripture and subject to the confirming testimony of the centuries of believers since the apostles. The Wesleyan societies were intensive group processes, interacting, interpersonally encountering, exceedingly self-disclosing, and personally open.

4. Marks of the Mutual Witness

The mutual witness of God's Spirit with my spirit in a community of prayer respects both God's grace and human freedom. If coerced by divine sovereignty,

[69]"The Witness of the Spirit, I," B 1:270–74, sec. 1.1–6.
[70]"The Witness of the Spirit, I," B 1:270–73, sec. 1.1–6.
[71]"The Witness of the Spirit, I," B 1:282–83, sec. 2.11–13.
[72]"The Witness of the Spirit, I," B 1:274–76, sec. 1.7–12.
[73]*CH*, B 11:468.

saving faith would not be human. It would disrespect humanity. If left to human hands, it would never be accomplished. That would disrespect God's way of saving humanity.

This cooperation of grace and freedom is quite different from the privatistic, reclusive presumption of my natural mind. It is not that my spirit takes charge of the Spirit of God, but rather that the Spirit advocates within my spirit.[74]

There are reliable marks set forth in Scripture that one is becoming a child of God. Among these visible signs are five in particular: repentance, faith, behavioral reversal, a sense of serene joy, and obedient keeping of the commandments.[75]

a. The Evidences of Repentance

When one truly *repents*, having been convicted of sin and in godly sorrow turned in faith to God, one need not wonder despairingly whether one is a recipient of God's saving love. Those who experience in themselves a syndrome of continual resistance to repentance still await the joy of the shared witness of the Spirit with our spirits.[76]

b. The Evidences of Faith

Faith trusts in God's pardon. This pardon is accomplished on the cross. Faith does not quibble with the Judge. It receives the gracious gift, which is entirely unmerited. There is nothing more to do than to thank God from the heart.

c. The Evidences of a Behavioral Reversal

True repentance elicits a fundamental *behavioral reversal*, a turning around of one's actual conduct in such a way that it bears fruit in the works of love. These joint witnesses are accompanied by palpable evidences of moral and behavioral change. The contrite of heart do not just keep on living as before.

Anyone can ask, "Have I undergone such a reversal of wretched behaviors that could be rightly described as a new birth of spirit?" If not, pray for the grace of repentance that enables readiness to receive the witness of the Spirit.[77]

d. A Joyful Sense of God's Presence

The new life is accompanied by joy, one of the fruits of the Spirit. Anyone can ask whether he or she is experiencing a *joyful sense of God's presence*, felicity in the Lord, precisely amid the keeping of the commandments. There has always been a focus in Methodist preaching on the joy of the reception of the Spirit. If absent, one of the marks of assurance is missing.[78] If present, it is not hard to recognize a yielding, humble, joyful spirit.

---

[74]"The Witness of the Spirit, I," B 1:275 – 77, secs. 1.11 – 2.2.
[75]"The Witness of the Spirit, I," B 1:277 – 84, secs. 2 – 5.
[76]"The Witness of the Spirit, I," B 1:278, sec. 2.4.
[77]"The Witness of the Spirit, I," B 1:274 – 76, sec. 1.6 – 12.
[78]"The Witness of the Spirit, I," B 1:279 – 80, sec. 2.6.

e. The Obedience of Faith

The new life is a life of obedience to God that actively serves the neighbor in love. Anyone can ask, "How willingly am I keeping the commandments of Scripture? Am I walking according to the Decalogue, telling the truth, not worshiping false gods, not committing adultery?" An honest negative points one back to square one — repentance.[79]

These are the evidences of new birth. Ordinarily repentance *precedes* the witness of the Spirit. Faith and a joyful sense of God's presence and the joyful fruits of the Spirit *accompany* the witness. The life of obedience *follows* the Spirit's witness.

Temptations remain, but they are not above the competence of grace to overcome them.

Wesley was confident that when we give ourselves these tests honestly within an accountable community of testimony and disclosure, they yield reliable knowledge. There is no reason for one to remain wholly in the dark about one's assurance of salvation. These are clear marks that one is becoming a child of God.[80]

5. The Witness of the Spirit, Discourse II

Two decades later, Wesley wrote another discourse on the same text and the same theme — the conjoint witness of God's Spirit and our spirits. The text, again, is Romans 8:16: "The Spirit itself beareth witness within our spirit, that we are the children of God" [Homily #11 (1767), B 1:285 – 98; J #11, V:123 – 34]. This is normally called Discourse II.

a. The Dual Witnesses

Here the witness of the Spirit is again summarily defined as the "inward impression on the soul whereby the Spirit of God immediately and directly witnesses to my spirit that I am the child of God, that Jesus Christ has loved me and given himself for me and that all my sins are blotted out and that I, even I, am reconciled to God."[81]

All who study Holy Writ know that there is an inward testimony of the Spirit whose mission is to bear fruit by engendering faith active in love.

All this is thoroughly Protestant. But Wesley thought one aspect of the order of salvation — assurance of salvation — had not been given sufficient attention in some forms of Protestant preaching. This was a great gift neglected. For God has permitted an experience of the complete correspondence between the testimony of the Holy Spirit and our own spirit. This is no innovation, and it is no secret. It is clearly testified in Romans 8:16.

b. The Right of the Laity to Hear Reliable Scriptural Testimony

A great privilege of those born of God is to know assuredly that they are saved by

[79]"The Witness of the Spirit, I," B 1:280, sec. 2.7.
[80]"The Witness of the Spirit, I," B 1:278 – 80, sec. 2.4 – 7.
[81]"The Witness of the Spirit, II," B 1:287, sec. 2.2.

grace. Every believer has a right to know that this inward testimony is being reliably heard, received, and brought into personal appropriation in a felt process.

This inner testimony can be inchoately intuited by human knowledge, but not with the clarity of saving grace. It is known negatively by conscience. It can be observed and analyzed by critical reason. But the full range of this cooperative testimony requires the witness of the written Word.

Anyone can examine the Scripture text. But the full recognition of this dual witness can come only from the Spirit's work in repentance and faith. This scriptural promise can be confirmed by heartfelt examining of one's own experience. That believers may know the salvation of God is the entitlement of all who sincerely believe.[82]

Wesley considered assurance so intrinsic to salvation that all who have repented and believed the gospel and trusted God's gracious love are being enfranchised to know their reconciliation to God.[83] There is no need for believers to meander in the bewilderment of the wilderness state as to whether God's saving grace is being offered to them.[84]

c. Learning through Scripture to Listen

Few who attest saving grace would disagree that there is an indirect witness of the Spirit that may involve conscience, or rational reflection. But Wesley viewed the dual witness of the Spirit with our spirits as intrinsic to saving faith and to conversion.

We have to learn how to listen rightly for this consolation and summons.[85] It requires the joint disciplines of Scripture study, using means of grace, sacraments, and prayer. The Spirit is trying to get through to us by all these means. This homily seeks to help persons learn to listen for that inward testimony. No one can do this for another. Each must listen for himself.

d. Countering Aberrations and Falsifications

Even the Spirit's work of assurance can be falsified, counterfeited, and perverted. Wesley reminded his hearers that the internal testimony of the Spirit must be constantly tested against the written word of Scripture and correlated with an honest examination of conscience.[86] Even this does not eliminate the possibility of self-delusion, though these checks are useful in reducing its likelihood.[87]

God has given these two witnesses to secure against delusion — a direct and an indirect witness.[88] Their purpose is to assure us that we are children of God.[89]

---

[82]"The Witness of the Spirit, II," B 1:286 – 88, sec. 2.
[83]B 9:61, 100, 376; *JJW* 2:49.
[84]EA, J VIII:22 – 25.
[85]"The Witness of the Spirit, II," B 1:287 – 88.
[86]"Heavenly Treasure in Earthen Vessels," B 4:161 – 62; J VII:345.
[87]Letter to "John Smith," March 25, 1747, *LJW* 2:100 – 105.
[88]"The Witness of the Spirit, II," B 1:288 – 96, secs. 3, 5.
[89]"The Witness of the Spirit, II," B 1:297, sec. 5.2 – 3.

Individual experience alone is insufficient proof. Rather, the function of experience in the Christian life is to confirm what is found in Scripture, not invent something wholly contrary to Scripture.[90] Though some may fancy they experience what they do not, this cannot stand as discounting testimony against those who have fully used these means of grace. A false profession by one does not invalidate a true profession of the witness of the Spirit by another.[91]

The true witness of the Spirit is known by the fruits of love, peace, and joy. Lacking these fruits, the testimony is likely to be unreliable or intermittent.[92] "Let none ever presume to rest in any supposed testimony of the Spirit which is separate from the fruits of it," and "let none rest in any supposed fruit of the Spirit without witness."[93]

6. The Imperative to Teach Assurance

a. Assurance in the First Centuries of Christianity

Using the apostles and the earliest Christians as a measure of truthful testimony, Wesley argued that the consensual tradition immediately following the New Testament continued this witness. The early believers knew about assurance. They wrote about it. They experienced it under persecution. They preached it.

With regard to the conviction of assurance, Wesley was convinced that "the whole Christian church in the first centuries enjoyed it. For though we have few points of doctrine explicitly taught in the small remains of the ante-Nicene Fathers, yet I think none that carefully reads Clemens Romanus, Ignatius, Polycarp, Origen, or any other of them, can doubt whether either the writer himself possessed it or all whom he mentions as real Christians."[94]

Wesley could have extended this list to include Clement of Alexandria, Anthony of the Desert, Athanasius, and Cyril of Alexandria. Wesley had read enough in the original Greek and Latin sources to say confidently: "or any other of them." Readers of the first centuries of Christian exegesis can easily recognize its imprint on their view of the Christian life.[95]

Believers in Wesley's connection of spiritual formation in particular need to be clear about this teaching, "because it is one grand part of the testimony which God has given them to bear" to all humanity. Indeed, through Methodists "this great evangelical truth has been recovered, which had been for many years well nigh lost and forgotten."[96]

Many Wesleyan hymns were written on the theme of assurance. Wesley thought

---

[90]"The Witness of the Spirit, II," B 1:287 – 90, sec. 2.5 – 3.5.

[91]"The Witness of the Spirit, II," B 1:296 – 97, sec. 5.1 – 2.

[92]"The Witness of the Spirit, II," B 1:297 – 98, sec. 5.3 – 4; so are false prophets known by their fruits, *SS* 2:16.

[93]"The Witness of the Spirit, II," B 1:297 – 98, sec. 5.3 – 4.

[94]Letter to Richard Tompson, July 25, 1755, *LJW* 3:137.

[95]This is evident from the exegesis of the epistles of John, Acts, Rom. 5 – 8, and other Pauline epistles. It can be confirmed by reviewing these passages in *ACCS*.

[96]"The Witness of the Spirit, II," B 1:285, sec. 1.4.

that the assuring witness of the Spirit was a doctrine that had not been sufficiently explicated in previous Protestantism. Since it had been misunderstood, he considered it the destiny of the Methodist societies to carry this revitalized teaching to the whole church.

b. A Quintessential Wesleyan Doctrine

The doctrine of the assuring witness of the Spirit is a quintessentially Wesleyan doctrine. Though hardly distinctive to this community, the doctrine of assurance is nevertheless one that Wesleyans in three successive centuries have thought exceedingly important and often central to their teaching mission. This tradition of preaching sought to make clear that God not only gives us this merciful gift of justifying grace through the Son on the cross, but that God also works through the Spirit to attest the meaning of the Son's mission and bring it to full actualization in us.[97]

This sense of empowerment was especially needed in an environment in which many thought they were being taught in the eternal decree of election that no personal responsiveness or volitional faith was required. The secularizing equivalent of this theological determinism is naturalistic determinism. Some advocates of double predestination were admonishing believers not to get involved in a subjectivist introverted monologue since the decision about their salvation had already been made before eternity, and since what happens within our own spirits is an entirely ancillary if not inconsequential matter. In chapter 6, we will examine Wesley's teaching on grace and predestination. In this section on the work of the Spirit, we focus on assurance.

Those who neglect this teaching may turn religion into a routine matter of going to church without that which makes the church meaningful: the experience of new life in the Spirit. Those who claim to have received this testimony yet remain uncharitable and arrogant negate by their behavior what they attest in their words.

7. The Witness of Our Own Spirit

Integral to this teaching is the witness of our own spirit. Wesley wrote a separate homily on this subject, using 2 Corinthians 1:12 as his text: "Our rejoicing is this, the testimony of our conscience, that in simplicity and godly sincerity, not with fleshly wisdom, but by the grace of God, we have had our conversation in the world" [Homily #12 (1746), B 1:299 – 313; J #12, V:32 – 44].

Sustained reception of saving grace hinges on that special form of evidence provided by conscience. A good conscience gives inner testimony of sincere responsiveness to preparatory and justifying grace. The ground of the Christian's joy is the serenity, faith, hope, and love that come out of *the testimony of a good conscience*, which assures us that we have been single-minded and sincere in God's sight and have conducted ourselves in the world, not in the strength of carnal wisdom or worldly cunning or shrewdness, but by the grace of God.[98]

---

[97]B 1:81; 3:210; *CH*, B 7:532, 535, 687.

[98]"The Witness of Our Own Spirit," B 1:300 – 301, secs. 1 – 4.

a. Natural Conscience

It is evident from Romans 1 and 2 that Paul thought that all rational human beings have a form of self-awareness usually called conscience. The experienced faith we have described is confirmed by "the testimony of conscience."

Conscience is that form of consciousness by which we excuse or accuse ourselves morally. Wesley said, by conscience "I mean that every person capable of reflection is conscious to himself, when he looks back on anything he has done, whether it be good or evil."[99] Everybody has it.

No rational being living in time can do without it. It is a standard aspect of human consciousness. All rational agents have this capacity to discern whether one is doing right or wrong according to the light of one's own conscience. All rational beings have a mode of consciousness by which one says to oneself that what one is doing is proportionally acceptable or not. It is a moral sense, which according to Paul is universally given. Such awareness is intrinsic to consciousness, for it is simply the moral part of consciousness, that part of consciousness that makes a moral judgment about the decency, truth, and appropriateness of one's behavior.[100]

b. Scripture as the Rule of Christian Conscience

Christians, like others, know when their conscience says to them that something they are doing is not right. Conscience is a universal human function, but Christians are attuned to conscience in a particular way—under the guidance of Word and sacrament.

Conscience troubles everyone from time to time, but Christians it disturbs in special ways, because Christians have a consciousness shaped by the requirement and grace of God as revealed in history and attested in Scripture.[101] "The Christian rule of right and wrong is the Word of God, the writings of the Old and New Testament.... This is a lantern unto a Christian's feet... the whole and sole outward rule whereby his conscience is to be directed in all things."[102]

How does the conscience of the Christian function, and how is it formed? Christian conscience is shaped by the history of salvation. It is honed by the daily reading of the sacred text. When Paul speaks of a good conscience void of offense, he means a conscience decisively shaped by the address of God as attested in the history of redemption. This history is made clear in Holy Writ. No understanding of right and wrong is adequate to the Christian that has not been contoured by the attestation of Scripture to the Word of God in Jesus Christ.[103]

c. The Regenerate Conscience Void of Offense

A Christian conscience void of offense is a conscience living by faith on the

[99]EA, B 11:49, sec. 14.
[100]"The Witness of Our Own Spirit," B 1:301–2, secs. 3–5.
[101]B 2:125; 3:11, 118.
[102]"The Witness of Our Own Spirit," B 1:302–3, sec. 6.
[103]*LJW* 6:19.

sole foundation of Christ's atoning work,[104] instructed by the revealed and written Word, capable of self-examination, able without pretense to confess before God one's sin, which attests that one's actual moral behavior is consistent with one's heartfelt beliefs and public confession.[105]

Conscience is transformed when it comes under the influence of the living Christ, Scripture, the community of faith, preaching of the Word, and communion with God. There is a sharp distinction in Wesley's mind between natural conscience, which everyone has, and Christian conscience, which is instructed by Scripture, grace, and God's saving work. In this redeemed community, we share our faith and experience, disclose to others the ways the Spirit is working in us, use our reason, and listen to Scripture better to discern God's revelation in the whole of history.[106]

The regenerated, Christ-shaped conscience does not let us off cheaply. It tells us the truth about ourselves. When we listen to it with sincerity, we either hear it acquitting or accusing us. Paul would not have commended a conscience void of offense if that were wholly impossible. Conscience is a mode of consciousness intrinsic to the witness of our own spirit to ourselves. Our own spirit bears witness within an accountable community of faith that it is not offending against the holiness of God.[107]

d. By Grace We Have Our Day-by-Day Walk in the World

Either you have a conscience void of offense or you have a conscience that keeps on offending you. Paul is proposing a day-by-day walk without offense to the law of God, assuming that one's behavior is constantly being embraced by the atoning work of God. There is no way to have a good conscience without the atonement. No Christian can enjoy a conscience void of offense without God's forgiving word, but that must not become an open door for license or pretending that one is above the law.[108]

We are called to conduct ourselves in the world, and in this community of prayer and moral accountability, not with fleshly wisdom, but by the grace of God. Our conversation within the world — our daily movement through the world is a walk by grace, a conversation that may attest simple purity of heart, godly sincerity, relying on God's reconciling love, with a heart focused single-mindedly on accountability to God.[109]

e. Grace-Filled Simplicity, Purity of Heart, Holiness, Godly Sincerity

The ground of Christian joy is unmerited grace. The faithful are drawn to a single intent: becoming answerable to the gracious, sovereign God in daily behavior.[110] That is what it means to live the *simple life.*

---

[104]"The Witness of Our Own Spirit," B 1:304 – 5, sec. 8.
[105]*LJW* 7:209; *SS* 1:226.
[106]*SS* 1:221.
[107]B 1:270 – 74, 299 – 313.
[108]*LJW* 7:209; cf. *LJW* 6:19; *SS* 1:226.
[109]B 3:271 – 72; 4:375 – 76.
[110]"On a Single Eye," B 4:120 – 30.

Even though it may complicate our life in the world, it simplifies things profoundly if one is simply being accountable to God.[111] Simplicity has "a single intention of promoting his glory and doing and suffering his blessed will."[112]

Purity of heart is an expression of this simplicity. It desires God in all things, loving nothing more than God. This enables a walk of *holiness* that reflects the holiness of God to the degree that grace penetrates human finitude. This walk occurs by godly sincerity, and thereby recovering the moral image of God.[113] *Godly sincerity* is doing all to the glory of God, referring all one's aspirations to God with unblemished intent.[114]

"Simplicity regards the intention itself, sincerity the execution of it ... as actually hitting the mark which we aim at by simplicity ... that all our actions flow on in an even stream, uniformly subservient to this great end; and that in our whole lives, we are moving straight toward God, and that continually."[115] "Seek one thing, and you will be far less troubled with unprofitable reasonings."[116]

Living this life of simplicity results in joy even amid suffering, a gladness that emerges out of a life of the obedience of faith.[117] What the Spirit through conscience wants to do for us is take us step-by-step through a life of receptivity of grace by which our resistances to divine love are day by day being overcome.

f. Holiness and Happiness

Holiness and happiness are intrinsically joined. Those who want to live the happy life do well to realize that it is precisely this life of day-by-day resisting temptation and living with simple accountability before God that bears the fruit of human happiness. Wesley had a very uncomplicated notion of happiness: holiness.[118]

The joy that we have in the Christian life is confirmed by the testimony of our own conscience. The Christian's conscience keeps on witnessing not just of the law, but of the gospel, not just of God's judging requirement upon us, but of Christ's love that enables us to fulfill those requirements. Happiness is not premised on the basis of economic or psychological ("fleshly") wisdom, but on the basis of the inner testimony of the Spirit confirmed by conscience.[119] Only on this basis can we enter into this joy.

It is by the grace of God we have had our conversation in the world, not by virtue of a natural joy arising out of a seared or callous conscience, but a joy in obedience, elicited by grace, a joy the world is not capable of inventing.[120]

---

[111]"The Witness of Our Own Spirit," B 1:306–8, secs. 11–13.

[112]"The Witness of Our Own Spirit," B 1:307, sec. 12; "A Single Intention," B 4:371–77.

[113]"An Israelite Indeed," B 3:286, sec. 2.4.

[114]"The Witness of Our Own Spirit," B 1:309–10, sec. 16; cf. 1:134–35, 207–8, 263–64, 288–89, 207–8, 3:286.

[115]"The Witness of Our Own Spirit," B 1:307, sec. 12.

[116]Letter to Miss Bishop, June 12, 1773, J XIII:24.

[117]*CH*, B 7:94–95, 308–98, 494–96.

[118]"The Witness of Our Own Spirit," B 1:309–13, secs. 16–20.

[119]"The Witness of Our Own Spirit," B 1:308, sec. 14.

[120]"The Witness of Our Own Spirit," B 1:310–13, secs. 17–20.

F. The Firstfruits of the Spirit

Paul taught that there is no condemnation for sin to those who have by faith received God's pardon in Jesus Christ. Wesley shows how this divine pardon applies to past, present, and future sins, so long as accompanied by faith. Even our defects drive us closer to God. This means that sins of infirmity and all things outside of the person's power to change cannot diminish joy in the Spirit.

This homily is an extension of Wesley's teaching on the witness of the Spirit with our spirits. Wesley's text is Romans 8:1: "There is therefore now no condemnation to them which are in Christ Jesus, who walk not after the flesh, but after the Spirit" [Homily #8 (1746), B 1:233–47; J #8, V:87–97]. The path ahead may be summarized in this order:

There Is No Condemnation for:	Therefore, the Imperative Is:
Past sins	Do away with guilt.
Present sins	Avoid committing new sins.
Inward sin, though natural corruption remains	Be not afraid to know all the evil of your heart.
Defects that drive one closer to God	Do not despair of defects.
Sins of infirmity	Let Satan gain no advantage.
Anything not in one's power to change	If you sin, take it to the Lord.

1. Those Who Walk after the Spirit

a. They Walk Not after the Flesh

Those engrafted in Christ, dwelling in him, united with him, *walk not after the flesh*, which "signifies corrupt nature."[121] Having "crucified the flesh with its affections and lusts," even if they "feel the root of bitterness in themselves, yet are they endued with power from on high to trample it continually," so that they are no longer bound to sin.[122]

"They are led into every holy desire, into every divine and heavenly temper, till every thought which arises in their heart is holiness unto the Lord," speaking "always in grace, seasoned with salt," and doing "only the things which please God," so "in the whole course of their words and actions" they bear "the genuine fruits of the Spirit of God, namely, 'love, joy, peace, long-suffering, gentleness, goodness, fidelity, meekness, temperance.' "[123]

[121] "The First-Fruits of the Spirit," B 1:235, sec. 1.2.
[122] "The First-Fruits of the Spirit," B 1:236–37, sec. 1.2–3.
[123] "The First-Fruits of the Spirit," B 1:236–37, sec. 1.4–6; Zech. 14:20–21; Gal. 5:22–23; Col. 4:6.

b. For Them There Is No Condemnation

The recipient of divine pardon is liberated from slavery to sin, redeemed from bondage. The Redeemer pays the debt for the enslaved. Having been crucified with him, those who live in him have been resurrected with him and so walk after the Spirit and bear the fruits of the Spirit.[124]

There is now no condemnation for those who are in Christ — no condemnation either of past or present sin, or for inward sin, defects, infirmities, or involuntary failings. The six imperatives that follow this indicative are summarized in the table on page 132.

2. The Meaning of Freedom from Condemnation

a. If Freed from Past Sin, Away with Guilt

There is no condemnation for any *past* sin. Those whose lives are hid in Christ no longer have to bear the dismal burden of compulsively recollecting their former moral debts and value negations. Nothing that freedom has distorted is beyond this divine reconciling activity. All former guilt-eliciting acts are taken up into the pardon of God.

Since God remembers our past sins no more, we are invited to quit remembering them. It is absurd to continue dwelling on a debt that has been paid. We are called and enabled to feel no condemnation, "no sense of guilt, or dread," having the peace of God ruling in our hearts.[125]

So long as the faithful believe and walk after the Spirit, they are not condemned either by God or by their own hearts. Guilt and condemnation are no longer fitting categories for those who live by faith in God's redeeming love and share by faith Christ's death and resurrection. As we trust in God's revealed righteousness, faith wipes away all past moral marks against the self.[126]

b. If Freed from Present Sin, Then Do Not Commit New Sin

"It is for freedom that Christ has set us free. Stand firm, then, and do not let yourselves be burdened again by a yoke of slavery" (Gal. 5:1 NIV). The moral imperative not to commit sin derives from the evangelical indicative that God has freed us from sin.

If we are free from all *present* sin, then we are called not to commit new sin. That is a commitment that can only be fulfilled by praying for grace and being willing to receive it. To the extent that we in our stubbornness decide to continue to collude with temptation, we return by choice once again to live under condemnation. Insofar as we continue in sin, we are called to pray anew for the grace of repentance.[127]

---

[124]"The First-Fruits of the Spirit," B 1:235 – 37, sec. 1; cf. FA, B 11:292; 1:160 – 65, 283 – 88; 11:171 – 72, 178, 197.

[125]"The First-Fruits of the Spirit," B 1:237, sec. 2.1 – 2; *JJW* 2:250.

[126]"The First-Fruits of the Spirit," B 1:243 – 44, sec. 3.

[127]"The First-Fruits of the Spirit," B 1:238, 244, secs. 2.4, 3.3.

c. No Condemnation for Inward Sin though Natural Corruption Remains

The roots of sin are being dug up, uprooted. We are being called by new life in Christ to go to the very underpinnings of our old, sinful life and change those behaviors and intentions. It is "too plain to be denied" that the corruption of fallen nature "does still remain, even in those who are the children of God by faith," who have remaining in them "the seeds of pride and vanity, of anger, lust and evil desire."[128]

Though the corruption of the old Adam remains, it does not rule. The new life in Christ frees us from *inward* sin. This is the interior dimension in which the Holy Spirit comes to dwell in us and rule from the inside out. The aim is to reflect the love and goodness of God. This is possible by grace alone.

Of these Paul speaks as "infants in Christ" (1 Cor. 3:1 NIV). Still they are not condemned. Though they grow "more sensible day by day that their 'heart is deceitful and desperately wicked'; yet so long as they do not yield thereto, so long as they give no place to the devil ... God is well-pleased with their sincere though imperfect obedience."[129]

d. The Imperative

Wesley provides the corresponding imperative: "Fret not thyself because of ungodliness, though it still remain in thy heart. Repine not because thou still comest short of the glorious image of God." "Be not afraid to know all the evil of thy heart, to know thyself as also thou art known."[130] God's desire is that we know ourselves accurately.

> Show me, as my soul can bear,
> The depth of inbred sin:
> All the unbelief declare,
> The pride that lurks within![131]

To be the child of this Father is to be invited to trust that God "will withhold from thee no manner of thing that is good," so do not fear looking deeply into your own failings, provided you do not let the shield of faith be torn away from you.[132]

e. There Is No Condemnation for Defects That Drive One Closer to God

Even when believers are "continually convinced of sin cleaving to all they do ... yet there is no condemnation to them still, either from God or from their own heart[s]. The consideration of these manifold *defects* only gives them a deeper sense

[128]"The First-Fruits of the Spirit," B 1:239, sec. 2.5.
[129]"The First-Fruits of the Spirit," B 1:240, sec. 2.6; Jer. 17:9.
[130]"The First-Fruits of the Spirit," B 1:245, sec. 3.4.
[131]Charles Wesley, *HSP* (1742), p. 209; *PW* 2:263.
[132]"The First-Fruits of the Spirit," B 1:245–46, sec. 3.4.

that they have always need" of the crucified Advocate who ever lives to make intercession for them. "So far are these from driving them away from him in whom they have believed, that they rather drive them the closer."[133]

f. If There Is No Condemnation for Sins of Infirmity, Let Not the Adversary Gain an Advantage

"By 'sins of infirmity,' I would mean such *involuntary failings* as the saying a thing we believe true, though in fact it prove to be false; or the hurting our neighbor without knowing or designing it, perhaps when we designed to do him good." Though deviating from the perfect will of God, these involuntary infirmities "do not bring any guilt on the conscience of 'them which are in Christ Jesus.' "[134]

Even those being made "perfect in love ... still need his Spirit, and consequently his intercession, for the continuance of that love from moment to moment. Besides, we should still be encompassed with infirmities, and liable to mistakes ... even though the heart was all love.... As long as he remains in the body, the greatest saint may say: 'Every moment, Lord, I need the merit of thy death.' "[135]

The corresponding imperative: Do not let the adversary gain an advantage from your all-too-keen awareness of your involuntary infirmities. Do not let your weakness or folly shake your "filial trust in God.... Do not lie there, fretting thyself and bemoaning thy weakness.... Leap and walk."[136]

g. There Is No Condemnation for Anything Not in One's Power to Change

" 'There is no condemnation' to them for *anything whatever which is not in their power to help*, whether it be of an inward or outward nature, and whether it be doing something or leaving something undone.... There is no guilt, because there is no choice."[137]

Sins of surprise are those in which I am quietly or unconsciously overtaken. Wesley argued that to the extent I collude or cooperate or concur in a behavioral pattern that leads to sin, then I am to that extent accountable. Then I must return to petition for forgiveness. This is why the Christian life is paradoxically a life of daily repentance, even while it is going on toward full maturity.[138] Even when "surprised into what [your] soul abhors," if you are "overtaken in a fault, then grieve unto the Lord.... Pour out thy heart before him"[139]

This is the promise of the Spirit for all. Without slackening the good work of natural conscience, the Christian conscience is transformed by the power of grace.

[133]"The First-Fruits of the Spirit," B 1:240, sec. 2.7; Heb. 7:25, italics added.
[134]"The First-Fruits of the Spirit," B 1:241, sec. 2.8, italics added.
[135]To James Hervey, *LJW* 3:380.
[136]"The First-Fruits of the Spirit," B 1:246–47, sec. 3.5.
[137]"The First-Fruits of the Spirit," B 1:241, sec. 2.9, italics added.
[138]"The First-Fruits of the Spirit," B 1:242, sec. 2.11.
[139]"The First-Fruits of the Spirit," B 1:247, sec. 3.6.

Further Reading on the Work of the Spirit in Assurance

Banks, Stanley. "Witness of the Spirit." *AS* 14, no. 1 (1960): 48 – 60.

Bence, Clarence Luther. "Salvation and the Church: The Ecclesiology of John Wesley." In *The Church*, edited by Melvin Dieter and Daniel Berg, 297 – 317. Anderson, IN: Warner, 1984.

Burtner, Robert W., and Robert E. Chiles. *A Compend of Wesley's Theology*, 89ff., 168ff. Nashville: Abingdon, 1954.

Collins, Kenneth. *A Faithful Witness: John Wesley's Homiletical Theology*, 57 – 82. Wilmore, KY: Wesleyan Heritage, 1993.

———. "New Birth and Assurance." In *Wesley on Salvation.* Grand Rapids: Zondervan, 1989.

Howard, Ivan. "The Doctrine of Assurance." In *Further Insights into Holiness*, edited by K. Geiger. Kansas City: Beacon Hill, 1963.

Jones, Howard Watkins. *The Holy Spirit from Arminius to Wesley*. London: Epworth, 1929.

Jones, Ivor H., and Kenneth B. Wilson, eds. *Freedom and Grace.* London: Epworth, 1988.

Kirkpatrick, Dow, ed. *The Holy Spirit.* Nashville: Tidings, 1974.

Langford, Thomas. *Practical Divinity: Theology in the Wesleyan Tradition.* Chap. 6, "Holiness Theology." Nashville: Abingdon, 1982.

McDonald, William. *John Wesley and His Doctrine.* Boston: McDonald and Gill, 1893.

McGonigle, Herbert. "Pneumatological Nomenclature in Early Methodism." *WTJ* 8 (1973): 61 – 72.

Noll, Mark. "John Wesley and the Doctrine of Assurance." *Bibliotheca Sacra* 132 (1974): 195 – 223.

Oswalt, John N. "John Wesley and the Old Testament Concept of the Holy Spirit." *RL* 48 (1979): 283 – 92.

Slaate, Howard. *Fire in the Brand.* Chap. 7. New York: Exposition, 1963.

Smith, Timothy L. "The Doctrine of the Sanctifying Spirit in John Wesley and John Fletcher." *PM* 55, no. 1 (1979): 16 – 17, 54 – 58.

———. *Whitefield and Wesley on the New Birth.* Grand Rapids: Zondervan, 1986.

Starkey, Lycurgus M. "The New Birth." In *The Work of the Holy Spirit*. Nashville: Abingdon, 1962.

Watkin-Jones, Howard. *The Holy Spirit from Arminius to Wesley.* London: Epworth, n.d.

Williams, Colin. "New Birth and Assurance." In *John Wesley's Theology Today*, 98ff. Nashville: Abingdon, 1960.

Wynkoop, Mildred Bangs. *Foundations of Wesleyan-Arminian Theology*, 302ff. Kansas City: Beacon Hill, 1967.

———. "Theological Roots of Wesleyanism's Understanding of the Holy Spirit." *WTJ* 14, no. 1 (1979): 77 – 98.

Yates, Arthur S. *The Doctrine of Assurance, with Special Reference to John Wesley.* London: Epworth, 1952.

Young, Frances. "The Significance of John Wesley's Conversion Experience." In *John Wesley: Contemporary Perspectives*, edited by John Stacy, 37 – 46. London: Epworth, 1988.

CHAPTER 5

Grace: Preceding, Accompanying, and Perfecting Salvation

A. The Doctrine of Grace

Wesley's doctrine of grace is in most ways Augustinian. It sees God's favor at work throughout the whole narrative of salvation. (1) Common grace is present in the whole of nature and history, preceding all acts of human decision. (2) Saving grace is given in Jesus Christ and received by faith alone. (3) Completing grace is given through the Holy Spirit to nurture the life of faith toward holy living.

As in Augustine's Confessions, Wesley celebrates the grace that comes before and leads to justification, the saving grace that converts the soul through God the Son, and the sanctifying grace that perfects the broken life through the constant care of God the Spirit.

1. The Grace That Prepares the Will for Justifying Faith

a. How God Leads the Broken Will to Pardon

Preparatory grace is the grace that seeks to make the way clear for faith. It enables seekers to come toward repentance, but until repentance and faith, it has no saving power. However far from saving grace, seekers can always pray for the grace that may lead them to choose to cooperate further with saving grace. But no one is saved by preparatory grace. This chapter clarifies the sharp distinction between prevenient grace and saving grace.

By God's gracious work of preparation, the will may gradually be drawn to move toward saving grace. The person then may freely and increasingly become a willing and active participant in receiving the conditions for justification: repentance and faith.

b. The One Grace of the One God Taking Various Forms

Sin has had devastating consequences on the capacity of freedom to act in its best interests. Grace is present quietly in the earliest signs of gestation of the new birth of freedom.

Since God is one, there is only one grace: God's grace. It is that unsurpassable attribute of God by which he shows unmerited favor to sinners. There are not three separable graces, but only one, moving from the devastation of sin toward God's saving action, and finally toward the perfecting of that grace in holy living. This one grace of God manifests itself in distinguishable gifts and operations. The richest manifestation is seen in those gracious operations of God that result in the salvation of sinners

Freedom grows through stages. Preparatory (or prevenient) grace is the lowest gear in the drive train of grace that enables one to move from inertia so that one may gradually be brought up to speed. When we are dead in our sins, we have no way of raising ourselves to new life. Preparatory grace makes this miracle possible. It is the grace that brings initial recognition that a more decisive new stage may be possible, even if only vaguely imaginable.

c. The Grace That Seeks to Coax the Sinner toward Faith Prior to Faith

No fallen creature has power to do good work pleasing to God "without the grace of God by Christ *preventing* us" (*nos praeveniente*), that is, going before us.[1] Grace is always to be found working way out ahead of us, and only then "working with us when we have that good will" by which we may cooperate with ever-fresh new offerings of grace. Today we use the term *prevent* to mean obstruct, hinder, or stop. But in Latin usage it meant to prepare, make ready, to go before (the Latin root *prevenire* does not mean to thwart but to precede).

Since the fall of freedom, no one spiritually dead is able to choose that which is his truest good. Nonetheless, persons still have a "degree of liberty" that allows them to be self-governing, "otherwise we were mere machines, stocks and stones."[2] This autonomy, however, does not enable persons to turn to God by means of their own resources. God the Spirit works within the limitations of our fallen human freedom to draw us toward salvation.

This work of the Spirit is the form of grace that Wesley called "going before grace," or "prevening grace." The Latin root makes this clearer. Prevenient grace is treated as an article of faith in the Articles of Religion. Prevenient grace is moving the sinner toward the fullness of grace even before its saving implications are recognized.

Since the term *prevenient* is archaic, and since its history of controversy has led to nuances misleading to some readers, I prefer the term *preparatory grace*, which is thoroughly consistent with Augustine's teaching and Wesley's restatement of it, provided the point is constantly held that *no one is saved by prevening grace.* To be saved is to come to that saving grace of which preparatory grace is modestly an anticipation.

d. The Winsomeness of Grace

The sinner is at liberty to resist grace but not to initiate grace. *Preceding* (prevenient) grace elicits the inception of a preliminary good will toward grace, while

[1]XXV, art. 8.

[2]"Heavenly Treasure in Earthen Vessels," B 4:163, sec. 1.1.

cooperating grace works within the constricted settings of broken human freedom to turn it around, redeem, and enable the will to be responsive to God's own good will.

There is no sufficient scriptural understanding of the depth of sin without affirming at the same time the eternal winsomeness of the grace of God drawing sinners always toward ever more appropriate and fitting responses to the holy love that constantly works to open up the possibility of repentance. But of itself the fallen will cannot simply turn itself around and will to do good.[3]

2. The Doctrine of Grace and Free Will in the Articles of Religion, Article 8

The title of the eighth article, "On Free Will," might more accurately be called "Grace and Free Will": "The condition of man after the fall of Adam is such that he cannot turn and prepare himself, by his own natural strength and works, to faith, and calling upon God; wherefore we have no power to do good work, pleasant and acceptable to God, without the grace of God by Christ preventing [i.e., going before] us, that we may have a good will, and working with us, when we have that good will."

This is Reformation teaching, as well as Anglican and Methodist teaching. It is especially enshrined in the constitution of American Methodism as unalterable doctrine. There is no natural strength that can call faith into being. That would be the arch-heresy called Pelagianism, against which Augustine and classic Western ecumenical teaching has struggled.

None can repent without grace. No good work is acceptable to God without grace. God works to draw us to himself. God's wooing of the sinner toward faith comes before faith. This grace is necessary to awaken even the desire for faith. It is the work of God the Spirit in order that we may move toward a good will, which is dependent on saving grace. The preparatory grace works with us so that when we come to faith, we will have that good will that is acceptable to God.

The grace that precedes freedom is that grace that helps us to receive more grace, which prepares our will so that we may first become aware of our acute predicament, which Paul compares to the inertness of death. Only with this grace can we come toward that repentance that is prior to that faith that is lived out in love to God and neighbor.[4]

3. On Working Out Our Own Salvation

A much-loved homily in early Methodist preaching was Wesley's teaching "On Working Out Our Own Salvation." It best shows how grace works within the confines of fallen freedom. The text is Philippians 2:12 – 13: "Work out your own salvation with fear and trembling. For it is God which worketh in you both to will and to do of his good pleasure" [Homily #85 (1785), B 3:199 – 209; J #85, VI:506 – 13].

[3]"Praying for a Blessing," *CH*, B 7:178 – 88.
[4]PCC 43 – 47, J X:228 – 31.

a. We Can Work Because God Is Working in Us

By "working," Wesley does not here refer to our autonomous working, but grace working within us. "Our own" does not refer to that which we initiate or devise but which God enables so as to become "our own."

Preparatory grace plays a crucial role in the Wesleyan teaching of grace.[5] There are no treatises where this important teaching is more concentrated than in the homilies "On Working Out Our Own Salvation" and "On Conscience."

God's preliminary working in us precedes and enables our cooperating with God. What appears to be a contradiction (that grace elicits freedom) contains a call to action that attests the ground of its action. *We can work because God is working in us.*[6] Readers of Augustine will readily recognize Wesley's indebtedness to him in this homily.

God's prevenient grace works quietly in all humanity, since the Holy Spirit is present to all, though most powerfully among a vital community of believers where the Word is preached. "No one sins because he has not grace, but because he does not use the grace he hath."[7] All are called to be ready to stir up whatever grace is in them that more grace will be given.

Preparatory grace works in every domain in which original sin is working. The deficiencies of human willing do not negate the sufficiency of grace offered. Even when rejected, never is God's grace insufficient to God's unfolding purpose. Assuming the depth of the drastic human predicament as spelled out in "The Doctrine of Original Sin," it is impossible without grace to make the least motion toward God.[8]

b. God Works in Us Both to Will and to Do

God works in us both *to will and to do* his good pleasure. That "removes all imagination of merit from man.... God breathes into us every good desire, and brings every good desire to good effect."[9]

God is *inwardly* at work in us, operating in us, actively present in our inner lives, enabling our *outward* acts. Grace works within to convert our passions so as to transform and reorder them in relation to the love of God and humanity. Out of that reordering, the fruits of faith emerge in good works.[10]

All phases of salvation are permeated by grace that we may be led both to will and to do. Willing and doing lead Wesley to make a distinction between inward and outward actions: inward religion (holiness of heart) is grounded in God's work in us "*to will*" (*to telein*, "to desire, wish, love, intend"). Outward religion (holiness of life)

[5]"This grace prompts our first wish to please God, our first glimmer of understanding concerning God's will," and our first slight recognition of having sinned against God. United Methodist *Book of Discipline* (Nashville: Abingdon, 1988), para. 68, 46.

[6]"On Working Out Our Own Salvation," B 3:199 – 201, proem.

[7]"On Working Out Our Own Salvation," B 3:207, sec. 3.4.

[8]"On Working Out Our Own Salvation," B 3:202 – 3, sec. 1.

[9]"On Working Out Our Own Salvation," B 3:202 – 3, sec. 1.1 – 2.

[10]"On Working Out Our Own Salvation," B 3:202 – 3, sec. 1.3.

is grounded in God's giving us the energy "*to do*" (*to energein*, "to energize, execute, actualize") his good pleasure.[11] This energy that comes from God "works in us every right disposition, and then furnishes us for every good word and work."[12]

c. No One Works without Grace

When Paul says to "work out your own salvation," he does not imply that one may work *without* the preparatory grace of God, but rather only *with* it. Yet the coworking (*sunergia*, cooperation) design of grace asks for our responsive willing, through which it is God who is working concurrently in us to will and do God's own good pleasure.[13]

No stage of saving faith, not the slightest motion, is a matter of merited or self-initiated goodness. God comes our way not when we merit it, but before we merit it, precisely while we are yet sinners. God is helping us come to the desire to do the good through preparatory grace, then to enable a result of good action from that good will.[14]

God comes personally to humanity in the form of a servant.[15] The good news calls each hearer to have that mind that was also in Christ Jesus, who though he was in the form of God counted not equality with God as something to be grasped (Phil. 2:1–6).

This pivotal christological passage concludes with the imperative, which calls us to *work out our own salvation*, not with any implication that salvation is our work, but that it involves our free response to grace. We are to work because it is God who is working in us to enable our working.

d. With Fear and Trembling

We are called in response to work out our own salvation *with fear and trembling*, taking with utter seriousness what God is doing for us in advance.[16] This responding is occurring repeatedly and daily in the life of faith. For each particular hearer, this remains a personal task. Grace plants seeds that one may either attend or ignore. Saving grace does not occur by simple, unilateral, absolute fiat, as if to ignore whether one is cooperating or not.[17]

e. God Works, Therefore You Can Work

Since God is working in you, you are called to share responsively in the work of grace, as grace gives you opportunity. Knowing all, God knows more than we do how much we are proportionally able to respond. Grace comes in a way fitting to our situation. God does not coerce our willing, but reaches deeply into our willing

[11]"On Working Out Our Own Salvation," B 3:202, sec. 1.1–2.
[12]"On Working Out Our Own Salvation," B 3:203, sec. 1.3.
[13]"On Working Out Our Own Salvation," B 3:202–3, sec. 1.
[14]"On Working Out Our Own Salvation," B 3:202–3, sec. 1.2.
[15]*CH*, B 7:468.
[16]B 4:523; *LJW* 5:257; 6:258.
[17]"On Working Out Our Own Salvation," B 3:204–5, sec. 2.2.

to prompt, guide, and enable it. The illuminating, wooing, and inward convicting of the will is God's own work.[18]

All this prompting and encouraging, given time, will bear fruit leading toward repentance and faith. "Faith is *the work of God*; and yet it is *the duty of man* to believe. And every man may believe the will, though not *when* he will. If he seek faith in the appointed ways, sooner or later the power of the Lord will be present, whereby God works, and by His power man believes."[19] Grace is patient. The "appointed ways" are clear: reading Scripture accompanied by the Holy Spirit, prayer, and the attendance of common worship to hear the preached Word.

f. God Works, Therefore You Must Work

The indicative of grace requires the imperative of obedience. If God is for us, we ought to work in response to God's work in us. God is working; we are called to work. What God is doing enables us to do.

God works in us, so we are called to cooperate with his working in us.[20] We are to work with "singleness of heart ... utmost earnestness of spirit, and with all care and caution, and secondly, with the utmost diligence, speed, punctuality, and exactness."[21]

Wesley did not have a passive, idle, lethargic, quietistic notion of saving grace. Its reception requires energetic work, earnest prayer, spirited study of Scripture, and active good works. It is not as if God zaps us with grace apart from our responsive cooperation. Every subsequent act of cooperating with grace is premised on God's preceding grace, which elicits and requires free human responsiveness.[22]

4. Preparing, Convicting, Justifying, and Sanctifying Grace

The well-designed order of the work of grace was once familiar to Wesley's connection of spiritual formation: prevening, convicting, justifying, and sanctifying grace. This order is drawn from and found abundantly in the ancient ecumenical tradition. We have fallen from our original condition of uprightness, yet within this fallenness, grace is at work to free us from guilt and sin. The diverse outworking of grace is phased in four dimensions:[23]

a. Prevenient Grace

The saving work of God begins not by our being attentive, but by grace that attends us and awakens our attentiveness. The focus is not first of all on our coop-

[18]"On Working Out Our Own Salvation," B 3:204, sec. 2.1.
[19]Letter to Isaac Andrews, January 4, 1784, *LJW* 7:202.
[20]"On Working Out Our Own Salvation," B 3:201, proem 4.
[21]"On Working Out Our Own Salvation," B 3:205, sec. 2.2.
[22]"On Working Out Our Own Salvation," B 3:208, sec. 3.7.
[23]"On Working Out Our Own Salvation," B 3:203, sec. 2.1; "Principles of a Methodist," J VIII:373 – 74.

erative initiative by which we imagine ourselves coming to God, pleading to cooperate. Rather, the initiative comes from grace preparing us (prevening) prior to our first awakening to the mercy and holiness of God.[24] Grace resists our resistances.

Preparatory (or prevenient) grace elicits "the first wish to please God, the first dawn of light concerning his will, and the first slight transient conviction of having sinned against him."[25] Grace works ahead of us to draw us toward faith, to begin its work in us.

Even the first fragile intuition of conviction of sin, the first intimation of our need for God, is the work of preparing grace, which draws us gradually toward wishing to please God. Grace is working quietly at the point of our hope and desire. It may bring us in time to despair over our own righteousness. It will challenge our perverse dispositions, so that our distorted wills cease gradually to resist the gifts of God.

Grace works to convict freedom of its fallenness and its need for a total reversal through repentance. This is compared to a death-to-life turnaround that is possible only in view of God's justifying grace that meets us on the cross, of which we in time may become aware.

At each stage, we are called to receive and respond to the grace being incrementally given. Preparatory grace does not justify anyone but readies all for justification. It elicits the desire for faith. Faith is the sole condition of justification. The chief function of preparatory grace is to bring the person to a state of nonresistance to subsequent forms of grace. Prevenient grace is that grace that goes before us to prepare us for more grace, the grace that makes it possible for persons to take the first steps toward saving grace.[26]

b. Convicting Grace

Prevening grace leads toward convicting grace, which begins not with our self-initiated determination to repent but by the grace that awakens a determination to repent.[27] Prevenient grace brings us to the exact point of attentiveness to our own personal responsibility for sin. It asks for works appropriate to repentance. That does not mean that works evidencing repentance are justifying works, since no work justifies, but that the threshold of grace is being entered by penitence.[28]

Convicting grace enables one to grow closer toward repentance, toward greater knowledge of oneself as sinner, aware of how far away from God one is. Convicting grace brings one to despair over one's own righteousness under the law and leads to repentance, which turns around one's intentionality.[29]

---

[24]B 1:35, 57, 74–76, 80–81; 2:156–57; 3:203–4.

[25]"On Working Out Our Own Salvation," B 3:203, sec. 2.1.

[26]"On Working Out Our Own Salvation," B 3:203–4, sec. 2.1.

[27]B 1:200–201, 291–92, 350–52, 477–81; 2:22–23; *CH*, B 7:180–84, 210–34.

[28]B 3:204; *SS* 1:185–86.

[29]"On Working Out Our Own Salvation," B 3:203–4, sec. 2.1.

c. Justifying Grace

Wesley's distinction between justification and sanctification is simple: "By justification we are saved from *the guilt of sin and restored to the favor of God*; by sanctification we are saved *from the power and root of sin and restored to the image of God*."[30] This one sentence is well worth memorizing. Those who grasp it have laid hold of the heart of Wesleyan teaching on salvation.

By justification God has worked for us to pardon us. Justifying grace calls us to trust the one who takes our sin upon himself on the cross.[31] God works through justifying grace for us to make us aware that his favor is addressed personally to us. We respond in simple trust in his promise, which proceeds toward a process of growth in responsiveness, which is sanctification.[32]

We cannot take grace seriously without taking into account the depth, subtlety, and recalcitrance of the history of sin. In the Wesleyan tradition, however, there is a strong commitment not just to talk about how bad things are, how deeply enmeshed in evil, but how God the Spirit is at work in human history to elicit responses by which that predicament can be transformed.[33]

d. Sanctifying Grace

By sanctifying grace, our salvation is being brought toward full moral and behavioral fruitfulness. In sanctification we are *saved from the root of sin and restored to the renewed image of God.* The best way of thinking of *imago* is as mirror, so as to image or mirror the goodness of God within human finitude.

Sanctifying grace is not merely an awareness of God's pardon (the central concern of justifying grace). Rather, it is further bent on actively digging into and dislodging the roots of sin, cutting those roots, either gradually or quickly, whether by sawing or snipping.

This enables the believer actually to live out the glorious liberty of the children of God.[34] It offers new life in the family of God. The eviction of sin calls for the rooting out of willfully chosen habits of the sin, which is formally or juridically overcome in the saving grace of faith.

In this way, sanctifying grace seeks to go to the very root of sin behaviorally and practically to uproot the sin and draw the person again toward the way of holiness.[35] This is a defining Wesleyan doctrine. God the Spirit does not leave us alone with justifying grace as if to tempt us to licentiousness, but intends functionally to reclaim the whole of our broken lives. That has implications both for personal and social life.[36]

---

[30]B 3:204; J VI:509, italics added.
[31]B 1:381; 2:583–84.
[32]*LJW* 4:201.
[33]"On Working Out Our Own Salvation," B 3:203–4, sec. 2.1.
[34]*LJW* 3:189; 7:152; 8:147.
[35]B 2:582–84; 3:53–54.
[36]"On Working Out Our Own Salvation," B 3:203–4, sec. 2.1.

Natural finitude and physical infirmities are not strictly speaking sin, which is willful negation of a known command of God. So sanctifying grace does not have as its purpose the ending of either finitude or physical diseases and infirmities. Any of these may become a spur or a means of increasing faith, hope, and love.

5. Issues in the Reception of Grace

Wesley took pains to answer carefully a number of issues pressed upon him by his critics:

a. Whether Grace Works Gradually or Instantaneously

Grace works both by gradual and instantaneous means.[37] Wesley could not deny that some in the evangelical revival were apparently experiencing the Spirit's perfect work as coming to them in an instantaneous flood of consummating grace.[38] Knowing that grace could work powerfully to change life radically in a single sweeping experience, he could not thereafter ignore it, for it had become a fact of revival history.[39] Seeing the fruits of faith active in love in them, and a remarkable purity of heart, he could not deny instantaneous grace.

Nor did Wesley want to deny that grace works quietly and gradually and over a period of time, patiently within the wayward paths of human freedom. He knew that many such as himself were involved in a lengthy process of receiving it gradually. It had a beginning at Aldersgate, but it continued throughout his life.

Meanwhile, believers learn to cooperate daily with grace by using the means of grace: by searching the Scriptures, which attest the history of grace; by attending Holy Communion, which brings grace near; by becoming attentive to conscience; and by sharing in common prayer, godly admonition, and good counsel.[40]

b. Whether Freedom Is Causally Bound

It is a false placing of the question to ask whether we are free or bound by causal chains. Grace is working precisely amid natural causality to enable freedom.[41] The doctrine of grace is an argument for human freedom. It would be more absurd if God had worked in a costly way to free us, yet we remained automatons or puppets.[42] God would not work in us to free us were we not created with the capacity for freedom, which though now fallen into sin, can be redeemed and reconstituted by grace.

The heart of Wesley's reasoning: *God works in you, therefore you can work; God works in you, therefore you must work.* There is a moral imperative for us to work,

[37]*LJW* 2:280; 7:267.
[38]B 11:368–69; *JJW* 1:454–55; JWO 53–54; *SS* 1:298; 2:239.
[39]*LJW* 2:280; 7:267.
[40]"On Working Out Our Own Salvation," B 3:204, sec. 2.1.
[41]"A Thought upon Necessity," J X:474–80.
[42]"The Deceitfulness of the Human Heart, B 4:150–52, proem.

to respond to the grace given. Justification comes to us as a radical gift, but having been given as a total gift, it calls for our total response. If it is being made possible for us to cooperate with justifying and sanctifying grace toward our salvation, then we must do it. If God the Son gives himself utterly to us, we are called to respond utterly to him.

God does not by fiat save us, but wishes to save us with our willing, cooperative action. If God is working in us so that we *can* work, we *must* work.[43]

c. Resisting Quietism

Wesley concluded his homily by quoting Augustine: "He who made us without ourselves will not save us without ourselves."[44] God does not will to save us without our will.

Wesley resisted quietism as much as antinomianism. He had benefited immensely by dialogue with the Moravians, but when he got to know them well, he realized that there was one aspect he refused to accept: a quietism that said God is going to do it for us, so let us just sit back and do nothing.

Wesley never sat anywhere very long. He was constantly on the move. Much of it was on horseback. In fact, some estimate that Wesley traveled 250,000 miles by horse.

As God creates us *ex nihilo* without any cooperation of our own, for no one makes an application to be born, so God recreates our freedom to love, rescuing us from our fallen condition of unresponsive spiritual deadness. As natural birth is a radical gift, so is the new birth a radical new way of life. God does not desire to bring us into this new birth without our cooperation.

d. The Three Functions of the Law of Believers Living under Grace

Preparatory grace breaks down our resistance to other forms of grace. It enables us to move toward subtler and more inclusive levels of reception of grace. Preparatory grace brings us to despair over our own righteousness under the law, teaching us that we cannot without grace perform the works of the law adequately.[45]

The law has three functions: (1) The law curbs our native anarchic temptations. It says to human self-assertion: "No, go no further. Intrude no further than this line on the well-being of the neighbor." (2) The law leads us to despair over our righteousness. If we had only the law without grace, we would be entirely miserable. (3) The law brings us into a fuller life of participation in Christ.[46]

Preparatory grace works through the law in all these ways.[47]

[43]"On Working Out Our Own Salvation," B 3:208–9, sec. 3.7.

[44]"On Working Out Our Own Salvation," B 3:208, sec. 3.7; Augustine, Sermon 169, 11.13.

[45]"On Working Out Our Own Salvation," B 3:206–9, sec. 3. Here Wesley is relying to a large degree on Reformation teaching, but more particularly on classical Anglican formularies.

[46]"On the Origin, Nature, Properties, and Use of the Law," B 2:4–19.

[47]"On the Origin, Nature, Properties, and Use of the Law," B 2:1–19.

B. Common Grace and Conscience

1. Common Grace

a. What God Is Doing for Us in Nature and History

On scriptural grounds, Wesley taught:

> Some great truths, as the being and attributes of God, and the difference between moral good and evil, were known, in some measure, to the heathen world. The traces of them are to be found in all nations. So that in some sense, it may be said to every child of man, "He hath showed thee, O man, what is good, even to do justly, to love mercy, and to walk humbly with thy God." With this truth he has, in some measure, "enlightened every one that cometh into the world."[48]

Here is a decisive point of contact with the history of religions and a theology of world religions, and in particular with the Reformed tradition on common grace from Calvin to Kuyper.

Wesley had read a translation of the Qur'an and some of the Vedas, and he had a very rough precursory knowledge of Buddhism. His views on comparative religion were largely shaped by Hebrew-Christian Scripture as received through patristic exegesis. But as a voracious reader, he was reading the leading primary translated texts in the history of religions that were known in the eighteenth century. He cannot be condemned for not knowing what we must learn today.

The common and prevening grace working in other religions accordingly is understood as the veiled and flawed intimation of the Way, the Truth, and the Life in Jesus Christ. He viewed the arena of world religions not as something outside the grace of the one who meets us in the incarnation. The same Triune One was working in a preparatory way throughout history to elicit saving faith.

b. Grace of the Omnipresent God Is at Work Everywhere

Common grace is present throughout the whole human condition. Grace is not stingy. It is present in every time and place that human beings inhabit. It works everywhere to call freedom to repentance wherever human beings live and struggle. It silently addresses their will, imagination, and reason. It works precisely amid the constant intergenerational and social transmissions of sin. Grace works every moment, both before and after the subjective dynamics of faith, both without and within the circle of faith, though differently in each. In this way, common grace is found in all nations, in every child of man and woman, in all who love mercy.

Due to the diversity of gifts, all persons are not being given the same specific graces at any moment, for the Spirit is distributing different gifts to different persons according to emergent needs.[49] God does not make us accountable for a grace not given to us. God makes us accountable only for that grace that in fact is given to us.[50]

[48]"On Working Out Our Own Salvation," B 3:199, proem; cf. *ENNT* on Acts 17:24 and Rom. 1:19–20.
[49]B 1:149–55; 2:268, 410; 3:263–66; *CH*, B 7:583.
[50]"On Working Out Our Own Salvation," B 3:206–9, sec. 3.

2. Reorienting Wesley's Teaching of Grace within Classic Reformation Teaching

A fair discussion of this subject requires delving into Wesley's family background in the Puritan and Reformed traditions.

a. The Puritan and Reformed Impact on Wesley through His Mother, Susannah, and His Maternal Grandfather, Samuel Annesley

Since Wesley's teaching on grace has been unfairly contrasted with Reformed teaching, it is necessary to allow his own texts to correct some of these cartoons. This is best done by setting forth Wesley's texts in his close relation to Augustine, Calvin, and sixteenth- to eighteenth-century Reformed theology on these issues.

Much of the Reformed side of Wesley's teaching came directly from his remarkable mother, Susannah. She was the daughter of the Annesleys, a prominent Puritan family. The family had suffered persecution under the royal government after the Cromwellian period.

Wesley had read Calvin early and continually, and I think carefully. More so, he had absorbed the writings of many of the moderate Calvinist and English Puritan divines who had decisively been shaped by Calvin.

John Calvin strongly set the pattern for the entire English scene of religious discourse in the century before Wesley. Among those Puritan or Reformed Anglican teachers whom Wesley showed evidence of having read with significance were John Owen, Phillip Doddridge, Richard Baxter, John Goodwin, William Perkins, Jeremy Taylor, Lancelot Andrewes, and Joseph Hall.

But the more lasting Reformed theology influence by far came from his parents, both of whom had Presbyterian and nonconformist backgrounds. This is a story that belongs within the narrative of Wesley's teaching on grace and predestination.

Wesley's maternal grandfather and grandmother had close ties to Reformed Puritan theology. His grandmother was the daughter of a renowned Puritan lawyer who served as a representative in Cromwell's Long Parliament. John Wesley's mother, Susannah Annesley, came from a staunch Puritan family. Her father, Samuel Annesley, was a Presbyterian minister, rector of Cliffe. He had preached before the parliament. He had received a doctor of civil law degree from Oxford and had the unusual record of having been a Dissenter within both the reigns of Charles I and Cromwell.

Susannah's father refused in 1662 to take the repressive Oath of Obedience to the established church according to the Act of Uniformity. It required the reordination of many Puritan pastors and marked the beginning of the period of the Great Persecution. The Annesley family suffered severely because of it. Reverend Annesley, along with many other Puritan ministers, were ejected from their livings.

After much persecution, Susannah's father was relicensed as a Presbyterian minister in 1672 at Spitalfields, where he taught the Calvinist and Reformed teaching of "Christ and holiness, holiness and Christ" until his death in 1696. So Susannah was brought up within the confession of the vital core of leadership of Puritan nonconformity. Most were supporters of the Westminster Confession, now a hallmark of classic Presbyterian teaching, and all were Calvin-influenced teachers.

Susannah herself was well read in the Puritan divines. In accord with the education Susannah was getting in a select Anglican academy, however, she returned at the age of thirteen to the Anglican Church from which her father had been ejected. This caused some consternation in the Presbyterian family of Spitalfields.

Susannah later married John Wesley's father, Samuel Wesley. Samuel Wesley was then a brilliant but impoverished theological student in the dissenting ministry at Mr. Veal's Academy.[51] Tiring of the conflicts between Dissenters and the established church, Samuel Wesley became a postulant and student of Exeter College, Oxford, was ordained as a priest of the Church of England in 1689, and was later appointed to the parish of Epworth in Lincoln, where Susannah had nineteen children, one of whom was John Wesley.

After the "Glorious Revolution" of 1688, the conflict continued. Following the invasion from Holland by William of Orange, the Catholic king of England, Wales, Scotland, and Ireland, James II, fled to France. The conflict between William of Orange and James II festered in the years between 1688 and the Act of Settlement in 1701. This conflict figured symbolically into an episode of conflict between Susannah and Samuel Wesley.

We learn of a serious but telling political conflict before John's birth, serious enough to threaten the continuity of his parents' marriage. It reveals the passion of the conflict between the nonconformist intuitions of his mother and the establishment conscience of his father: In 1702 Susannah refused to utter "Amen" in response to Samuel's prayer of blessing for William Prince of Orange, who had become king following the flight of James II in 1688. Susannah regarded William as a usurper with no real right to the throne. Samuel replied: "If that be the case, you and I must part, for if we have two kings, we must have two beds." Samuel retreated to London for months until the death of William of Orange, who was followed by Queen Anne, upon whose legitimacy both Samuel and Susannah could agree. Susannah was pregnant three months later with John in 1703.

This glimpse of a Puritan influence in Wesley's background is recounted to show where John Wesley got much of his Puritan, Calvinist, and nonconformist tendencies—largely from his mother but also from his scholarly, high church, Anglican father. Now back to Wesley's writings.

b. The Influence of Augustine and Calvin on Wesley's Teaching on Grace

Calvin's doctrine of common grace forms the background of Wesley's teaching of preparatory grace that precedes saving grace. This teaching stood on the shoulders of Augustine, whose writings are saturated with a high doctrine of grace, just as we have seen in Wesley.

[51] Edward Veal, Stepney, England, d. 1683.

Augustine wrote of a grace that Adam enjoyed before the fall but not after. When Pelagius emphasized the natural ability of man, he was firmly opposed by Augustine and the classic Christian consensus. The example of Christ, in Pelagius's view, is limited essentially to illumining this natural ability without clearly requiring special saving grace.

Wesley, like Augustine, emphasized the total inability of fallen man to raise himself to righteousness without divine grace, as we will see in his longest treatise, *The Doctrine of Original Sin*.

The questions to which the doctrine of common grace responds are still familiar: How can the unregenerate to some extent have reliable knowledge and act in ways commonly called good in varied human cultures? How can Christian believers explain the comparatively orderly life of the world even under the conditions of sin? How does natural man, despite sin, retain some knowledge of nature and history, and possess some capacity to distinguish between good and evil in the form of conscience? What accounts for the persistent hunger for God in human history that manifests itself in the universal history of religions? What are Christians to say about the monotheist religions: Judaism and Islam?

c. Common Grace Does Not Save from Sin

Wesley taught the absolute dependence of humanity on the grace of God to renew the image of God lost in Adam's fall. This grace stands ready to illumine the mind, convert the will, and draw fallen human beings toward divine pardon and holy living. Wesley argued that grace is the necessary condition to the performance of any good act. Any deed that does not spring from faith is, without grace, tainted with sin, because it does not come from the right motive and does not fulfill the righteous purposes of God. Without the faithful reception of the grace of God, no good deeds suffice for righteousness or salvation.

Calvin, along with Augustine and later Wesley, maintained that the natural man can of himself do no good work whatsoever and strongly insisted on the particular nature of saving grace. Calvin developed alongside his doctrine of particular grace the doctrine of common grace.

Common grace, in Calvin's view, does not justify, pardon, or sanctify human nature. On this Calvin and Wesley are in thorough agreement. Common grace curbs the destructive power of sin and maintains in some measure the moral order of the universe. Thus, common grace tends toward an orderly life, distributing in varying degrees gifts and aptitudes among men. Common grace encourages the rational development of science and art, and showers untold blessings on unjustified sinners.

My view of the closeness of Calvin and Wesley may be disputed by some well-intentioned Reformed thinkers, but I intend to show through his texts how Wesley tracks explicitly the path of Augustine and Calvin on common grace.

This is important in the present environment, since one of the most divisive issues among evangelicals is the supposedly wide difference between Calvin and

Wesley on these points. This is due in part to the fact that the least read of Wesley's texts by Reformed evangelicals are *On the Doctrine of Original Sin* and his detailed discussions on predestination and election. More of this study will be devoted to these revealing treatises than in most Wesleyan interpreters of recent times. But this is an absolutely necessary corrective to unnecessary divisiveness among the evangelical family of churches. Wesley described his difference with Calvin as only "a hair's breadth."[52]

d. Wesley Consistent with Later Reformed Theology on the Necessity of Grace

In later Reformed theology, the doctrine of common grace (*gratia communis*) came into more general use to express the idea that this grace extends to all men. It complements but does not conflict with Calvin's teaching on the particular grace (*gratia particularis*) that is given to those who repent and believe so as to live the redeemed life.

Abraham Kuyper distinguished between three types of common grace in orthodox Reformed teaching:

1. a universal common grace that extends to all physical creation,
2. a general common grace that applies to all human creatures, and
3. a covenant common grace shared by all who live under the divine-human covenant.

Other Reformed theologians, including from Owen and Edwards to Alexander, Warfield, and Bavinck, have expanded on the theme of common grace.

In all of these mentioned, including Wesley, the grace commonly bestowed on all creation and history falls short of a saving effectiveness. Common grace never removes the guilt of sin. It does not renew human nature. It only has a restraining effect on the corrupting influence of social and personal sin.

It is completely contrary to Wesley's intent to think of grace as natural to humanity or inherent in our fallen nature. Grace remains a radical gift wholly unmerited by us in our natural fallenness. Grace comes before any of our natural competencies or responses.[53]

It is contrary to fact to claim that Wesley ascribes to common grace saving significance. That cannot be supported by the Wesley texts. Nor is it the case that moderate Arminianism in general claims to be perfectly able on the basis of common grace to turn to God in repentance and faith. That cannot be found in the writings of Arminius.

More importantly, the Canons of Dort reject the error of those who teach "that the corrupt and natural man can so well use the common grace (by which they understand the light of nature), or the gifts still left him after the fall, that he can

[52]Letters, May 14, 1765, *LJW* 4:297.
[53]"On Working Out Our Own Salvation," B 3:202–3, sec. 1.

gradually gain by their good use a greater, that is, the evangelical or saving grace, and salvation itself."[54] Wesley consistently agreed with Dort on this.

e. Grace Not Nature: Pelagius Strongly Disavowed by Wesley

Wesley's Augustinian arguments on preparing grace are not about man's natural ability, or about nature as such working of itself, but about grace working through nature. "The will of man is *by nature free only to evil*," wrote Wesley. Yet "every man has a measure of free-will restored to him by grace."[55]

Grace is not a teaching about natural free will: "Natural free-will, in the present state of mankind, I do not understand: I only assert that there is a measure of free-will supernaturally restored to every man, together with that supernatural light which 'enlightens every man that comes into the world.' "[56]

Preparatory grace is sometimes misunderstood in a Pelagian sense as natural human ability. This erroneous reading understandably makes Lutheran and Reformed evangelicals uneasy. The misreading seems to portray Wesley as if he asserts what he specifically denies: that he is secretly speaking of some universal natural capacity to do good. Wesley's preachers knew very well that "there is no one who does good, not even one" (Rom. 3:12 NIV), apart from grace. Wesley's Reformed critics who have not thoroughly examined Wesley's *The Doctrine of Original Sin* have worried unnecessarily that Wesley's Augustinian talk of prevenience tempts believers to imagine that they might of their own initiative contribute to their salvation. When we cooperate with the unmerited grace of God's saving act on the cross, we do not forget that it is precisely grace that enables our cooperation. On behalf of greater unity within the evangelical family, we must overcome those misreadings.

Though not intrinsic to freedom, grace is constantly present to freedom as an enabling, wooing gift. That does not reduce grace to an expression of nature. Grace remains grace. It is not something we possess by nature. It is given us. Yet grace is given abundantly to everyone, from the Paleolithic mound makers of Georgia to the forest Hottentots of Africa.

Everywhere human beings exercise freedom, there grace is working to elicit, out of the distortions of fallen human nature, responses of faith, hope, and love. Preparatory grace remains a teaching that can be twisted so as to imagine that Wesley was covertly affirming the very Pelagianism he so frequently denied.

Common grace bestows on fallen humans the conditions for experiencing some preliminary knowledge of the existence of God and his attributes. Common grace works to offer all humanity the possibility of reflecting on the fundamental fact

[54]Canons of the Council of Dort, 7.

[55]"Some Remarks on Mr. Hill's Review," J X:392, sec. 16, italics added.

[56]PCC, J X:229–30, sec. 45; similarly, Wesley asserted that both he and Fletcher "absolutely deny natural free-will. We both steadily assert that the will of man is by nature free only to do evil. Yet we both believe that every man has a measure of free-will restored to him by grace." "Some Remarks of Mr. Hill's 'Review of All the Doctrines Taught by Mr. John Wesley,'" J X:392.

that God is and is good and holy.[57] This does not constitute a saving knowledge of God as such, but only the opening of the door for the readiness to receive by faith, saving grace in Jesus Christ.[58] One can be shaped by common grace and moved by preparatory grace and still know nothing yet of the saving grace that knows of the incarnation, cross, resurrection, repentance, faith, hope, and love.

3. The Relation of Grace and Conscience

a. Conscience Defined

Conscience is "that faculty whereby we are at once conscious of our own thoughts, words, and actions, and of their merit or demerit, of their being good or bad, and consequently, deserving either praise or censure"[59] Conscience is a mode of consciousness, in which one is aware of the goodness or badness of one's own actions. All humans have that mode of consciousness. No sapient person is wholly lacking in the capacity to review morally one's own behavior. All who have consciousness have this facility of looking at oneself and saying, "That was passable; that was not so good."[60]

If you posited freedom without the conscience that is intrinsic to freedom, you would never have the capacity for freedom to assess its own behavioral decisions. Conscience is the capacity to judge oneself, present in all human beings, regardless of how acculturated.

Preparatory grace works through conscience. Conscience is capable of being distorted, yet God works steadily and step-by-step to ready persons for further grace.

Conscience is universally present in common humanity not as a gift of nature but of grace that mercifully leads us back to our true selves. Conscience is not merely a natural function lacking in common grace but rather "a supernatural gift of God," transcending all his natural gifts.[61] While preparatory grace is "vulgarly called 'natural conscience' ... it is more properly termed 'preventing grace,'"[62] in the sense that it comes before saving grace and is strictly distinguished from the saving grace of justification. Through the prevening grace of moral awareness, persons are drawn toward repentance and clearer self-knowledge. To assign this function to a hypothesized "natural conscience" is a vulgar description of it, because it fails to acknowledge conscience as the gift of grace refracted through the varieties of human cultures. This operation of conscience must be augmented by a "convincing grace" that leads to repentance.[63]

In conscience we experience not a natural liberty to do good, but to glimpse some hope for it. Conscience tells us that something is missing in our fallen nature.

---

[57]"The Imperfection of Human Knowledge," B 2:568 – 69, proem.
[58]B 1:118, 213.
[59]J VII:187.
[60]"On Working Out Our Own Salvation," B 3:207, sec. 3.4.
[61]"On Conscience," B 3:481, sec. 1.1 – 4.
[62]"On Working Out Our Own Salvation," B 3:207, sec. 3.4.
[63]"On Working Out Our Own Salvation," B 3:204, sec. 2.1.

That something is the grace of divine pardon. In this way, Christ who is the end of the law is being inscribed ever anew on our hearts by the preliminary discernment of the difference between good and evil.

This teaching of preparatory grace served as a structural foundation for Wesley's teaching about baptism. Though he affirmed adult baptism, he would also view infant baptism as expressing the prevenience of grace, that grace is at work even before responsiveness or the age of accountability in confirmation. The inclusion of families into God's converting activity is expressed in this anticipation of saving grace when the person comes to an age of accountability. The welcoming of the child in the community of faith corresponds to circumcision as an act of initiation. It brings one initially into the community of faith but awaits an age of accountability in which the circumcision of the heart is experienced in conversion.

The knowledge that stems from conscience does not necessarily include specific awareness of the Christian gospel, though through families it may also be early formed by the spiritual disciplines arising from Scripture's witness to the history of revelation. Rather, it involves "some discernment of the difference between moral good and evil," along with "some desire to please God, as well as some light concerning what does really please him, and some convictions when they are sensible of displeasing him."[64]

b. Only the Son Saves

Only the Savior saves, though conscience may draw the sinner closer to the possibility of repentance.

"For though in one sense it may be termed natural, because it is found in all men; yet, *properly speaking, it is not natural, but a supernatural gift* of God, above all his natural endowments. No, it is not nature, but the Son of God, that is 'the true light, which enlighteneth every man that cometh into the world.' "[65]

There is no excuse for spurning whatever level of grace is given. "For allowing that all the souls of men are dead in sin by nature; this excuses none, seeing there is no man that is in a state of mere nature; there is no man, unless he has quenched the Spirit, that is wholly void of the grace of God. No man living is entirely destitute of what is vulgarly called natural conscience."[66]

We have previously dealt with saving grace and will deal further with sanctifying grace in chapter 9. Now we turn to the subject of predestination, to which Wesley gave considerable attention.

[64]"Heavenly Treasure in Earthen Vessels," B 4:169, sec. 1.1.
[65]"On Conscience," B 3:482, sec. 1.5, italics added.
[66]"On Working Out Our Own Salvation," B 3:207, sec. 3.4.

Further Reading on Grace

Callen, Barry L. *God as Loving Grace.* Nappanee, IN: Evangel, 1996.

Cho, John Chongnahm. "John Wesley's View of Fallen Man." In *Spectrum of Thought,* edited by Michael Peterson, 67–77. Wilmore, KY: Francis Asbury Press, 1982.

Collins, Kenneth. "Prevenient Grace and Human Sin." In *Wesley on Salvation.* Grand Rapids: Zondervan, 1989.

Dorr, Donal. "Total Corruption and the Wesleyan Tradition: Prevenient Grace." *Irish Theological Quarterly* 31 (1964): 303–21.

Dunning, H. Ray. *Grace, Faith and Holiness.* Kansas City: Beacon Hill, 1988.

Harper, Steve. "Prevenient Grace." In *John Wesley's Theology Today.* Grand Rapids: Zondervan, 1983.

Langford, Thomas. "Wesley's Theology of Grace." In *Practical Divinity: Theology in the Wesleyan Tradition,* 24–48. Nashville: Abingdon, 1982.

Lawton, George. "Grace in Wesley's Fifty-Three Sermons." *PWHS* 42 (1980): 112–15.

Luby, Daniel Joseph. *The Perceptibility of Grace in the Theology of John Wesley: A Roman Catholic Consideration.* Rome: Pontificia Studiorum Universitas A.S. Thomas Aquinas in Urbe, 1994.

Nicholson, Roy S. "John Wesley on Prevenient Grace." *Wesleyan Advocate* (1976): 5–6.

Nilson, E. A. "Prevenient Grace." *LQHR* 184 (1959): 188–94.

Smith, J. Weldon, III. "Some Notes on Wesley's Doctrine of Prevenient Grace." *RL* 34 (1964): 68–80.

Wood, A. Skevington. "The Contribution of John Wesley to the Theology of Grace." In *Grace Unlimited,* edited by Clark Pinnock, 209–22. Minneapolis: Bethany Fellowship, 1975.

The Order of Salvation

Collins, Kenneth J. *The Scripture Way of Salvation: The Heart of John Wesley's Theology.* Nashville: Abingdon, 1997.

Deschner, John. *Wesley's Christology.* Dallas: SMU Press, 1960; reprint with foreword, Grand Rapids: Zondervan, 1988.

Williams, Colin. "The Order of Salvation: Prevenient Grace." In *John Wesley's Theology Today,* 39ff. Nashville: Abingdon, 1960.

God's Grace and Human Responsibility

Cobb, John B., Jr. *Grace and Responsibility: A Wesleyan Theology for Today.* Nashville: Abingdon, 1995.

Gunter, W. Stephen. *The Limits of "Love Divine": John Wesley's Response to Antinomianism and Enthusiasm.* Nashville: Kingswood, 1989.

Houghton, Edward. *The Handmaid of Piety and Other Papers on Charles Wesley's Hymns.* New York: Quack Books in association with the Wesley Fellowship, 1992.

Hulley, Leonard D. *To Be and To Do: Exploring Wesley's Thought on Ethical Behavior.* Pretoria: University of South Africa, 1988.

———. *Wesley: A Plain Man for Plain People.* Westville, South Africa: Methodist Church of South Africa, 1987.

Marquardt, Manfred. "John Wesley's 'Synergismus.'" In *Die Einheit der Kirche: Dimensionen ihrer Heiligkeit Katholizitat und Apostolizitat: Festgabe Peter Hein*, 96 – 102. Weisbaden: Steiner Verlag, 1977.

Schilling, Paul. "John Wesley's Theology of Salvation." In *Methodism and Society in Theological Perspective*, 44 – 64. Nashville: Abingdon, 1960.

CHAPTER 6

Predestination

A. How Wesley Taught Predestination and Election

Contrary to some stereotypes, Wesley had doctrines of predestination and election. They were not, however, that form of absolute double predestination that was attested by the Synod of Dort.

1. Whether the Subject Matter Is Relevant to Preaching

The subject of predestination, if vexatious to approach, is even more arduous to master. Only two subjects in the Wesley literary corpus place serious intellectual burdens on the ordinary reader, and this is one of them (original sin being the other). In both cases, Wesley is enmeshed in a complex polemical engagement with Dissenters who were exercising considerable influence within the Methodist societies. He could not afford simply to ignore the challenge. Though Wesley did not fixate on predestination, he took care to preach on it occasionally in places where it was under debate.

Though predestination is hardly an urgent question today, one need only sample the literature of the late eighteenth and early nineteenth centuries to see how fiercely it was debated. Even today it remains as a key theological hazard in conversations between Anglican-Arminian-Wesleyan evangelicals and Reformed evangelicals, including some Baptists with their special focus on eternal security.

Though predestination has an antiquarian ring to modern ears, the deeper issue remains profound for anyone who wishes to think scripturally about the omniscience, eternity, and sovereignty of God. Its crucial questions are these: How can saving grace be made available without coercing human freedom? How can the omniscient God who already sees all future and past moments fail to know who is to be saved in a future time?

Evading or ignoring this debate altogether is tempting, though to do so would be ill-advised. It remains a theme that draws together a host of basic issues that still trouble the divided body of Christ. It yields a flood of light on correlated teachings on human existence, freedom, divine sovereignty, and providence.

2. To the Very Edge of Calvinism

a. The Doctrinal Minutes of August 2, 1745

From the doctrinally defining Minutes of August 2, 1745: "Q23. Wherein may we come to the very edge of Calvinism? A. (1.) In ascribing all good to the free grace of God. (2.) In denying all natural free will, and all Power antecedent to grace. And (3.) In excluding all merit from man; even for what he has or does by the grace of God."[1] Note carefully: these are all doctrines central to Calvin's teaching, and they are all strongly affirmed by Wesley and made standard doctrine among Methodists by being included in the early Doctrinal Minutes that formed the core of Methodist doctrinal standards:

> No human act is truly free prior to divine grace.
> No human good is done except by the free grace of God, denying all natural free will and all power antecedent to grace.
> No merit claimed by any man is fitting to grace, even for what he does by divine grace.

In all of these crucial points, Wesley was citing ancient ecumenical teaching that Calvin would confirm ten centuries later. The Second Council of Orange of AD 539 stated these views consensually, which Wesley confirmed:

1. Canon 20. That a man can do no good without God.
2. Canon 6. If anyone says that God has mercy upon us when, apart from his grace, we believe, will, desire, strive, labor, pray, watch, study, seek, ask, or knock, but does not confess that it is by the infusion and inspiration of the Holy Spirit within us that we have the faith, the will, or the strength to do all these things as we ought; or if anyone makes the assistance of grace depend on the humility or obedience of man and does not agree that it is a gift of grace itself that we are obedient and humble, he contradicts the apostle who says, "What have you that you did not receive?" (1 Cor. 4:7), and, "But by the grace of God I am what I am" (1 Cor. 15:10).
3. Canon 18. That grace is not preceded by merit.

When Wesley is mistakenly portrayed today as a Pelagian or semi-Pelagian, the portrayer owes it to fairness to read *The Doctrine of Original Sin*. When Wesley is portrayed as a cheery humanistic type of Arminian who supposedly stressed the natural abilities of man, the critic reveals ignorance of the defining Doctrinal Minutes of August 1745 instructing all preachers in Wesley's connection.

b. The Doctrinal Minutes of August 24, 1743

In August 24, 1743, Wesley attempted a doctrinal *eirenicon* (peace-making effort) with Whitefield, which is even more amazing to those who might not have noticed Wesley's high doctrine of election:

---

[1]Minutes, August 1745, J VIII:285; JWO 152; cf. JWO 347 – 50, 425 – 28, 447 – 50.

With regard to ... Unconditional Election, I believe, That God, before the foundation of the world, did unconditionally elect certain persons to do certain works, as Paul to preach the gospel: That He has unconditionally elected some nations to receive peculiar privileges, the Jewish nation in particular: That He has unconditionally elected some nations to hear the gospel ... : That He has unconditionally elected some persons to many peculiar advantages, both with regard to temporal and spiritual things: And I do not deny (though I cannot prove that it is so), that He has unconditionally elected some persons [thence eminently styled "The Elect"] to eternal glory. But I cannot believe, That all those who are not thus elected to glory must perish everlastingly; or That there is one soul on earth who has not, [nor] ever had a possibility of escaping eternal damnation."[2]

These key points are thoroughly in accord with Calvin:

God unconditionally elects certain persons to do certain works.
God unconditionally elects some nations, notably Israel, to peculiar privilege.
God unconditionally elects some to peculiar advantages both temporal and spiritual.
He does not deny that God elects some to eternal glory, though he cannot prove it.

What Wesley cannot believe is also plainly that, again harking to conciliar Western Christianity in the Second Council of Orange:

Some are elected by God to perish everlastingly.
No soul is without the possibility of escaping eternal damnation by grace.

Those who treat Wesley as a soft Arminian opponent of unconditional election need to read the Doctrinal Minutes, which became Standards of Doctrine. Only the last two require futher debate with some Calvinists. Wesley stood with the ancient patristic tradition of exegesis (Origen, Cyril of Alexandria, Augustine in most ways) that was definitively formulated at the Second Council of Orange, which affirmed predestination to life but not a double predestination that would predestine to everlasting punishment so as to ignore the work of grace.

Wesley's last two reservations were debated in the period of the Second Council of Orange (AD 539) after Augustine's struggle against Pelagianism. The Council agreed with most of Augustine's points against Pelagianism but not double predestination.

3. Questions on Wesley's Omission of the Predestinarian Article

Wesley struck entirely article 17 of the Anglican Thirty-Nine Articles, on predestination and election. This cannot imply that by omitting it he rejected all its

[2]*JJW* 3:85; cf. *CH*, B 7:134, 35, 701. For comments favorable to Calvin and Calvinism, see B 1:453; *LJW* 6:146, 153, 210.

aspects, for some phrases in the article he would approve wholly, such as that "we must receive God's promises in such wise as they be generally set forth to us in Holy Scripture." But he struggled to explain the article's contention that God, before the foundation of the world, had "decreed by his counsel, secret to us, to deliver from curse and damnation those whom he hath chosen in Christ out of mankind." This language was not considered sufficiently indisputable to be sustained as a central confession for American Methodists.[3]

In his letter to James Hervey, Wesley argued that Anglican article 17 of the Thirty-Nine Articles "barely defines the term [predestination], without either affirming or denying the thing; whereas the Thirty-first totally overthrows and razes it from the foundation."[4] Writes Wesley, "Mr. Sellon has clearly showed, that the Seventeenth Article does not assert absolute predestination.... *I never preached against the Seventeenth Article, nor had the least thought of doing it.* But did Mr. Hill never preach against the Thirty-first Article," which explicitly asserts God's saving intent for all humanity?[5]

The seventeenth Anglican article is actually an affirmation of election. It is a moderate, not a radical, doctrine of election. In his *eirenicon* with Whitefield,[6] Wesley argues that some are predestined to life by the everlasting purpose of God. Only the elect are brought to everlasting salvation, as vessels made to honor, having been called according to God's purpose by his Spirit working in due season. They by grace obey this calling, are justified freely, and are made sons of God by adoption. The elect are made like the image of Christ, walking in good works, and at length, by God's mercy, receiving everlasting happiness. This teaching is said by the Anglican article 17 to be "full of sweet, pleasant and unspeakable comfort to godly persons," because it establishes and confirms faith, fervently kindling love to God. Yet for "curious and carnal persons, lacking the Spirit of Christ," they will "have continually before their eyes the sentence of God's predestination," so as to warn them against the "recklessness of most unclean living." Wesley himself subscribed to this article as a priest of the Church of England and did not inveigh against it, but did not press it upon the 1784 Conference of American Methodists.

Wesley's quarrel with double predestinarianism was not directed primarily against the Anglican formulary, but more so against the much harsher conceptions of the later Reformed tradition following Dort.

4. The Paradox of the Eternal Decree

Wesley affirmed that the eternal love of God motivated the incarnation. Due to

---

[3]*LJW* 1:23, 279; 2:69, 88, 192; 3:200, 249.

[4]*LJW* 3:379; Anglican article 31 is on "The One Oblation of Christ Finished upon the Cross," which confesses that "there is none other satisfaction for sin but that alone" (*DSWT* 122).

[5]"Some Remarks on Mr. Hill's 'Review of All the Doctrines Taught by Mr. John Wesley,' " J X:383, italics added; cf. "Answer to Roland Hill's Tract," *LJW* 5:213, 329; 6:305–6; *JJW* 5:476; B 1:206n.; 4:7n.; and "Remarks on Mr. Hill's Review," B 1:206n., 451n., 643n.; 4:7n.; 9:402–15.

[6]B 3:542–45, 590–98; 11:407–9, 500–501.

God's foreknowing of the history of sin, God decided from all eternity, before the foundation of the world,[7] that the Son should become man in order that all humanity might be offered the choice of believing or not believing in God's love, and as a result of that choice, eternal life or separation from God.[8]

In Wesley's view, a healthy teaching of predestination implies not unilaterally or deterministically "a chain of causes and effects," but a providential ordering of phases of the divine will in time, the incremental "method in which God works, the order in which the several branches of salvation constantly follow each other."[9] Wesley taught predestination as scripturally received, but for Wesley this is more a celebration of providence, divine foreknowledge, and divine sovereignty than of absolute decree.

The paradoxical idea of an eternal decree that presupposes the fall of freedom is possible on the premise of God's eternal foresight, wherein all events in time are viewed as eternally present by the all-knowing God. God does not need to wait till freedom decides to fall to envision a plan of redemption, because God sees from eternity that man will fall, and hence the remedy can be envisioned from before the foundation of the world.[10] "Salvation remains conditional, but it is salvation with an eternally grounded content."[11]

In resisting a mechanistic view of the divine decrees, Wesley stressed God's foreknowledge of free choice of sin by sinners. According to Deschner, "When Wesley thinks of the fall in the context of sanctification, a supralapsarian motif can suddenly appear: *God not only foresees the fall and provides a remedy; God decrees, foresees, and permits the creation, fall and incarnation in order to effect His overriding purpose, that man should be made holier and happier than Adam before the fall!*"[12]

In a letter of May 14, 1765, Wesley wrote, "Just so my brother and I reasoned thirty years ago, 'as thinking it our duty to oppose [absolute double] predestination with our whole strength; not as an opinion, but as a dangerous mistake, which appears to be subversive of the very foundation of Christian experience, and which has, in fact, given occasion to the most grievous offenses.' "[13] He regarded double predestination as "the very antidote of Methodism ... the most deadly and successful enemy which it ever had ... a lie ... [which does] strike at the root of Methodism, grieve the holiest of your friends, and endanger your own soul."[14]

[7]"The Signs of the Times," B 2:521 – 23, sec. 1.1; *ENNT* on 1 Tim. 1:9.

[8]*WC* 19.

[9]"On Predestination," sec. 4, B 2:416; cf. 1:87, 327, 375 – 76, 413 – 21; 3:545 – 48; JWO 349 – 50, 425 – 26.

[10]*WC* 20; PCC, J X:237 – 38.

[11]Ibid.

[12]*WC* 22, italics added.

[13]*JJW* 5:116.

[14]J XIII:150.

B. A Hair's Breadth from Calvin

1. God Freely Gives All Things

The text of the homily "Free Grace" is Romans 8:32: "He that spared not his own Son, but delivered him up for us all, how shall he not with him also freely give us all things?" [Homily #110 (1739), B 3:542–63; J #128, VII:373–86].

a. With the Son God Freely Gives Us All Things

To those who may have wondered in what sense Wesleyan evangelicals are different from Calvinists, this homily offers some leading indicators. There are in fact only a few differences. Wesley was very close to Calvin in most ways, so much so that he could concede to John Newton that "holding Particular Election and Final Perseverance is compatible" with "a love to Christ and a work of grace." He wrote in his Letters that he never differed from Calvin more than a "hair's breadth."[15]

But in this homily, the distance from the Synod of Dort to the Wesleyan revival is clear. Those who grasp accurately these fine distinctions will see instantly why Wesleyans are so close to Calvinists in doctrinal definition yet farther away in temperament with respect to grace in providence.[16]

b. Classic Consensual Teaching

With the exception of a few traditional Calvinists, many contemporary Reformed evangelicals have not rigorously followed the double predestinarian teaching of Dort. Especially among mainline Presbyterians, absolute double predestination has not often been preached. It remains a reclusive doctrine today, even among traditions that once fought diligently for it. But there still remain today rhetorical echoes of this debate reverberating from the eighteenth century.

Central to the teaching task in the Wesleyan revival was the classic pre-Augustinian consensual reformulation of the understanding of the relation of grace and freedom. This homily on "free grace" is addressed to Methodist societies as a warning against the unintended consequences of absolute double predestinarian teaching. This was the first round of many on predestination, the commencing shot of a long controversy.

There were in the societies some who strongly believed in predestination teaching. George Whitefield and Augustus Toplady and others within the Methodist orbit held fiercely to many aspects of predestinarian teaching. Wesley's argument with Calvinists would recur intermittently for over forty years, from 1739 in the free grace controversy to 1778 and following with the defiant publication of the *Arminian Magazine.* But it is best to draw conclusions about his usage of the term *Arminian* based on his own writings rather than those of later disputants.

[15]Letters, May 14, 1765, *LJW* 4:297; cf. B 1:453; *LJW* 6:146, 153, 210.

[16]See also *LJW* 5:238, 250, 322, 344; 6:34–35, 75–76; and Letter to Thomas Maxfield, B 9:422–23.

By *Arminianism* Wesley referred to a moderated Calvinism, tempered in the joyful doctrine of divine grace that elicits and encourages free, cooperative, human responses. This teaching of grace has different temperament from some severe versions of absolute double predestination. During much of this four-decade debate, he was content to view predestination as an arguable, though abusable, opinion.

Meanwhile, Wesley's theology retained most other standard features of Reformed exegesis excepting its most extreme hyper-Augustinian elements, some of which failed to gain either early or later ecumenical consensus.

Aware that this sermon would awaken controversy, he sought divine guidance.[17] In his preface "To the Reader" prior to his homily on "Free Grace," Wesley stated that he felt "indispensably obliged to declare this truth to all the world," hoping that responses would come "in charity, in love, and in the spirit of meekness."[18]

c. God's Atoning Work on the Cross "For Us All"

In what sense can it be said that God the Father "spared not his own Son, but delivered him up for us all"? The atoning work of Christ on the cross is directed to all humanity (Rom. 8:32), whether or not it is voluntarily received and thus made effectual. The gift that comes with the atoning deed is the grace that freely draws us toward acceptance of that gift.

This is not a teaching of universal salvation. It is about the universal offer of atonement. It leaves room for freedom to ignore or reject it. It is consistent with Jesus' teaching on hell, as we will later see.

The Wesleyans and double predestinarians agreed that grace produces good fruit and that works as such do not justify. The burning issue remained whether the atoning work of saving grace is offered to all or some. In the midst of the swirling activity of the revival, Wesley argued that the free sovereign grace of God is in all and for all.[19] Wherever humanity is struggling with sin, God's free grace is enabling sufficient strength for that struggle.[20]

The beginning point is the sovereign freedom of God to share his mercy with all humanity. While we were yet sinners Christ died for the ungodly. While dead in our sins, God did not spare "his own Son, but delivered him up *for us all*" (Rom. 8:32 KJV, italics added).

This is not a grace that is decreed to operate only in some, but *in all*. Grace, whether preparatory or cooperating, is offered sufficiently and freely *to all*, even when we reject it. No one is saved by prevenient grace, but only by justifying grace, as we have seen.

---

[17]Letters, to James Hutton and the Fetter Lane Society, April 30, 1739, 25:640. Outler judged Wesley insensitive to his own active role in the controversy (B 3:543). The irony of this passage is the phrase "by lots."

[18]"Free Grace," B 3:544.

[19]B 1:122.

[20]"Free Grace," B 3:544, secs. 2–4.

d. While We Were Yet Sinners

The irony of amazing grace is this: the atoning grace in Christ is freely given to all, precisely *while we were yet sinners.* All humanity comes under the condemnation of sin, yet while we were dead in sins, God freely was giving us all things.[21]

Justifying grace does not depend on any human merit, good works, tempers, good desires, good purposes, or intentions. Yet grace elicits a good willing that animates good works. Good works are the fruit of grace, not its root, the effects of grace, not its cause.[22]

2. The Practical Temptations of Predestination

The key premise of double predestination is that God ordained some to eternal salvation and some to eternal damnation, predestining both. Thus, "by virtue of the eternal, unchangeable, irresistible decree of God, one part of mankind are infallibly saved and the rest infallibly damned, it being impossible that any of the former should be damned, or that any of the latter should be saved."[23] In this view, there are two decrees of God, salvation for the elect and damnation for the damned. That is the "double" in double predestination.

The premise of the predestination of some individuals to life is easier to argue than the corollary premise that God pretemporally elected some to death.

Whatever one calls it — the divine decrees, election, predestination, or reprobation — the argument comes down to a harsh point: God before time not only foresees but decides all who will be elected and all who will be damned.[24]

Wesley thought it delusive to imagine that one could take a harmless speculative taste of the double predestinarian hypothesis but ignore the consequences.[25]

3. Eight Problematic Tendencies of Double Predestination Preaching

The price of absolute double predestinarian exegesis is far too high not only for moral accountability but for theodicy, evangelism, the attributes of God, the goodness of creation, and human freedom. Wesley set forth a series of arguments to show that absolute double predestination could not be a scriptural doctrine of God:

1. Absolute double predestination may work to *make preaching unnecessary* and absurd. Why should one preach if it is already decided before time by divine decree that about which the seeker is asked to decide? Preaching appears vain if the decisive matter of human response to grace is already settled from the beginning of time.[26]

2. Predestination tends to *undermine holy living.* It takes away the primary

[21]"Free Grace," B 3:545 – 46, secs. 3 – 5.
[22]"Free Grace," B 3:545, sec. 3.
[23]"Free Grace," B 3:547, sec. 9, as in the Synod of Dort.
[24]"Free Grace," B 3:545 – 47, secs. 5 – 8.
[25]"Free Grace," B 3:545 – 48, secs. 4 – 10.
[26]"Free Grace," B 3:548, sec. 11.

motive to follow after the holiness commended in Scripture — "the hope of future reward and fear of punishment," so that hearers believe falsely that their lot is already invariably cast. It thereby undermines the desire for holiness and active cooperation with grace, which is the purpose of preaching the Word and administering the sacraments.[27]

Suppose I am ill and know that I am destined to live or die, regardless of what is done. An extreme predestinarian might plausibly conclude that I have no need of faith, hope, and love, because my lot is already cast. Similarly Wesley argued that a person who understood himself to be predestined is tempted to feel no need either to repent or to grow in godliness.

3. Contrary to its claim, predestinarian preaching may tend to *obstruct the consoling work of the Spirit* out of which the comfort of religion flows. Among those prone to realistic self-examination, the preoccupation inevitably tends to focus on despair. It is neither consoling nor morally challenging to assert that God decides who will be saved unilaterally apart from all human responsiveness.[28]

Not only reprobates but sincere questioners may be left to despair. Whatever its intention, the doctrine refocuses attention subjectively upon whether an individual is elected, rather than whether God elects to love humanity in Christ. It tends to lead believers to pride and sinners to despair. It tends to minimize the importance of moment-by-moment dependency on the witness of God's Spirit for assurance. Under this premise, admonition to the elect becomes superfluous, and admonition to the damned ludicrous.[29]

Wesley thought that double predestination teaching has a dubious history of increasing sharp tempers and coldness of heart toward those thought to be excluded from grace, tending to thwart meekness and love. "Does it not hinder the work of God in the soul, feed all evil and weaken all good tempers?"[30] Wesley thought that evangelical testimony does better to stand empathically in the shoes of the reprobate, grasp the depths of his despair over fulfilling the requirements of the law, and there address to him the word of free grace.[31]

4. Predestination tends to *destroy zeal for works of mercy*, such as feeding the hungry. One has reduced incentive for clothing the naked or visiting the prisoner if his or her election is unassailable. Why bother to do good works if one is already securely elected, irreversibly right with God? Wesley had seen enough of acquisitive Puritans and mean-spirited Dissenters to be convinced that predestinarian arguments tend toward an ill-tempered antinomianism.[32]

Though Calvin himself never intended to discourage good works, his followers at times have been tempted to conclude that if predestined, a person can more

[27]"Free Grace," B 3:548 – 49, sec. 12.
[28]"Free Grace," B 3:549 – 50, secs. 13 – 15.
[29]"Free Grace," B 3:549, secs. 13 – 14.
[30]Letter to Lady Maxwell, September 30, 1788, *LJW* 8:95.
[31]"Free Grace," B 3:549 – 51, secs. 13 – 17.
[32]"Free Grace," B 3:550 – 51.

easily rationalize his preferred position and reinforce injustices with a self-righteous demeanor. The doctrine invites a cheaper solution than the scriptural requirement for faith working in love.[33]

5. Predestinarian tenets have a tendency to undermine the need for any actual history of revelation by *trivializing historical revelation* so as to make it absurd and superfluous. Why does one really need any history of revelation or the cross if all is settled from the beginning?[34]

6. Furthermore, its exaggerations are *based on flawed exegesis.* The analogy of faith is the surest basis of interpreting Scripture: allow the clear teachings of Scripture to interpret and validate ambiguous or controverted teachings of Scripture in a balanced way. Those who take double predestinarian premises as the key to all other biblical testimony find it increasingly hard to state an apologetic for other crucial biblical teachings, such as obedience, faith, hope, and love. They may cite texts on election while systematically ignoring those on God's atoning act for all humanity. Wesley was convinced that the exaggerations of this doctrine in his time were not a balanced reading of Scripture, but in a narrower, nonconsensual tradition of interpretation that does not account for the fuller witness of Scripture as received by the pre-Augustinian ancient church. In this way, the predestinarian premise wrongly ratchets Scripture toward seeming to contradict itself. For it is Scripture that so often appeals to responsible freedom and calls all to respond to God's saving action. If God has decreed every detail from the beginning, it makes a sham out of those texts that emphasize a decisive response to grace. Confounding the analogy of faith by pitting Scripture against Scripture, predestination may increase the difficulty of the exegete in making sense out of many biblical teachings.[35]

7. Some predestination preaching is *prone to a kind of blasphemy.* It too easily makes of God a liar and Jesus a hypocrite, by dangling salvation before all, yet allowing only a tiny in-group of the elect to receive it, misrepresenting Christ as a deceiver in his promises to care for all. If the Father does not primordially intend that all should be saved, the Son's words to that effect are a mockery. This kind of preaching presents God as taunting his helpless creatures by offering that which he does not intend to make possible, by pretending a boundless compassion for all, which turns out to be restricted.[36]

8. By austere predestination teaching, *the moral attributes of God are subverted.* The sovereignty of God is supposedly affirmed by destroying other moral attributes of God — mercy, compassion, truth, justice, and love. "This is the blasphemy for which (however I love the persons who assert it) I abhor the doctrine."[37]

It makes the premise of the veracity of God difficult to defend. How can one be

[33]"Free Grace," B 3:551, sec. 18; cf. 1:481.
[34]"Free Grace," B 3:551 – 52, sec. 19.
[35]"Free Grace," B 3:552 – 54, secs. 20 – 22.
[36]"Free Grace," B 3:554 – 59, secs. 23 – 30.
[37]"Free Grace," B 3:558 – 59, sec. 29.

just or merciful who makes a decree to damn prior to any possible responsiveness? The merciful God appears as a capricious tyrant more deceptive and cruel than the devil himself, and the human person an automaton.

Double predestination makes the devil's work unnecessary. If true, God would be worse than the devil. Scripture teaches that God's sovereignty is directed by his love and views love as God's foremost attribute. Absolute predestination disorders the primacy of God's love among the divine attributes.[38]

C. Wesley's Own Teaching of Predestination: Its Positive Aspects

1. The Homily "On Predestination"

The text for the homily "On Predestination" is Romans 8:29 – 30: "Whom he did foreknow, he also did predestinate to be conformed to the image of his Son.... Whom he did predestinate, them he also called: and whom he called, them he also justified: and whom he justified, them he also glorified" [Homily #58 (1773), B 2:413 – 21; J #58, VI:225 – 30]. Here Wesley states a positive view of the scriptural teaching of predestination.

Wesley did not deny every conceivable view of predestination, but only that hyper-Augustinian view tempered by the Second Council of Orange. He thought the extreme position of the Council of Dort was flawed exegesis, hence in spirit unscriptural, unreasonable, and lacking ancient ecumenical consent.

Wesley's own predestinarian teaching is grounded textually in Romans 8:29 – 30: "For God knew his own before ever they were, and also ordained that they should be shaped to the likeness of his Son, that he might be the eldest among a large family of brothers; and it is these, so fore-ordained, whom he has also called. And those whom he called he has justified, and to those whom he justified he has also given his splendour" (NEB).

Wesley gleaned from this text a carefully tempered doctrine of predestination that preserves grace-enabled freedom. While such passages should inspire humility, they tend instead among some to elicit uncharitable hubris. Theodore Beza's supralapsarian explication of this passage is the infelicitous logical outcome of an opinionated fixation upon divine sovereignty.[39]

[38]PCC 45 – 48, J X:229 – 31; 1 John 4:8b; on the doctrine of absolute decrees, see B 2:416; 545 – 47; cf. *LJW* 5:83; 6:296; 7:99.

[39]Acknowledging this as a difficult Pauline text, Wesley mused about whether Peter might have had this text in mind when he noted that Paul's "letters contain some things that are hard to understand, which ignorant and unstable people distort, as they do the other Scriptures, to their own destruction" (2 Peter 3:16 NIV). Subsequently, predestination became, in Wesley's view, a doctrine that "many of the most learned men in the world and not the 'unstable' only, but many who seemed to be well established in the truths of the gospel, have, for several centuries, 'wrested' to their own destruction" (B 2:415).

2. Divine Foreknowing

a. Elected according to the Foreknowledge of God

God freely wills grace to all, but not all decide to receive this incomparable gift. Wesley did not reject altogether the scriptural teaching of God's electing love, but set forth a view of election that did not require the double decree premise.[40]

Accordingly, God's choice of the faithful seeks our confirming choice of God. God sets before us life and death. The soul that chooses life shall live, and the soul that chooses death shall die. The pivot is choice. Persons are not made reprobate because God wills them to be damned, but because they respond deficiently to sufficient grace.[41]

God offers grace freely to all who will receive it, forcing grace upon none. Wesley followed a traditional ancient consensual way of understanding the predestination texts: They point to God's foreknowledge of those who would believe, as those who are "chosen according to the foreknowledge of God" (1 Peter 1:2 NIV).

The elect are not elected without either grace or freedom. They are elected with the foreknowledge of God, but without a decree that crushes the invitation to say yes to grace. Election does not disrespect God's gift of human freedom. The faithful are elected "according to the foreknowledge of God." They are not elected according to an absolute double predestinarian decree. This requires further inquiry into the relation between foreknowing and predetermining.

b. Whether God's Foreknowing Implies Predetermining

God's knowing differs from human knowing in time. God is simultaneously aware of all events in time, since only God is eternal and omniscient. God is already foreknowing of all who are responding negatively or positively to free grace.

To God, all time is eternally present. Hence even our temporal notions of foreknowing and afterknowing are strictly speaking not the way God sees time, but only egoistic expressions based on our lack of knowing.

From creation to consummation, God knows what is in the hearts of all people.[42] *It is precisely God's foreknowing that defines, interprets, clarifies, and explicates the otherwise obscure meaning of God's foreordaining will.*[43] Note the sequence: "whom he did foreknow, he also did predestinate to be conformed to the image of his Son (Rom. 8:29 KJV).[44]

Thus scriptural election is "according to the foreknowledge of God," not according to our limited human experience of flowing time. God's foreknowing extends to every aspect of our memory, motivation, and imagination. This is no problem for the omniscient and omnipresent God, who sees and knows all inward contingencies of every person in every moment.

---

[40]"On Predestination," B 2:417–24.
[41]"Free Grace," B 3:549–59, secs. 14–30.
[42]"On Predestination," B 2:416–17, sec. 5.
[43]"On Predestination," B 2:420–21, sec. 15.
[44]"On Predestination," B 2:418, sec. 7.

We do not sin *because* God knows it in advance, but God knows it because of his eternal precognition of time. Our choices to sin are known by God who knows every aspect of all moments of time without dishonoring human freedom. As one may know the sun is shining, yet that knowledge does not cause the sun to shine, so God knows that a person sins.[45]

God's foreknowing in no way absolutely necessitates human action; it simply foreknows human actions, their determinants and consequents. God's foreknowing recognizes our sin but does not unilaterally cause it. At one level of causality, God is the first cause of every effect, the first mover of every motion. But God himself has created free human beings who have their own forms of causality. That is what freedom means. Take that away and you have automatons, not free human beings.

c. God's Eternal Will Cannot Be Temporally Bound to Linear Temporal Sequences

One can best discern the meaning of Romans 8:29 – 30 by rethinking its terms in reverse order from last to first — from glorification backward in time toward foreknowing. Among all those saved, there is not one who has not been purchased by the blood of Christ. No one is justified without being called, first with an outward call and then an inward call. No one is finally called without being conformed to the image of the Son by faith. No one is sanctified by grace without this being foreknown by God, since God sees past times as present and is himself present at every step along the way.

The moral image of God is thereby being freely expressed or rejected in those who are called. All this occurs by God's eternally foreknowing providence[46] so as to enable them to share in the eternal blessing.[47] This doctrine is based on 1 Peter 1:2 and Romans 8:29 – 30. Thus, the apostle is not describing in Romans an unalterable series of cause-effect interactions with each layer building on the previous one, viewed deterministically. He is not delineating "a chain of causes and effects . . . but simply showing the *method in which God works*," the providential arrangement by which the order of salvation steadily unfolds, so the work of God may be considered "either forward or backward — either from the beginning to the end, or *from the end to the beginning*."[48]

This is a profound view of predestination. It is regrettable that Methodist preaching and apologetics in the nineteenth century did not defend it adequately. It is clearly expressed in the Wesley homily "On Predestination." So to say that Wesley has no doctrine of election and no doctrine of predestination is to misread him entirely.

[45]"On Predestination," B 2:417, sec. 5.

[46]On dispensations of grace within this plan, see B 3:492 – 93; *LJW* 5:268.

[47]"On Predestination," B 2:418 – 20, secs. 7 – 14.

[48]"On Predestination," B 2:416, sec. 4, italics added. This is a salient anticipation of Wolfhart Pannenberg's view of proleptic eschatological reasoning, from the end to the whole. See *Revelation as History* (New York: Macmillan, 1968).

God witnesses all eternity at once, observing everything in an "eternal now," innocent of the charge that his knowing makes him the direct causative agent of evil.[49] Double predestinarian exegesis binds God too tightly in a crude linear conception of time. Wesley amended this presumption by appealing to the transtemporal nature of God, for whom there is no before or after.

d. Sustaining Moral Accountability within the Premise of Divine Foreknowing

God wills eternal life to the faithful by grace according to God's foreknowledge. God's elect have been "chosen *according to* the foreknowledge of God the Father, through the sanctifying work of the Spirit, to be obedient to Jesus Christ" (1 Peter 1:2 NIV, italics added).

The cause of sin is the sinner, not God, the giver of freedom. The sinner absurdly turns away from God in sin. Lacking freedom, no one could be held morally responsible. Having freedom is what we mean by being a person.

God sees from eternity who will and will not accept his atoning work. God does not coerce the acceptance of his offer. The atonement is available for all but not received by all.

Wesley was convinced that this reading of the Pauline text was consensually received by the Ante-Nicene Fathers and only then clarified further in the post-Augustinian period. It is orthodox patristic consensus of both East and West. It is especially seen in the apostolic fathers, notably in Clement of Alexandria, Origen, and Gregory of Nyssa, as well as in Athanasius, John Chrysostom, Cyril the Great, and the early ecumenical conciliar tradition.[50]

3. The Destiny to Conform to the Son's Image

God's predestining will has as its goal to conform those whom he did foreknow "to the image of his Son" (or to be "shaped to the likeness of his Son," NEB). All of any future time who freely and truly believe in the Son are promised that they will be conformed to the Son's image, saved from outward and inward sin, and enabled to walk in the way of holiness.

Those so foreknown and in this sense predestined are in time effectually called outwardly by the word of his grace and inwardly by the Spirit, justifying them freely and making them children of God. The divine decree is that "believers shall be saved, those whom he foreknows as such, he calls both outwardly and inwardly — outwardly by the word of his grace, and inwardly by his Spirit."[51]

Wesley's argument for God's electing and predestining grace is a unique argument, seldom referenced in the harsh polemics between Reformed and Methodist teachings in America. This formulation solves many otherwise thorny problems

[49]"On Predestination," B 2:417, sec. 5.

[50]DPF X:265; cf. Council of Ephesus, AD 431; Second Council of Carthage, AD 529; see my discussion of the predestination texts in *The Transforming Power of Grace* (Nashville: Abingdon, 1993).

[51]"On Predestination," B 2:418, sec. 8.

of his sanctification teaching. It means that those who seek the holy life but do so inadequately can take comfort in God's electing love.

Those called freely are offered justifying grace freely and sanctifying grace to be received freely. Sanctification of the believing life occurs as the believer is conformed to the image of the Son. The conforming process, which aims in time toward the complete yielding of the will to God, comes to full fruition in glorification: "having made them 'meet to be partakers of the inheritance of the saints in light,' he gives them 'the kingdom which was prepared for them before the world began.'"[52]

"Whom he predestined" means those whom he foreknew to be believers who would ultimately respond to their effectual calling by grace. God foreknows their repentance, faith, and sanctification, even when they cannot see it. From God's point of view, the past tense is merely a way of speaking. For God's "fore"-knowing is an eternal now — "to speak after the manner of men: for in fact there is nothing *before* or *after* to God."[53]

a. The Substance of This Election Found in Susannah Wesley's Letter of 1725

The substance of this homily, preached in Ireland in 1773, echoes the letter of John Wesley's mother, Susannah, to John in his Oxford days:

> I do firmly believe that God from eternity hath elected some to everlasting life. But then I humbly conceive that *this election is founded on his foreknowledge*, according to that in the 8th of Romans: ..."Whom in his eternal prescience God saw would make a right use of their powers, and accept the offered mercy ... he did predestinate, adopt for his children, his peculiar treasure. And that they might be conformed to the image of his Son, he called them to himself, by his external Word, the preaching of the gospel, and internally by his Holy Spirit."[54]

This brilliant insight of Susannah Wesley remained firm in her son's mind. It awaited 1773 to become a clearly expressed argument.

In this way, scriptural teaching is not inconsistent in asserting both that "He that believeth shall be saved; he that believeth not shall be damned," and that God wills to save all. "O that men would ... be content with this plain account of it, and not endeavor to wade into those mysteries which are too deep for angels to fathom."[55]

D. Predestination Calmly Considered

In his most detailed essay on predestination, Wesley initiated the colloquy with predestinarian teaching by letting Scripture texts on predestination speak for themselves. He had an empathic gift for entering into dialogue with those different from

[52]"On Predestination," B 2:418 – 19, sec. 10.
[53]"On Predestination," B 2:418, sec. 7.
[54]Letter from Susannah Wesley to John Wesley, August 18, 1725, B 25:179 – 80, italics added.
[55]"On Predestination," B 2:421, sec. 16.

himself. This dialogue is found in a carefully argued essay on "Predestination Calmly Considered" [1752; JWO:427–72; J X:204–59]. It is accompanied by numerous direct quotations from standard predestinarian sources.

Wesley was not wholly lacking a reprobation teaching but insisted that it be grounded in providence and grace, and that grace lead freedom, not coerce freedom. He held that God is just in judging those who have freely rejected his gift of grace. Wesley did not advise his connection of spiritual formation to disdain predestination altogether. Rather, he sought its proper scriptural grounding.

1. The Puzzle of Irresistible Grace

a. The Experiential Ground of Irresistibility Teaching

Wesley offered an experiential explanation of the psychological tenacity of predestinarian teaching in speaking of irresistibility. His point of inquiry is not the logic of predestination but the feelings that accompany it. He was convinced that the idea had profound roots in the experience of believers redeemed by the radical power of grace. Those who had experienced the compelling power of grace in *themselves* tend to infer that God always works irresistibly in *every* believer. Wesley thus credits predestination with a certain psychological plausibility and power: the compelling feeling that God is calling one so powerfully to grace that it seems irresistible.[56]

Under such circumstances, it may seem that the posture of freedom is entirely passive and that grace is simply and unilaterally filling the soul with mercy. It is understandable that they leap to the inference that grace makes us completely inert rather than cooperating agents working out our own salvation in fear and trembling in order to receive the grace given. This psychological deduction prematurely assumes that the only way to interpret what has happened to me is to suppose that God chose this path from the beginning before the foundation of the world, destining some to salvation and some to reprobation. This experience then becomes systematized into a whole structure of exegesis, logic, and thought.[57]

In this way, Wesley turns the tables on extreme pietism, noting that it is too experientially and emotively oriented. His telling indictment is addressed directly to those most prone to make it against others.

b. The Spirit Does Not Work Coercively

There is no height or strength of holiness from which it is impossible to fall. But by grace anyone who has fallen may by repentance find forgiveness. Wesley admitted that God *"may* possibly, at *some times,* work irresistibly in *some souls,*" but one cannot infer from that "that he *always* works thus."[58]

The ordinary work of the Spirit is not coercive. That the Spirit can be resisted is evident from Acts 7:51 on stiff-necked people. Yet God is patient.

[56]PCC 1–4, JWO 427–28.
[57]PCC 1–4, JWO 427–28.
[58]PCC 81, JWO 468, italics added; cf. *LJW* 5:83; B 2:489–90; *JJW* 3:85–86; JWO 427–28, 448ff., 469–70.

c. Countering the Premature Systematization of a Falsely Simple Experiential Deduction

Wesley entered into a careful systematic review of predestinarian arguments, texts, and reasonings. Though Wesley is often dismissed as an unsystematic experiential preacher who lacks the internal cohesion of a systematic thinker, this treatise on predestination shows his love for rational congruence.

A central purpose of this exposition is to show the interior coherence of his theological system. "Predestination Calmly Considered" is not one of his typical brief teaching homilies, but a deliberately rational exercise. It shows that the aging former Oxford don could engage in detailed doctrinal reflection and think economically in an orderly way when the occasion demanded.

At first glance, it may seem as if the predestinarian system is more rationally ordered and its opponents weak on argument. A prevailing logical clarity and moral certainty seems to permeate predestinarian thought, where it is God who does all the deciding from the outset and only then works out its consequences in unconditional reprobation, absolute election, irresistible grace, and eternal perseverance. Those who hunger for an uncomplicated account of the divine-human relation and a less nuanced theology may have hidden psychological preferences. Especially if divine sovereignty is the central point in theology, the logic of predestinarian exegesis seems unassailable. But those who seek to understand the intimate inward dialogue of grace and freedom look for a more interactive explanation, hence more complex and less inevitable.

Wesley sought a more subtly harmonized and more personalized form of predestination reasoning. Many factors cry out for consideration besides simply God's omnipotent power. The grace-freedom interface requires more intricate forms of reasoning than the arguments of the absolute decrees of double predestination.

The covenant relation is more dialogical than monological. It is more dialectical than deductive. The interactive reasoning of mutuality requires a more rigorous and multifaceted analysis. It is finally left with fewer absurdities than its simpler alternative, a predestinarian system that at first glance appears to be utterly consistent.[59]

2. Letting Predestinarian Teachers Speak in Their Own Words

Usually Wesley preferred to let predestinarian sources speak for themselves. He cited frequently the Paris Confession of Faith of 1559, Calvin's *Institutes*, Dort's Decrees of 1618, and the Westminster Confession of 1646.[60]

When in a debating temperament, Wesley became very textually focused. In the heat of a polemical showdown, however, Wesley sometimes trimmed and edited the predestinarian voices so as to leave out some of their most crucial disclaimers

[59]PCC 1–16, JWO 427–33; cf. B 9:423, 520–21.
[60]PCC 1–9, JWO 427–30.

— that God was not the author of sin, or that the freedom of the redeemed will is still preserved by the doctrine of election.[61]

By 1752 Wesley was faced with a two-hundred-year tradition of election teaching. He found its classic Reformed expression in Calvin's *Institutes*. On this doctrine, he recapitulates Calvin's view: "All men are not created for the same end, but some are fore-ordained to eternal life, others to eternal damnation. So according as every man was created for the one end or the other, we say he was *elected* (i.e., predestinated to life) or *reprobated* (i.e., predestinated to damnation)."[62] He often quotes Westminster: "By the decree of God, for the manifestation of his glory, some men and angels are predestinated unto everlasting life and others foreordained to everlasting death."[63]

Wesley defined the doctrine of double predestination as follows: "Before the foundations of the world were laid, God of his own mere will and pleasure fixed a decree concerning all the children of men who should be born unto the end of the world. This decree was unchangeable with regard to God and irresistible with regard to man. And herein it was ordained, that one part of mankind should be saved from sin and hell, and all the rest left to perish for ever and ever, without help, without hope."[64]

That is the view Wesley was trying to make a fair account of and rebut with detailed textual analysis. Wesley's task was formidable: Inquire into how grace meets and guides human freedom precisely amid freedom's resistances. To do this he had to ask whether the predestinarian's scriptural exegesis is balanced and valid, and to what degree the predestinarian ends up undermining the divine attributes of justice, wisdom, love, and veracity.

He maintained that those who assert unconditional election are stuck logically also with unconditional reprobation.[65] If one maintains that only the elect are saved, then it follows that those whom God did not choose to elect are necessarily destined to be damned. "Go now and find out how to split the hair between thy being reprobated and not elected."[66] Wesley appealed to Calvin's own logic that "election cannot stand without reprobation. Whom God passes by, those he reprobates."[67] "Unconditional election cannot appear without the cloven foot of reprobation."[68]

3. The Condition of Divine Election

a. Two Senses of Election in Scripture

In challenging this teaching, it is necessary to distinguish two complementary

---

[61] JWO 425 – 26.
[62] PCC 7, JWO 429; Calvin, *Institutes*, 3.21.5.
[63] PCC 7, JWO 429.
[64] PCC 14, JWO 432.
[65] *JJW* 2:353; 3:84 – 86.
[66] PCC 12, JWO 431.
[67] *Institutes* 3.23.1; PCC 9, JWO 430.
[68] PCC 15, JWO 432.

biblical senses of election. First, election in Scripture may refer to *a personal divine appointment to accomplish a particular task*, such as God's election of Cyrus or Paul. This does not imply eternal happiness. Judas, for example, was called to be a disciple, yet not saved, holy, or blessed.[69]

In other passages, election refers to *election to eternal happiness.* Such election to eternal happiness is not unconditional, for it is conditioned upon its faithful reception.[70] Those who have faith may share in God's electing love. Lacking faith, one does not share in God's electing love.

b. God's Choice in the Cross and Human Choice in Response

Subjectively viewed, the decisive factor is one's own choosing — always by grace alone through faith — in response to God's electing love for all.[71] As with the people of Israel, the full circle of an effective, actualized teaching of election calls for and requires human confirmation of the election of God.[72] In this way, election in Scripture refers not exclusively to God's unilateral choice, but also to grace-enabled human responsiveness to God's choice.[73]

Eternal happiness in Scripture is not an absolute pretemporal divine choice. Rather, it is grounded in God's own choice to love all humanity, addressed freely to all, and awaiting the timely response of all:

Wedding guests who fail to respond, lose their invitation (Matt. 22:8).
Those inattentive to wisdom find that she will spurn them (Prov. 1:23 – 29).
Israel was instructed that "if you forsake him, he will forsake you" (2 Chron. 15:2 NIV).
The people were given a choice of a blessing or a curse, depending on how they keep the command of God (Deut. 11:26 – 28).
God keeps his covenant love with those who love him and keep his commands (Deut. 7:12).
Only when we choose to build the house on the rock of grace do we find a foundation that does not fall (Matt. 7:24 – 25).[74]

c. God Sets Limits

To those who responded that Wesley was making salvation conditional, he answered that it was not he who was setting limits, but the revealed Word of God that has explicitly defined what is necessary for the reception of the covenant.[75]

"*If* you ... are careful to obey my commands ... I will keep my covenant with you." "*If* you reject my decrees ... I will set my face against you" (Lev. 26:3, 9, 15, 17

[69]PCC 16, JWO 433.
[70]PCC 17, JWO 433.
[71]*JJW* 5:116.
[72]JWO 433 – 34; cf. "Principles of a Methodist," B 9:59 – 63.
[73]PCC 19, JWO 434.
[74]Ibid.
[75]B 11:108 – 17, 444 – 57; *SS* 1:128.

NIV, italics added). God has "done all which was necessary for the conditional salvation of all mankind; that is, *if* they believe."[76] If, if, if — all conditional statements.

"I am justified through the righteousness of Christ, as the price; through faith, as the condition. I do not say ... faith is that *for which* we were accepted; but ... faith is that *through which* we are accepted. We are justified, we are accepted of God, for the sake of Christ, through faith."[77] My salvation is conditional upon my response.

But God's atoning act on the cross is not conditional. God's gift on the cross cannot be finally obliterated by any particular person's disbelief. The gift of the Son is objectively given on the cross whether received or not. What happened on the cross is for all, yet only some respond in faith, hope, and love to the electing love of God.

4. Distinguishing Precognition from Preordination

It is only God, "to whom all things are present at once, who sees all eternity at one view." Only God has the omniscience to speak precognitively of believers freely responding to grace as the "elect from the foundation of the world."[78] God has prescient awareness of how our wills are going to respond, for God is eternal, all-seeing, present to future time as well as past, and grasps the consequences of specific acts of freedom. But that does not imply that God unilaterally determines our acts of freedom.

God, who is incomparably the ground and giver of all things, could have made the world differently, but not in such a way that would be inconsistent with his own intent as Creator. God has freely, omnipotently chosen to create this world, the one we see, a real world, not a fantasy. Within this world there are natural causes in a complex order of causality, and free beings in this world whose decisions are not reducible to external determinants alone, but due in part to self-determination within the webbing of causality.[79] The permission of freedom is within the range of the affirmation of God's omnipotence.[80]

5. Whether Unconditional Election Is a Scriptural Doctrine

a. All Are Invited, Few Accept

Unilaterally decreed reprobation is not consistent with the scriptural teaching that all are invited to salvation. God originally intends and is willing that all should be saved.[81] Let Scripture speak:

[76]"An Extract from A Short View of the Difference between the Moravian Brethren, (So Called,) and the Rev. Mr. John and Charles Wesley," J X:202.

[77]"Some Remarks of Mr. Hill's 'Review of All the Doctrines Taught by Mr. John Wesley,'" J X:390, italics added.

[78]PCC 17 – 18, JWO 433. This assumes a critical distinction between precognition and preordination. God has preknowledge of futurity based on God's eternity. Only God knows how our freedom will spell itself out. But that does not deny that freedom is spelling itself out in self-determination. Wesley insisted that this freedom is not undermined but enabled by grace.

[79]JWO 474 – 76, 489 – 90.

[80]PCC 120, JWO 432 – 34.

[81]PCC 19, JWO 434.

It is not God's will that any should be lost, but rather that all would repent (2 Peter 3:9).
God bestows his riches upon all who call upon him (Rom. 10:13).
As Adam's sin leads to the condemnation of all, so Christ's obedience is offered for the reconciliation of all (Rom. 5:18 – 19).
The good news is to be proclaimed to all creation (Mark 16:15).
Christ died for all (2 Cor. 5:15).
Christ, the lamb takes away the sins of the world (John 1:29).

This is the intended remedy not only for our sins, but for the sins of the whole world (1 John 2:2). Wesley patiently worked through the texts (Matt. 22:9; Luke 19:41ff.; John 5:16, 34, 40; Acts 17:24; 1 Tim. 2:3 – 4; 4:10; James 1:5; 1 John 4:14) that show God came to save all, and died for all. All are atoned for, though few may accept. Christ is the propitiation for the sins of the whole world. What happened on the cross is not for some but all (Matt. 18:11; John 1:29; 3:17; 12:47; Rom. 14:15; 1 Cor. 8:11; 2 Cor. 5:4; Heb. 2:9; 2 Peter 2:1).[82]

b. The Eternal Decree

The eternal decree is that those who believe will be saved, not that those who are saved will believe. The parable of the potter and clay (Rom. 9:21) does not conclude for unconditional pretemporal reprobation, for "God has a right to fix the terms on which he will show mercy." God may show mercy to whoever meets the terms God defines for showing mercy regardless of previous privilege, even to the Gentiles if God so desires.[83]

The abridged code phrase God "hardened his [Pharaoh's] heart," upon deeper inspection, actually means that God "permitted Satan to harden it."[84] God permits obstinate believers to harden in their unbelief. That "no one can snatch them out of my Father's hand" (John 10:28 NIV) assumes that some have freely chosen by grace to follow and obey.

6. Challenging the Logic of Unqualified Determinism

a. Whether Divine Justice Is on Trial in the Court of Determinism

Does God justly condemn a free person to eternal damnation totally apart from any opportunity for that person to cooperate? "Justice can have no place in rewarding or punishing mere machines."[85] In Scripture, "God is pleased to appeal to man himself touching the justice of His proceedings."[86]

How can God be regarded as a just judge if an eternal decree has been made that does not take into account any capacity to accept or reject grace? Why should the Spirit be active in our hearts to enable this response if it is already predetermined?

[82]PCC 19 – 23, JWO 434 – 35.
[83]PCC 24 – 33, JWO 435 – 41.
[84]PCC 56, JWO 453 – 54.
[85]PCC 37, JWO 442.
[86]PCC 22, JWO 435; J X:216.

God's justice does not damn anyone except those who refuse the grace being freely offered to them.[87]

b. Demeaning God's Justice

If absolute predestination to reprobation is true, then the sincerity of God's promises is put in question. For how could God be straightforward in his call to all to repent if repentance were impossible or already absolutely negated by a pretemporal divine decree? One who is not given the power to do good cannot justly be condemned for not doing good. One cannot justly be condemned of sin if the means to escape sin are not present. Who could be justly condemned for doing evil if he could do only evil?[88] Unbelief could not be the basis of the condemnation of those who did not have the power to believe.[89]

God's sovereignty is manifested through free will, not undermined by it.[90] Double predestination may be pressed in such a way as to debase both God's justice and human freedom.[91] It may inadvertently demean God's sovereignty, mercy, veracity, and sincerity, making absurd all preaching aimed at repentance and faith. The sovereignty of God must be viewed not abstractly but in conjunction with God's other attributes.

c. God Is Unchangeable in His Covenant

God's unchangeableness is expressed precisely through his constant, responsive love. God is unchangeable in his will to save those who respond in faith.[92]

"God's unchangeableness with regard to his decrees is this: he has unchangeably decreed to save holy believers and to condemn obstinate, impenitent unbelievers." "Unchangeably he loveth faith and unchangeably hateth unbelief."[93]

God is *unchangeable* precisely with regard to his decree to save those who respond to his love in faith.

In his incomparable *faithfulness*, God will perform what he has promised, will keep his covenants, which from the outset require and enable human responsiveness.[94]

---

[87]Ibid.

[88]PCC 31, JWO 439; J X:221.

[89]PCC 35–36, JWO 441; J X:223.

[90]*LJW* 6:287; 1:184.

[91]Monotheletism is that heresy that viewed the Christ as having only one will. Orthodoxy speaks of two wills in the God-man, a human will and a divine will to which the human will is freely yielded in constant consecration. Wesley regarded double predestination as a novel form of monotheletism, assuming that only one will is present in conversion and that will is God's.

[92]PCC 58, JWO 455.

[93]PCC 58–59, JWO 455; J X:238.

[94]PCC 59–78, JWO 455–67.

7. The Wisdom, Justice, Mercy, Sovereignty, and Faithfulness of the Unchangeable God

a. Divine Sovereignty Does Not Deny Divine Mercy

The incarnation shows that God comes to us humbly. The wisdom of God adapts itself to our human condition. God works not by duress, but gently in our hearts, reproving, grieving, wooing, like a lover trying to invite and draw and persuade the beloved. It is a wiser God who offers salvation to humanity without forcing salvation upon them, who enables human self-determination and welcomes the free interactive play of human choice, than one who would simply create a closed world in which freedom is a cruel illusion.[95]

God by grace saves humanity first by enlightening everyone who comes into the world with an understanding of good and evil by means of common grace; then by convicting grace reproving when the will falls into evil; then by moving the will gently, not coercively, to respond cooperatively; then by wooing the will, by nurturing good desires into our hearts, by setting life and death before us, and by seeking to persuade us to choose life.[96]

b. The Eternal Decree Is to Save or Condemn According to Our Response

The human person is not a stone or a cannonball that does not act but is merely acted upon. No one holds a cannonball responsible for what it effects. Similarly, one impelled by a force he cannot resist cannot be held accountable either for reward or punishment.[97] The best metaphors for grace eliciting freedom are not drawn from billiard-ball natural causality, but from the interpersonal, interactive, dialogical sphere in which one person addresses and appeals to another's freedom.

God's glory is not magnified by demeaning God's attributes. It is unconvincing that God's justice is glorified because in his sovereign will he has preordained persons to sin. What would one say of a man who, though he could save millions with just one word, chooses rather to save only a few, refusing to save the others by saying, "I will not because I will not"?

Neither does it commend God's mercy to argue that God has acted in such an arbitrary way.[98] The sovereignty of God rightly appears "in fixing from eternity that decree, 'He that believeth shall be saved,'" in "all the general circumstances of creation," in "allotting the natural endowments" of humanity, and in "dispensing the various gifts of his Spirit," but not in pretemporally damning some while saving others.[99]

---

[95]PCC 51–52, JWO 449–50.
[96]PCC 52–54, JWO 450–52.
[97]PCC 37, JWO 442; J X:224.
[98]PCC 52–53, JWO 450–51.
[99]PCC 53–56, JWO 451–53.

8. Free Will Defended

Wesley held to the freewill defense that God creates freedom, and freedom chooses evil in its own struggle against God, who is the author not of sin but of freedom, which is created good even if prone to fall. No creature capable of mirroring the image of God can be considered an automaton.

Human freedom is created to mirror within the limits of finitude the freedom of God. Only through freedom can the goodness of God be consciously and rationally reflected, unlike inorganic matter, which can only refract God's goodness inertly, without speech or reason.[100]

Take away freedom and you take away the greatest expression of God's glory in creation. Scripture repeatedly calls each of us to choose between death and life, good and evil (Gen. 3:17; Deut. 7:9 – 12; Matt. 7:26). Freedom is capable of glorifying and reflecting God in ways that inanimate creatures are incapable.

Wesley took special delight in quoting back to Reformed advocates the language of the Westminster Assembly, which allowed that "God hath endued the will of man with that natural liberty that is neither forced, nor by an absolute necessity of nature, determined to do good or evil."[101]

9. Wesley's Rejection of Semi-Pelagianism

a. The Creator's Glory Is in Created Freedom

The hypothesis that God saves us without our freedom is not more exalting to God than that God saves us with and through our freedom. It is not more glorifying to God to save an automaton irresistibly than to save a free agent by such grace as one may either concur with or resist.[102]

Some argue that if human free will is given any power at all, such power is taken away from God, and thus God would not have the whole glory of the work of salvation, but some would fall to the human will. Wesley answered, against all hints of semi-Pelagianism, that the power "to work together with him" by grace is wholly from God.

The creation of the free person who may "work together with God" is the ground for the greater glorification of God, for such power to work has come from God. God does not exclude human freedom from cooperating with his grace, but rather creates, redeems, and newly enables human freedom.[103]

b. No Cooperation with God Possible without Grace

One could not cooperate with God had not the power and possibility of cooperating come from God. So it is no offense to grace to say that grace enables human freedom to cooperate with grace. The right use of freedom, far from detracting from the glory of God, enhances God's glory.

[100]PCC 49, JWO 447.
[101]Westminster Confession IX.1.
[102]PCC 49, JWO 448; J X:231.
[103]PCC 43 – 49, JWO 446 – 48.

By cooperation Wesley was not implying that fallen freedom retains a natural capacity to reach out and take the initiative and establish a restored relation with God. Rather, by cooperating grace he means that human freedom by grace is being enabled to cooperate interactively with God's saving plan.[104] It is the coworking through grace of human willing with the divine willing.[105]

10. Falling from Grace

Those who having once truly believed and been endued with the faith that produces a good conscience, may later fall (Ezek. 18:24; 1 Tim. 1:18 – 19).

Those once grafted into the good olive tree may later be broken off through willful unbelief (Rom. 11:16 – 22). Branches that "do not remain in [Christ]" are cast forth and burned (John 15:6 NIV). Those having once known Christ can again become entangled in the world (2 Peter 2:20). Those who have been made partakers of the Holy Spirit and have produced fruits of the Spirit may nevertheless fall from grace back into former pollutions (Heb. 6:4 – 6; 10:29).[106]

Even those most actively receiving sanctifying grace may yet fall (Heb. 10:26 – 29). We share finally in Christ only if we hold to our first confidence (Heb. 3:14). We are instructed to take care that we do not lose what we have (2 John 8), to hold fast so that no one seizes the crown (Rev. 3:11).[107] Grace is almighty but not irresistible.[108]

11. The Synod of Dort and Wesley Compared

a. Dort Articles 1 – 5

Wesley did not contest Dort's article 1 of the first main point that "since all people have sinned in Adam and have come under the sentence of the curse and eternal death, God would have done no one an injustice if it had been his will to leave the entire human race in sin and under the curse, and to condemn them on account of their sin."

Wesley could not disagree with article 2, that God showed his love: he sent his only begotten Son into the world, so that whoever believes in him should not perish but have eternal life; nor with article 3, which quotes Romans 10:15: "And how can anyone preach unless they are sent?" (NIV).

Similarly on article 4, Wesley firmly held to these Pauline teachings that "God's anger remains on those who do not believe this gospel. But those who do accept it and embrace Jesus the Savior with a true and living faith are delivered through him from God's anger and from destruction, and receive the gift of eternal life."

There is nothing objectionable either to article 5 that "the cause or blame for this unbelief, as well as for all other sins, is not at all in God, but in man. Faith in Jesus Christ, however, and salvation through him is a free gift of God. As Scripture

[104]JWO, Introduction, 13 – 16; cf. 119, 425.
[105]PCC 43 – 49, JWO 446 – 48.
[106]PCC 68 – 79, JWO 458 – 68.
[107]PCC 73 – 78, JWO 463 – 67.
[108]PCC 81, JWO 468.

says, 'It is by grace you have been saved, through faith, and this not from yourselves; it is a gift of God' (Eph. 2:8). Likewise: 'It has been freely given to you to believe in Christ' (Phil. 1:29)."

b. Dort Articles 6 – 10

Excepting the first sentence of article 6, that "the fact that some receive from God the gift of faith within time, and that others do not, stems from his eternal decision," Wesley concurred with Dort that God "graciously softens the hearts, however hard, of his chosen ones and inclines them to believe." In his homily "On Hell," he tacitly agrees that " by his just judgment he leaves in their wickedness and hardness of heart" those who have resisted grace. Nor did he preach against the Anglican article 17 that souls are comforted by the eternal counsels of God, in language similar to Dort.

Wesley's resistance begins to focus on the first sentence of article 7, that "before the foundation of the world, by sheer grace, according to the free good pleasure of his will, he chose in Christ to salvation a definite number of particular people out of the entire human race, which had fallen by its own fault from its original innocence into sin and ruin."

Wesley had no reason to object to most of article 9, which affirms that grace is given "not on the basis of foreseen faith, of the obedience of faith, of holiness, or of any other good quality and disposition," for that would amount to works-righteousness. His comments on Ephesians 1:4 show that he has a different interpretation from Dort on "he chose us (not because we were, but) so that we should be holy and blameless before him in love."

c. Dort, Remaining Articles

If the term "unmerited grace" were substituted for "election," Wesley would hold especially dear Dort articles 13 and 14 on assurance and its fruits.

In their awareness and assurance of this election, God's children daily find greater cause to humble themselves before God, to adore the fathomless depth of his mercies, to cleanse themselves, and to give fervent love in return to him who first so greatly loved them. This is far from saying that this teaching concerning election, and reflection upon it, make God's children lax in observing his commandments or carnally self-assured. By God's just judgment, this does usually happen to those who casually take for granted the grace of election or engage in idle and brazen talk about it but are unwilling to walk in the ways of the chosen.

By God's wise plan, this teaching concerning divine election has been proclaimed through the prophets, Christ himself, and the apostles, in Old and New Testament times, and has subsequently been committed to writing in the Holy Scriptures. Today it is also taught in God's church, for which it was specifically intended. This teaching must be set forth with a spirit of discretion in a godly and holy manner at the appropriate time and place without inquisitive searching into the hidden ways of the Most High. This must be done for the glory of God's most holy name and for the lively comfort of his people.

Wesley disagreed with much though not all of article 15 on reprobation, that God has decreed to leave sinners "in the common misery into which, by their own fault, they have plunged themselves; not to grant them saving faith and the grace of conversion; but finally to condemn and eternally punish them (having been left in their own ways and under his just judgment), not only for their unbelief but also for all their other sins, in order to display his justice." Wesley firmly held with Dort that God's just reprobation of sin does not at all make God the author of sin.

Wesley agrees with much of article 16, which says this:

> Those who do not yet actively experience within themselves a living faith in Christ or an assured confidence of heart, peace of conscience, a zeal for childlike obedience, and a glorying in God through Christ, but who nevertheless use the means by which God has promised to work these things in us — such people ought not to be alarmed at the mention of reprobation, nor to count themselves among the reprobate; rather they ought to continue diligently in the use of the means, to desire fervently a time of more abundant grace, and to wait for it in reverence and humility.

Ironically, Wesley's teaching on "children of believers" (article 17) is, excepting its double predestination premise, largely the same as Dort, that "by virtue of the gracious covenant in which they together with their parents are included, godly parents ought not to doubt the election and salvation of their children."

The purpose of this exercise is to make clear just how narrow and how wide is the "hair's breadth" from Calvinism. It is often taken to be infinitely wide, but this exercise shows that it is more limited than many critics have imagined.

E. A Dialogue between a Predestinarian and His Friend

1. Whether Sin Is Made a Necessity by Double Predestination

Addressed to predestinarians in a conversational style, Wesley is here approaching them as a friendly but tough-minded partner in dialogue. The text is found in "A Dialogue between a Predestinarian and His Friend" (J X:259 – 66).

The purpose of this dialogue is to answer predestinarians who in debate often claim that "that is not what predestinarians say." In order to counter this, Wesley uses direct quotes from leading Reformed writings (notably Zwingli,[109] Calvin,[110] the Westminster Catechism, Peter Martyr,[111] Jerome Zanchius,[112] Johannes Piscator,[113] and William Twisse[114]) as a composite of predestinarian partners in dialogue. All were respected spokespersons for Reformed teaching on predestination.

[109]"On Divine Providence," B 2:534 – 50.

[110]*Institutes* 1.16.3, 8; 1.17.5; 3.23.1 – 2, 6; 3.24.8, 12 – 13.

[111]Commentary on Romans.

[112]"On the Nature of God."

[113]"Disputation on Predestination."

[114]*Vindiciae Gratiae Potestatis et Providentiae Dei*, 3, 22.

a. Does God Make Sin Necessary?

Wesley identifies the central premise of absolute predestination according to its own key sources: that God from eternity ordained all that has come to pass, with no exceptions, extending also to human actions.[115] Calvin wrote, "The wills of men are so governed by the will of God that they are carried on straight to the mark which he has foreordained."[116]

The consequent trend of such an argument tends to make sin a necessity. According to this argument, God made Adam and Eve for the very purpose that they would be tempted and fall into sin. God's decree is grounded not in his foreknowledge but in his will. All but the elect are predestined by God to reprobation. Why does God call upon the reprobate to repent? Only that they may become more deaf and blind? If the number and identity of the reprobate are fixed before time, there can be no meaning in calling them to repentance.[117]

The predestinarian is left with three options: to equivocate, to swallow all these assertions and honestly try to avow them, or to renounce them altogether, freely affirming free grace to all. Wesley had come to the conclusion that the first two required a sacrifice of both intellect and moral prudence.[118]

b. God Foresaw but Did Not Mandate the Fall

Wesley conceded that God foresaw the fall but not that he directly ordained it. God permitted but did not mandate the fall by divine decree.

It would indeed be a "horrible decree" if God preordained Adam's fall, or caused sin, or diminished the glory of God in the creation of human freedom.[119] Absolute unconditional election and reprobation cannot be found in Holy Writ. It bears the dismal fruit of the burning of Michael Servetus.[120]

Wesley contrasted the permissive will of God, which places the responsibility for rebellion and possibility of obedience squarely on the human agent who willfully shuns or embraces the compassionate and universal offer of grace, with the predestinarian assertion of the irresistibility of God's will. If the fall occurred "not only by the permission, but also by the appointment of God,"[121] then sin occurs by necessity.

c. Reclaiming the Pre-Augustinian Consensual Tradition

More subtle and more difficult to argue is the pre-Augustinian Eastern patristic teaching of free grace meeting free will. Wesley was not inventing this interpretation but reincorporating it within the Protestant teaching of justification through grace by faith, which becomes active in love.

---

[115]DPF, J X:260.
[116]Calvin, *Institutes* 1.16.8.
[117]DPF, J X:259–64.
[118]DPF, J X:260.
[119]DPF, J X:261–62; *JJW* 6:131.
[120]DPF, J X:266.
[121]DPF, J X:261, quoting Calvin, *Institutes* 3.24.8.

The pre-Nicene teaching of grace gently coaxing freedom was rediscovered in the eighteenth century by Wesleyan evangelicalism. Wesley realized that Protestants who resist the inconsistencies of predestination are likely to be stereotyped wrongly as "semi-Pelagians," who ignore the absolute necessity of grace. He warned that those who are afraid of hard names are probably going to be averse to discipleship.

When Calvinists appealed to a hyper-Augustinian mode of anti-Pelagian exegesis, Wesley had ready a counterappeal to the Eastern church fathers before Pelagius (Clement of Alexandria, Origen, Athanasius, and the early Augustine). Those who wish to see Christian theology in its most mature and pristine stage must search in the sources prior to Augustine's belated fifth-century fight with Pelagianism. They must go beyond the fifth-century Western Latin tradition of divinity to an earlier period.

The Pelagian challenge rightly required an astute rejoinder. Augustine answered it deftly. But for a broader corrective to less heinous excesses, we must look to the pre-Augustinian consensus of antiquity as stated by Irenaeus, John Chrysostom, Gregory of Nyssa, and Gregory Nazianzen. This was a form of argument familiar to the early Eastern and Western orthodox traditions, and especially valued by the Anglican tradition by which Wesley had been nurtured.

In its extreme form, the double decrees of predestinarianism, as well as the modern determinists, seemed to Wesley to have more affinity to Islamic determinism than Augustine's view. For the first four centuries of church history, the Eastern church was against all views of fixed determinism.[122] "Augustine speaks sometimes for [absolute double predestination] and sometimes against it. But all antiquity for the four first centuries is against [it], as is the whole Eastern Church to this day; and the Church of England, both in her Catechism, Articles, and Homilies. And so are divers of our most holy Martyrs, Bishop Hooper and Bishop Latimer in particular."[123]

In an evangelical environment arguably dominated by nonconformists and Dissenters, Wesley was once again appealing to the ancient Christian consensus before Pelagius's outrageous remarks elicited Augustine's retaliation.

2. "The Consequence Proved"

In "The Consequence Proved" (1771; J X:370–74), Wesley responded to a tract written by predestinarian Augustus Toplady, which asserted that "one in twenty, suppose, of mankind are elected; nineteen in twenty are reprobated. The elect shall be saved, do what they will; the Reprobate shall be damned, do what they can."[124]

When an outcry emerged "that no such consequence follows from the doctrine of absolute predestination," Wesley followed Toplady's argument through to

[122]*LS*, pt. 2.

[123]DPF, J X:265. According to Chrysostom, Judas had been earlier "a child of the kingdom" who had received the promise from Jesus himself, "but afterwards he became a child of hell" by his own willful choice, so even Judas was not predestined to reprobation.

[124]"The Consequence Proved," J X:370.

its logical conclusion: "I calmly affirm, it is a fair state of the case; this consequence does naturally and necessarily follow" as stated by Toplady.

If God's love is unconditional and immutable, and election is fixed, the nonelect cannot be reprobated for sins "they never had.... For it cannot be a sin in a spark to rise, or in a stone to fall."[125] If it was never "in their power to love God and their neighbor," how can they be held responsible? Their unbelief cannot reasonably be termed "obstinate" if they never had a possibility of removing it. "How then can the Judge of all the earth consign them to everlasting fire, for what was in effect his own act and deed?"[126]

Wesley from youthful days had an allergic reaction to double predestination: "I never did believe it, nor the doctrines connected with it, no, not for an hour. In this, at least, I have been consistent with myself.... I believe no decree of reprobation.... I believe no decree of preterition.... I do not believe ... any such absolute election, as implies that all but the absolutely elect shall inevitably be damned.... I do not believe the doctrine ... of infallible perseverance.... I do not believe salvation by works."[127]

F. Serious Thoughts upon the Perseverance of the Saints

Faith active in love is the sole condition for God's fulfillment of his covenant promise of salvation to the believer. Can a believer who has been justified return to a state of nature as if prior to justification and annul the effects of justifying grace in his life? Answering presents "great difficulties."[128] The issue is resolved only by careful examination of texts that admit of debatable interpretations. Some of these are examined in "Serious Thoughts upon the Perseverance of the Saints [(1751) J X:284–98].

1. Whether a Believer Can Make a Shipwreck of Faith

God's covenant with Israel was conditional on the people keeping God's law. The point is realistically stated in Ezekiel: "But if a righteous person turns from their righteousness and commits sin and does the same detestable things the wicked person does, will they live? None of the righteous things that person has done will be remembered. Because of the unfaithfulness they are guilty of and because of the sins they have committed, they will die" (Ezek. 18:24 NIV).

Paul speaks of those who holding to faith and having had a good conscience, have made a shipwreck of their faith (1 Tim. 1:18–19). Shipwreck is a metaphor of total loss.[129] "He that believeth shall be saved" does not imply that one cannot cease

[125]"The Consequence Proved," J X:372.
[126]"The Consequence Proved," J X:373–74.
[127]"Some Remarks of Mr. Hill's 'Review of All the Doctrines Taught by Mr. John Wesley,'" J X:379.
[128]"Serious Thoughts upon the Perseverance of the Saints," J X:285.
[129]"Serious Thoughts upon the Perseverance of the Saints," J X:287.

to believe, having once believed. Those who believe and continue believing in faith active in love "shall be saved; he that believeth not," if he continue in unbelief, "shall be damned."[130]

2. The Falling Away of Believers

Wesley's argument on perseverance is based on his understanding of the *saint* (*chasid, hagios*, Heb. *chasid)*, namely one

who loves the Lord (Ps. 31:23)
whose way God preserves (Prov. 2:8)
whose death is precious to the Lord (Ps. 116:15)
set apart from the profane world
endued with the faith that purifies the heart
who maintains a good conscience
grafted into the good olive tree, the church
who is a branch of the true vine, Christ
who so effectually knows Christ as to have escaped the pollutions of the world
who sees the light of the glory of God in the face of Jesus Christ
who, having been made a partaker of the fruits of the Holy Spirit, lives by faith in the Son, sanctified by the blood of the covenant[131]

Such is the saint, according to Scripture. But can such a saint *fall away* from faith? By falling away, he means that a believer may not only fall into occasional sin, but fall so far as to perish everlastingly.

Each of these above elements of the scriptural definition of the *hagios* is conditional upon faith, whose ground is sufficiently supplied by grace. One must continue in faith, not having faith just at one moment, but continually in time (1 Tim. 1:18–19). God who alone is unchangeable will carry out his promise to enable purity of heart to grow on the condition of faith.

One who has been baptized into the church can fall away. One who has served splendidly as a branch of the True Vine can be cut off (John 15:1–6). One who has begun responding to sanctifying grace can fall from that grace (Heb. 6:4, 6; 10:26–29). Wesley concludes that "a saint may fall away" having believed, so as finally to perish.[132]

No promise of God is ever offered so unconditionally that the response one makes to it is irrelevant. No promise can be claimed until the condition is met: "perform the condition, and the promise is sure. Believe, and thou shalt be saved."[133]

God's righteousness is not found exclusively in forensic and imputed metaphors, but also is at work through the nurturant metaphors, working behaviorally toward

[130]"Serious Thoughts upon the Perseverance of the Saints," J X:288.
[131]"Serious Thoughts upon the Perseverance of the Saints," J X:285.
[132]Ibid.
[133]"Serious Thoughts upon the Perseverance of the Saints," J X:290.

the making righteous of the believer, toward the fit maturation of those who believe. Wesley took the premise of grace much further into the dynamics of human freedom than did the continental Reformation, without relaxing a high view of God's sovereign grace or the depth of the human predicament.

3. Turning Away from God

a. Perseverance Conditional on Faith Active in Love

Jesus lamented Jerusalem's refusal of him (Luke 13:34). While the hyper-Augustinian tradition taught irresistible grace, the pre-Augustinian Eastern tradition insisted on human responsiveness to resistible grace. Otherwise Scripture could not meaningfully call the believer to avoid an "unbelieving heart that turns away from the living God" (Heb. 3:12 NIV). It was in this tradition that Wesley intentionally stood.[134]

"Not that I deny, that there are exempt cases, wherein 'The o'erwhelming power of saving grace' does, for a time, work as irresistibly as lightning."[135]

In a *Journal* entry of August 24, 1743, Wesley wrote lucidly on this point:

> That the grace which brings faith, and thereby salvation into the soul, is irresistible at that moment: That most believers may remember some time when God did irresistibly convince them of sin: that most believers do, at some other times, find God irresistibly acting upon their souls. Yet I believe that the grace of God, both before and after these moments, may be, and hath been, resisted; and that, in general, it does not act irresistibly; but we may comply therewith, or may not.[136]

The promises of salvation and perseverance are conditional on the continued reliance of the believer on preparatory, convicting, cooperating, and sanctifying grace. One forfeits the right to receive the promise when one ceases to have faith.[137] Wesley sought to preserve the scriptural teaching of the universal significance of the atonement without leading to an unscriptural assertion of the universality of faithful obedience.[138]

b. Assured of Perseverance as Long as Faith Persists

Believers are assured of their perseverance as long as they do not neglect the condition of the covenant: actively trusting in its promises.[139] It is not within human power to turn to God without grace, but it remains within human power to reject the grace offered.[140]

It is challenging enough for the infant to learn to walk but more challenging for

[134]*LJW* 5:83; B 2:489 – 90; *JJW* 3:85 – 86; JWO 427 – 28, 448 – 49, 468 – 69.
[135]"The General Spread of the Gospel," B 2:489, sec. 12.
[136]*JJW* 3:85.
[137]B 1:233 – 34; 3:156, 169; B 9:407; 11:398; *SS* 2:149.
[138]"Serious Thoughts upon the Perseverance of the Saints," J X:292 – 98.
[139]*LJW* 5:83.
[140]"Serious Thoughts upon the Perseverance of the Saints," J X:290 – 94.

the youth to stay on the arduous path through many temptations. Few are willing to stay the long journey.

On November 26, 1790, Wesley wrote to Adam Clarke: "To retain the grace of God is much more than to gain it; hardly one in three does this. And this should be strongly and explicitly urged on all who have tasted of perfect love. If we can prove that any of our local preachers or leaders, either directly or indirectly, speak against it, let him be a local preacher or leader no longer."[141]

Wesley did not want anyone in leadership in his connection who had serious doubts about the power of the Spirit completely to reshape human life. The teaching remains the centerpiece of Methodist revivalism.

4. Thoughts on Salvation by Faith

a. Why Unconditional Predestination Puts Faith in Jeopardy

In a mature reflection of 1779, "Thoughts on Salvation by Faith" (J XI:492 – 95), Wesley maintained that he and his brother had held to a fixed course for over forty years following Aldersgate on the centrality of "our constant theme": "By grace are ye saved through faith" (Eph. 2:8). "It was our daily subject, both in verse and prose ... we could hardly speak of anything else, either in public or private."[142] For this we were "stoned in the streets, and several times narrowly escaped with our lives ... and painted as unheard-of monsters."

Yet because they so emphasized faith active in works of love, the Wesleys were accused of salvation by works. But their steady purpose for forty years was to hold together salvation by grace through faith "so as not to contradict that other expression of the same apostle, 'Without holiness no man shall see the Lord.' "[143] Without "personal holiness ... none who is not himself conformed to the law of God here, 'shall see the Lord' in glory." This is apostolic testimony that "all the labored evasions of Witsius" cannot invalidate.[144]

b. The Unconditional Decree Excludes Both Faith and Works

Wesley was puzzled about the all-or-nothing tendency within predestination teaching "when a thought shot across my mind, which solved the matter at once: 'This is the key: Those that hold everyone is absolutely predestinated either to salvation or damnation see no medium between salvation by works and salvation by absolute decrees.' It follows, that whosoever denied salvation by absolute decrees, in so doing (according to this apprehension) asserts salvation by works."[145] It would be a peculiarly myopic exegesis to conclude that anyone who denies predestination must be asserting salvation by works.

Wesley shrewdly reasoned that *if salvation is by absolute decree, it is not by*

[141] Letter to Adam Clarke, November 26, 1790, *LJW* 3:633.
[142] "Thoughts on Salvation by Faith," J XI:492 – 93.
[143] TSF, J XI:495.
[144] Letter to James Hervey, *LJW* 3:383.
[145] TSF, J XI:493, quotation marks amended.

works, but neither can it be by faith, "for unconditional decree excludes faith as well as works."[146] If one admits to the scriptural condition that "he that believeth shall be saved," then there must be an element of free, responsible cooperation in the work of grace, for there is no faith that does not work by love freely responding to grace.[147]

This is why "we must expect, all who hold unconditional decrees will say [that] we teach salvation by works," since their premise prevents them from conceiving a third alternative.[148] He concluded that "none shall finally be saved by any faith but that which worketh by love both inward and outward holiness."[149] In this way, classical Christian teaching "stands opposite to the doctrine of the *antinomians* on the one hand, and to that of *justification by works* on the other."[150]

Further Reading on Predestination

Cell, George Croft. "The Very Edge of Calvinism." In *The Rediscovery of John Wesley*, 242 – 72. Reprint, New York: University Press of America, 1935.

Gunter, W. Steven. *The Limits of Divine Love: John Wesley's Response to Antinomianism and Enthusiasm.* Chap. 14, on conditional election, 227 – 67. Nashville: Kingswood, Abingdon, 1989.

Pinnock, H. Clark, ed. *A Case for Arminianism.* Grand Rapids: Zondervan, 1989.

Rack, Henry. "Horrible Decrees." In *Reasonable Enthusiast*, 420 – 71. London: Epworth, 1989.

Shipley, David C. "Wesley and Some Calvinist Controversies." *Drew Gateway* 25, no. 4 (1955): 195 – 210.

Walls, Jerry L. "The Free Will Defense: Calvinism, Wesley, and the Goodness of God." *Christian Scholar's Review* 13 (1983): 19 – 33.

[146]TSF, J XI:494.
[147]Ibid.
[148]Ibid.
[149]TSF, J XI:495.
[150]FA, pt. 1, B 11:111, sec. 2.4.

CHAPTER 7

The Doctrine of Salvation by Faith

Soter is the Greek word for Savior, and soteriology is the study of salvation. Wesley seldom used professional terms like *soteriology*. He was committed to plain speaking for ordinary people. But in practice his most important contributions were on the teaching of salvation.

We have previously discussed Christology. This chapter takes us further into the saving work of Jesus Christ.

Wesley's first forty-four homilies were later designated Standard Sermons and considered normative for teaching in the Wesleyan connection of spiritual formation. Most of these focus explicitly on the basic themes of salvation. He called for a present, deliberate decision in response to God's gracious action.

Wesley neither sought nor pretended to make any novel contribution to a Christian theory of salvation. All key questions of salvation teaching were in his view apostolically derived and clarified in the ancient ecumenical consensus. They have survived relatively intact through centuries of challenge. Wesley resolved only to magnify experientially the moral, personal, and societal outworkings of the biblical calling of God to repentance and faith.

Step-by-step Wesley clarified how one estranged from God is drawn from the natural man (living according to nature) to the legal man (living according to the law) and to the evangelical man (living according to the gospel). This distinction is our point of entry into his soteriology.

A. Grace Moves through Three Stages

1. Natural Man, Legal Man, and Evangelical Man

a. The Spirit of Bondage and of Adoption

The text of Wesley's powerful and poetic homily "The Spirit of Bondage and of Adoption" is Romans 8:15: "Ye have not received the spirit of bondage again to fear; but ye have received the Spirit of adoption, whereby we cry, 'Abba, Father' " [Homily #9 (1746), B 1:248 – 66; J #9, V:98 – 111]. It was preached from his father's tombstone and is all about saying, "Abba."

This is among the most important of Wesley's discourses and is worthy of intensive study to grasp structurally the argument of a whole series of crucial teaching homilies on salvation. Much else will fall into place for readers who grasp its core design.

The unconscious form of the spirit of bondage is the natural state, the conscious form is the legal state, and the spirit of adoption is the evangelical condition of being adopted into the family of God as child of the Father. The text, Romans 8:15, assumes a three-stage transit of human existence, the first of which is natural self, in which the bulk of humanity dwells.[1]

Learning as a sinner to say from the heart, "Father," is central to the freedom of the Christian life. This personal address belongs to evangelical existence. But how does one make the unlikely move from the unconscious condition of sin through sin-consciousness to the joy of faith, hope, and love?[2]

b. The Human Condition: Natural Man

The organization of the homily follows a classic Pauline-Augustinian sequence of three basic phases of the maturation of the human condition: natural, legal, and evangelical (see chart on pages 193–94).

Augustine had previously analyzed the threefold transition from the capacity of natural reason in its fallenness to servitude under the divine requirement, to freedom in Christ.[3] Luther had similarly analyzed the passage from the natural fallen condition of unawareness of sin to bondage under the law, to humanity under grace.[4]

Strictly speaking, in Luther there are only two uses of the law: to curb sin and to lead to a recognition of sin. But the Formula of Concord set forth three uses of the law in article 6: that "thereby outward discipline might be maintained against wild, disobedient men [and that wild and intractable men might be restrained, as though by certain bars]"; that "men thereby may be led to the knowledge of their sins"; and that "after they are regenerate ... they might ... have a fixed rule according to which they are to regulate and direct their whole life"[5] These three correspond largely to Wesley's sequence from natural, to legal, to evangelical existence.

Calvin similarly wrote of three uses of the law. It works (1) by "exhibiting the righteousness of God — in other words, the righteousness which alone is acceptable to God — it admonishes every one of his own unrighteousness, certifies, convicts, and finally condemns him."[6] (2) It acts "by means of its fearful denunciations and the

---

[1]"The Spirit of Bondage and of Adoption," B 1:250, sec. 1.3.
[2]"The Spirit of Bondage and of Adoption," B 1:249, proem 1.
[3]*The Spirit and the Letter.*
[4]Martin Luther, *The Freedom of a Christian, MLS,* 42–85; for further reference to Luther by Wesley, see *JJW* 1:409, 467, 475; B 2:78, 556–57; 3:335, 449, 505; 11:318–19; JWO 366–67.
[5]Triglot Concordia, Formula of Concord, Epitome 6.1.
[6]Calvin, *Institutes* 2.7.6.

consequent dread of punishment to curb those who, unless forced, have no regard for rectitude and justice."[7] (3) "The third use of the Law ... has respect to believers in whose hearts the Spirit of God already flourishes and reigns.... For it is the best instrument for enabling them daily to learn with greater truth and certainty what that will of the Lord is which they aspire to follow, and to confirm them in this knowledge."[8]

Those who have had the privilege of reading *Kierkegaard* will recall his three basic stages along life's way: the aesthetic pleasure-principle stage, the ethical-choice stage, and religious consciousness, which deals primarily with the problem of suffering (with religious consciousness A as the pathos of the natural religion expressed by Socrates, and religious consciousness B as the evangelical consciousness of those whose life is hid in Christ).[9] Wesley preceded Kierkegaard in astutely analyzing the psychological dynamics of these transitions.

Tillich's language may be used to translate the same sequence, moving from autonomous human existence unaware of its estrangement to the heteronomous awakening of awareness of estrangement from oneself, and finally toward the theonomous capacity to enter into estrangement without being estranged, wherein one accepts one's acceptance, grounding oneself in the ground of being, so that one is no longer estranged from oneself, even though the remnants of estrangement may continue.[10]

c. Wesley's Treatment of This Progression from Natural to Legal to Evangelical Life

The following table conveys the essential elements of Wesley's version of the three stages. Those who take more than a glimpse to grasp these correlations will find the rest of the doctrine of salvation a snap. It is worthwhile to meditate on these stages, which will be further discussed below.

Three Stages of the Divine-Human Relationship

NATURAL The Spirit of Bondage	**LEGAL The Spirit of Bondage unto Fear**	**EVANGELICAL The Spirit of Adoption**
Aesthetic: What I want to do	Ethical: What I ought to do	Religious: What God does for me
Unaware of moral danger Sleeping	Aware of bondage as if facing an abyss Awakening	Aware of bondage being transcended Reposing

continued on next page.

[7]Ibid., 2.7.10.
[8]Ibid., 2.7.12.
[9]Sören Kierkegaard, *Stages along Life's Way* (Princeton, NJ: Princeton University Press, 1988).
[10]Paul Tillich, *Systematic Theology*, 3 vols. (Chicago: University of Chicago Press, 1951).

Continued previous page.

NATURAL The Spirit of Bondage	**LEGAL The Spirit of Bondage unto Fear**	**EVANGELICAL The Spirit of Adoption**
Attempted avoidance of suffering Lacking faith Autonomy Blameless lack of dread Easy self-ignorance	Tragic moral choices deepen suffering Faith of the servant Heteronomy Dreadful blame Odious self-knowledge	Joy amid suffering Faith of the son or daughter Theonomy Overcoming of dread by faith Gracious freedom
False peace of the naturalized self Fantasized liberty Wrestling in utter darkness Neither conquers nor fights Sins willingly	Internal war within the moral self Bondage Seeing the painful light of hell Fights but does not conquer Sins unwillingly	True peace of the reconciled self True liberty Beholding the joyous light of heaven Fights and conquers Does not sin willingly
Prevenient grace Neither loves nor fears God Naïveté Supposed freedom	Convicting grace Only fears God Death of naïveté Slavery to sin	Justifying grace Loves as God loves New birth Children of a new inheritance

A century before Kierkegaard and two before Tillich, Wesley had developed his own version of the stages along life's way, or three states of human existence, largely dependent on Pauline exegesis.

These stages appear in many of Wesley's writings, but no place more clearly than in "The Spirit of Bondage and of Adoption." The same sequential structure is evident in "The Almost Christian" and the altogether Christian;[11] the legalistic faith of the servant and the faith of the son adopted into the family of God; the righteousness of the law and the righteousness of faith. It recurs in crucial sermons on salvation by grace through faith, notably "Scriptural Christianity," "Justification by Faith," "The Witness of the Spirit," and "The New Birth."

In all of these homilies, Wesley was working primarily out of Paul's letter to Rome. Each of these classic interpreters is operating out of an exegetical memory of Romans 1 and 2, which begins with the natural human condition and natural reason then views the human condition under bondage to the law (Rom. 2 and 3); then the transition in 3:24ff. into evangelical existence, with the remainder of Romans setting forth new life in Christ. Wesley's focus is on Romans 8.

[11]See section 7 below; B 1:131 – 34.

2. Natural Man

a. The Natural State of Fallen Humanity

The characteristic feature of the natural condition in which sin has come to feel at home is a bondage that is unconscious of its plight, analogous to the state of moral sleep, or ethical unconsciousness — unawareness of any serious moral hazard.[12]

Think of a child playing near a cliff. Unawareness of the danger does not make the situation less dangerous, but more. This is the condition of the natural self. While one is playing perilously on the edge of a measureless moral abyss (final judgment), one remains totally unaware of it. The abyss is the righteousness of the requirement of God impinging on all actions.

A powerful series of metaphors (family alienation, legal condemnation, spiritual death) rhetorically illumine ways in which in actual history all human progeny have together fallen from their created nature into a relentless chronicle of sin.[13] By seeking only pleasure and evading any awareness of personal accountability, the falsely naturalized fallenness of the self follows hedonic criteria, remains morally unserious about oneself, not yet having come to any recognition of one's actual moral condition before God or any serious realization of one's own self-deceptions.[14]

In this naturalized condition of fallen humanity, the self reclines in complete unawareness of the judgment and claim of God, hence remains largely unaware of its very self. There is no dread of moral inadequacy, much less of divine justice, no anxiety about moral insolvency. One does not have enough understanding of oneself even to stand in awe of the divine claim. The imagination fancies itself blameless. The prevailing presumption is of innate goodness, canopied under a self-congratulatory attitude that converges around one's own achievements.[15]

b. The Sleep of Moral Ignorance

This "natural man" (or woman) remains ethically asleep. There is no consciousness of moral jeopardy. This person experiences life as secure and peaceful, feeling nothing awry. There is no thought that one is harming anyone else, no awareness of any deep structural or familial or national or cultural brokenness, no hint of any unretraceable lostness.[16]

This chronically fallen condition is rightly described as a condition of "ignorance" in which one is uninformed of oneself as a morally problematic being. Wesley thought that this ignorance never glares so strongly as in persons of learning, among whom he had spent so much of his life (1716 – 46).[17] The ethos of the

[12]B 2:19; cf. Sören Kierkegaard, *The Sickness unto Death: A Christian Psychological Exposition for Upbuilding and Awakening*, Kierkegaard's Writings, vol. 19 (Princeton, NJ: Princeton University Press, 1983), pt. 1.

[13]Cf. B 1:250 – 55, 263 – 66, 401 – 2, 433 – 34; 2:76 – 77; 4:171 – 72.

[14]"The Spirit of Bondage and of Adoption," B 1:252, sec. 1.2.

[15]Ibid.

[16]"The Spirit of Bondage and of Adoption," B 1:249, sec. 1.1.

[17]"The Spirit of Bondage and of Adoption," B 1:253, sec. 1.4.

university tends to accentuate this ignorance inasmuch as it may be the least likely place to become aware of the depth of one's own moral bankruptcy. More education does not of itself offer a solution to this dilemma but may reinforce its hubris. Nowhere are people more confident of themselves morally than in academia, where the imagination prevails that inveterate sinners are perfectly capable of thinking of themselves as having the unhindered capacity to talk rationally about their abilities and freedom and their capacity to reason their way out of the human predicament through education, cleverness, and invention.

c. The Dead Soul

To "men of reason" (the knowledge elite) Wesley spoke bluntly: "Your soul is utterly dead in sin, dead in pride, in vanity, in self-will, in sensuality, in love of the world. You are utterly dead to God. There is no intercourse between your soul and God.... You have no spiritual 'sense exercised to discern spiritual good and evil.'... My soul is distressed for you ... you are 'seeking death in the error of your life.'"[18]

Such is "natural" humanity—natural in the sense of the fallen nature. The natural man dwells in a chronic sense of deluded self-congratulation about human wisdom and goodness. His focus is on natural gratification, ego strength, and self-affirmation, guided confidently by the pleasure principle and the avoidance of pain. One is likely to think of oneself at this stage as a good person, expecting others to think well of him.[19]

Wesley used biting irony to describe this natural man clothed in self-deceit, who understands himself to be free from vulgarity, prejudice, enthusiasm, bigotry, and superstition. He fancies himself as walking in a kind of natural liberty, as a freely self-actualizing person. Such are the imaginations of the natural self, largely unaware of the turbulent history of sin.

d. Raising the Consciousness of the Self-Deceiver

Put in terms of modern social-location thinking, one remains quite unaware of one's social sin, racism, cultural prejudices, gender-centricity, or expressions of economic interest. One does not see how deeply enmeshed one is in these self-deceptions. There is no personal sense of alienation from the neighbor, much less the neighbor's Creator. If a serious or disturbing thought comes, one finds a way of bypassing it.[20] It never occurs to him that he himself is the person who is stumbling toward death.[21]

There is no striving against sin, because there is no recognition of oneself as a sinner. Wesley thought this condition characterized the bulk of humanity—a state of moral numbness, of relative unconsciousness.

Such a person may be a nominally religious person, a quite decent sinner, a

[18]EA, sec. 50–51, B 11:64; cf. JWO 49–50, 128–29, 405.
[19]"The Spirit of Bondage and of Adoption," B 1:253, sec. 1.5.
[20]"The Spirit of Bondage and of Adoption," B 1:253–54, sec. 1.6.
[21]"The Spirit of Bondage and of Adoption," B 1:254, sec. 1.7.

person who attends religious services and displays the form of godliness though not its power, whose consciousness of sin is so slight as to be unregisterable on any scale.[22] "Consciousness raising" for Wesley is a radical movement from natural unawareness of sin toward growing moral awareness.[23] At this stage one neither loves nor fears God.

How does it happen that the moral drifter moves toward becoming morally serious? Each person's story is unique.[24]

3. Legal Man: Life under the Law

a. By Some Awful Providence God Touches the Heart

"By some awful providence, or by His word applied with the demonstration of His Spirit, God touches the heart of him that lay asleep in darkness and in the shadow of death." Something happens to shake the sleeper out of this moral stupor. The eyes of moral understanding are suddenly open to how one is colluding with corruption, injustice, and inhumanity.[25]

A horrid light breaks in upon the soul, as if gleaming from a bottomless pit. Awareness of one's sin is magnified when understood in the presence of one whose holiness is a consuming fire. God's justice is first glimpsed then relentlessly beheld as an all-encompassing conflagration.[26] Though once at peace, now errant freedom is increasingly grieved. This trouble is itself a maturation process. At long last moral awareness is making some headway. Having been lulled into a false peace, one is now impelled toward a consciousness of danger.

The possibility of repentance emerges. The need for vast change is dreadfully grasped. A hint of contrition is beginning to dawn by providential grace. This may be a phlegmatic process or an abrupt event. The cycle is extremely variable, here in a moment, there by degrees. There is no way to predict how providence will move in one's life to spur one toward repentance. Not everyone makes the transition. Some who glimpse the edge of the precipice pretend they see nothing.

b. A Fearful Thing to Fall into the Hands of the Living God

The pith of legal consciousness: I behold each of my actions as if standing in the presence of the Holy One who intends to render judgment according to my works on the final day for every idle word, for all the false imaginations of my heart. The most secret recesses of my soul are easily penetrated by God's holy knowing. Nothing is hidden from its light. It is a fearful thing to fall into the hands of the living God.

The gravity and magnitude of God's requirement is now grasped in a way that

[22]B 1:688 – 91; 3:313 – 14; 4:57 – 58; 11:63 – 64, 237 – 40, 251 – 52, 258 – 60, 483 – 84; *CH*, B 7:188 – 93, 194 – 200; FA, B 11:250 – 51, 268, 273.

[23]B 1:330n.

[24]"The Spirit of Bondage and of Adoption," B 1:254 – 55, sec. 1.7 – 8.

[25]"The Spirit of Bondage and of Adoption," B 1:255, sec. 2.1; cf. 2:4, sec. 4.1.

[26]"The Spirit of Bondage and of Adoption," B 1:255, sec. 2.1; cf. 5:443.

was never before recognized under the conditions of hedonic, natural dreaming. The law teaches what God requires, what we ought to do, without imparting the power to do it. Not only does the law require "Thou shall not commit adultery" as an outward act, but inwardly. "Thou shall not kill" is intensified inwardly when it calls me to deal with the causes of my anger. The law itself, intended for good, in the hands of the sinner merely moves me into a deepened syndrome of self-alienation.

God is not fooled by the self-deception that has prevented me from seeing myself. I recognize that the whole self is sick, the whole heart faint.[27] A floodlight is shining on my sin. It is not shining on God's mercy at this point. I feel myself to be naked, as if all things were open to him with whom I have to do, all pretenses cut through. Everything in me is exposed, open to the All-Knowing One with whom no chicanery is possible. Whereas previously I had felt clothed in a kind of fantasy of innocence, now I experience radical vulnerability, with fig leaves stripped away.[28]

c. The Awakening of Guilt

From this follows one of Wesley's most searching psychological descriptions of the dynamics of emerging guilt. His most stunning visual metaphor of the law-judgment syndrome is his fantasy of himself as being *cleft asunder* as in a sacrifice, as if the piercing requirement of God were literally splitting him apart, opening up the whole self.[29]

Consciousness becomes trapped in a whirling entanglement of guilt and fear of punishment.[30] No matter how one strives to improve, one is drawn further into its vortex. Amid this anguish and guilt, one senses with the psalmist that "there is no one who does good, not even one" (Ps. 14:3 NIV; cf. Rom. 3:10). The law is breathing down our necks so heavily as to expose every recess of sin. It presses at every point, outwardly concerning our behavior and inwardly concerning our motivations, never giving respite.

d. The Spirit of Bondage unto Fear

It is this condition that Paul called *the spirit of bondage unto fear*, where one is captive to the alienating forces of guilt and dread. One experiences "paradigmatic guilt,"[31] where even some trivial value negation becomes symbolic of one's whole life-alienation, where some trivial event reflects the total guilt that I feel in the cosmos. A small slice of experience serves as a window upon the vast burden of human history's guilt.

What has happened to the exultant freedom of will I once thought I had as my natural hedonic self? Aware of my imprisonment by my own will, I feel the anguish

[27]"The Spirit of Bondage and of Adoption," B 1:255 – 56, sec. 2.2.

[28]"The Spirit of Bondage and of Adoption," B 1:255 – 56, sec. 2.2 – 3.

[29]"The Spirit of Bondage and of Adoption," B 1:256, sec. 2.3. As one who has been cleft asunder in open-heart surgery, I find this an especially poignant metaphor.

[30]*SS* 2:246 – 48, 261.

[31]See Thomas C. Oden, *The Structure of Awareness* (New York: Abingdon, 1969), pt. 1, chaps. 2 – 3 on paradigmatic guilt.

of a wounded spirit. The pleasures I once loved, I take no delight in. They pall upon the taste. There is a nausea that pervades this syndrome of vulnerability, fear of punishment, fear of death, despair of lostness in the clutches of the demonic, sorrowing over blessings lost, the feeling of being cursed to remorse and despair. Now I feel condemned, despairing over any capacity to change myself, fearing final judgment of the just Judge. Having fallen from the former blithe unawareness of sin, this intense awareness is felt as slavery to despair.[32]

This is legal consciousness, humanity under the law. Working out of Romans 7, Wesley does not hold back in his description of the human predicament under the law. Under bondage to the law, I am in a prison of my own making. The more I struggle against my fetters, the more I feel my bondage. I bite at the chains but do not break them.[33] I picture myself trying to climb out of this morass by following the law perfectly, to get myself back to square one of the original condition that was lost. But the law proves too encompassing. I never quite fulfill it. Before the eternal Holy One, I am always inadequate — the same despair Luther described in "The Bondage of the Will."[34]

e. O Wretched Man That I Am!

"O wretched man that I am! who shall deliver me from the body of this death? I thank God through Jesus Christ our Lord.... There is therefore now no condemnation to them which are in Christ Jesus, who walk not after the flesh, but after the Spirit" (Rom. 7:24 – 8:1).[35]

Only on this recognition is one prepared to hear this good news, though one may have heard it prosaically a thousand times. Only at the point of feeling the depth of this personal condemnation is one able to grasp the relevance of God's atoning work, and that it is *for me. Me.*

Those who have not been through the rigor of this personal moral awakening, who have never stood under the judgment of God, are not yet sufficiently formed by convicting grace to hear the gospel. The verdict of pardon is only pertinent to one who is standing guilty before the judge. The good news is of an unmerited act of pardon.[36]

4. Evangelical Existence: Humanity under Grace

a. From the Curse of the Law to the Glory of the Gospel

The Spirit of convicting grace draws us toward justifying grace.[37] The possibility of repentance matures precisely as one takes seriously the depth of this alienation.

[32]"The Spirit of Bondage and of Adoption," B 1:257, sec. 2.6; 2:233 – 35; 3:211 – 26.
[33]"The Spirit of Bondage and of Adoption," B 1:257 – 59, sec. 2.6 – 9.
[34]*MLS*, 166 – 207; *SS* 2:255.
[35]"The Spirit of Bondage and of Adoption," B 1:258, sec. 2.8.
[36]"The Spirit of Bondage and of Adoption," B 1:258 – 60, sec. 2.9 – 10.
[37]B 1:200 – 201, 291 – 92, 350 – 52, 477 – 81; 2:22 – 23; 3:204; *CH* 7:180 – 84, 210 – 34; *SS* 1:185 – 86, 257.

At some point, by some providential circumstance, the way of repentance is offered to those who have experienced the sting of the law. This is not possible for the "natural man."

This new life is offered in a timely, hearable way. It normally is offered when the Word is clearly preached or the Scripture read under the guidance of the Spirit.

By pardon I am offered the possibility of cutting to the root of sin, going right to the source of it. I receive the good news by renouncing the whole sordid life of this former bondage. I receive new life by repenting and believing.

Only then is it possible for this bondage to end so that the believer is no more trapped in the life of sin. There is no condemnation; the new life is under grace. Every day lived under grace is the life of one who is daily finding the favor of God within God's own way of righteousness.[38]

b. How Does This Happen?

How does it occur that one moves beyond this desperate pit into new life? God's justifying action reaches into the middle of this human condition.

God takes responsibility for us in our sin, becoming sin for us in the sense that in his sacrifice on the cross he takes our sin upon himself. We share in that death, the death of Christ, and in his resurrection.

Faith is affirmative response, a yea-saying to that grace offered to all through the cross.

What happens on the cross is a finished act. By the Spirit it becomes imparted by a grace-enabled free response. Trust in unmerited grace is the first step toward a full life of response to God.[39] It constitutes a new birth of spiritual life.[40]

c. A Reprise of the Stages along Life's Way

The fallen and naturalized self neither loves nor fears God. The legal self only fears God. The evangelical self under grace can now love as God has loved us, becoming a child of God, not merely a servant. The bondage is overcome by divine grace, whereby a new relation to God beyond law is made possible.

This is the center of Wesley's teaching of God's saving action, unfolding in three stages of the work of grace.

d. Salvation and Baptism

In volume 3, Wesley's teaching of baptism will be examined, but for now we note that the command of God is not only to repent and believe, but to repent, believe, and be baptized (Acts 2:38). To be baptized means to participate by grace in the death and resurrection of Jesus Christ. By baptism the faithful enter into new life in the Spirit. As children of the Father and not merely servants in the Father's

[38]"The Spirit of Bondage and of Adoption," B 1:258 – 60, sec. 2.9 – 10; *CH* 7:201 – 10.
[39]B 1:118, 404, 662 – 63; 2:167; 3:119; 4:26.
[40]"The Spirit of Bondage and of Adoption," B 1:260 – 63, sec. 3.

house, they share in adoption as sons and daughters in the family of God. Baptism begins this life.

By receiving Holy Communion again and again, this new life is nurtured. If baptism is analogous to birth, the Lord's Supper is analogous to a constant feeding of the reborn life, which bears the fruits of the Spirit.

5. The Spirit of Adoption

Adoption and assurance are closely linked teachings of the Wesleyan evangelical revival. The Spirit does not fail to attest our sonship and daughterhood when we receive justifying grace by faith. That is what the Spirit is communicating to us: we are children of this Abba, whose Son takes our sin upon himself. The Father accepts the self-offering of the Son for us.[41]

We thus are invited to move immediately and directly from the spirit of bondage to the spirit of adoption by which we enter into a new family on the premise of a new spiritual birth. We are no longer servants or slaves to sin, but children entering into an inheritance.[42] That inheritance, eternal life with God, is offered to be gladly received.

This adoption into the family of God is inwardly felt as a radical, assured gift, insofar as we listen to the testimony of the Spirit certified in the written Word and in our hearts. We are confident of the divine-human reconciliation by this testimony of the Holy Spirit witnessing within our own spirits that we are children of God, attesting the truth of the cross, the mission of the Son made known through the power of the Spirit.[43]

6. Evangelical Freedom

a. Light to Walk Freely

To live under the gospel is to experience oneself as free. This is not in a falsely fantasized liberty of moral ignorance, but a true liberty to love the neighbor grounded in pardon. It is not only liberty from guilt but also for the life of faith active in love that the cross makes credible. By this the power of sin is broken. Sin may remain in fragmented forms amid the redeemed life, but its primal vitality is broken. It has no power over the faithful though its consequences and effects lie strewn all about.[44]

Now there is no condemnation. Light shines upon the reconciled soul. God, who commanded light to shine, shines in the heart so as to attest the pardon of God. This is what Wesley designates evangelical life, life under grace, a new life of peace where one does not experience condemnation. This light shines from the spirit of adoption into the family of God.

Note that there is a surprising parallel of opposites between the natural and

[41]"The Spirit of Bondage and of Adoption," B 1:260–63, sec. 3.
[42]"The Spirit of Bondage and of Adoption," B 1:423–24; 3:497–500.
[43]"The Spirit of Bondage and of Adoption," B 1:260–63, sec. 3.
[44]Ibid.

evangelical stages — between the imagined liberty of the natural self and the true liberty of the evangelical self. The freedom lost in moral despair and ambiguity is now regained in a more profound form. The peace that had been dissipated is regained in a deeper form — *shalom*, reconciliation with God, ending the tyranny of guilt and remorse, overcoming the spirit of bondage unto fear.[45] The false peace of the natural self is contrasted with the true peace of the reconciled self.[46]

b. Abba, Father

This renewed person is enabled to call God "Abba." Every step of life becomes receivable as the gift of this Father. God is welcomed not solely as righteous Judge who places the radical claim of the law upon us, but as merciful, caring, disciplining, correcting, loving Abba.

God still is the Holy One whose requirement has not diminished, but now we understand that God has taken our sin upon himself by his active obedience to the law and by his suffering obedience on the cross in which we participate by faith. So we share in this new life of freedom, peace, light, truth, and pardon, clothed in the righteousness of Christ. All of these metaphors are taken captive to the truth made known on the cross.[47]

In this state of trust, I am now wholly at rest, though no longer in a moral daze. My eyes are realistically open to the history of sin, yet with the renewed serenity that comes from trusting God's pardon.

c. Preached from His Father's Gravestone

The sequence moves from ignorance of self to incriminating evidence of one's collusion with sin and finally toward liberating grace.

The pivotal homily "The Spirit of Bondage and of Adoption" was preached on June 10, 1742, at Epworth, where Wesley's father had served for years as parish priest. More strikingly, it was preached in the graveyard adjacent to the church, from his father's tombstone! It is about learning how to say, "Abba, Father." Wesley spoke about the reconciling love of his heavenly Father in loving and respectful recollection of his own father.

This is among the most theologically lucid of Wesley's homilies. It is filled with moving images: the sleep of the fallen state, the wretched man, light gleaming from a bottomless pit, the light to walk in freedom, the joy of the redeemed life.

It shows how conversion moves from deception to recognition and then to the glorious liberty of the sons and daughters of God, from *false peace to no peace to true peace.* Much of his revival preaching had to do precisely with clarifying these transitions.[48]

---

[45] *SS* 1:288.
[46] "The Spirit of Bondage and of Adoption," B 1:262, sec. 3.5.
[47] "The Spirit of Bondage and of Adoption," B 1:264, sec. 4.1.
[48] "The Spirit of Bondage and of Adoption," B 1:265 – 66, sec. 4.3 – 4.

7. The Distinction between Almost and Altogether

The memorable difference between the almost Christian and the altogether Christian is taken up in a homily on Acts 26:28: "Almost thou persuadest me to be a Christian" [Homily #2 (1741), B 1:131–41; J V:17–25].

The *almost* Christian has the form but not the power of godliness, as contrasted with the *altogether* Christian who walks daily in the way of evangelical life by the steady, habitual reception of justifying and sanctifying grace.[49] This is one of the most preachable of all Wesley's sermons.

Our text is the surprising comment of King Agrippa to Paul under arraignment.[50] Paul was preaching, and the king was listening. He answered: "Almost thou persuadest me to be a Christian." This prompted Wesley to explore the difference between almost and altogether hearing and believing in God's reconciling love.

a. The Almost Christian

The almost Christian has the *form* of piety and religion, but without its *power*. Its power flows from God's pardon and the spirit of holiness.[51]

This person may keep the sabbath, not lie, and do good, all with unflagging sincerity.[52] The almost Christian may be seeking a more just social order, not fornicating, not stealing, and this with all earnestness.[53] He may attend to public worship, receive the means of grace, and do no harm to anyone.

What is missing? A desire to serve God? No, that desire may be fervent. A strong sense of religious commitment? No, the sense of duty may be felt so strongly as to appear oppressive.[54] The fear and death accompanying the law is not Christianity.

Why then almost and not altogether a Christian? What is lacking is that which is necessary and sufficient to the Christian life: *full trust in God's merciful self-disclosure.*

b. What Is Lacking in the "Almost" Christian?

The almost Christian may come conceptually to the brink of evangelical existence and still never have felt the full import of what God has done for him. This person may appear to be a thoroughly decent person, even an intensely moral character. But something is missing.

Implied in being "almost a Christian" is that humane honesty found wherever people are paying attention to truth and justice, seeking fairness to all, telling the truth, and seeking to be attentive to the less fortunate. These qualities even

[49]"The Almost Christian," B 1:131–33, sec. 1; cf. "Scriptural Christianity," B 1:167, sec. 2.5; cf. FA, B 11:176, 267–68, 536–37.

[50]*JJW* 2:478; 3:484.

[51]"The Almost Christian," B 1:132, sec. 1.4; cf. "Hypocrisy in Oxford," B 4:400, sec. 2.2; cf. B 1:508; 2:465; 3:317.

[52]"The Spirit of Bondage and of Adoption," B 1:264, sec. 4.1.

[53]"The Almost Christian," B 1:135, sec. 1.9.

[54]"The Almost Christian," B 1:132, sec. 1.

Philistines expect of good persons.[55] "So true it is that the faith of a devil and the life of a heathen make up what most men call a good Christian!"[56]

For many years, Wesley himself lived with utmost rigor as an almost Christian, lacking the joy of saving grace. He pointed candidly to his own earlier demeanor as a prime example of the almost Christian.[57]

c. The Altogether Christian

The "altogether Christian" is infused with the love of God, which is always being made active and tangible in the love of the neighbor through faith. The Christian is one who altogether loves God, whose affections are wholly turned to the one who gives life.

Enabled by the undistracted *love of God*, one is free to view all other goods in relation to the one giver of all creaturely goods, each one of which is capable of being (precisely because good) falsely worshiped.

All loves are now loved in relation to the love of God. The love of God "engrosses the whole heart ... takes up all the affections ... fills the entire capacity of the soul, and employs the utmost extent of all its faculties," when one is "crucified to the world."[58]

d. Freedom to Love

The pardoning love of God frees me to give full attention to *the love of the neighbor*, the person who meets me next. Having been loved in a costly way by God as sinner, I am made ready to become radically responsive to the next one that comes along my path, the one I now see before me. I do not choose the neighbor. He meets me unexpectedly, happens to me, comes instantly before my eyes as a surprising gift. Person-to-person meeting occurs in joyful awareness of the final I-Thou meeting.[59]

The altogether Christian lives by *faith*, by trusting in God's own righteousness made known on the cross. Faith is not merely intellectual assent to an idea of God or conceptual proposition, but far more the immediate entrusting of oneself to a person, God the Son, Jesus Christ, by the power of the Spirit.[60] Faith is *the sure trust and confidence in God that by the merits of Christ my sins are forgiven and I*

[55]Ibid.

[56]"Hypocrisy in Oxford," B 4:399, sec. 1.9.

[57]"The Almost Christian," B 1:131 – 35, sec. 1; cf. *JJW*, January 29, 1738: "I who went to America to convert others, was never myself converted to God," but a note was added later: "I am not sure of this." In his January 4, 1739, journal entry, he repeated that he was "not a Christian now" in the sense that he was conscious that he had not yet attained to perfect love. Five months after Aldersgate he wrote to his brother: "I was not a Christian till the 24th of May last past" (assuming the distinction between the faith of a servant and the faith of a son). Cf. letter to Charles, June 17, 1766; and "In What Sense We Are to Leave the World," sec. 2.3.

[58]"The Almost Christian," B 1:137, sec. 2.1; Gal. 6:14.

[59]"The Almost Christian," B 1:138, sec. 2.2.

[60]"The Almost Christian," B 1:138 – 39, sec. 2.3 – 6.

am reconciled in favor with God.[61] Out of this confidence, there ensues a grateful spontaneous inclination to follow God's calling and receive God's gifts, insofar as it lies within my power.[62]

Faith has as its consequence a comprehensive reordering of life in a new birth in which the self is no longer locked into guilt and fear but freed to love the neighbor.[63] Such is the life of the altogether Christian who, being regenerated, is daily receiving new life in Christ.

B. Terms of Salvation

1. The Way to the Kingdom

The text of the homily on "The Way to the Kingdom" is Mark 1:15: "Repent ye and believe" [Homily #7 (1746), B 1:217 – 32; J #7, V:76 – 86].

The terms of salvation are repent and believe. Early in the gospel narratives, these terms are unambiguously stated: "The kingdom of God has come near. Repent and believe the good news!" (Mark 1:15 NIV). To those who sincerely ask about the way to the kingdom, Scripture answers directly: repent and believe.[64]

a. The Kingdom of God as True Religion

To ask about the kingdom of God is to ask about the nature of true religion, which is a heart right toward God and humanity.[65] The kingdom is true religion in practice, not merely as outward act, tenet, or doctrine.[66] True religion is behaviorally defined and is not adequately grasped in terms of outward ceremony, moral preachment, or conceptual argument about religion.[67]

The kingdom of God is not meat or drink or any exterior good or outward thing, but righteousness, joy, and peace in the Holy Spirit (Rom. 14:17).[68]

b. Love of God and Neighbor: Two Branches of True Religion

1. The first great branch of true religion is that *active love of God* that finds all one's happiness in God, delighting in the Lord, desiring none beside God, giving the whole heart to God without a rival.[69]

---

[61]"The Almost Christian," B 1:137 – 40, sec. 2; "The Doctrine of Salvation," "Faith and Good Works," sec. 14.

[62]B 1:418 – 19, 634 – 35, 9:101 – 2.

[63]"The Almost Christian," B 1:138 – 42, sec. 2; Gal. 5:6; "The Law Established through Faith, I," sec. 2.3.

[64]Preached from Wesley's father's tombstone, the first of the series of "tombstone sermons" at Epworth, June 6, 1742.

[65]B 1:217 – 25; 3:520.

[66]*LJW* 5:5.

[67]"The Character of a Methodist," sec. 1; "A Caution against Bigotry," sec. 2.3. That this does not imply theological indifferentism is evident from "The Doctrine of Original Sin," B 1:220n., secs. 3.1, 4.4.

[68]"The Way to the Kingdom," B 1:221, sec. 1.7; *LJW* 2:269 – 70; 8:218.

[69]"The Way to the Kingdom," B 1:221, sec. 1.7 – 8; "The Righteousness of Faith," sec. 2.9.

2. The second is to *love the neighbor* as oneself, every soul God has made, even those unseen, "not excepting him whom thou knowest to be evil and unthankful, him that still despitefully uses and persecutes thee," all to be loved "with the same invariable thirst after his happiness" just as one thirsts for one's own happiness.[70] Such love fulfills the law by an inward righteousness that is not puffed up and an outward righteousness that actively does good to all.[71]

c. Peace with God

The heart made right toward God and the neighbor empowers holiness, which welcomes and engenders happiness, for it begets peace and joy in the Holy Spirit (Rom. 14:17). This is a *peace* that only God can give and the world cannot take away, a peace that passes natural understanding because it is spiritually discerned, a peace that banishes fear. It is inwardly attested by the hushed witness of the Spirit that one is a child of God (Rom. 8:16).

Peace with God means reconciliation with the Holy One with whom one has been long estranged. This *shalom* is a key evidence of the kingdom of God and of true religion. Only God bestows this peace. Once bestowed it is not expended or depleted except by our own decision to ignore or reject it. Grace enables this peace to be sustained as long as faith is receptive to it.[72] It is a taste of the world to come. It enables a life of righteousness, peace, and joy, a blessed life that already anticipates the bliss that is to come eternally for those who love the Lord.[73]

d. Joy in Right Living

This peace brings *joy* wrought in the heart by the Holy Spirit, enabling that calm, humble delight in God that is made possible by the divine-human reconciliation effected on the cross. One is made happy by the awareness that one's sins are entirely covered by grace.[74]

Such happiness and holiness conjoined is an intimation of the reign of God. It is called the kingdom of God because God is reigning in our hearts. Those who allow God to set up his throne in their hearts find themselves instantly filled with righteousness, peace, and joy[75].

This kingdom is also called the kingdom of heaven because heaven is opening up our closed souls, coming to us in the Son who descends from heaven to bring us back with him to the presence of God the Father. This reign of God is at hand every instant. With the Son's coming, its time is fulfilled. It is not far away for those who repent and believe its promise.[76]

---

[70]"The Way to the Kingdom," B 1:222, sec. 1.8 – 9.
[71]FA, B 11:250 – 51, 268, 273; *CH*, B 7:194 – 200.
[72]B 1:349, 458, 477; 2:162; *SS* 2:394.
[73]"The Way to the Kingdom," B 1:231, sec. 2.11 – 13.
[74]"The Way to the Kingdom," B 1:223 – 24, sec. 1.11.
[75]"The Way to the Kingdom," B 1:224, sec. 1.12.
[76]Letter to a Gentleman at Bristol, January 6, 1758, *LJW* 3:246 – 48.

e. Repentance the Porch, Holiness the Temple of Religion

To repent one must first recognize oneself as sinner.[77] *Metanoia* is a 180-degree turning: from sin to grace.[78] Repentance involves that moral seriousness about oneself that readies the soul to turn joyfully to the mercy of God.[79] This is the first step to enter into the realm of the reign of God. In a letter to Thomas Church, Wesley summarized the way to salvation: "Our main doctrines, which include all the rest, are three — that of Repentance, of Faith, and of Holiness. The first of these we account, as it were, the porch of religion; the next, the door; the third, religion itself."[80] The temple itself is the holy life of faith active in love.[81]

1. "By *repentance* I mean conviction of sin, producing real desires and sincere resolutions of amendment."[82] By "*fruits* meet for repentance," Wesley means "forgiving our brother, ceasing from evil, doing good, using the ordinances of God, and in general obeying Him according to the measure of grace which we have received. But these I cannot as yet term good works, because they do not spring from faith and the love of God."[83]

2. Faith is distinguishable but not separable from repentance and showing the seriousness of repentance: "Although both repentance, and the fruits thereof, are in some sense necessary before justification, neither the one nor the other is necessary in the same sense, or in the same degree, with faith.... For none of these has so direct, immediate a relation to justification as *faith*."[84]

Faith is the reception of God's mercy. Faith is not bare intellectual assent, but trusting that the Word spoken on the cross and in the resurrection is for me, addressed personally to me, and able to change me thoroughly.

One who repents and believes has his feet already on the path to true religion, which is the love of God addressing us in the needs of the neighbor, where loving responsiveness is made possible through faith.[85]

Faith is necessary to justification, while "repentance remotely, as it is necessary to faith.... And the fruits of repentance still more remotely, as they are necessary to the increase or continuance of repentance. And even in this sense, they are only

---

[77]"The Way to the Kingdom," B 1:225, sec. 2.1; cf. "Of Repentance and Obedience," from discussion of Roman Catechism, J X:94 – 102; B 1:47, 245, 335 – 37, 403, 480 – 81, 653; 2:230 – 31; 4:299 – 300.

[78]Since *repentance* means a true and deep knowing of oneself, the further one progresses in the reception of sanctifying grace, the more aware one is of one's sin. See "The Righteousness of Faith," sec. 2.6; and "The Repentance of Believers."

[79]"The Way to the Kingdom," B 1:225 – 27, sec. 2.1 – 2; "The Righteousness of Faith"; cf. B 1:126 – 27, 252 – 53, 335 – 36; 3:113; 4:411 – 12.

[80]Letter to Thomas Church, June 17, 1746, *LJW* 2:268. Note the same sequence in "The Spirit of Bondage and the Spirit of Adoption."

[81]Letter to Thomas Church, June 17, 1746, *LJW* 2:268; cf. 7:396 – 97.

[82]Letter to Thomas Church, February 2, 1756, *LJW* 2:187, italics added.

[83]Letter to Thomas Church, February 2, 1756, *LJW* 2:187; cf. J IX:112.

[84]"The Spirit of Bondage and of Adoption," B 1:253 – 54, sec. 1.6.

[85]"The Way to the Kingdom," B 1:230 – 31, sec. 2.9 – 13; cf. Hymns on Praying for Repentance, *CH* 7:188 – 201, and Hymns for Mourners Convinced of Sin, *CH* 7:210 – 34.

necessary on supposition — if there be time and opportunity for them."[86] The walk toward the kingdom begins with repentance that continues with faith.[87]

3. Holy living confirms that the repentant believer is dwelling in the temple — the reign of God. The holy life that follows repentance and faith is the temple — to be treated further under the section on sanctification.

C. By Faith

Three of Wesley's definitive homilies on faith were published in 1788: "On Faith" (B #106), "On the Discoveries of Faith" (B #117), and "Walking by Sight and Walking by Faith" (B #119).

Their common theme: what the eye of faith can see, the natural senses cannot. Faith is a vital spiritual sense that enables the believer to live spiritually, seeing beyond the visible to the invisible, eternal sphere.[88]

1. On Faith, Hebrews 11:6: Faith's Types and Stages

The text of the homily "On Faith" is Hebrews 11:6: "Without faith it is impossible to please him" [Homily #106 (1788), B 3:491 – 501; J #106, VII:195 – 202]. This homily discusses different types of faith, ranging from the faith of the heathen to saving faith.

Several providential dispensations of grace are seen in the gradual coming of faith into human history, in accord with the finite human capacity to receive grace:[89]

the general revelation of God's existence and justice to all people, commonly termed the *heathen* dispensation of grace to all who believe there is a Giver of life to be sought;

the historical revelation to the people of Israel through the law, the *Mosaic* dispensation entrusted with the oracles of God;

the *expectation of the coming* of the Christ as exemplified prototypically in John the Baptist, who was able to recognize the Lamb of God, and who preached repentance pointing to another yet to come; and finally

the *coming of the fullness of faith in Jesus Christ*, the Christian dispensation of those who have received the spirit of adoption.[90]

2. Types of Rudimentary Faith Distinguished from Saving Faith

Within the frame of these overlapping dispensations, it is possible to enumerate a number of types of rudimentary faith that are distinguishable from the faith that saves.

[86]"Principles of a Methodist Farther Explained," J VIII:428, sec. 2.1; cf. "The Scripture Way of Salvation," B 2:162 – 69, sec. 3; B 1:349, 458, 477; 2:162; *SS* 2:394.

[87]Letter to Thomas Church, February 2, 1745, *LJW* 2:224 – 25, sec. 2.1; cf. 2:188; 5:168.

[88]B 4:30 – 38, 53 – 56; EA, B 11:46 – 47, 54; JWO 275 – 76, 293 – 95, 386 – 88, 395 – 96.

[89]Relying upon John W. Fletcher, *The Doctrines of Grace and Justice*, 1777, sec. 1, pp. 1 – 13.

[90]"On Faith, Hebrews 11:6," B 3:493, proem 3.

a. The General Faith of Rational Creatures

1. While the empirical scientist is not usually thought of as a person of faith, there is a faith commitment in scientific inquiry. For it takes an immense axiomatic leap to enter into the realm of scientific inquiry by assuming the intelligibility of nature and the risk of hypothesis. Scientific belief often proceeds with the radical, unexamined faith assumption that the material world of causality can be meaningfully investigated.[91]

2. As to the rationalistic faith typical of academics, some lean toward the hedonic-sensual type, having "a downright appetite to mix with mud."[92] Others are more inclined toward an idealist-moral faith, who, though they may hold that God exists apart from matter, reject any knowledge of God through the history of biblical revelation. In either case, both hedonic and moral rationalists, having voluntarily turned from hope in God, cling stubbornly to their own self-defined versions of rudimentary faith, distinguishable from the faith that saves.[93]

b. The Faith of the Heathen

The primitive faith of the nations (or heathen faith) functions without divine revelation in the history of Israel, except as it is anticipatively grasped through reason and conscience. Lacking illumination rather than sincerity, the goodness of the heathen often shames those communities gathered by divine revelation in history.[94] "To believe the being and attributes of God is *the faith of a heathen*."[95] It functions according to that light of conscience and reason that it has received.

3. The Theistic Faith of Judaism and Islam

a. The Faith of Islam

The theistic and moral faith of Islam at times puts Christians to shame.[96] Wesley spoke of the writings of the medieval Muslim mystic Abu Bakr Ibn Al-Tufail as containing "all the principles of pure religion and undefiled," as one who had been "taught of God, by his inward voice, all the essentials of true religion,"[97] insofar as religion is conceived in the theistic sense.

b. The Faith of Judaism

Wesley distinguished the faith of Judaism from that of Christianity in this way: "To believe the Old Testament and trust in Him that was to come was the faith of

[91]For some this takes the form of assuming that "there is nothing but matter in the universe," "On Faith, Hebrews 11:6," sec. 1.1.

[92]"On Faith, Hebrews 11:6," sec. 1.2.

[93]Ibid.

[94]B 1:119; 3:494–95; *SS* 1:39.

[95]Letter to Theophilus Lessey, January 1787, *LJW* 7:362, italics added.

[96]"On Faith, Hebrews 11:6," B 3:500, sec. 2.3; cf. *LJW* 6:118; *CH* 7:608; *LJW* 1:277; 5:250; 6:123, 371.

[97]"On Faith, Hebrews 11:6," B 3:494, sec. 1.4; Wesley knew him as Hai Ebn Yokton. He had read in 1734 *The Life of Ebenezer Yokton, An Exact Entire Mystic.* Cf. "Original Sin," sec. 2.4.

a Jew. To believe Christ gave himself for me is the faith of a Christian."[98] Wesley was not inclined to pass harsh judgment on modern Jews, leaving all judgment to God. Though "the veil is still upon their hearts" as to recognition of *Mashiach*, the Anointed One, "it is not our part to pass sentence."[99] It is clear, however, that there is wonderful faith in the people of Israel who received the historical revelation of God through Moses and throughout the history of Israel and the prophets, leading to the messianic hope.

Of the faith of Jews, Charles Wesley wrote affectionately: "Justly they claim the softest prayer from us."[100] Of their historical expectation of a renewed Israel, he wrote:

> Rebuilt by his command,
> Jerusalem shall rise.
> Her temple on Moriah stand
> Again, and touch the skies.
> Send then thy servants forth,
> To call the Hebrews home,
> From east, and west, and south, and north,
> Let all the wanderers come;
> Where'er in lands unknown
> The fugitives remain,
> Bid every creature help them on,
> Thy holy mount to gain.
> ... With Israel's myriads sealed
> Let all the nations meet,
> And show the mystery fulfilled,
> Thy family complete.[101]

4. Nascent Christian Faith

a. The Faith of John the Baptist

Pointing more definitely toward the coming Messiah so as to bridge Old and New Testaments, is the proto-Christian preaching of repentance seen in the unique and singular faith of John the forerunner, the Baptist, a faith peculiar to himself, anticipatory of faith in the Son through the Spirit.[102]

b. The Faith of Orthodox Teaching

1. The formally orthodox faith of medieval scholasticism conceptually contains all that is necessary for salvation, conceived as the faith of assent, even though it at times has added dogmas not revealed in Scripture and has often not measured up to the conditions of repentance, belief, and holy living.

---

[98]Letter to Theophilus Lessey, January 1787, *LJW* 7:362; cf. *LJW* 7:307.
[99]"On Faith, Hebrews 11:6," B 3:495, sec. 1.6.
[100]*CH* 7:615.
[101]*CH* 7:617.
[102]"On Faith, Hebrews 11:6," B 3:494–95, sec. 1.3–6.

2. Similarly, the formally orthodox faith of Protestant and Catholic scholasticism is right to believe neither more nor less than what is found in Scripture as necessary to salvation. Yet in both Protestant and Catholic orthodoxy, insofar as faith is treated primarily as conceptual conviction of truths, it does not reach the depth of saving faith.

Faith viewed as mere cerebral acknowledgment of abstract propositional truth does not save, for even the devil may be aware of the truth of revelation, that God has come into our midst. This is what Wesley called "the faith of devils."[103]

Wesley did not deny that many in the church of Rome and in the churches of Protestantism have received the saving faith that works through love. But he was also aware of a dismal neglect of the proclamation of saving faith in both traditions.[104] Head faith is not heart faith. Routinized correct teaching, though correct, is not saving faith.

c. The Servile Faith of a Servant

To those with the servile faith of a servant, who fear God but have not learned to love God as Father, or dwell in holy living in the family of God, Wesley says: "You have already great reason to praise God that he has called you to his honorable service. Fear not. Continue crying unto him; 'and you shall see greater things than these.' "[105]

The faith of the servant, or faith that still hovers ambiguously under the law, brings one closer to the fear of God and the working of righteousness.[106]

The servant has a different place in the family than the son or daughter. The faith of the servant is preparatory to receiving adoption by the conviction that "the life I now live in the body, I live by faith in the Son of God, who loved me and gave himself for me" (Gal. 2:20 NIV).[107]

5. Saving Faith

The filial faith embraced by sons and daughters is rather "properly and directly a divine conviction whereby every child of God is enabled to testify, 'The life that I now live, I live by faith in the Son of God, who loved me, and gave himself for me.' "[108]

At the twinkling of an eye, whenever this occurs, the believer is "living at that very moment in a state of acceptance," not as a servant but as a son or daughter freely adopted into the family of God. "They will receive the *faith* of the children of God by his *revealing* his only-begotten Son in their hearts."[109]

Because you are sons and daughters, "God hath sent forth the Spirit of his Son

[103]On the faith of devils, see B 1:119 – 20, 138 – 39; 9:52 – 53; *SS* 1:38, 63, 284.
[104]"On Faith, Hebrews 11:6," B 3:495 – 97, sec. 1.7 – 10.
[105]"On Faith, Hebrews 11:6," B 3:497, sec. 1.11; John 1:50.
[106]"The Spirit of Bondage and of Adoption," sec. 4.3 – 4.
[107]"On Faith, Hebrews 11:6," B 3:498, sec. 1.12.
[108]"On Faith, Hebrews 11:6," B 3:497, sec. 1.11.
[109]"On Faith, Hebrews 11:6," B 3:498, sec. 1.12.

into your hearts, crying, 'Abba, Father'; that is, giving you a childlike confidence in him, together with a kind affection toward him." This inward witness of the Spirit "the servant hath not. Yet let no man discourage him; rather, lovingly exhort him to expect it every moment."[110] In whatever proximate degree of faith they have thus far received or secured, they are called to press on fully to receive the Spirit of adoption as children of God.[111]

The history of religions reveals a panoply of varied modes of embryonic faith. These are often mixed with the idolatry endemic to the history of sin. They are thus viewed not negatively but positively as making ready for faith in God's own coming. "There is no reason why you should be satisfied with the faith of a materialist, a heathen, or a deist; nor indeed with that of a servant ... press on till you receive the Spirit of adoption."[112]

The next two homilies follow and extend this teaching of saving faith.

6. "On the Discoveries of Faith"

The text of the homily "On the Discoveries of Faith" is Hebrews 11:1: "Now faith is ... the evidence of things not seen" [Homily #117 (1788), B 4:28–38; J #110, VII:231–38]. Here Wesley distinguishes sense knowledge from saving faith.

a. Sense Knowledge

Though some think that ideas are innate to persons, Wesley agreed with Locke that "there is nothing in the understanding which was not first perceived by some of the senses."[113] All the knowledge of nature that we have acquired is derived from the senses.[114]

The five senses have different degrees of extension, so that sight extends farther than hearing — one may see the moon but not hear the meteor that strikes it — and hearing much farther than smelling, tasting, or feeling.[115] But none of the empirical senses, however astute, can reach beyond the finite world of time and space.[116] The dwelling place of the senses is *the visible world.*

b. Faith's Knowing

Faith, beholding the evidences of what is not seen, unlike the physical senses, reaches *beyond the visible world.*[117] Just as we have seen in the homily on "The Scripture Way of Salvation," faith is "the demonstrative evidence of things unseen,

[110] "On Faith, Hebrews 11:6," B 3:496–98, secs. 10–12, italics added. On the etymology and interpretation of *elenchos*, see B 2:160–61, 167–68, 368–69; 4:187–88; 9:95, 177; FA, B 11:106–7, 444.

[111] On degrees of faith, see B 3:175–76; 3:491–98; 9:111, 164–65; *LJW* 2:214; 5:200; *JJW* 1:481–83; 2:328–29; JWO 68–69, 356–62.

[112] "On Faith, Hebrews 11:6," B 3:498, sec. 13.

[113] Aristotle, *On the Soul* 3.7 (430); 4:29n.; EA, B 11:56, sec. 32.

[114] "On the Discoveries of Faith," B 4:29, sec. 1.

[115] "On the Discoveries of Faith," B 4:29–30, secs. 1–2; EA, B 11:46–47, sec. 7.

[116] "On the Discoveries of Faith," B 4:30, secs. 2–3.

[117] *CH* 7:194–95, 315–18, 489–90, 515–16.

the supernatural evidence of things invisible, not perceivable by the eyes of flesh, or by any of our natural senses or faculties ... whereby the spiritual man discerneth God."[118] The discerning appropriation of invisible evidences occurs by faith.

God has appointed faith to "supply the defects of sense." Faith's task begins where the natural senses end.[119] Being given an ability to see things not seen is of "the very essence of faith; love and obedience, the inseparable properties of it."[120]

c. The Evidence of Things Not Seen

What sort of knowing requires the evidence of things unseen? Such matters as the origin and destiny of the soul, the spiritual creation, the incarnation, the moral attributes of God, the Trinity, and the coming judgment are known by faith. These may all be mistaken as mere intellectual ideas. More accurately, they refer to that reality to which those ideas properly refer.

By faith one knows that one has a soul, created in the image of God, and that having fallen from that image, one is "totally unable to quicken [one's] own soul."[121] By faith one knows, grasps, and "sees" so to speak, that there are other orders of spiritual creation, some of whom blessedly dwell with God, and others who resist God in misery and unrighteousness.[122] By faith one knows that God, who transcends all creatures, was made flesh and died for our salvation. By faith one knows that God is infinite in power, wisdom, justice, mercy, and holiness.

By faith the one God is known as Father, Son, and Spirit.[123] By faith we perceive that the righteous dwell with Christ. Faith looks toward the coming final judgment when the righteous will inherit the kingdom and the wicked will depart to the dissolution epitomized by fire.[124] The Spirit prepares us for this kingdom by convicting us of sin and teaching us to fear God's judgment and trust God's love.[125] Sense experience yields only minimal formal knowledge of these matters. For true faith these are forms of evidence of things unseen.

d. The Growth of Saving Faith from Strength to Strength

Insofar as we have learned to obey God out of fear, we have the faith of a servant, as seen in the previous homily. But we are called to press on until we learn to obey God out of grateful love, which is the great privilege of the children of God.

The Spirit attests to our spirits our adoption as sons and daughters of the reconciling Father.[126] Beginning with new birth, the faith of the child of God grows toward spiritual maturity in "the faith of the fathers," being delivered from doubt

[118]EA, B 11:46, sec. 6; B 1:119–21, 138–39; *LJW* 4:174–76; 3:385.
[119]"On the Discoveries of Faith," B 4:30, sec. 4.
[120]Minutes, 1744, June 25, Q8, JWO 138.
[121]"On the Discoveries of Faith," B 4:30–31, sec. 5.
[122]"On the Discoveries of Faith," B 4:31, sec. 6.
[123]"On the Discoveries of Faith," B 4:31–32, sec. 7.
[124]"On the Discoveries of Faith," B 4:32, sec. 8.
[125]"On the Discoveries of Faith," B 4:34, sec. 11.
[126]"On the Discoveries of Faith," B 4:35–36, secs. 13–14.

and fear,[127] and from "all inward as well as outward sin, from evil desires and evil tempers, as well as from evil words and works."[128]

Healthy faith grows steadily through gradual stages, from being a babe in Christ, still having anxieties and guilt, toward growing up as a maturing person gradually coming better to refract the holiness of God in one's behavioral life.[129]

As maturing persons in Christ, they continue to grow from strength to strength, with the knowledge of God's Word abiding in them, toward "the consciousness of the divine favour without any intermission," leading toward full confidence that walks in the hope of dwelling and reigning with God eternally.[130] Praying without ceasing and taking up their cross daily,[131] they are "able to comprehend, with all saints, what is the breadth, and length, and depth, and height; and to know the love of Christ, which passeth knowledge" (Eph. 3:18 – 19). "The more we exert our faith, the more 'tis increased."[132]

7. Walking by Sight and Walking by Faith

The third of this series of homilies on faith shifts the textual focus from Hebrews 11:1 (evidence of things not seen) to 2 Corinthians 5:7: "We walk by faith, not by sight" [Homily #119 (1788), B 4:48 – 59; J #113, VII:256 – 64]. Faith walks by a different kind of knowing than empirical sense knowledge that is known by sight.

a. Walking by Faith

Those who have been dead in trespasses have been quickened and given new senses to behold spiritual things. Adopted into the family of God as sons and daughters, they no longer walk by fear in a servile relationship with the Lawgiver.[133] No one can begin to walk by faith until first born of the Spirit. One is thereby given new senses to discern the requirement of faith.[134] "'By this faith we are saved' from all uneasiness of mind, from the anguish of a wounded spirit, from discontent, from fear, and sorrow of heart."

Christians "walk by faith, not by sight" (2 Cor. 5:7), not by the five physical senses alone, but by the grace-enabled new sensibilities of saving faith. This homily offers a concise description of the life that proceeds step-by-step by faith insofar as a person lives by grace.[135]

No one can give this faith to himself. He can only receive it from God. "The

[127]"On the Discoveries of Faith," B 4:36, sec. 15.
[128]"On the Discoveries of Faith," B 4:37, sec. 16.
[129]*LJW* 2:215; 3:213 – 321; JWO 231 – 34.
[130]"On the Discoveries of Faith," B 4:37 – 38, sec. 17.
[131]*SS* 2:292.
[132]Minutes, 1744, June 25, Q13, JWO 138; cf. *CH* 7:690 – 94.
[133]"Walking by Sight and Walking by Faith," B 4:49, sec. 1; cf. "The Witness of the Spirit, 1," sec. 1.12; "On Faith, Hebrews 11:6," sec. 1.10.
[134]"Walking by Sight and Walking by Faith," B 4:49, sec. 2.
[135]"Walking by Sight and Walking by Faith," B 4:49 – 52, secs. 1 – 9.

more you labor so to do, the more you will be convinced, 'it is the gift of God.'"[136] Lacking this new birth from above, one walks solely by sight, knowing only what the five senses reveal.[137] Nothing of the invisible world, full of God, is directly accessible to sight, sound, smell, touch, or taste.[138] Our external senses serve us in our clay houses, but there is far more to life than body.[139] Physical senses "have nothing to do with the invisible world: they are not adapted to it."[140]

b. The Light That Enlightens This Walk

A succession of degrees of faith may be seen in the progression from the glimmering light of crude faith of primitive cultures, from the faith of Noah through the faith of Socrates.[141]

Some inkling of God's presence remains in all generations of the history of religions. But all these "lights" together avail no further than faint twilight when compared to the full light of day of the revelation by which we can walk by faith in the Son. These forms of anticipatory faith are fulfilled by faith in God's own coming in Jesus Christ.[142]

Faith illumines where the senses fail. Walking by faith "opens eyes" to the life that is "hid with Christ in God."[143] The things that are seen are temporal, things not seen, eternal. Those who live by faith walk each step by faith, judging each situation in relation to the invisible. They sojourn in the temporal world but as citizens of an eternal city. They do not love the world or the things of the world, but desire chiefly the glory that abides forever, seeking in the general tenor of their lives "the things that are above."[144]

True religion does not consist in moral decency or harmlessness, however admirable they may be. Nor does it consist in the formal observance of divine ordinances. True religion is "no less than living in eternity and walking in eternity; and hereby walking in the love of God and man — in lowliness, meekness, and resignation. This, and this alone, is that 'life which is hid with Christ in God.' He alone who experiences this 'dwells in God, and God in him.'"[145] True religion is to live and walk in the love of God and humanity by faith, so as to do God's will on earth as in heaven. Yet precisely this is regarded as madness by those who walk only by sight.[146]

---

[136] EA, B 11:47 – 48, secs. 8, 10.

[137] B 3:327; 4:30, 48 – 52, 288.

[138] "Walking by Sight and Walking by Faith," B 4:50 – 51, secs. 4 – 7.

[139] "Walking by Sight and Walking by Faith," B 4:50, sec. 6; cf. "Sermon on the Mount, 8," sec. 21.

[140] "Walking by Sight and Walking by Faith," B 4:50, sec. 6; cf. "Witness of the Spirit, I," sec. 1.12; and "On the Discoveries of Faith," sec. 8.

[141] "Walking by Sight and Walking by Faith," B 4:51 – 52, secs. 8 – 10.

[142] "Walking by Sight and Walking by Faith," B 4:53 – 54, secs. 11 – 12.

[143] "Walking by Sight and Walking by Faith," B 4:54, sec. 13.

[144] "Walking by Sight and Walking by Faith," B 4:56 – 57, secs. 16 – 17.

[145] "Walking by Sight and Walking by Faith," B 4:57, sec. 18.

[146] "Walking by Sight and Walking by Faith," B 4:57 – 58, sec. 19.

Walking by faith is contrasted with dissipation, the dull art of forgetting God. This dissipation ends in studied inattention to the whole invisible world known by faith.[147] Those who walk by faith flee from dissipation, being steadily attentive to God, having God in all their thoughts, eternity always before their eyes, having constant regard for that which remains unseen.[148] Such is the life that walks by faith, not sight.

[147]"Walking by Sight and Walking by Faith," B 4:58, sec. 20.
[148]"Walking by Sight and Walking by Faith," B 4:59, sec. 21.

CHAPTER 8

Regeneration

A. New Birth

Regeneration is the birthing work of God the Spirit by which the pardoned sinner becomes a child of God, loving and serving God with the affections of the heart, so as to receive the Spirit of adoption by whom we are enabled to say, "Abba, Father."[1]

1. The Regenerating Work of the Spirit

a. New Life Quickened by Faith

The new birth brings into being not only a new life, but a new will and a new beginning for the redeemed affections. A new spiritual nature is being offered by the mercy of God so that one is born again into a new capacity better to mirror the original image of God in humanity.[2] God's image in humanity, having become distorted by the intergenerational history of social and individual sin, original and actual, in this way is being renewed by the life-giving power of the Spirit.[3] The regenerating work of the Spirit allows our earthen vessels to yield so as to reflect anew the love, power, and goodness of God. This new life is quickened by faith made active in love.

The new birth is the renewal of the whole person in righteousness by the power of the Spirit.[4] The work of the Spirit is acting at each discrete phase to renew and energize the whole life of the baptized faithful. That we are made partakers of the divine nature means that we share in God's own life through this regenerating grace.

b. From Pardon to New Birth

Four memorable formula sentences in "The New Birth" have marked Wesleyan teaching on the flow of grace from justification to new birth.

- The cross embodies God's act *for* us. The new birth makes effective the outworking of God's act *in* us.

[1]Letter to Rev. Mr. Potter, November 4, 1758, J IX:89–90; and to Rev. Mr. Downes, November 17, 1759, J IX:104.

[2]B 1:279, 415–16, 432–35; 2:186–201; 4:173; *CH*, B 7:234–83.

[3]*CH*, B 7:553–81.

[4]Letter to the Bishop of Gloucester, B 11:459–539.

- Justification changes the believer's *relation* to God. New birth changes the believer's inmost *motivation and disposition* of soul.
- Justification restores the whole person by pardon to *the favor of God*. New birth restores the whole person by faith to *the image of God*.
- Justification takes away the *guilt* of sin. New birth takes away the *power* of sin.[5]

c. Inseparable in Time, Distinct in Nature

The four sentences above summarize Wesley's doctrine of salvation. He explains: God's justifying act on the cross is conceptually distinct from our new birth of spirit yet inseparable experientially. These two are inseparable in point of time, yet distinct in nature. It is not that one first has a justification experience and then later has a regeneration experience. It is *amid*, not chronologically following, the reception of justifying grace that one is reborn.[6]

In this rebirth, the active agency is God's own Spirit imparting new life. The *imputation* of the gift of righteousness of the Son on the cross sets the context for an *impartation* — the actual subjective, motivational, and behavioral giving of new life through the Spirit. Faith *begins* by the gift of atoning grace by the Son and is *continued* in us through the sanctifying grace empowered by the Spirit. We experience in regeneration the personal *appropriation* of the gift formally and juridically offered on the cross.

2. Adoption into the Family of God

a. Legal, Biological, and Filial Metaphors Harmonized

Justification uses a *courtroom* metaphor to teach that by our trust in Jesus Christ we are in fact accounted righteous, having been freed from the guilt and the penalty of our sin.

Regeneration is a *biological* metaphor, a word picture of a birth into a new life that has a new spiritual nature, a new motivational life engendered by the grace and love of God. The moral nature of the penitent believer is being quickened, enlivened spiritually into a life capable of faith, hope, and love.

Adoption is a *filial* metaphor pointing to inclusion within the family of God. By adoption we mean that the pardoned sinner becomes a child of God, welcomed and freely adopted into the family of God, sharing in that family fully, heir of the inheritance of that family, inheritor of eternal life, and delivered from the power of the corruption that reigns in the history of sin. In this way the born-again metaphor is intimately connected with both the teachings of justification and adoption.

b. The New Family, the One Father

This adoption tells of a new relationship to God as Abba. The word picture is one of warmth, love, and belonging, showing that by our new relation and new life

[5] *LJW* 1:327; 3:358; 4:38, 65; *CH*, B 7:234 – 83; B 1:279, 415 – 16, 432 – 35; 2:186 – 201; 4:173; 11:520 – 27.

[6] "On God's Vineyard," B 3:506 – 8, sec. 1.6 – 10.

we have become his wanted children freed from the alien mastery of a creditor or oppressor, now having the witness of the Spirit that we are children of God. Adoption in the new family assumes a previous estrangement from the family that has now been overcome. The prodigal is again drawn back into the family, adopted into full rights of inheritance of that family.

We become sons and daughters as we are reborn into this family. At this table we are sustained daily by the preaching of the Word, sacramental life, and spiritual discipline. Even when we fall into sin, we are still supported by a community of faith that offers this Word, embodied in its sacrament and accompanied by its admonition, that brings us back into a restored and renewed relationship to God.

3. The New Birth

The key text of regeneration teaching is John 3:7: "Ye must be born again" [Homily #45 (1760), B 2:186–201; J # 45, VI:65–77]. The crucial term is "must."

The issues incisively examined in Wesley's homily "The New Birth" are these:

Is new birth the equivalent of justification?
What does it mean to die to sin?
What does it mean to be renewed in the image of God?
If we are so prone to fall, how are we made able to stand?
Why is rebirth necessary?
In what sense is it even possible that one may be born again?
How is new birth related to baptism?[7]

a. The Gracious Ordering of the Relation of Justification and New Birth

We are not first justified and then reborn, but by being justified we are reborn. The two metaphors are intimately woven together as one. We are not talking about a chronological sequence in which justification first comes and then at some later date regeneration occurs.

In the order of *time,* neither is before the other. Chronologically you cannot say that justification precedes new birth. But in order of *thinking,* i.e., logically, there is a distinction. God's justifying activity of imputing righteousness is the logical precondition and presupposition of the Holy Spirit's impartation of the gift of new life to us. Justification is God's work *for us,* which calls forth the work of the Spirit *in us* to bring to life our responsiveness to God's work for us.[8] These move together dynamically. Son and Spirit work together for our salvation.[9]

Justification is by grace alone through faith alone. New birth focuses special energy of grace poured out on the new life that begins in response to justifying grace.

The magisterial Protestant tradition has faithfully taught of justification, but

[7]"The New Birth," B 2:188, proem 2.

[8]"The New Birth," B 2:187, proem 1; cf. "The Great Privilege of Those That Are Born of God," proem 1; "Justification by Faith," sec. 2.1.

[9]"The New Birth," B 2:198, sec. 4.3.

the new birth has sometimes been insufficiently emphasized. But in Scripture it is a "must." Neither of these two teachings can be separated experientially. Holding them together is what the bands and societies of Wesley were seeking to do.[10]

b. Renewal in the Natural, Political, and Moral Image of God

We are not originally made to be sinners. We are made good by the Creator, and only then we choose to become sinners. But the fact that we are created good does not mean that we are created immutably good.[11] Here "we" refers to the whole of humanity.

There is a threefold working distinction in the Wesleyan evangelical tradition between the natural, political, and moral image of God in humanity. The original creation of humanity stood in the *natural* image of God by which human beings have free self-determining will and immortality. We are created in the image of God in the sense of having some measure of natural free will. When fallen, the will ceases being able to elicit moral good on its own initiative.[12]

By the *political* image of God is meant that human beings are permitted and called to bring tranquil order and governance to the world, to have responsible dominion or stewardship over the earth. We are created in the image of God in the sense of having some measure of political competence to organize society toward relative justice and decent governance.[13]

Most importantly, we are made in the *moral* image of God by being made for righteousness and holiness. What does it mean morally to refract the image of the holy God? Before the history of sin, human nature was like a diamond, beautifully capable of gloriously refracting the holiness of God. With the fall, that capacity for refraction has been radically marred and reduced. With the history of sin, the natural, political, and moral image of God in us has not been altogether lost but has been grossly disfigured by that history.[14]

4. Able to Stand, Liable to Fall

Human beings are created in the image of God *able to stand but liable to fall.*[15] "Liable" means we are apt to fall into temptation. Our freedom has this aptness, this susceptibility. Without this capacity, we would not be free.

Those who understand this distinction will be very far along in grasping Wesley's basic anthropology. In the prefallen condition, God gives the grace and power to human life to stand accountably before God so as to mirror this natural, political, and moral image; but this ability to stand was perpetually susceptible to mutation, forever alterable by freedom.[16]

---

[10]"The New Birth," B 2:187 – 88, proem.
[11]"The New Birth," B 2:189, sec. 1.2.
[12]"The New Birth," B 2:188, sec. 1.1.
[13]Ibid.
[14]Ibid.
[15]"The New Birth," B 2:189, sec. 1.2.
[16]"The New Birth," B 2:190, sec. 1.3.

No person is created immutable, for it is the very essence of personhood to be created with a free, self-determining capacity to change. In this mutability, human history did in fact change for the worse. That is the story of the fall. Whatever good is given in creation is vulnerable to fallenness, to failure of the will to hear and respond adequately to the command of God.[17] If able to stand, the liability to falling is not necessitated. If liable to fall, the ability to stand is not immutable.

5. Since All Have Died, All Must Be Reborn

a. The Inexorable Death That Follows from Sin

In Adam's fall and Eve's fall, something in all of us has died or is destined to die. The whole history of sin is a history of spiritual death that cannot awaken itself to new life.[18] This is the pervasive condition of the history of sin: spiritual death as exemplified prototypically by the case history of the first human beings. The death they died was not merely a death of the body, but a spiritual death in which life in God is lost and the image of God defaced.[19] The consequences of the first fall and each of our subsequent fallings of human freedom ripple on out to influence subsequent human sufferers.[20]

The answer to why we *must* be born again is best framed historically, not abstractly: we all actually share from the outset in this tangible history of sin and death. Every discrete act following from our freedom has become subject to corruption.[21] This is the grounding assumption of all regeneration teaching. All who in Adam die must be born anew to mirror once again the divine goodness. We must be born anew because we have died, in the sense that the most vital spiritual root of our humanity has perished. This does not mean that the moral image of God is totally lost, but radically disfigured and shattered, remaining only in fragmented form.[22]

b. The Jewish Precedent to New Birth Exemplified by John the Baptist

We get a refreshing glimpse of Wesley as a critical historical exegete in his homily "The New Birth." He was especially interested in the ways in which biblical metaphors were being refashioned in the period between the Old and New Testaments. He was intrigued by the analogies between Jewish circumcision and Christian baptism. The expression "being born again" was not an expression first used by Jesus in his conversation with Nicodemus, but already available to the late Judaic tradition, referring to non-Jews who had converted to Judaism.[23]

In that conversion, they went through a ritual cleansing process analogous to baptism as a preparatory act to circumcision and actual entry into the covenant

[17]"The New Birth," B 2:189, sec. 1.1.

[18]*DOS* IX:404–9.

[19]"The New Birth," B 2:190, sec. 1.3.

[20]"The New Birth," B 2:190, sec. 1.4.

[21]For further development of the effects of the fall, see "Original Sin," sec. 1.3; "On the Fall of Man"; "On Living without God," sec. 15.

[22]"The New Birth," B 2:190, sec. 1.4.

[23]"The New Birth," B 2:190–91, sec. 2.1–2.

community. When ritually cleansed, the converts were said to be born again. Converts into Judaism were baptized as a type of dying to an old way and being born into a new way of life.[24]

This tradition illumines the radical nature of what John the Baptist was doing. For John was baptizing not non-Jews but Jews! That is precisely what made the Christ's forerunner so controversial. Prior to the call of John, Gentiles could be converts to Judaism through this humbling ritual act of purification and cleansing that later became the pattern of Christian baptism. John's baptism was saying that the chosen people now must repent.[25]

6. The Mystery of Birth

a. Without Knowing How, We Know That We Are Reborn

How are we born again? Scripture does not offer an empirical description of the "how" of the new birth. Rather the opposite: we do not know how the Spirit works in this renewing process, but we do know *that* it happens.[26] While no one can disinterestedly describe the precise way the Spirit enables new birth, there can be little doubt that new life in Christ has come into being.

The basic scriptural analogy: the Spirit blows where he wills. Who can say where or how the Spirit moves or is going to move? Like wind, we know *that* the Spirit is there, but we cannot account for him precisely; no matter how much meteorological evidence we compile, there remain elements of chaotic absurdity in our conceptualities and vast holes in our data bases. God does not offer himself up neatly for our objective inquiry, for God being Spirit is not an object for our laboratory dissection. Objects are by definition visible. God is not reducible to anything visible.[27]

Before we are born, we have no way of conceiving how it might be to be born. If I am in my mother's womb, I may have some awareness that there is something outside my immediate environment but no actual knowledge of what is ahead for me. It is a maturing, unfolding surprise.[28] That analogy is like the transition going on when the Spirit is awakening one to faithful sonship or daughterhood in the family of God.[29]

The Spirit is moving us from a lack of spiritual awareness to a birthing in which one becomes unexpectedly aware of new life. New birth is "the change wrought in the whole soul by the almighty Spirit of God," when it is renewed after the image of God, "when the love of the world is changed into the love of God, pride into humility, passion into meekness," "whereby the 'earthly, sensual and devilish' mind is turned into 'the mind which is in Christ.'"[30] A new spiritual consciousness and

[24]"The New Birth," B 2:190 – 91, sec. 2.1 – 3.
[25]"The New Birth," B 2:191, sec. 2.3.
[26]"The New Birth," B 2:191, sec. 2.1.
[27]"The New Birth," B 2:191, sec. 2.2.
[28]"The New Birth," B 2:192 – 93, sec. 2.4.
[29]"The New Birth," B 2:193, sec. 2.4.
[30]"The New Birth," B 2:193 – 94, sec. 2.5; Phil. 2:5; James 3:15.

life are given that elicit a healing *shalom*, a serenity that results from reconciliation with God.

b. "You Must": Whether New Birth Is Requisite to Salvation

The text, "You must be born again" (John 3:7 NIV), provides the scriptural imperative for the necessity of regeneration.[31] A precise requirement is implied in the phrase "You must," in order to live within and toward the coming reign of God. The sinner cannot be restored into the image of God until having once again received the renewed capacity to refract the holiness of God by which human happiness is restored.[32]

As long as ungodly passions and tempers "reign in any soul, happiness has no place there. But they must reign till the bent of our nature is changed, that is, till we are born again."[33] "Gospel holiness is no less than the image of God stamped upon the heart."[34]

Nothing necessitated the fall of humanity. It was absurdly chosen.[35] There is no way to speak of the necessity of the new birth without recalling the fundamental predicament of human history (the enigma of sin) from its beginnings: Adam was given freedom and the sufficient grace to sustain a day-by-day walk in a trusting relation with God.[36] From that freedom, Adam fell, and with him his whole progeny, since freedom has consequences. Our abuse of our freedom makes problems for those who follow after us, since one cannot unwind history.

What Adam's fallen progeny need is a new birth of freedom.

c. Regaining the Original Capacity to Refract God's Holiness

"Without holiness no one will see the Lord" (Heb. 12:14 NIV). Those who lack the capacity to reflect God's holiness will remain unhappy, for holiness is the necessary precondition of a durable joy.[37]

The text contends for "the necessity of holiness" in order to glorify the Lord. This calls for a "new birth, since none can be holy except he be born again."[38]

To be happy finally is to live an accountable life before God, fully enjoying the source and end of all good. This blessedness is not fully grasped as a hedonic, humanistic, individualistic, narcissistic happiness, for it is always set within the frame of eternity.[39] The desired end of this birth is a growing life of holiness, salvation, and happiness, in which the image of God is being constantly renewed in the heart.

[31] *DOS* IX:307 – 14; cf. B 1:214.
[32] Letter to "John Smith," June 1746, *LJW* 2:71.
[33] "The New Birth," B 2:195 – 96, sec. 3.3.
[34] "The New Birth," B 2:194, sec. 3.1.
[35] "The New Birth," B 2:188, sec. 1.1.
[36] "The New Birth," B 2:189 – 90, sec. 2.3 – 4.
[37] "The New Birth," B 2:194, sec. 3.1.
[38] "The New Birth," B 2:195, sec. 3.2.
[39] "The New Birth," B 2:195, sec. 3.2 – 3.

7. The New Birth and Baptism

a. Whether Scripture Requires Baptism in the New Life

Baptism, strictly speaking, is not the same as rebirth. But the new life in Christ calls for the grace of baptism.

The command in Scripture is stated clearly by Peter in Acts 2:38: "Repent and be baptized, every one of you, in the name of Jesus Christ for the forgiveness of your sins. And you will receive the gift of the Holy Spirit" (NIV).

Baptism is the sign of regeneration.[40] Regeneration is the thing signified, and baptism is the sign.[41] Baptism points to that reception of regenerating grace, which is commanded in baptism in the name of the Father, Son, and Spirit.[42] Wesley cautions against an excessively spiritualized view of baptism that would diminish its physical expression: water, symbolizing death and burial in water, ritual cleansing by water, and the rising up into new life. There is no baptism without water as its abundant, life-giving, common cleansing physical expression.[43]

b. The Classic Christian Teaching of Baptism

The Anglican Articles to which Wesley ascribed commend baptism in explicit terms:

> Baptism is not only a sign of profession, and a mark of difference, whereby Christian men are discerned from others that are not christened, but it is also a sign of regeneration or new birth whereby, as an instrument, they that receive baptism rightly are grafted into the Church: the promises of forgiveness of sin, and of our adoption to be sons of God by the Holy Ghost, are visibly signed and sealed: faith is confirmed and grace increased by virtue of prayer unto God. (art. 27)

Elsewhere Wesley defines baptism:

> What is baptism? It is the initiatory sacrament, which enters us into covenant with God. It was instituted by Christ, who alone has power to institute a proper sacrament, a sign, seal, pledge, and means of grace, perpetually obligatory on all Christians.... The matter of this sacrament is water; which as it has a natural power of cleansing, is the more fit for this symbolical use. Baptism is formed by washing, dipping, or sprinkling the person, in the name of the Father, Son and Holy Spirit, who is hereby devoted to the ever-blessed Trinity. I say, by washing, dipping, or sprinkling; because it is not determined in Scripture in which of these ways it shall be done, neither by any express precept, nor by any such example as clearly proves it.... By baptism we enter into covenant with God.... By baptism we are admitted into the church, and consequently made members of Christ, its head. The Jews were admitted to fellowship by circumcision, so are

---

[40] B 2:196–200; 1:428–30; FA, B 11:107; cf. 11:253; JWO 321–25.
[41] FA, B 11:48–49; B 1:143, 415, 428–30; 2:196–200.
[42] "Of the Church," B 3:49–50.
[43] "The New Birth," B 2:196–97, sec. 4.1; cf. "Treatise on Baptism," 1756.

the Christians by baptism. We read in Galatians 3:27, "As many as are baptized into Christ," (in His name) "have thereby, put on Christ" (that is, are by participation united to Christ, and made one with Him). (See 1 Corinthians 12:13 and Ephesians 4:12.)[44]

Note these features of baptism:

- the initiatory sacrament
- instituted by Christ,
- entering us into covenant with God—
- a sign, seal, pledge,
- a means of grace
- obligatory on all Christians,
- the physical matter of which is water,
- having a natural power of cleansing,
- administered in the name of the Father, Son, and Holy Spirit,
- by which we are admitted into the church
- and consequently made members of Christ, its head.

c. An Outward and Visible Sign of an Inward and Spiritual Grace

Baptism is "the outward sign our one Lord has been pleased to appoint of all that inward and spiritual grace which he is continually bestowing upon his church. It is likewise a precious means whereby this faith and hope are given to those that diligently seek him."[45] More simply it is "an outward and visible sign of an inward and spiritual grace."[46]

The death and rebirth metaphors so prominent in regeneration are also profoundly embedded in baptism.[47] That is what baptism attests: going down into death and being raised anew with the risen Lord (Rom. 6).

New birth in the Spirit is made palpable and public in baptism, but it is more than a public confession; it is a work of grace. Baptism is accompanied by confession of sin and confession of faith, but it is effectual by grace through faith and faith's evidences of new birth. It calls for the complete renunciation of demonic powers.

So the life of the new birth is embryonically anticipated in baptism, even while not maturely or fully or experientially possessed.

Since baptism is a command of God in Scripture, it is an "effectual sign of grace."[48] It assists in effecting that of which it is a sign. But the person cannot simply claim that because one is baptized, one is therefore reborn. Why? "There may sometimes be the outward sign where there is not the inward grace."[49]

[44]"A Treatise on Baptism," JWO 319; J X:188, sec. 1.1.

[45]"Of the Church," B 3:49.

[46]Cf. the sixteenth-century Anglican divine, Richard Hooker, *Of the Lawes of Ecclesiastical Politie*, cf. BCP; Art. 29, On Baptism.

[47]"On Baptism," JWO 317–32.

[48]Westminster Confession, art. 25.

[49]"The New Birth," B 2:197, sec. 4.2.

d. Living Out Baptism in the New Life

Within the frame of reference of the historic teaching of Protestantism and especially that of the Anglican Church, Wesley assumed that with few exceptions most of his hearers, those who attended his revival meetings, were baptized. In his preaching, he repeatedly insisted that those who have been baptized are called to manifest their baptism. They must be born again in the sense of receiving actively and joyfully the very regenerating grace of the Spirit that baptism offers and to which it points.

The grace given with baptism is a participatory grace that looks toward further actualizing confirmation in our behavior and our choices. This is a standard article of Anglican teaching, that baptism is a means of grace. It is a proper ordinance of God by which the seed of the grace of regeneration is first planted.[50]

Baptism is the charter of redemption, a constituting liturgical moment that then asks to be lived out. Though baptized only once on a particular day, we keep on living daily. The grace of baptism points beyond itself as a visible event to this new birth and the beginnings of behavioral transformation.[51] So just showing your baptismal certificate is not enough. God wants to see a life lived out in response to the grace of baptism.[52]

Wesley: "I tell a sinner, 'You must be born again.' 'No,' say you, 'He was born again in baptism. Therefore he cannot be born again now.' Alas! What trifling is this? What if he was *then* a child of God? He is *now* manifestly a 'child of the devil'?...Therefore do not play upon words. He *must* go through an entire change of heart," without which "if either he or you die ... your baptism will be so far from profiting you that it will greatly increase your damnation."[53] There is little promise for one who claims the grace of baptism but does not live it.

e. Receiving the Whole Image of God through the Seal of the Spirit

"The being 'sealed by the Spirit' in the full sense of the word I take to imply two things: first, the receiving the whole image of God, the whole mind which was in Christ, as the wax receives the whole impression of the seal when it is strongly and properly applied; secondly the full assurance of hope, or a clear and permanent confidence of being with God in glory. Either of these may be given ... separate from the other. When both are joined together, then I believe they constitute the seal of the Spirit. But even this admits of various degrees."[54]

The wax is the physical expression of the receipt of grace. The seal is God's imprint on the soul. Its acceptance calls for receiving the whole image of God. Baptism is called for as a sign and seal of this acceptance. The grace of God is poured

[50]XXXIX, BCP; on the relation of baptism and subsequent decision, see *LJW* 4:235; 5:330; JWO 318–31; *CH*, B 7:646–48.

[51]B 3:435–36.

[52]"The New Birth," B 2:196–98, sec. 4.1, 2.

[53]FA, pt. 1, B 11:107, sec. 1.5.

[54]Letter to Hannah Ball, October 4, 1771, *LJW* 5:280; cf. B 9:64.

into the act of baptism in the form of promise. This act of receiving grace is accompanied by the "full assurance of hope."

8. Breathing Grace

Certainly a genuine gift is given to us in baptism, but grace has not thereby completed its work, but only begun it. The grace of baptism places us in this new community of response where this new circumcision of the heart is taking place. We ourselves must freely join in with God's Spirit working in us. Baptism enables and requires a renewal of our hearts, eliciting an inward change in us that seeks to become outwardly actualized in daily behavior.[55]

a. Beginning and Continuing

The analogies of birth and growth work are complementary. New birth is the *beginning* of the renewed spiritual life. One does not enjoy life or enter into this new family of God without spiritual birth. Birth in this sense simply means faith responding to the love of God on the cross. But one does not keep getting born and born and born. After one is born, one grows in the family, having been adopted into its inheritance.[56]

When you think of a fully matured intrauterine fetus, you have an unborn child that is completely potentiated and ready to come into full actualization as a human being, yet it is not until after birth that this one begins to breathe. The baby is born, begins breathing, and then keeps on breathing, in a *continuing* process that is the basis of constant growth. It is this constant growth process, this constant reception of grace, that Wesley is concerned to interpret and enable. Breathing is a pivotal symbol of our constantly receiving grace upon grace and ever anew responding to grace.

b. Breathing, Seeing, and Hearing Spiritually

Before birth one's eyes are not yet opened. *After birth* one begins to breathe, to see with one's own eyes, which existed previously but did not see, and to hear with one's ears the previously muffled sounds of providence.[57] Before birth the baby is *alive* in the womb. After birth the baby is *breathing* outside the womb. Breathing is a physical act that lends itself to become a metaphor of spiritual rebirth. The Spirit breathes life into the soul.

What new birth is all about is the birthing of these spiritual senses that have remained dormant prior to birth. Breathing, hearing, seeing spiritually are all gifts of the new birth by which one may now receive the breath of life, behold the Way, and hear the divine address.[58]

[55]"The New Birth," B 2:199, sec. 4.4. On the distinction between inward and outward sin, see B 1:239–40, 245–46, 336–44; 2:215–16.

[56]"The New Birth," B 2:191, sec. 2.3.

[57]"The New Birth," B 2:192, sec. 2.4; cf. "The Great Privilege of Those That Are Born of God," 1; FA, J V:24–26.

[58]"The New Birth," sec. 4.4, 2:199–201.

Imagine what it would feel like to be born — suddenly entering an unfolding world of free action. Upon birth one sees the world one has not seen before. In spiritual birth, one learns to hear in a new way, by listening to the words of Scripture and the voice of the Spirit in one's daily walk.

The new birth permits attentive hearing and alert seeing. A new sensory apparatus comes with faith. One's spiritual senses begin gradually to be activated by this new spiritual birth. That does not mean that they immediately all work maximally as if in mature spiritual hearing and seeing, but they commence seeing and hearing. Birth is just a beginning, but nothing else can occur until it happens.

c. The Continuity of Prenatal Life with Postnatal Breathing

The new birth is the entrance to the life in which one begins to grow in holiness.[59] Countering William Law, who had equated regeneration with progressive sanctification, Wesley argued that the new birth was the beginning point of growth in sanctification. "The same relation therefore which there is between our natural birth and our growth there is also between our new birth and our sanctification."[60] Thus, there is a precise distinction between regeneration and sanctification. It hinges on the difference between beginning and continuing. Regeneration is analogous to birth, sanctification to breathing.

The respiratory function that keeps us spiritually alive is a constant reception of grace, not a single momentary occurrence. Think of the sin of believers as returning voluntarily again into the stifling atmosphere of an oxygen-deprived smoke-filled room. Those who have repented, believed, been baptized, and fallen again may yet return to the freedom and open air of grace. Those who fall and stumble have the remedy of the Eucharist to complement the grace of their baptism.

If sin means voluntary transgression of a known law of God, then the life of grace means constantly being empowered by the Spirit to walk in the way of faith, trusting step-by-step in God's providing.[61]

Anyone who loves souls seeks a way of communicating with them candidly that they must be born again. Neither baptism, church attendance, nor moral renewal can take the place of the new birth.[62]

We now turn from the homily on "The New Birth" to the homily on "Marks of the New Birth."

B. Marks of the New Birth

The text for the homily "Marks of the New Birth" is John 3:8: "So is every one that is born of the Spirit" [Homily #18 (1748), B 1:415 – 30; J #18, V:212 – 23].

The Spirit intends to work a thoroughgoing victory over our sins. Part of what

[59]B 2:194 – 95, 198; 3:506 – 7, 4:521 – 22.
[60]"The New Birth," B 2:198, sec. 4.3.
[61]"The New Birth," B 2:198 – 201, sec. 4.3 – 4.
[62]"The New Birth," B 2:200 – 201, sec. 4.4.

makes classical Wesleyan teaching relatively distinctive among Protestant teachings is that Wesley held not to a perfunctory or minimal expectation of behavioral transformation, but to a consummate and radical expectation.

While God's saving work finally remains a mystery of grace, what becomes evident are marks and visible fruits of the new birth. As God works for our renewal, we are not left without plausible evidences of this work.[63] The first mark of the new birth is faith.

1. Faith

a. Born of the Spirit

Whoever from the heart *believes* that Jesus is the Christ is born of God. Regenerating, saving faith means not simply intellectual assent to propositions of revelation,[64] or speculative faith, but a disposition of the heart to trust in God that through the merits of Christ *my* sins are forgiven and I am reconciled to favor with God.[65] This is not to disavow the intellectual component of faith, but the course of faith runs deeper than intellectual assent. What happened on the cross is meritorious for me, so that what is objectively done for humanity is applied and received by me through faith.

Whoever is born of the Spirit and abides in the Spirit and is nurtured by the Spirit, remains free from sin as long as he or she trustingly receives the empowerment of grace through the Spirit. The fruit of faith is precisely power over sin, inward and outward, and thus peace with God and human happiness.

b. Abiding in the Spirit: God's Seed Remains in Him

Wesley addressed the crucial text "No one who is born of God will continue to sin, because God's seed remains in them; they cannot go on sinning, because they have been born of God" (1 John 3:9 NIV).[66] The only way to understand that text is to test it out experientially by finding out what it means to live practically by this regenerating grace. Only then will you see its fruit, which is freedom from sin. Wesley did not try to coerce the text to say that what the writer of 1 John really meant was that whoever is born of God does not commit sin *habitually.* He preferred to adhere closely to what the Greek text plainly says.[67]

"Seed" points to the reimplanted divine nature and image given the one born of God by faith and baptism, who is "inwardly and universally changed." This renewal promises the complete cleansing of the maturing self, moment by moment, by this justifying and regenerating grace. From this renewal we receive a sense of serenity,

---

[63]"The Marks of the New Birth," B 1:417, proem.

[64]FA, B 11:177.

[65]"The Marks of the New Birth," B 1:418, sec. 1.3.

[66]"The Marks of the New Birth," B 1:420–21, sec. 1.5–6.

[67]"By living faith, whereby God is continually breathing spiritual life into his soul, and his soul is continually breathing out love and prayer to God, [the believer] does not commit sin," *ENNT* 911.

consolation, and peace — not only a peace within ourselves, but a peace that transforms our relation to the neighbor toward whom we reach out in love.[68]

2. Hope

a. The Spirit Enables Hope

The second mark of the new birth is a lively hope that testifies that we are children of God, along with the testimony of conscience that we are walking in simplicity and godly sincerity. It is not simply a biblically informed conscience testifying that we are so walking, but it is the direct witness of God's own Spirit with our spirit that we are children of God that gives this assurance, a firm sense that we are adopted into the family of God, and that this inheritance is eternal life.

This dual testimony of my conscience with that of God's own Spirit in and with my spirit is what yields hope, which finally reaches toward the end-time judgment and consummation of divine glory.[69] The hope is ultimately to receive the inheritance that is the final gift of faith's journey.[70]

b. Joy in Hope

Intense joy is found in this hope. It is no dismal, depressing matter to share in this hope, as if focused despairingly on what one does not have. Rather, it is a serene, at times ecstatic, anticipatory reception of the gifts yet finally to be received — eternal bliss, the vision of God.[71]

Suffering is understood in relation to the providential purposes of God in history that are already in the process of being fulfilled. Meanwhile history is incomplete. The end of history is not yet. In this transient interim, faith elicits a living hope that sustains the believer through whatever drought or storm may come.[72]

This faith grounded in this hope leads to love.

3. Love

The third mark of the new birth is *love,* which pours itself out caringly for the neighbor. We care for the neighbor as we have been cared for by God. We love our enemies as God has loved us while we were enemies of righteousness.[73] Love, which bears the fruit of faith in relation to the neighbor, is especially tested in relation to one perceived as foe. Even the antagonist can now be viewed in relation to the coming final divine reconciliation. In this way, the believer is freed to love every person he or she meets in relation to the love of God, which is being poured out by the Holy Spirit in our hearts.[74]

---

[68]"The Marks of the New Birth," B 1:420, sec. 1.5.

[69]B 1:406 – 7, 411 – 12, 422 – 25; 2:223.

[70]"The Marks of the New Birth," B 1:422 – 23, sec. 2.1 – 3.

[71]"The Marks of the New Birth," B 1:423 – 25, sec. 2.4 – 5.

[72]"The Marks of the New Birth," B 1:422 – 25, sec. 2.

[73]*LJW* 5:101, 203, 258, 323.

[74]"The Marks of the New Birth," B 1:425 – 27, sec. 3.

4. Recognition of the Marks of the New Birth

Each one is called to earnest self-examination as to whether the marks of the new birth are being truly manifested: trusting in God, hoping amid suffering, and loving the neighbor in need. These are such visible evidences of new birth that no one need feel deprived of assurance of salvation or in the dark about one's reconciliation with God as Abba. By faith, hope, and love, we are living out in practice a life of responsiveness to God in a joyful constant answerability of the whole heart to the love of God.[75]

By these evidences, it is knowable that one, being born again, born of God, born of the Spirit, is a "child of God" by "the Spirit of adoption." These privileges "by the free mercy of God, are *ordinarily annexed to baptism* (which is thence termed by our Lord in a preceding verse, the being 'born of water and of the Spirit')."[76] Yet we are admonished not to say too cheaply, "I *was once* baptized, therefore I *am now* a child of God," or identify the new birth simply with the sacrament of baptism as such, as if to ignore behavioral responsiveness to the grace of baptism. For this forces any serious observer to ask whether "baptized whoremongers" are indeed living as children of God.[77]

C. The Great Privilege of Those That Are Born of God

A great privilege awaits those born of God. The text of the homily "The Great Privilege of Those That Are Born of God" is, again, 1 John 3:9: "Whosoever is born of God doth not commit sin." [Homily #19 (1748), B 1:431–43; J #19, V:223–33].

1. Relational and Real Change: Restoration of the Favor and Image of God

New birth begins the daily respiratory process of breathing in the grace and mercy of God and breathing out the energies of new life.

Justification is God's work on the cross for us, a completed work that implies an objective change in our relationship to God. As such it is not contingent on our decision. It is simply a gift.[78] That new *relation with God*[79] intends and seeks a *real change in us*, imperatively requiring a new spiritual life responsive to that gift. Justification is therefore a relational ("relative") change, while what follows after justification (new birth and growth in sanctifying grace) calls for real, substantive behavioral response.[80]

[75]"The Marks of the New Birth," B 1:427–30, sec. 4.
[76]"The Marks of the New Birth," B 1:417, proem, italics added.
[77]"The Marks of the New Birth," B 1:429, sec. 4.3.
[78]"The Great Privilege of Those That Are Born of God," B 1:431, proem 1–2.
[79]Wesley's term is *relative*, used archaically in the sense of relational.
[80]"The Great Privilege of Those That Are Born of God," B 1:431, proem 2.

a. The One God in Triune Form Acts to Restore

On the cross, God the Son established a new relationship between God the Father and fallen humanity. By new birth, we are actually being born into that relationship so that we may continue to grow in it, in a real behavioral change that is answerable to the relational change offered on the cross.

God the Spirit seeks to transform fully and in consummate detail the fallen person so that the image of God is being reflected in human conduct. The offering and receiving of this new life is what is meant by being born of God. In this way, the triune God is working economically and cooperatively to bring us this salvation by justification in the Son and sanctification through the Spirit.

Wesley sharpened this distinction: if by justification we are restored to the *favor* of God, by regeneration we are restored in the *image* of God. God's justifying action on the cross changes one's real relation to God. New birth changes one's inmost motivation and disposition of soul. If justification is God's action *for us in the Son,* new birth is the inauguration of God's action *in us through the Spirit.* Justification takes away the *guilt* of sin. New birth takes away the *power* of sin. When the image of God is restored, the power of sin is made null.[81]

b. Being Made Sensible to God

Once again in "The Great Privilege of Those That Are Born of God," Wesley worked off of the birth-growth analogy: The child in the womb has no knowledge of the world outside the womb even though that world surrounds him, because the senses are not yet fully functional. Likewise, the fallen self has little or no knowledge of the spiritual world because its spiritual senses are not yet activated, awakened, or ready to function. By analogy, the unregenerate self lives and "subsists by Him in whom all that have life 'live, and move, and have their being,' yet he is not *sensible* of God; he does not feel, he has no inward consciousness of His presence."[82]

One born of God is *made sensible to God,* and can employ never before used spiritual senses to come alive to grace. The newborn, "by a kind of spiritual reaction, returns the grace he receives in unceasing love, praise, and prayer."[83]

2. The Great Privilege of Those Reborn: The Grace Not to Sin

a. Sin as Voluntary Transgression of Law

What is the unique privilege of those born of God? "No one who is born of God will continue to sin" (1 John 3:9 NIV) as long as one shares in this responsiveness to grace, as long as one continues to breathe the invigorating air of grace.[84] The distinct

[81]"The Great Privilege of Those That Are Born of God," B 1:431 – 32, proem 2 – 4.

[82]"The Great Privilege of Those That Are Born of God," B 1:433 – 34, sec. 1.6.

[83]"The Great Privilege of Those That Are Born of God," B 1:435, sec. 2.1. Wesley was among the earliest known to use the term *re-action,* cf. *OED.*

[84]"Marks of the New Birth," B 1:419, sec. 1.3.

gift of the Christian life is to be delivered from the power of sin and thus prepared for the holy and happy life.[85]

"By 'sin,' I here understand outward sin, according to the plain, common acceptation of the word: an *actual voluntary 'transgression of the law'*; of the revealed, written law of God; of any commandment of God acknowledged to be such at the time that it is transgressed." It is just such offenses that those born of God are being enabled by grace to overcome.[86]

b. Grace Sufficient to Enable Not Continuing in Sin

Wesley wrote, "Does not St. Paul say plainly that those who believe do not 'continue in sin'? And does not St. John say most expressly: ...'For this purpose the Son of God was manifested, that he might destroy the works of the devil. Whosoever is born of God doth not commit sin.' ...It is not *we* that say this, but the Lord.... This is the height and depth of what we (with St. Paul) call perfection—a state of soul devoutly to be wished for by all who have tasted of the love of God."[87]

In promising that "whosoever is born of God doth not commit sin," Wesley was not imposing a new law that *requires* all believers not to commit sin. Rather, he was announcing the good news that grace *enables* believers not to sin.

c. The Responsibility Commensurable with the Privilege: Keeping Oneself from Temptation

The gift of the new birth is to be so steadily surrounded by sufficient grace that temptation can be continually turned aside. As long as this seed remains alive and nurtured in us, the adversary does not get close enough to us to do us mortal harm. So we are being guarded, hedged by grace from temptation and its consequent sin.[88]

Falling away begins with temptation, but keep in mind that temptation is by definition that which can be resisted. To be compelled is not the same as to be tempted. Temptation is a seduction to which we are idolatrously inclined but with which we are not necessitated to collude.

The faithful are not unconditionally protected from falling into sin, as we see in the biblical accounts of David's lust and Peter's denial. When we neglect grace and incline our hearts to evil, we lose faith, failing to listen attentively to the steady witness of the Spirit. This is a needless failure of the spiritual senses. We decide we do not want to breathe clean air but polluted air. And so we fall away. It is not guaranteed that once having received justifying grace, one can then forever rest easily in Zion, as if without human responsiveness. Freedom remains always vulnerable to temptation.[89] Resisting temptation is largely in our hands, but sufficient grace assists us in the resistance.

---

[85]"The Great Privilege of Those That Are Born of God," B 1:435–36, sec. 2.1.
[86]"The Great Privilege of Those That Are Born of God," B 1:436, sec. 2.2, italics added.
[87]EA, sec. 53–56, B 11:65–67.
[88]"The Great Privilege of Those That Are Born of God," B 1:436, sec. 2.2.
[89]B 2:142, 226.

d. No Fall Is Irremediable

One born of God who keeps himself under the constraint of grace may fall temporarily, but no fall is irremediable. Wesley's formula: though *liable to fall*, we remain *able to stand*.[90] We are being given the possibility of not committing sin by ever-sufficient grace: preparatory, justifying, and sanctifying. No temptation is so great that it cannot by grace be resisted.

One may receive this grace in one moment and succumb to temptation the next. There is no way to predict outcomes or to anticipate how freedom will react to the variable possibilities of grace meeting free agency in history. But the distinct privilege of the believer is to live the life of the new birth whereby sin has lost its absolute sway, though it continues to tempt freedom. Sin remains in the faithful but does not reign.[91]

3. Regression from Grace to Sin

a. How Grace Works against Regression

So long as one is living by faith, one is not committing sin. One may regress, however, from grace to sin in the following sequence: The seed remains in one born of God. The seed does not die. It may be reawakened by faith. Temptation arises within the conditions of finitude, amid the body/soul interface, escalated by demonic intensification.[92]

When that happens, we are admonished by the Spirit through conscience. By this admonition, we know we are children of our Father, not parentless waifs. Growth in grace can be arrested at any point at which faith ceases to respond trustingly to grace. Whenever we are tempted, the Spirit is always there to give counsel (Gk. *nouthesia*, "admonition"). Those attentive to the Spirit will hear early warning signals and not fall into sin insofar as faith is sustained. Those who collude with the temptation may fall into sin and grieve the Spirit.

Tempted freedom may gradually "give way, in some degree, to the temptation, which now begins to grow pleasing."[93] The Spirit is grieved, our faith is weakened, and our love for God cools. The Spirit warns more sharply. We may try to turn off conscience but seldom with undivided or enduring success.

b. Habitual Regression Not beyond the Power of Grace

We may turn away from the Spirit's address even more decisively so that evil tempers and wretched neurotic behavioral patterns begin to form and become habitual.[94] When this happens, it does not mean that we are ever completely out of

[90]"The Great Privilege of Those That Are Born of God," B 1:436–41, sec. 2.4–10.
[91]Ibid.
[92]B 1:438–41, 484, 693; 3:24–25, 156–71; 4:194, 533.
[93]"The Great Privilege of Those That Are Born of God," B 1:440, sec. 2.9.
[94]B 1:416, 420–21, 557–58.

the reach of the Spirit. Even then the Spirit does not abandon the fallen but continues to reprove, correct, and teach.

But whenever we reinforce toxic behavioral patterns, it becomes psychologically harder to hear the address of the Spirit. Finally, we may spin into a syndrome in which evil desires[95] spread so cancerously that the living power of faith, hope, and love virtually vanishes in a sea of despairing self-assertion, making us again prone to sin since the power of the Lord has left us; yet still the seed remains implanted and may be revitalized by faith.[96]

c. Daily Meeting Temptation

At each stage of falling, we are choosing, not being necessitated, to fall. Those who freely collude are at first free to cease to collude, but with more collusion they grow ever less free. It is our personal responsibility when we collude with temptation. Those born of God do not commit sin insofar as they do not choose to fall step-by-step into this syndrome of collusion with temptation.[97]

Those born of God are charged to keep themselves so that the adversary will not come within reach of touching them. Those born of God through justifying grace grow through this constant respiratory process, continuing to breathe in the ever-new daily life of grace and breathe out the works of love.[98]

Christian caregiving focuses on helping pardoned sinners meet temptation, so as not to collude with the demonic at the moment when tempted to pride or gluttony. Amid all snares, as long as faith remains, one has not turned away from saving grace. Even if faith remains in a weak form, one has not lost access to saving grace.

The faithful do well to examine carefully, in small accountable groups, specific ways in which they at early stages are beginning to be tempted. They are called to pray to be guarded against temptation and to pray for the means of grace by which temptation can be resisted.[99] It is therefore always an inward loss of faith that precedes outward, actual sin.[100] If we do not continue in love toward God and neighbor, the Spirit may seem to "gradually withdraw, and leave us to the darkness of our own hearts."[101]

Faith working by love leaves no room for inward or outward sin in a soul being made fully alive by grace.[102] This is the "great privilege."

[95]It is not that desire as such is evil, but that evil desires may be transformed into desires made holy by faith active in love; *SS* 2:362n.

[96]"The Great Privilege of Those That Are Born of God," B 1:440–41, sec. 2.9, 10; *SS* 2:275.

[97]"The Great Privilege of Those That Are Born of God," B 1:438–39, sec. 2.6–8.

[98]"The Great Privilege of Those That Are Born of God," B 1:438–41, sec. 2.6–10.

[99]"The Great Privilege of Those That Are Born of God," B 1:441–43, sec. 3.

[100]"The Great Privilege of Those That Are Born of God," B 1:442, sec. 3.2; cf. B 2:203, 206; *SS* 2:246.

[101]"The Great Privilege of Those That Are Born of God," B 1:442, sec. 3.3.

[102]B 1:559–60; 3:122–23, 303–4, 385–86, 612–13; JWO 68, 123–32, 231–32, 279–80, 376.

Further Reading on Salvation

Soteriology

Collins, Kenneth. "Convincing Grace and Initial Repentance." In *Wesley on Salvation.* Grand Rapids: Zondervan, 1989.

Mason, C. E. "John Wesley's Doctrine of Salvation." Master's thesis, Union Theological Seminary, 1950.

Schilling, Paul. "John Wesley's Theology of Salvation." In *Methodism and Society in Theological Perspective*, 44 – 64. Nashville: Abingdon, 1960.

Change of Heart

Brown, Robert. *John Wesley's Theology: The Principle of Its Vitality and Its Progressive Stages of Development.* London: E. Stock, 1965.

Clapper, Gregory S. *As If the Heart Mattered: A Wesleyan Spirituality.* Nashville: Upper Room, 1997.

———. *John Wesley on Religious Affections: His Views on Experience and Emotion and Their Role in the Christian Life and Theology.* Metuchen, NJ: Scarecrow, 1989.

———. *The Renewal of the Heart Is the Mission of the Church: Wesley's Heart.* Nashville: Upper Room Books, 1997.

Collins, Kenneth J. *John Wesley: A Theological Journey*. Nashville: Abingdon, 2003.

Fowler, James W. "John Wesley's Development in Faith." Chap. 6 of *The Future of the Methodist Theological Traditions.* Nashville: Abingdon, 1985.

CHAPTER 9

Sanctification

Since the teaching of sanctification is found abundantly in the ancient church tradition, it is viewed as a unique Wesleyan distinctive only by those inattentive to the patristic writers. It is also found persistently in all the classic Reformers — Luther, Calvin, and the Anglican formularies as well as the Puritan and Pietistic writers.

Emphasis on this doctrine became a leading feature of the Wesleyan legacy in the evangelical revival. The preaching of its full realization by grace in ordinary believers has impacted many forms of nineteenth-century revivalism, including charismatic, evangelical Catholic, Wesleyan, and Pentecostal traditions of preaching.

Many vectors of modern perplexities about Wesley focus here. One does an injustice to Wesley by viewing all his teaching in the light of this single point, yet those who disregard it miss something crucial in Wesley. In his *Plain Account of Christian Perfection*, Wesley reviewed four decades of his teaching on this subject. He considered his views throughout this time as consistent.

A. A Plain Account of Christian Perfection

1. Rooting Out Sin

a. Whether Consistently Taught

Wesley was convinced that he had not substantially changed his mind about sanctification and perfection teaching from his Oxford days until 1763 when he wrote *A Plain Account of Christian Perfection* (J XI: 366 – 446).

He thought he had consistently held to the expectation that the Holy Spirit intends to transform our behavior, not partially but completely, and if not now, in due time when we become more fully responsive. The doctrine went through modest changes of interpretation and defense, not of substance, but expression. It remained constant except for a few minor alterations that amount to little more than responses to challenges. Variable circumstances caused Wesley to argue the same case in different ways and to defend it against varied deconstructions.[1]

Wesley urged that all preachers in his connection of spiritual formation make a

[1]*PACP*, secs. 1 – 5, J XI:366 – 67.

point of teaching the way of holiness to believers "constantly, strongly and explicitly," and that all class leaders should be attentive to this doctrine and "continually agonize" for its experiential appropriation.[2]

b. The Grand Depositum

Wesley was convinced that Christian preaching in his time had not grasped the full implications of the work the Holy Spirit intends to do in us. Methodists were called upon not merely to teach but to live the holy life. His pastoral work sought to bring this life into full expression as an experienced reality.

Wesley considered this "the *grand depositum* which God has lodged with the people called Methodists and for the sake of propagating this chiefly he appeared to have raised them up."[3]

In the 1740 preface to *Hymns and Sacred Poems,* Wesley wrote, "This is the strongest account we ever gave of Christian perfection; indeed too strong in more than one particular."

Admitting that perfection teaching had led to some misunderstandings, he nonetheless insisted that "there is nothing we have since advanced upon the subject, either in verse or prose, which is not either directly or indirectly contained in this preface. So that whether our present doctrine be right or wrong, it is howsoever the same which we taught from the beginning."[4]

The two affirmations that invited misunderstanding, later to be refined, were (1) that those walking in perfect love "are freed from evil thoughts, so that they cannot enter into them"; and (2) that "they are, in one sense, freed from temptation; for though numberless temptations fly about them, yet they wound them not."[5] Answer: They are not freed from the challenge of temptation, but rather, from any necessity to fall, and are freed by sufficient grace to avert temptation. They situationally receive "unction from the Holy One which abideth in them, and teacheth them every hour, what they shall do."[6]

c. Kempis, Taylor, and Law

Three authors of the holy living tradition exercised a decisive influence on Wesley's early formation on this theme: Jeremy Taylor, Thomas à Kempis, and William Law. At age twenty-three (in 1725), Wesley read Anglican bishop Jeremy Taylor's *Rules and Exercises of Holy Living and Holy Dying,* which stressed the intentional resolution to lifelong purity of heart. Taylor called his readers to dedicate their entire lives wholly to God, every moment being seen in relation to eternity. He said, "Instantly I resolved to dedicate all my life to God."[7]

[2]*PACP*, sec. 26, J XI:443.
[3]"On Perfection," B 3:86 – 87, sec. 3.12.
[4]*PACP*, sec. 13, J XIV:381 – 82.
[5]The point here is not that temptation ceases objectively, but that it is being subjectively deprived by the grace-enabled, disciplined will of exercising unchecked power.
[6]*HSP* (1740), pref. 7, J XIV:324 – 25.
[7]*PACP*, sec. 2, J XI:366; see also B 3:123, 324, 580; 4:121 for reference to Bishop Taylor.

In 1726 when Wesley read *The Imitation of Christ* by Thomas à Kempis,[8] he was further arrested by the notion of simplicity of intention, that purity of affection where one loves but one thing, has one design in all that is spoken or done, and a single desire ruling all motives.[9] These gracious habits are "indeed 'the wings of the soul' without which she can never ascend to the mount of God."[10]

Wesley found the same centeredness of intent in William Law's *Christian Perfection* and *A Serious Call to the Devout and Holy Life.* He unequivocally decided that it was impossible to be a fractional Christian; one must yield all to God.[11] The rest of Wesley's long life expressed the embodiment of this teaching that he had deeply appropriated so early, first at home under the instruction of his mother, Susannah, and in his early twenties at Oxford before the time of his ordination.

d. Christ Is Forming the Believer both from Above and Below

The teaching of perfecting grace is not finally about the power of human freedom, but the power of grace totally to transform freedom.[12] This transformation is best understood as Christ's image forming in us and secondarily as our yielding ourselves to be formed by Christ.

From the point of view of Christ forming himself in us, Christian perfection is the mind of Christ entering into us and taking us into himself in union with himself. It assumes the ancient Christian teaching of Christ: truly divine, truly human.

Viewed from above, it is "all the mind which was in Christ enabling us to walk as Christ walked. It is the circumcision of the heart from all filthiness, from all inward as well as outward pollution."[13]

Viewed from below, perfecting grace is seen as an act of complete dedication, entire consecration, a radical and unreserved commitment of the self to the grace of the Spirit filling the soul. Grasped volitionally, "it is purity of intention, dedicating all the life to God. It is the giving God all our heart; it is one desire and design ruling all our tempers. It is the devoting, not a part, but all, our soul, body, and substance to God."[14]

Wesley's sanctification teaching is based explicitly on a cohesive chain of Scripture texts. In most ways, it is close to what some Reformed writers have called positional sanctification. There is a profound doctrine of sanctification in the Calvinist

[8]On Thomas à Kempis, see B 2:375; 3:39, 580; 4:105, 182; 9:85; *LJW* 3:213; 4:239, 293.

[9]On purity of heart, or simplicity of intention, see *LJW* 1:192; 2:190, 201; B 1:306 – 7, 510 – 14, 573 – 77, 608 – 9, 672 – 73, 698; 3:122 – 23, 287 – 89; 4:120 – 23, 371 – 77.

[10]J XI:367; Christian spirituality today is currently recovering this doctrine of simplicity of intention in writers like Thomas Merton, Henry Nouwen, and Richard Foster.

[11]*PACP*, sec. 4, J XI:367; "And by my continued endeavor to keep his whole law, inward and outward to the uttermost of my power, I was persuaded that I should be accepted of Him, and that I was even then in a state of salvation." John Emory edition of *The Works of the Rev. John Wesley* (1855), 3.71.

[12]B 2:97 – 121; 3:70 – 87; JWO 252 – 53; on crowning grace, see *CH*, B 7:49.

[13]J XI:444.

[14]*PACP*, sec. 5, J XI:366 – 67; cf. *LJW* 4:298. The holy living tradition from both Anglican and Puritan sources is crucial in this definition. Cf. B 1:20 – 22, 37; 4:268.

teaching of our sharing in the righteousness of Christ, assuming that our sanctification is already embedded in the justifying act of God.[15] This idea of sanctification Wesley strongly affirmed, yet with the warning that it might drift toward antinomian license. The only way he was refashioning it was by speaking steadily of the possibility and necessity of a full and unreserved consecration of the whole of one's redeemed powers for the remainder of one's life.[16]

Meanwhile Charles was writing hymns by which the societies were singing their way into celebrating the same teaching:

> In thee my wandering thoughts unite,
> Of all my works be thou the aim:
> Thy love attend me all my days,
> And my sole business be thy praise.[17]

In early 1738 while returning from Savannah, John Wesley wrote:

> O may thy love possess me whole,
> My joy, my treasure, and my crown!
> Strange fires far from my heart remove;
> My every act, word, thought, be love![18]

2. Against Pelagian and Manichean Distortions

Some objected that Wesley was exalting the human possibility by wrongly, even in a Pelagian manner, claiming that native humanity is of itself capable of achieving redemption. His reply made it clear that perfecting grace is a doctrine of grace, not anthropology or natural human competency. It is only by the power of grace that human willing is being reclaimed to its original purpose of righteousness, reflecting the image of God. There is not a shred of Pelagianism in Wesley.

Others objected that humanity is so far fallen into evil that talk of perfect love is ludicrous and that we had better be speaking of the redeemed will as still tending inevitably toward evil. To the Manichean claim that it is self-evident that the self is so evil that there is no full responsiveness to God on the earth, Wesley answered that while created humanity is profoundly fallen into sin, grace sufficiently reaches and addresses human follies with the intent of utterly transforming them.

The faithful are not perfect in knowledge nor free from weakness, finitude, or temptation, but the Christian life aims toward unblemished love of God and neighbor that is not intrinsically unrealizable. There is, however, no perfection that does not admit of continual increase. It is not a static notion but rather dynamic, a *teleiôsis* and not a *perfectus.* The Greek terms in Scripture are more fitting than their translation into Latin.

---

[15]Calvin, *Institutes* 3.11.10, 4:13; Commentaries, XVIII:561, XXIV:334; John Owen, *Works* 3:468 – 538; Thomas Goodwin, *Works*, V:85 – 95, 459 – 70; W. S. Chafer, *Systematic Theology*, V:283 – 85.

[16]*CH*, B 7:589 – 93.

[17]*HSP* (1739), 122.

[18]*PACP*, sec. 7, J XI:369.

"We are justified by *faith alone*, and yet by such a faith as is *not alone*" (in the sense of being fruitless).[19] "Faith alone is the condition of *present* salvation," on the assumption that when "faith is given, holiness commences in the soul; for that instant 'the love of God (which is the source of holiness) is shed abroad in the heart.'"[20] "This was the view of religion," which from the early age of thirty to the advanced age of seventy-four, Wesley said, "I scrupled not to term *perfection*. This is the view I have of it now."[21] But he never meant by perfection a static condition.

B. The Circumcision of the Heart

The text of the homily "The Circumcision of the Heart" is Romans 2:29: "Circumcision is that of the heart, in the spirit, and not in the letter" [Homily #17 (1733), B 1:398–414; J #17, V:202–12].

Before going to Georgia, on the first day of the year in 1733, Wesley preached at St. Mary's, Oxford, on what it means to be a Jew inwardly. The key idea is best captured in the Pauline text: "A person is not a Jew who is one only outwardly, nor is circumcision merely outward and physical. No, *a person is a Jew who is one inwardly; and circumcision is circumcision of the heart*, by the Spirit, not by the written code" (Rom. 2:28–29 NIV, italics added).

1. On Being a Jew Inwardly

a. Circumcision of the Heart Defined

Being a Jew inwardly, or "circumcision of the heart," is defined as that habitual disposition of soul to walk by faith in the way of holiness. It implies so trusting in the coming righteousness of Christ as to be renewed in the spirit of our minds that the body, as temple of the Spirit, manifests the holiness of God fully and without blemish. It implies being cleansed from sin, from corruption of both flesh and spirit, and in consequence being drawn toward those character qualities of Christ Jesus.

Only by complete trust in the atoning work is one enabled to fulfill the command to be perfect as our Father in heaven is perfect. It is accompanied by the confirmation of one's hope for reconciliation through the testimony of one's conscience, and through the testimony of the Holy Spirit to our spirit.

Circumcision of the heart is total commitment of the heart to God. Let every thought, word, action, and movement of the heart be ordered in relation to this source and end of our existence so that everything we do tends to the glory of God, loving all things in relation to the one worthiest of our love. All loves are loved in relation to the love of this one. We are called first to love God unreservedly, that all that we love may come into the orbit of this centering love. In this way, the will is reordered so that all created things tend toward the glory of the

[19]A Letter to the Rev. Mr. Home, B 11:454, sec. 2.3.
[20]FA, pt. 1, B 11:130, sec. 3.10.
[21]*PACP*, sec. 6, J XI:369.

Creator. Nothing thought to be good is pursued except in relation to the one who is eternally good.

Circumcision of the heart means complete consecration, entire sanctification. Those circumcised of heart are constantly being effectively renewed in the Spirit of Christ.[22] This is not the circumcision of the flesh, but of the heart, for it is out of the heart that all words and deeds come.

b. Sharing in the Covenant Community

Circumcision has its origin in the Hebraic rite by which infant males were brought into the covenant community, set apart as consecrated members of the people of God. Circumcision of the heart is a metaphor that reveals how God the Spirit is giving us a new birth so as to place us in a new covenant community.[23]

The New Testament debate about circumcision had to do with what is meant by one's entry into the covenant community. Baptism functions in analogy with circumcision, except that it is a rite not just for males, but for all men and women who share in Christ's death and resurrection.[24] The Torah had promised that "the LORD your God will circumcise your hearts and the hearts of your descendants, so that you may love him with all your heart and with all your soul, and live" (Deut. 30:6 NIV). "A promise is implied in every commandment of God."[25] What God commands, God offers sufficient grace to do.

Jesus attested that the sum of the law is to love the Lord with all your heart, mind, and strength and the neighbor as yourself, so that whatever one fears, desires, seeks, or avoids is viewed in relation to the Giver of life. Circumcision of the heart (as distinguished from "outward circumcision or baptism, or any other outward form") is a way of talking about the heart being set apart for the love of God and the neighbor.[26]

2. Being Sustained Daily in Humble Repentance, Faith, Hope, and Love

a. Descent with Christ: Daily Humbling to Repentance

Those circumcised in heart are characterized by a daily mortification,[27] a dying to the world's idolatries, a profound meekness and "lowliness of mind," that makes way for faith, hope, and love.

The penitent life that burns away pride and self-deception readies the heart for saving faith, which allows and calls us to hope that the Spirit will provide us with the means of grace that leads to "Love divine, all loves excelling."[28]

---

[22]"The Circumcision of the Heart," B 1:401 – 2, proem 1 – 3.
[23]JWO 318 – 31.
[24]"The Circumcision of the Heart," B 1:402 – 9, sec. 1.
[25]"On Perfection," B 3:80, sec. 2.11.
[26]"The Circumcision of the Heart," B 1:402, sec. 1.
[27]B 2:245; *SS* 1:165; 2:289.
[28]*LJW* 1:248; 2:107, 110, 186.

Grace must first remove the pride that blocks us from hearing the word of God's mercy. Through this *humbling*, we become aware of how far our own natural capacities have fallen away from the goodness of God, and how we really cannot save or adequately help ourselves.[29]

Repentance brings the realistic self-awareness that "in our best estate we are, of ourselves, all sin and vanity ... that there is no whole part of our soul, that all the foundations of our nature are out of course."[30]

Sanctifying grace works to cleanse the person from multiple layers of inveterate egocentricity. The tendency to see everything from one's own self-assertive point of view is being cut away. Circumcision is a cutting image, an incision that carries over metaphorically into the life of repentance. What happens in circumcision is a cutting away of a part of the male generative organ by which life is spawned, a sanctification metaphor, whereby this most crucial engendering function is being set aside for a holy purpose.

b. Ascent with Christ: Daily Growth toward Faith, Hope, and Love

From the humility of repentance, there may follow by grace *faith*, which is a sure trust in Christ who redeems us from our sin and reconciles us to God.[31]

Faith leads to *hope* that quietly expects the Spirit to do his promised work in us. Hope is the expectation that the Spirit desires to provide us with sufficient means of grace by which our lives can be thoroughly reordered.[32] Unless we rejoice in hope that we are heirs of God's promise, we will not rise above our persistent weaknesses and impediments and truly be led by the Spirit toward self-denial and taking up of the cross. Hope perseveres by "a lively expectation of receiving all good things at God's hand."[33]

Love completes the circle, fulfills the law, so that the love of God with all of one's heart, mind, and strength and love of neighbor as oneself are not only envisioned but enabled.

3. Whether One Baptized Can Be Half a Christian

a. Either/Or

"Half a Christian" is an oxymoron. One either believes the good news or one does not. What follows from that is either radically transforming of one's behavior or falls short of unfeigned faith. One is either altogether a Christian, adopted into the family of God, or still trapped in the syndromes of being almost a Christian, with the servile, legalistic, wage-counting relation of a servant.[34]

Becoming a Christian at heart means not merely that one has received the grace

---

[29]B 1:403 – 4, 409 – 10, 479 – 80.

[30]"The Circumcision of the Heart," B 1:403, sec. 1.2.

[31]"The Circumcision of the Heart," B 1:410, sec. 2.2.

[32]"The Circumcision of the Heart," B 1:411 – 12, sec. 2.5 – 8.

[33]"The Circumcision of the Heart," B 1:406, sec. 1.9.

[34]"The Almost Christian," B 1:131 – 35, sec. 1; J V:17 – 25.

of baptism, but that one having received it understands what the grace of baptism means. Christians are those who, having been baptized, take seriously the full consequences of their baptism.

Those who have received the grace of baptism remain free to deny or disregard or forget or ignore the meaning of their baptism. Their mouths are not stopped. They are not forcibly prevented from falling from grace. The grace of baptism points quietly toward the new birth, toward daily sharing in Christ's death and resurrection. Whether sanctifying grace is palpably experienced by those who have been once formally baptized depends not on whether God offers sufficient grace, but on whether they receive it.[35]

It appears as a hard saying to one dead to God and alive to the world to be called to "live wholly unto God." Who without grace is ready to die to the world? "Unless it be so qualified in the interpretation as to have neither use nor significance," the hearer will turn away, thinking such thoughts "foolishness."[36] To teach such things "runs the hazard of being esteemed" as "a setter forth of new doctrines," most having "so *lived away* the substance of that religion, the profession whereof they still retain, that no sooner are any of those truths proposed"[37] that distinguish true from false religion than they cry out, "You are bringing some strange ideas to our ears" (Acts 17:20 NIV).

b. Counting All Else Dross

It is useful here to recall the questions on sanctification embedded in the sermon "Catholic Spirit" (#39), where the centerpiece of that homily, in order to avert latitudinarian distortions, has a telling series of questions addressed to anyone whose life is hid in Christ:

> Is thy faith *energoumene di agapes* — filled with the energy of love? Dost thou love God? I do not say "above all things," for it is both an unscriptural and an ambiguous expression, but "with all thy heart, and with all thy mind, and with all thy soul, and with all thy strength"? Dost thou seek all thy happiness in him alone? And dost thou find what thou seekest? Dost thy soul continually "magnify the Lord, and thy spirit rejoice in God thy Saviour"?
>
> Is God the centre of thy soul? The sum of all thy desires?
>
> Art thou accordingly "laying up" thy "treasure in heaven" and "counting all things else dung and dross"? Hath the love of God cast the love of the world out of thy soul? Then thou art "crucified to the world." "Thou art dead" to all below, "and thy life is hid with Christ in God." If so then your heart is as my heart [so give me your hand]."[38]

This is the catholic spirit.

---

[35] "The Circumcision of the Heart," B 1:402 – 9, proem 3, sec. 1.
[36] "The Circumcision of the Heart," B 1:402, proem 2.
[37] "The Circumcision of the Heart," B 1:401, proem 1; Acts 17:18 – 19.
[38] "Catholic Spirit," B 2:88, sec. 1.14.

C. The Character of a Methodist

1. Assertions and Disclaimers

a. Whether Behavioral Descriptions of Sustained Responsiveness to Grace Are Disclosed in Scripture

In 1739 Wesley set forth distinguishing marks of the people labeled "Methodists," a term he did not like or choose, but knew had stuck, and with which he was willing to let providence do its work.[39] He hoped that with increased discernment, those who "hate what I am *called*, may love what I *am* by the grace of God."[40]

His essay on "The Character of a Methodist" (1739, J VIII:339 – 47) stands as his best early descriptive statement of perfecting grace. What follows is Wesley's clearest delineation of the Christian life of complete steady responsiveness to saving grace. He persisted in forming his thoughts around the ironic text "not as though I had already attained" (Phil. 3:12).

It must not be assumed that Wesley claimed smugly that he himself had attained what he was seeking to implement and enable in others. He never publicly asserted that he himself was living the life of complete responsiveness that he was convinced he was finding in many whose lives had been totally reshaped by the revival.[41]

Later when William Dodd charged him with claiming that "A Methodist, according to Mr. Wesley, is one who is perfect, and sinneth not," Wesley retorted, "This is not 'according to Mr. Wesley.' I have told all the world I am not perfect; and yet you allow me to be a Methodist. *I tell you flat I have not attained the character I draw.* Will you pin it upon me in spite of my teeth?"[42]

b. Nonstarters in Defining the Altogether Christian

By a series of disclaimers as to what a Methodist (or altogether Christian) is not, Wesley sought to avert misconceptions. One seeking to live the life of sustained accountability to God cannot be instantly differentiated by clothing, eating habits, quaint words, gestures, vocabulary, or anything external. There are indeed few outward indicators or body-language clues, as might be the case with many other more predictably uniformed pietists.[43]

What distinguishes a "Methodist," in Wesley's sense, are not political or intellectual opinions or any sentiments that do not strike at the root of Christianity. Nor is a Methodist distinguished by the holding of a single special precious doctrinal interpretation or accent that defines all other doctrines.

On such matters, one is well advised to think and let think, urging honest

[39]Cf. Letter to the Bishop of Gloucester, B 11:531 – 34; *LJW* 1:152, 158, 262; 2:375, 380; 8:47.

[40]"The Character of a Methodist," J VIII:339, proem 4.

[41]"The Character of a Methodist," J VIII:339 – 40, proem 1 – 4.

[42]Letter to the Editor of *Lloyd's Evening Post*, March 5, 1767, *LJW* 3:43 (italics added); i.e. "in spite of what I have said."

[43]"The Character of a Methodist," J VIII:340 – 41, secs. 1 – 3.

respect for differing sincere opinions.[44] If such outward evidences do not distinguish a Methodist, what does?

c. So What Is a Methodist?

Wesley preferred to look at it behaviorally. Have you ever seen someone who, so far as you can see, wholeheartedly loves God? That, says Wesley, is what he means by a "Methodist." What distinguishes the Methodist in Wesley's sense is praying without ceasing; loving the Lord with all one's heart, soul, mind, and strength; serving the neighbor in need; and not being enamored with the vices of the world. The love of God is shed abundantly abroad in such a heart.[45]

God's grace is the joy of his life, the source of life's meaning and value. He rejoices in God's gifts even amid disabilities, crying out with the psalmist: "Whom have I in heaven but you? And earth has nothing I desire besides you. My flesh and my heart may fail, but God is the strength of my heart and my portion forever" (Ps. 73:25–26 NIV).[46]

God's all-encompassing love has cast out his fear. In everything he gives thanks, saying the Lord gives and the Lord takes away; blessed be the name of the Lord. Whether in comfort or distress, sickness or health, life or death—from his heart he gives thanks to the one to whom he has committed all. Anxious about nothing, he does not despair or compulsively try to secure his future.[47]

d. Behavioral Marks of Genuine Christianity

The fully consecrated believer is happy in the divine love that has justified him, claimed him as a son or daughter for adoption into the family of God, and begotten him to a living hope. In whatever state he finds himself, he is content and poised to follow God's will. The works of the flesh are being supplanted by the fruits of the Spirit. All desires are toward God.[48]

What other behavioral marks evidence a complete believer?

He has cast his cares on one who infinitely cares for him.

He continually presents himself on the altar before God as a living sacrifice in response.

All his talents are committed to the practical service of the neighbor, doing whatever is at hand to the glory of God, whether in commerce, family, recreation, or religion, rejoicing in doing what God requires, not from fear but from gratitude.[49]

His heart is set at liberty.

He delights in God's commandments.

---

[44]"The Character of a Methodist," J VIII:340–41, secs. 1–4.
[45]"The Character of a Methodist," J VIII:341–43, secs. 4–8.
[46]"The Character of a Methodist," J VIII:341, sec. 5.
[47]"The Character of a Methodist," J VIII:342–43, secs. 6, 7.
[48]"The Character of a Methodist," J VIII:342, secs. 6, 7.
[49]"The Character of a Methodist," J VIII:343, sec. 9.

He loves the nearest one at hand as himself, regards the neighbor in relation to the love of God, loves even the supposed enemy without class distinction or social, racial, or gender partiality.
He provides for the neighbor's good as earnestly as his own. If it is not within his power to do good to those who hate him, he does not cease to pray for them.
He prays without ceasing, with God as constant companion.
Whatever things are good, wholesome, of good report, or just, he thinks on those things.
He has fundamentally one desire: to serve his neighbor as God has loved and served him.[50]
He does not love the world. No matter how deteriorated the environing culture, this person is focused on valuing each one he meets in relation to God.
The ways of the world do not bring him to despair.
The love of God is cleansing his heart from every unkind temper and malignant affection.[51] Love has reclaimed his life, reaching into every crevice of his volition, driving out hatred, contentiousness, and pride, and awakening kindness, longsuffering, and humility.
He has a single eye, and because his eye is single, his whole body is full of light.[52]
God's reign has begun in him. In all this he finds no grounds for self-congratulation.[53]

These are qualities that grow in the character of those fully alive to God.

2. This Is "Plain Old Christianity"

This is what a Methodist is — a Christian not in name only but in heart and life, renewed inwardly and outwardly in the image of God.[54] The marks of a Methodist are those found in anyone whose life is hid in Christ. What we have in these descriptions are the same characteristics manifested in one whose life is shaped by unfeigned responsiveness to God. It is not a different list. The Methodist is neither more or less than one who takes such promises with complete seriousness.[55] This is "plain old Christianity," and Methodists are not distinguished from other Christians in any other way.[56] They are merely seeking wholeheartedly to live the Christian life.[57]

Wesley derived this pattern of Christian perfection primarily from the Scriptures and secondarily from the pre-Nicene writers who spoke of it so cogently. In March 1767, Wesley wrote: "Five- or six-and-thirty years ago [1729] I much

[50]"The Character of a Methodist," J VIII:343 – 44, secs. 8 – 10.
[51]"The Character of a Methodist," J VIII:343, sec. 9; B 3:110 – 11.
[52]On singularity of intent, see B 1:573 – 77, 608 – 9, 672 – 73; 4:120 – 23, 371 – 77.
[53]"The Character of a Methodist," J VIII:343 – 44, secs. 10 – 11.
[54]*LJW* 2:71 – 75; 4:237; B 3:202 – 3; 4:275, 398; 9:35.
[55]"The Character of a Methodist," J VIII:346 – 47, secs. 16 – 18.
[56]"The Character of a Methodist," sec. 17, J VIII:346. Methodism is described as "plain old Bible religion," B 9:469; cf. *LJW* 4:131.
[57]"The Character of a Methodist," J VIII:347, sec. 18.

admired the character of a perfect Christian drawn by Clemen Alexandrinus.[58] Five- or six-and-twenty years ago [1739] a thought came into my mind of drawing such a character myself, only in a more scriptural manner, and mostly in the very words of Scripture; this I entitled *The Character of a Methodist.*"[59]

D. Christian Perfection

1. Not as Though I Had Already Attained

The leading text of this homily is Philippians 3:12: "Not as though I had already attained, either were already perfect"[60] [Homily #40 (1741 or earlier), B 2:97 – 124; J #40, VI:1 – 22].

a. Perfecting Grace in Scripture

Perfecting grace is admittedly a difficult doctrine to express perfectly. By 1741 Wesley was receiving thoughtful challenges and having to fend off serious objections. At times he must have been tempted to give up altogether on defending this tenet. Some in the connection were wondering why such a controversial and falsifiable doctrine should be taught at all.

The intractable answer for Wesley was that this teaching is found constantly in Scripture. Even if *teleiotēs* (perfecting grace) should cause offense among some, it could not be denied as a recurrent scriptural term. It defies being sidestepped or parsed in the Scripture texts. It echoes so frequently through the language of Scripture that it cannot be circumvented without abandoning a central theme of Holy Writ. Were it not so deeply embedded in so many beloved texts from Jesus, and from the Pauline, Petrine, and Johannine traditions, it might be more conveniently ignored or discarded. But its prevalence as a scriptural theme constrained Wesley's conscience.[61]

As a result of answering these arguments, Wesley began to shape the teaching more confidently. The Spirit is determined to renew the self totally, rejecting all halfway measures. Those who are receiving regenerating grace by the Spirit are being freed not only from all outward sin at the time of new birth but also from inward sin so as to grow toward the fullness of Christ.[62]

b. Perfecting Grace, Not Perfected Grace: The Greek Teleiotēs

The Greek *teleiotēs* (Col. 3:14; Heb. 6:1) has been commonly translated "perfec-

[58]Clemen Alexandrinus, *Christ the Educator* and *Stromateis.*

[59]Letter to the editor of *Lloyd's Evening Post,* March 5, 1767, *LJW* 5:43.

[60]Paul had just implied in verse 12 that he had not already laid hold of perfection and had not already arrived at this goal, when he then called upon his hearers in verse 15: "Let us therefore, as many as be perfect [*téleioi,* "full grown, spiritually mature, ripe in understanding"], be thus minded." To solve the seeming contradiction between verses 12 and 15 is the concern of Wesley's reflection.

[61]Letter to William Dodd, March 12, 1756, *LJW* 3:167 – 72.

[62]B 1:239 – 40, 245 – 46, 336 – 44; 2:215 – 16.

tion" but also under metaphors of maturation and completeness. The Christian life is not a static *perfectus* in the sense of no further possible improvement, but a dynamic *teleiotēs* in the sense of the most excellent conceivable contextual functioning of the developing person.

The Latin term *perfectus* tends to contort and caricature the earlier Greek language tradition of *teleiotēs*. Since English is rooted far more in Latin than Greek, this becomes a fate-laden difference.

Wesley himself was working constantly out of the Greek text, not the Latin Vulgate or the King James Version in his daily meditations on Scripture. Therefore, when we say "perfect" in our modern vocabulary, our Latinized English language yields to us a static notion of perfection. Wesley's references to "perfection" instead assumed the Greek notion of a perfecting (not perfected) grace. It is consecration to "a never-ending aspiration for all of love's fullness," as found especially in the pre-Augustinian Eastern church writers.[63]

c. In What Ways It Is Improper to Say That Christians Are Perfect: What **Teleiotēs** *Is Not*

Wesley learned by rough experience to qualify his words carefully. He patiently went through a detailed list of stipulations, indicating *what Scripture does not mean* by *teleiotēs*.

(1) Not Freedom from Ignorance

The Scripture promise of perfecting grace does not command or imply freedom from *ignorance*. The full reception of grace can occur in one who remains normally limited in knowing (since finite knowledge is intrinsic to the nature of human finitude). No finite human person is capable of infinite knowledge. Reason offers only proximate knowledge of "things relating to the present world."[64] The saints may know more than most about the ways of God, but still there is much more that they as ordinary human beings "know not."[65]

(2) Not Free of Mistakes Due to Finitude

The perfecting grace of which Scripture speaks is not free from *mistakes*, which are an unavoidable consequence of our finitude and ignorance. Those walking with full maturity in love make mistakes of fact and perception.[66] When John said, "Ye know all things" (1 John 2:20 KJV), his intent was "all things needful for your souls' health."[67] "Every one may *mistake* as long as he lives.... The most perfect have continual need of the merits of Christ, even for their actual transgressions, and may well say, for themselves as well as their brethren, 'Forgive us our trespasses.'"[68]

[63]Outler, Introduction; "Christian Perfection," B 2:98, sec. 1.1.
[64]"Christian Perfection," B 2:100 – 102, sec. 1.1 – 4.
[65]"Christian Perfection," B 2:101, sec. 1.3.
[66]JWO 254 – 58, 284 – 90.
[67]"Christian Perfection," B 2:102, sec. 1.4 – 5.
[68]Minutes, 1758, August 15, JWO 177.

(3) Not Freedom from Infirmities

The mature reception of perfecting grace does not imply freedom from *infirmities*.[69] By "infirmities," Wesley points to such things as slowness of understanding, poor memory, dull apprehension, or flawed speech.[70] These are not matters of moral decision, except as they have been habitually formed by collusions of freedom with temptation.

(4) Not Freedom from Temptation

Nor does perfecting grace deliver the faithful from *temptation*. As Jesus was tempted, so are we. Trials and temptations continue to surround any who walk in this way, but each must be dealt with contextually by receiving grace upon grace.[71] Whatever the temptation, there is always a way open to deflect it.

(5) There Is No Absolute Necessity to Sin

No necessity is laid upon us to sin. "The trials which a gracious Providence sends may be precious means of growing in grace, and particularly of increasing in faith, patience, and resignation."[72] No matter where one is in the sequence of stages of growth in grace, one never gets to the point where it is impossible to sin or inconceivable that one might again fall into neglect.

All these false premises misjudge what the Scripture means by full responsiveness to God's grace.

Anyone whose feet are on the path of holiness will be guarding continually against the subtleties of spiritual pride and seeking to gain early victory over each temptation to sin as it arises. Only as one responds wholly to the will of God does sin lose its power. Those who are so responding to grace that grace is exercising increasing influence within the will are prepared for whatever emerges. "The world, the flesh, and the devil are put under his feet; thus he rules over these enemies with watchfulness through the power of the Holy Spirit."[73]

2. What *Teleiotēs* Is

a. In What Way Believers Are Being Perfected by Grace in This Life

The unchallenged dominion of sin has been broken in those newly born from above. There is no ground on which to legitimize continued sin in the life of the believer.[74]

The full and sustained maintenance of a way of life utterly dependent on faith is not intrinsically impossible. If so, the call to holiness in Scripture would be absurd.[75]

[69]B 1:241–42; 2:482–83; 4:166–67.
[70]"Christian Perfection," B 2:103, sec. 1.7.
[71]"Christian Perfection," B 2:104, sec. 1.8.
[72]Letter to Hester Ann Roe, October 6, 1776, *LJW* 6:234.
[73]Confession, art. 11, United Methodist *Book of Discipline* (1988), 72.
[74]"Christian Perfection," B 2:106, sec. 2.3.
[75]"Christian Perfection," B 2:107, sec. 2.7.

No believer is being asked to seek holiness apart from grace, but rather to reflect contextually insofar as possible the holiness of God.[76] God is holy. It is possible for God's redeemed creatures proximately to image, as in a mirror, the goodness and holiness of God.[77] This mirroring normally occurs in stages that often move through a series of crises.

b. Each Stage Has a Perfection Applicable to That Stage

Those who look for a developmental doctrine of sanctification will find this homily the best place to examine it. Here Wesley shows how the Christian life may be viewed in terms of progressive stages of growth from newborn to adolescence to young adulthood to older adulthood.

Each stage has a perfection applicable especially to that stage. It is not as if there is a maturity for neonates that is also applicable to young adults. No one expects an adolescent to express the kind of responsibility expected of a wise grandmother. Rather, there is a peculiar maturity that pertains to being a child and a different maturity that pertains to being an adolescent, and still a different one that pertains to being an adult.

While the perfecting of love is often associated with mature age, Wesley specifically pointed out that there is a completeness that even newborn babes have, since the notion of maturity must be understood contextually within the frame of reference of what is possible at a given stage of development.[78]

Yet grace is one, not many, since it is the gift of the one God.

c. Like a Baby's Growth, Sanctification Is a Process

"The generality of believers in *our* Church (yea, and in the Church of Corinth, Ephesus, and the rest, even in the Apostolic age) are certainly no more than babes in Christ; not young men, and much less fathers. But we have some, and we should certainly pray and expect that our Pentecost may fully come."[79]

All these points make it clear that we have here a doctrine of *teleiotēsis* (dynamic perfecting grace) rather than *perfectus* (static perfection).[80] The key idea is not that of getting to a fixed state of perfection in a motionless sense — a very un-Wesleyan notion, but rather being in a continuing process of growth in grace that has multiple moments of completion and fulfillment, where the reflection of inexhaustible love occurs at many points (in principle any point) along the way.

The process of receiving sanctifying grace, since it is a process, is never capturable as a still photograph, but must be a history that can be conceived only narratively and lived out personally.

---

[76]*JJW* 2:90, 275; 5:283 – 84.
[77]"Christian Perfection," B 2:105 – 9, sec. 2.1 – 10.
[78]"Christian Perfection," B 2:105 – 6, sec. 2.1 – 2.
[79]*LJW* 6:221; cf. B 1:503.
[80]"Christian Perfection," B 2:105 – 6, sec. 2.1 – 2.

d. Why Claiming "I Have No Sin" Misunderstands the Atonement

The first epistle of John does not misunderstand this dynamism in saying, "If we claim to be without sin, we deceive ourselves" (1:8 NIV), for to say, "I have no sin," is to imply I have no need of the atoning work of God the Son to cleanse me from all sin. To stand in no need of Christ is to deceive oneself and make God a liar. But if we do confess that we have sinned, God will not only forgive but also cleanse us so that we may go and sin no more.

Having been made dead to sin, Christians are now alive to righteousness. Living without sin is the privilege of every Christian, who is being invited and enabled by grace to move gradually through this and that temptation seeking a consummate victory over each evil thought or temper.[81]

Jesus was tempted yet without sin. Insofar as the risen Lord lives in the life of the believer, how could it be otherwise than that the believer is fully freed from sin?[82] However far one travels on the way of holiness, there is always room the next moment to go further, to grow from grace to grace. There is no perfection that does not admit of continual increase, of further growth in grace. However matured, it is always further maturing, perpetually in process.[83]

The *teleiotēs* of which Scripture speaks does not imply that no further progression is possible, but that the faithful are going on from strength to strength. Paul says that they behold the love of God first as a faint image in an indistinct mirror and only gradually are changed into this image from glory to glory by the Spirit of the same Lord.

3. On Perfection

The text the homily "On Perfection" is Hebrews 6:1: "Let us go on unto perfection" [Homily #76 (1784), B 3:70 – 87; J #76, V:411 – 24]. This is the most penetrating account of Wesley's matured doctrine of perfection. In this late offering, dated 1784, the elderly Wesley gathered a lifetime of clarifications and disclaimers together in concentrated scope.

a. God's Perfection and the Perfect Love of Believers

We do not speak here of that perfection that is possible only for God, for we are not God. Thus, "the highest perfection which man can attain, while the soul dwells in the body, does not exclude ignorance, and error, and a thousand other infirmities."[84] If so, all children of Adam and Eve need the work of God on the cross to atone for every transgression of the requirement of God.[85] Key scriptural descriptions of grace perfecting ordinary humanity are abundantly exhibited in the sacred text.

[81]"Christian Perfection," B 2:117; 3:313 – 15, 320 – 21, sec. 2.21.
[82]"Christian Perfection," B 2:116 – 18, sec. 2.22 – 24.
[83]"Christian Perfection," B 2:121, sec. 2.30.
[84]"On Perfection," B 3:72 – 73, sec. 1.1 – 2.
[85]Ibid.

Christian perfection occurs within the theater of human history, not angelic creation. The life of perfect love within this world is neither angelic nor Adamic perfection, for we are corporeal creatures who have fallen from grace into a specific history of sin. Angels are not as liable to make perceptual mistakes as human beings in time and space.

b. Its Center Is Love

"It is all comprised in that one word, *love*"—love toward God and neighbor.[86] Christian perfection implies "loving God with all the heart, so that every evil temper is destroyed and every thought and word and work springs from and is conducted to that end by the pure love of God and our neighbor."[87]

So to love is thereby to have the mind that is in Christ (Phil. 2:5), to bear the fruits of the Spirit of love (Gal. 5:22–23). One who loves puts on a new humanity renewed after the moral image of God that is "true righteousness and holiness" (Eph. 4:24 NIV), walking in the way of inward and outward righteousness with holiness of life issuing from holiness of heart (1 Peter 1:15).[88] It is the sacrificial offering of our very selves on the altar of grace, so as to participate in the Son's once-for-all sacrifice for sin and share finally in salvation from all sin (Matt. 1:21).[89]

One who is crucified with Christ, in whom dwells the mind that was in Christ, "loveth his neighbor (every man) as himself; yea, as Christ loved us; them in particular that despitefully use him and persecute him.... Indeed, his soul is all love, filled with the bowels of mercies, kindness, meekness, gentleness, long-suffering."[90] "'Faith working by love' is the length and breadth and depth and height of Christian perfection."[91]

4. The Danger of Confusing Sin with Finitude

a. Creaturely Finitude as Such Is Not Sin

"There is no such perfection in this life, as implies ... a freedom from ignorance, mistake, temptation, and a thousand infirmities necessarily connected with flesh and blood."[92]

The question of the possibility of full responsiveness to grace turns significantly on the definition of sin. Wesley thought that those who rail against the possibility of perfect love have a tendency to redefine sin as involuntary. The confusion of sin with finitude has caused mischief. This confusion lies at the heart of much of the debate about perfecting grace.

In Scripture, however, sin is characteristically a voluntary transgression of a

[86]"On Perfection," B 3:74, sec. 1.4.

[87]Minutes, 1758, August 15, JWO 177; cf. EA, B 11:66–67; FA, B 11:278.

[88]*LJW* 3:380; 5:56; B 11:239, 416.

[89]"On Perfection," B 3:74–76, sec. 1.4–12.

[90]*HSP* (1745), J XIV:329, pref. 5.

[91]*HSP* (1739), J XIV:321, pref. 5; B 1:559–60; 3:122–23, 303–4, 385–86, 612–13; JWO 68, 123–32, 231–32, 279–80, 376.

[92]*HSP* (1745), J XIV:328, pref. 1.

known law.[93] The apostle John assumes that "sin is the transgression of the law" (1 John 3:4). The assumption is that each collusion with temptation could have been chosen otherwise.

b. If Sin Is Willed Transgression, Then It Is Not Absolutely Decreed as Necessary

Some breaches of God's requirement are not strictly speaking sin because they are not willed. Some may be due to unavoidable illnesses, spontaneous mistakes, and the limiting conditions of human finitude. With such a definition, miscalculations of judgment, infirmities, and ignorance can be reasonably distinguished from deliberate, voluntary sin.

Wesley found it difficult to believe that any earnest reader of Scripture could "deny the possibility of being saved from sin" in the sense in which he is using the word *sin* as voluntary. Sin at some level always has a voluntary component or aspect. Sin is willfully done and without coercion. It is willing to fall into temptation.[94]

There is nothing in the teaching of perfecting grace that suggests that anyone is exempt from human weakness, ill health, events, and consequences of which one is unaware, or from imprecisions common to human finitude. All these are sharply distinguished from intentional negations of a known requirement of God — the scriptural sense of the word *sin*.

5. Whether There Are Living Exemplars of the Life of Holiness

a. Does Holy Living Exist?

In answer to the objection that there are no living exemplars, Wesley conceded there are not many, that some are false, and that others having received such holiness have lost it. Nevertheless, he thought some had experienced it over many years.[95] True, they may not measure up to the hyper-skeptic's uncritical idea of perfection as sinless in every sense. They never could if the skeptic defines the standard of perfection as already intrinsically impossible.[96]

Wesley thought that there were persons in the range of honest observation and experience who fully, consistently, and in a sustained manner walked in the way of holiness, loving the neighbor in relation to God, loving God with their whole mind, strength, and spirit.[97]

But can we empirically locate anyone who lives such a life? Have any such species ever been actually sighted or held up to rigorous scrutiny or examination? To Charles he conceded in 1767: "If there be *no living witnesses* of what we have

[93]On the volitional character of sin, see B 1:181, 124, 233, 315, 416; 3:71, 85.
[94]"On Perfection," B 3:79 – 80, sec. 2.9.
[95]"On Perfection," B 3:81 – 83, sec. 2.12 – 15.
[96]"On Perfection," B 3:83, sec. 2.16.
[97]"Short Account of the Life and Death of the Rev. John Fletcher," J XI:364.

preached for twenty years, I cannot, dare not preach it any longer."[98] If it turns out that there are no living saints and cannot be any, that would run contrary to repeated apostolic reference to living saints.

b. Why Saints Prefer Anonymity

Assuming that he knew some who were living the life of complete responsiveness to divine love, Wesley answered that for good reason he would not name them, nor would they wish to be named. If named, then cynical detractors would mercilessly pounce on their infirmities, weaknesses, mistakes, all of which those who are living responsively to sanctifying grace are admittedly still subject to. The piranha press would enjoy nothing more than to have a saint to try to devour.

There is another obvious reason why the best exemplars of the Christian life are never found advertising themselves as such. By this display, they would evidence a pride precisely contrary to the life they would be seeking to embody. Nonetheless, Wesley was convinced that there were indeed persons who, unadvertised, embody the Christian life.

Wesley could not believe that the life so clearly promised in the gospel was intrinsically impossible. That would make it a cruel joke. Yet this remains a potentially hazardous teaching insofar as it tempts pride and is easily confused with pretending to erase the limits of finitude.

c. Herod's Search

Wesley was convinced that there were godly persons in his own connection of spiritual formation who were living a life hidden in Christ, fully accountable to sanctifying grace, but he was not willing to write out a list for others to vilify. Where there are saints, we do them no favor by issuing a press notice.

> To some that make this inquiry one might answer, "If I knew one here, I would not tell you. You are *like Herod, you only seek the young child to destroy it.*" But to the serious we answer, "There are numberless reasons why there should be few, if any indisputable examples. What inconveniences would this bring on the person himself, set as a mark for all to shoot at! What a temptation would it be to others, not only to men who knew not God, but to believers themselves! How hardly would they refrain from idolizing such a person! And yet how unprofitable to gainsayers! For if they hear not Moses and the prophets ... neither would they be persuaded though one rose from the dead."[99]

To Charles he wrote on July 9, 1766, warning against "setting perfection too high. That perfection which I believe, I can boldly preach; because I think I see five hundred witnesses of it. Of that [impossible, too lofty, supposed] perfection which you preach, you think you do not see any witnesses at all." Why then not "fall in plumb

[98]Letter to Charles Wesley, February 12, 1767, *LJW* 5:41.
[99]Minutes, 1747, June 17, Q12, JWO 170, italics added; Matt. 2:16 – 18; Luke 16:31.

with Mr. Whitefield," who asks with imprecise criteria: "Where are the perfect ones?" If you accept skewed, insurmountable, impossible-to-fulfill criteria, "there are none upon earth; none dwelling in the body ... no such perfection here as you describe.... Therefore ... to set perfection so high is effectually to renounce it."[100]

d. Why Be So Fond of Sin?

Wesley mused that the opposers of this teaching were willing to concede most of its key points as long as the Latin-based term *perfection* could be strictly avoided. They are willing to "allow all you say of the love of God and man; of the mind which was in Christ; of the fruit of the Spirit; of the image of God; of universal holiness; of entire self-dedication; of sanctification in spirit, soul, and body; yea, and of the offering up of all our thoughts, words, and actions, as a sacrifice to God; — all this they will allow [if] we will allow sin, a little sin, to remain in us till death."[101]

The homily culminates with a searching series of rhetorical questions: Why should detractors become so furious at those who are seeking complete responsiveness to grace? What rational objection can one have to people who love God with all their hearts? What explains our being so adverse to receiving the whole fruit of the Spirit? Why be so fond of sin?[102] Even if wrong in our exegesis, let us be left to live with our mistakes, lest we give up the contest against sin altogether.

Wesley continued to insist that this was why the Methodist people were called forth, to show in their behavior that the holy life is possible. They are those called to make plausible this scriptural teaching experientially.

Meanwhile, it remains very much a question of conscience for modern preachers in Wesley's connection to decide whether or how to present these teachings. No pastor who understands that the Eucharist is for sinners is likely to ask laity to show evidences of complete accountability to God. Clergy can preach on full accountability to God but not a static perfection.

6. Whether Instantaneous or Gradual

a. The Seed Planted in an Instant

How long does it take a farmer to plant a seed? Only a moment. But how long does it take the seed to grow? Only over time. Inward sanctification begins "in the moment we are justified, the seed of every virtue is then *instantaneously* sown in the soul. From that time, the believer *gradually* dies to sin and grows in grace. Yet sin remains in him, yea, the seed of all sin, till he is sanctified through in spirit, soul, and body."

To those who do not expect it sooner, sanctification is "ordinarily not given till a little before death," but we ought to expect it sooner, aware that "the generality of believers [whom we have hitherto known] are not so sanctified till near death."

[100]*LJW* 5:20.
[101]"On Perfection," B 3:85, sec. 3.10.
[102]"On Perfection," B 3:86 – 87, sec. 3.12.

"Yet this does not prove that we may not today" receive sanctifying grace before death.[103]

b. A Gradual Work Preceding and Following That Instant

Wesley did not rule out an instantaneous work of the Spirit by which one fully receives the seed of the regenerated life, which then grows in time and bears ever-new fruit.[104] "I believe this perfection is always wrought in the soul by a simple act of faith; consequently, in an *instant.* But I believe *a gradual work, both preceding and following that instant.*"[105]

When critics accused Wesley of a view of sanctification that too abruptly "finishes the business of salvation once for all," Wesley replied: "I believe a gradual improvement in grace and goodness [is a] testimony of our present sincerity toward God."[106]

> Neither, therefore, dare we affirm (as some have done) that this full salvation is at once given to true believers. There is, indeed, an instantaneous (as well as a gradual) work of God in the souls of his children; and there wants not [is no lack of], we know, a cloud of witnesses, who have received, in one moment, either a clear sense of the forgiveness of their sins, or the abiding witness of the Holy Spirit. But we do not know a single instance, in any place, of a person's receiving, in one and the same moment, remission of sins, the abiding witness of the Spirit, and a new, a clean heart.[107]

c. Brief Thoughts on Christian Perfection

On January 27, 1767, Wesley wrote a single page of morning reflections that he called "Brief Thoughts on Christian Perfection," in which he set down these points on "the manner and time" of receiving perfection grace: "By perfection I mean the humble, gentle, patient love of God and our neighbor, ruling our tempers, words, and actions." He wished to correct "several expressions in our Hymns which partly express, partly imply" the impossibility of falling from grace. "I do not contend for the term *sinless*, though I do not object against it.... As to the time. I believe this instant generally is the instant of death, the moment before the soul leaves the body. But I believe it may be ten, twenty, or forty years before. I believe it is usually many years after justification; but that it may be within five years or five months after it."[108]

---

[103]Minutes, 1745, August 2, Q1–4, JWO 152–53, italics added. For further reference to the distinction between instantaneous and gradual sanctification, see B 1:35, 350–51; 2:160, 168–69, 220; 3:178; *LJW* 5:16, 333.

[104]*LJW* 5:16, 333; B 2:168–69; 3:178.

[105]"Brief Thoughts on Christian Perfection," 1767, italics added; FA, B 11:70–71, 137–38; B 3:204.

[106]LLBL, B 11:338, sec. 7, against charge made by Edmund Gibson, bishop of London; B 1:201.

[107]*HSP* (1740), J XIV:326, pref. 9. Later this would cause some difference of opinion between John and Charles Wesley. To Charles he wrote on February 12, 1767: "Is there or is there not any instantaneous sanctification between justification and death? I say, Yes; you (often seem to) say, No." *LJW* 3:41.

[108]"Brief Thoughts on Christian Perfection," J XI:446.

E. The Doctrinal Minutes[109]

1. Refining the Definition of Sanctification

The minutes of the earliest conferences from 1744 to 1747 are foundational for what later would be called "Larger Minutes" or "Doctrinal Minutes."[110]

All basic Methodist doctrines were hammered out in dialogical form through conversation. The preachers came together under Wesley's leadership and made certain theological and disciplinary decisions.[111] These conversations established consensually agreed teachings at an early stage on key doctrinal themes: justification, salvation by faith, and especially sanctification.

Sanctification is the work of the Spirit by which God by grace seeks completely to mend the broken human condition, to bring our stunted lives to fulfillment, not partially, but wholly in a victory over all sin in this life, through a genuine renewal of all the redeemed powers of believers.[112] It is that movement of faith that radically and continually commits the will by grace to trust in Christ's righteousness.

Sanctification, which begins at the moment of justification, is given to all who earnestly desire it. Faith is its sole condition.[113] It is loving God with our whole being, all inward sin being removed.[114] Sanctification was defined in the 1747 Conference Minutes in this way: "to be renewed in the image of God, in righteousness and true holiness," faith being "both the condition and the instrument of it. When we begin to believe, then salvation begins. And as faith increases, holiness increases till we are created anew."[115] Faith has not abrogated the call to holiness,[116] nor has faith rescinded the requirement embedded in the text "Without holiness no one will see the Lord" (Heb. 12:14 NIV).[117]

a. Pardon and Purity of Heart

It is not as if one is first justified by faith and then separately sanctified by some-

[109]JWO 134–76.

[110]The conference records or minutes of early conferences are sometimes referred to as the "Doctrinal" or "Large" or "Larger Minutes." The minutes of the first six conferences were published in 1749 under the title "Doctrinal Minutes," along with a separate tract called "Disciplinary Minutes" (Dublin: S. Powell, 1749). In this edition, Wesley had rearranged and systematically abstracted all the doctrinal decisions of the conferences from 1744 to 1747. Six editions of "Large Minutes" were published during Wesley's lifetime, an incremental compendium of the minutes from 1744 to 1753. Well into the twentieth century, British Wesleyan candidates for ministry were required to read and subscribe to the "Large Minutes," using the 1797 edition as a standard, *JJW* 3:302n.; B 20:177. Wesley himself, along with a committee of preachers, edited the minutes of 1780. They "considered all the articles, one by one, to see whether any should be omitted or altered," *JJW* 6:289. After 1765 the minutes were published annually in order to "do all things openly," *JJW* 6:301. Cf. *LJW* 5:52, 228, 252, 259, 262; 6:215; 7:40, 210, 255, 375; 8:68, 149.

[111]*DSWT* 21–29.

[112]*The Pentecost Hymns of John and Charles Wesley*, ed. Timothy L. Smith (Kansas City: Beacon Hill, 1982), 1–85.

[113]B 11:130, 133.

[114]Minutes, 1747, June 16, JWO 167–72.

[115]Minutes, 1744, June 26, Q1–2, JWO 140.

[116]"The Law Established through Faith, I," B 2:26, sec. 2.1.

[117]B 11:115–16.

thing other than faith. One is justified and sanctified by the same faith, which from the beginning is becoming active in love.[118]

In this way faith remains the operating premise of all subsequent acts of reception of sanctifying grace. If salvation begins with pardon, it continues with an ongoing life of holiness, which finds its full maturation only in the celestial city. The life of faith begins with justifying grace and continues with a process of habitual growth in grace. Faith does not just occur at the beginning of this process but continues throughout the life that ensues.

Pardon is salvation begun; holiness is salvation by faith continued.[119] The justified are pardoned and received into God's favor so that insofar as they continue in faith, they are promised eternal happiness with God.[120]

This differs in tone from the early period of Oxford Holy Club theology, which tended to view sanctification as the premise of justification. By 1738 Wesley had come to understand more profoundly the radical nature of the Protestant doctrine of justification by grace through faith, especially as manifesting itself in an emotive life of joy in the fruits of the Spirit.

"Being made perfect in love" means "loving the Lord our God with all our mind and soul and strength," so much so that one does not sin insofar as one is born of God.[121] While we cannot be certain of identifying those made perfect in love, short of martyrdom these are the "best proofs which the nature of the things admits ... unblamable behaviour ... [wherein] all their tempers, words, and actions were holy and unreprovable."[122]

2. How Sanctification Teaching Counters Antinomian Resistance to Using the Means of Grace

a. Do Not Make Void the Law through Faith

Antinomianism is "the doctrine which makes void the law through faith," holding that "Christ abolished the moral law," and that "Christian liberty is liberty from obeying the commandments of God; that it is bondage to do a thing because it is commanded; that a believer is not obliged to use the ordinances of God or to do good works."[123]

Countering antinomian tendencies, Paul taught that no one "can be justified or saved by the works of the law, either moral or ritual," including "all works that do not spring from faith in Christ." More precisely, the law that Christ has abolished is "the ritual law of Moses."[124] "Does not the truth of the gospel lie very near both to

[118]On the relation of justification and sanctification, see B 1:124, 187, 191, 431–34; 2:158, 418; 3:505–7; 4:519–21.

[119]*SS* 2:451–53; 2:163–64; 3:178.

[120]B 3:266.

[121]Minutes, 1744, June 26, Q6–8, JWO 141.

[122]Minutes, 1744, June 26, Q9, JWO 141.

[123]Minutes, 1744, June 25, Q19–26, JWO 139–40; *JJW* 3:503–11.

[124]Minutes, 1744, June 25, Q19–26, JWO 139–40.

Calvinism and antinomianism? Indeed it does, as it were, within a hair's breadth. So that 'tis altogether foolish and sinful, because we do not quite agree either with one or the other, to run from them as far as ever we can." Wesleyans agree with Calvin "in ascribing all good to the free grace of God, in denying all natural free-will and all power antecedent to grace. And, in excluding all merit." We come to "the very edge of antinomianism ... in exalting the merits and love of Christ," and "in rejoicing evermore."[125]

The faithful await the gift of full salvation by attending "the general means which God hath ordained for our receiving his sanctifying grace. These in particular are prayer, searching the Scripture, communicating [Eucharist], and fasting."[126]

b. Against the Antinomian Interpretation of Perfecting Grace

"There is no such perfection in this life, as implies ... a dispensation from doing good, and attending all the ordinances of God."[127] They are to be repudiated who teach a supposed perfection that turns away from the privilege "as oft as they have opportunity, to eat bread and drink wine in remembrance of Him; to search the Scripture; by fasting, as well as temperance, to keep their bodies under and bring them into subjection; and, above all, to pour out their souls in prayer, both secretly, and in the great congregation."[128]

The Doctrinal Minutes give instructions on how to seek this sanctifying grace so as to elicit an undivided and completely sound way of holy living — by searching the Scriptures, keeping the commandments, and using the means of grace. The Spirit intends to penetrate and dwell in every fissure of our broken human lives. The inhibitions to full salvation lie in ourselves, not in God's own Spirit.

"Good works follow this [justifying] faith, but cannot go before it. Much less can sanctification, which implies a continued course of good works, springing from holiness of heart. But entire sanctification goes before our [final] justification at the last day."[129] The Spirit's mission is to fully refashion broken human life prior to, and not on, the last day, and not merely to passively await final judgment.

A fair number of Charles Wesley's hymns were written specifically either to prove or guard Christian doctrine against enthusiasts and Antinomians who "cause the truth to be evil spoken of."[130] Wesley admonished Thomas Maxfield's antinomianism for "using faith rather as contradistinguished from holiness than as productive of it."[131]

---

[125]Minutes, 1745, August 2, Q22 – 25, JWO 151 – 52.

[126]Minutes, 1745, August 2, Q6 – 11, JWO 153.

[127]*HSP* (1745), J XIV:328, pref. 1.

[128]*HSP* (1745), J XIV:328, pref. 2.

[129]Letter to Thomas Church, February 2, 1745, *LJW* 2:187; cf. 1:318 – 19. This assumes a distinction between the full pardon that occurs with faith in justifying grace and the final administering of that full pardon on the last day in "final justification."

[130]*HSP* (1762), J XIV:334, pref.; cf. *CH*, B 7:269n.

[131]Letter to Thomas Maxfield, November 2, 1962, *LJW* 4:193.

3. Whether the Full Reception of Sanctifying Grace Is Possible in This Life before the Article of Death

The overarching term "entire sanctification" was definitively explicated in the Doctrinal Minutes of June 16, 1747.[132]

Entire sanctification is more commonly realized by the faithful near death, but it can be received earlier. Nothing tests living faith like dying. No experience brings us closer to a more radical penitence. Hence the fullest sanctification is often not realized until near death, for death is always the final challenge and trial of faith.[133] Nonetheless, grace is sufficient to allow it to be received before death. Otherwise, one might be encumbered by the curious assertion that one must first die before one walks in the way of holiness.

On the basis of his experience in the revival, Wesley thought that many who were justified at one point in their life were never fully tested in faith until they neared death, where they were finally prepared to embody this life of holiness. But he never insinuates that one must wait until death before sanctifying grace is made available.[134] The controversy on sanctification hinged crucially around the question of "whether we should expect to be saved from all sin before the article of death," which the Doctrinal Minutes assert as a scriptural promise.[135]

The Minutes concede "that many of those who have died in the faith, yea, the greater part of them we have known, were not sanctified throughout — not made perfect in love — till a little before death," and "that the term 'sanctified' is continually applied by St. Paul to all that were justified.... Consequently it behooves us to speak almost constantly of the state of justification, but rarely, at least in full and explicit terms, concerning entire sanctification."[136]

Wesley was convinced that some actually attain the perfect love promised in the Scripture. It is the Scripture that drew him toward these sanctification promises. He heard in the prayers of the church and the promises of Scripture the hope of a full manifestation of grace. He was convinced that he had met living saints in the revival, people walking fully in the way of holiness and living unreservedly the life of perfect love prior to death.[137]

4. Should Perfect Love in This Life Be Attested?

a. Neither to Be Inveighed Against nor Preached Overmuch

The Minutes show agreement that entire sanctification does not need to be preached all the time, yet must not be avoided or abandoned. Wesley did not

[132]See also B 3:169, 174–79; 2:122–24; *SS* 1:151; 2:172–91, 457.

[133]*LJW* 1:120; 6:213; 11:528.

[134]Minutes, 1747, June 16, JWO 169.

[135]Minutes, 1747, June 17, Q3–8, JWO 168–69, from Deut. 30:6; Ezek. 36:25, 29; Eph. 3:14–19, 5:25, 27; 2 Cor. 7:1; John 17:20, 23; 1 Thess. 5:23.

[136]Minutes, 1747, June 17, Q2, JWO 167–68.

[137]*JJW* 2:90, 275; 5:283–84; 8:307.

require preachers in his connection to preach it, but they were required not to inveigh against it.

Even today it remains a strong tradition in interpreting Methodist doctrinal standards that one should not preach against *teleiotēs* in a Methodist pulpit, though no one is forced to preach in favor of it.

Admittedly, when these terms are translated into modern moral categories, little of this seriousness pervades the contemporary ethos, except perhaps in the sphere of social transformation, and even there it is often poorly formed. But it is a deep stratum of evangelical history, which one will often hear echoing even in supposedly secularized places.

b. A Caution on Testimony to Perfecting Grace

There are plausible grounds on which we are "apt to have a secret distaste to any who say they are saved from all sin," especially "if these are not what they profess," but this revulsion may come "partly from our slowness and unreadiness of heart to believe the works of God."[138]

The way of holiness must be attested with reserve: "Suppose one had attained to this, would you advise him to speak of it? Not to them who know not God; it would only provoke them to contradict and blaspheme."[139] Those who believe they are receiving perfecting grace do well to speak of their own experience with deep humility, modesty, meekness, and humble self-awareness. Young preachers if speaking publicly on Christian perfection are advised not to do so too minutely but rather in terms of clear scriptural promises.[140]

The Doctrinal Minutes recommend that the preachers not preach on perfecting grace constantly, even though it is constantly to be expected. It should be treated chiefly in the presence of those who have readiness to hear it without engendering unnecessary distortions. Entire sanctification should be preached

> scarce at all to those who are not pressing forward,
> to those who are, always by way of promise,
> drawing rather than driving.[141]

Since the judgmental or "harsh preaching" of perfection tends to "bring believers into a kind of bondage of slavish fear," "we should always place it in the most amiable light, so that it may excite only hope, joy and desire."[142]

Though promised to all, it remains difficult to communicate without misconstructions. The Methodist societies should seek to elicit a response to perfecting grace in all but not to make it a contentious point of constant railing for those not rightly prepared to understand it. Union with Christ, purity of heart, and godliness

---

[138]Minutes, 1747, June 17, Q15, JWO 171.
[139]Minutes, 1747, June 17, Q13, JWO 170.
[140]Minutes, 1758, August 15, JWO 177.
[141]Minutes, 1745, August 2, Q6 – 11, JWO 153; i.e., wooing rather than compelling.
[142]Minutes, 1747, June 17, Q16, JWO 171.

cannot be neglected or diluted, but perfecting grace can be preached sparely and prudently, depending on the context. Wesley asked all preachers in his connection the question still asked in Methodist ordinal services: "Do you expect to be made perfect in love in this life?"[143]

c. Scriptural Teaching on the Extent of Grace

A central teaching of Scripture concerns the radical extent of the promise of grace, so much so that perfecting grace is not doctrine merely permissible in Scripture, but integral to the gospel. God promised to "redeem Israel from *all* their sins" (Ps. 130:8 NIV, italics added). From all their impurities and idols they are promised cleansing (Ezek. 36:25). Christ loved the church and gave himself for her that he might "present her to himself as a radiant church, without stain or wrinkle or any other blemish, but holy and blameless" (Eph. 5:27 NIV). The Son of God was manifested that he might destroy all sin (1 John 3:8). Jesus prayed that his followers might all be one, and that they would be made perfect in love (John 17:22 – 23). Herein is our love made perfect, that we may have boldness in the day of judgment, because as he is, so are we in this world (1 John 4:17).

The call to "be perfect, therefore, as your heavenly Father is perfect" (Matt. 5:48 NIV) is a command given to living, not dead men. It would not have been commanded if impossible to fulfill. On the basis of these texts, there can be no doubt that the Scriptures are describing present Christian life, not merely an abstract description of a life that never happens. Yet we should be keenly aware of "the sinful nature which still remains in us," "but this should only incite us the more earnestly to turn unto Christ every moment."[144]

d. A Question for Ministers of the Gospel: Are You Going on to Perfection?

Those who come up for "full connection" as preachers in the Wesleyan tradition are asked a weighty series of questions not merely about Christian perfection as an idea, but more so about their own appropriation of it: "Have you faith in Christ?" "Are you going on to perfection?" "Are you earnestly striving after it?" "Are you resolved to devote yourself wholly to God and His work?"[145] By the time postulants in Wesley's connection are commissioned to preach, they must have thought carefully about these questions. And these questions remain troubling to some. Therefore postulants are not to be ordained without answering from the heart, "Are you going on to perfection?" The answer must be personal and truthful.

What has been said above about full responsiveness to grace, and what follows,

---

[143]United Methodist *Book of Discipline* (1988), 232.

[144]Minutes, 1747, June 17, Q19 – 21, JWO 171.

[145]United Methodist *Book of Discipline* (1992), para. 425. "These are the questions which every Methodist preacher from the beginning has been required to answer upon becoming a full member of an Annual Conference. These questions were formulated by John Wesley and have been little changed throughout the years," 227n.

seeks to frame the context in which a preacher's conscience is to be instructed and by which one's own answer might be made more meaningful.

Wesley's instruction does not seek prematurely to ease conscience but to inform it. Each must answer from the soul (*ex anima*) before God. Those who have not yet developed a defensible view of sanctification on which they are willing to stand and which they are willing to defend do well to study carefully this whole chapter on Wesley's teaching of sanctification and perfection. It is not out of order to quote Wesley directly in answering these questions.

A recent disciplinary rubric softens the way for modern ordinands. It protects them from making a hard landing. Upon the examination for full connection, the bishop is instructed to "explain to the conference the historic nature of the following questions, and seek to interpret their spirit and intent."[146] This language has embedded in it a studied, intentional ambiguity. On the one hand, some, by explaining its historic nature, exalt it as normative; on the other hand, others, by showing its historic importance, by implication show that it belongs to the past and perhaps does not need to be taken too seriously since it is just a historical document. It deftly allows for either interpretation. The hearer is left to conscience to judge the questions as either archaic or perennially pertinent.

The intent of the Doctrinal Minutes indicates that these questions prior to "full connection" must be taken to heart and in their plain sense. There can be no doubt that these questions have been asked of Methodist preachers in full connection from the early days of the Methodist revival. They are as serious now as then.

5. The Confession, Article 11

For many in the Wesleyan tradition, including all United Methodists, the leading confession from the Evangelical United Brethren tradition stands as a constitutionally unrevisable summary of doctrine in the Wesleyan tradition. Article 11 of the confession carefully defines sanctification and perfection and provides disclaimers about perfection. It deserves to be carefully studied by all who teach in the Wesleyan tradition. Following is a summary of the gist of its content.

Sanctification is the work of God's grace, not an expression of human ability. It assumes the work of the Spirit by which those who have been born again by justifying grace are cleansed from sin in their thoughts, words, and acts. God's work of grace does not intend partially but wholly to cleanse from sin.

Two metaphors complement each other: cleansing and empowerment. We are being empowered and enabled to live in accordance with God's will and to strive for holiness. "We believe sanctification is the work of God's grace through the Word and the Spirit by which those who have been born again are cleansed from sin in their thoughts, words, and acts, and are enabled to live in accordance with God's will, and to strive for holiness without which no one will see the Lord."[147]

[146]United Methodist *Book of Discipline* (1992), para. 425.

[147]Confession, art. 2; cf. *LJW* 8:256.

Entire sanctification is complete responsiveness to perfecting grace. It is a right ordering of perfect love, righteousness, and true holiness, which every regenerate believer may obtain, by being delivered from the power of sin, loving God with all the heart, soul, mind, and strength, and the neighbor as oneself.

"Through faith in Jesus Christ this gracious gift may be received in this life." The way of holiness is not simply a road to be walked after death, but rather received in this life. The Spirit works in this receptive process "both gradually and instantaneously" by means of a gift and a giving process. This perfecting grace "should be sought earnestly by every child of God."[148]

It is doubtful that those who inveigh against the teaching of perfecting grace can in good conscience lead and preach in Methodist pulpits. The model deed of 1763 made clear that the doctrinal standards that apply to Methodist preaching should be judged in relation to the first four volumes of the earliest edition (1746) of the sermons, and Wesley's *Explanatory Notes upon the New Testament*, which contain this teaching.[149] Those offend against Wesley's teaching who inveigh against perfecting grace. It is not implied that one cannot have a particular theory or opinion about it. One may, provided that scriptural promises are not attacked.[150]

6. The Unique Doctrinal Status of the Methodist Protestant Disciplinary Article on Sanctification

Appended to the Twenty-Five Articles in all United Methodist *Disciplines* is an unnumbered article on sanctification adopted by the uniting conferences of 1939 and 1968. It has a special status, having been received from the Methodist Protestant church tradition, which upon union was included in the *Discipline* as an article of faith. Arguably, it is not expressly protected by the restrictive rules and is not strictly speaking one of the Twenty-Five Articles of Religion though constitutionally appended to them. Nonetheless, it has appeared in every *Discipline* since unification (1939) and remains a concise and useful statement of that sanctification teaching generally accepted among Wesleyans.

In this article, sanctification is defined as the renewal of our fallen nature by the atoning work of the Son and by the attesting work of the Spirit, received through faith, enabling the cleansing from *all* sins. We are not only delivered from the guilt of sin but washed from its pollution, saved from its power, and enabled through grace to love God with all our hearts and to walk in his holy commandments blamelessly.

---

[148]Confession, art. 11.

[149]For Wesley's explanation of the teaching purpose of these sermons, see his pref., *DSWT* 90–93.

[150]*DSWT* 21–53.

Further Reading on the Work of the Spirit in Sanctification

Arnett, William M. "The Role of the Holy Spirit in Entire Sanctification in the Writings of John Wesley." *WTJ* 14, no. 2 (1979):15 – 30.

Cary, Clement. "Did Mr. Wesley Change His View on Sanctification?" In *Entire Sanctification*, edited by S. Coward. Louisville: Herald, 1900.

Collins, Kenneth. *A Faithful Witness: John Wesley's Homiletical Theology*, 138 – 47. Wilmore, KY: Wesleyan Heritage, 1993.

Dayton, Donald W. *Discovering an Evangelical Heritage*. 1976; reprint, Peabody, MA: Hendrickson, 1988.

———. *The Theological Roots of Pentecostalism*. Metuchen, NJ: Scarecrow, 1987.

Dieter, Melvin E. "The Wesleyan Perspective." In *Five Views of Sanctification*, edited by Melvin E. Dieter, 11 – 46. Grand Rapids: Zondervan, 1987.

Dorr, Donal. "Wesley's Teaching on the Nature of Holiness." *LQHR* 190 (1965): 234 – 39.

Dunnam, Maxie D. *Going on to Salvation: A Study of Wesleyan Beliefs*. Nashville: Abingdon, 2008.

Dunning, H. Ray. *Reflecting the Divine Image: Christian Ethics in Wesleyan Perspective*. Downers Grove, IL: InterVarsity, 1998.

Harper, Steve. "Transformation (Effects of Salvation)" and "Growth in Grace." In *John Wesley's Theology Today*. Grand Rapids: Zondervan, 1983.

Jones, Charles E. *The Charismatic Movement: A Guide to the Study of Neo-Pentecostalism with Emphasis on Anglo-American Sources*. Metuchen, NJ: Scarecrow, 1992.

———. *A Guide to the Study of the Holiness Movement*. Metuchen, NJ: Scarecrow, 1974.

———. *A Guide to the Study of the Pentecostal Movement*. 2 vols. Metuchen, NJ: Scarecrow, 1983.

———. *Perfectionist Persuasion: The Holiness Movement and American Methodism, 1867 – 1936*. Metuchen, NJ: Scarecrow, 1974.

Lindström, Harald G. A. *Wesley and Sanctification*. Nashville: Abingdon, 1946.

Miley, John. *Systematic Theology*. Vol. 2. Chap. 8 on sanctification. New York: Hunt and Eaton, 1892 – 94.

Monk, Robert. "Sanctification." In *John Wesley: His Puritan Heritage*, 107ff., 118ff. Nashville: Abingdon, 1966.

Outler, Albert C. *The Wesleyan Theological Heritage, Essays*. Edited by T. Oden and L. Longden. "A Focus on the Holy Spirit," 159 – 75. Grand Rapids: Zondervan, 1991.

Page, Isaac E., and John Brash. *Scriptural Holiness: As Taught by John Wesley*. London: C. H. Kelly, 1891.

Runyan, Theodore, ed. *Sanctification and Liberation*. Nashville: Abingdon, 1981.

Weems, Lovett Hayes. *The Gospel according to Wesley: A Summary of John Wesley's Message*. Nashville: Discipleship Resources, 1982.

CHAPTER 10

On Remaining Sin after Justification

A. On Sin in Believers

1. When Sin's Power Has Been Broken, How Can It Return?

The text for the homily "On Sin in Believers" is 2 Corinthians 5:17: "If any man be in Christ, he is a new creature" [Homily #13 (1763), B 1:314–34; J #13, V:144–56]. Sin's power has been broken, but what if sin returns to dwell in the believer?

No willful sin is consistent with life in Christ. "If a believer wilfully sins, he thereby forfeits his pardon. Neither is it possible he should have justifying faith again without previously repenting."[1] One may "forfeit the gift of God either by sins of omission or commission."[2] This "forfeit" is always remediable by the grace of repentance. Hence, with Wesley as with Luther, the whole life of the believer is repentance. This repentance may be ordinarily received at the Lord's Table. There it should be preceded by genuine repentance and faith. For Christ "cannot *reign* where sin *reigns*; neither will he *dwell* where any sin is *allowed.* But he is and dwells in the heart of every believer who is fighting against all sin; although it be 'not yet' purified according to the purification of the sanctuary.' "[3] Where sin appears to be too powerful, pray for grace to struggle against it. The believer is not intimidated by the power of sin, because he or she already knows that sin's power has been broken.

a. Whether Regenerate Believers Commit Sin

Wesley had repeatedly stressed the power bestowed by sufficient grace on justified and regenerate believers not to commit sin, a central feature of the holy living tradition.[4]

The controversy that emerged around this idea came from those formed by the Lutheran tradition of *simul justus et peccator*[5] and by the Calvinist tradition that stressed the perseverance of the saints and the irresistibility of grace. It also was in

[1] Minutes, 1744, June 25, Q9, JWO 138.
[2] Minutes, 1744, June 25, Q11, JWO 138.
[3] "On Sin in Believers," B 1:323, sec. 3.8.
[4] As in "The Circumcision of the Heart" and "The Great Privilege of Those That Are Born of God."
[5] B 1:233, 245n.

tension with those Moravians who were teaching "sinless — even guiltless — perfection, as if the power not to sin meant the extirpation of all 'remains of sin.' "[6] No. Sin remains but does not reign.

Wesley proposed an alternative that hinged decisively on the distinction between voluntary and involuntary transgressions, "between 'sin properly so called' (i.e., the [deliberate] violation of a known law of God — mortal if unrepented) and all 'involuntary transgressions' (culpable only if unrepented and not discarded when discerned or entertained)."[7] There remained a tension, however, between Wesley's preaching of the great privilege (not to commit sin) and the realities of postconversion life where sin remained even though it was not reigning.[8]

b. Wesley's Ecumenical Intent to Hold Close Both the Ancient Christian Fathers and the Reformation

Wesley persisted in holding the ancient ecumenical holy living tradition in the closest possible relation to the Reformation tradition of justification by grace through faith alone. When he shifted from one to another focus, he sometimes sounded as if the other was for a moment neglected; but seen as a whole, the corpus seeks to bring them into the closest integration.

By 1763 the need was evident to sort out these relationships with greater clarity, so he wrote homily #13, "On Sin in Believers," "in order to remove a mistake which some were laboring to propagate: there is no sin in any that are justified"[9] (followed four years later by its sequel, homily #14, "The Repentance of Believers"). This homily corrected the inference that might be unfairly drawn from some of Wesley's earlier sermons that after conversion the believer is de facto so entirely free from sin that there is no further possibility of sin (or even of finite error!), or that the presence of sinful desires proves one's lack of faith.[10] Keep in mind that the "great privilege of those born of God" is precisely that they are no longer bound to the *reign* of sin. This homily is a crucial addendum. Those who preach on Christian perfection should carefully read this and its companion homily as a corrective to the exaggerated fringes of several sermons on entire freedom from sin.[11]

Much of the confusion had been spawned by "well-meaning men" under the direction of Nicholas von Zinzendorf, who imagined that "even the corruption of nature *is no more* in those who believe in Christ."[12] When pressed, they allowed that

[6]"On Sin in Believers," Outler's introduction, 1:314; on Wesley's rejection of sinless perfection, see EA, B 11:65 – 66, 338 – 41; B 1:318 – 34, 416 – 21; 9:53 – 55, 397 – 98.

[7]"On Sin in Believers," B 1:315, sec. 1.5. This stands in the tradition of the medieval scholastic distinction between moral and venial sin, and between voluntary and involuntary transgression. On the distinction between deliberate and indeliberate, see JWO 258 – 59, 287.

[8]"On Sin in Believers," B 1:319, sec. 1.6. This was a theme that Wesley would repeatedly explore from one angle or another; see "The First-Fruits of the Spirit," sec. 3.4 – 5; "Christian Perfection," sec. 2.3 – 5; "Wandering Thoughts," sec. 3.6; "On Temptation," sec. 1.5.

[9]*JJW*, March 28, 1763.

[10]See also B 1:65, 335 – 52; 2:164 – 67.

[11]See also B 1:233, 245 – 46, 314 – 34, 336 – 47, 435 – 41; 2:165 – 66; 4:157, 212.

[12]"On Sin in Believers," B 1:319, sec. 1.5.

"sin did still remain *in the flesh*, but not *in the heart* of a believer. And after a time, when the absurdity of this was shown, they fairly gave up the point, allowing that sin did still *remain*, though not *reign*, in him that is born of God."[13]

c. Combating Despondency

Wesley was trying to protect earnest believers against despair over deep-rooted sin. Some who having experienced justifying faith had then often experienced a backsliding despondency were disturbed over whether they still had saving faith. His purpose was to show that the struggle against sin continues after justification. It would become a serious problem of pastoral care if each time one fell from faith one would then intensely despair over whether one had ever or ever would again receive saving grace. Wesley was countering that forgiveness is constantly being offered and that one is never made absolutely immune from falling.

The idea that the justified person is free from all remnants of sin and temptation is a novel teaching (hence spurious, viewed apostolically) never found in the primitive church, patristic writers, or central history of the Church of England.[14]

2. A Caution to Those Who Deny Sin in Believers, Using Scripture, Experience, Tradition, and Reason

Wesley built his case on the basis of quadrilateral criteria. Only in a few places can the quadrilateral method be seen deliberately at work: here, in "On Sin in Believers," and in *Original Sin*, and in the *Appeals*.[15] Accordingly, he offered four types of argument, from *Scripture*, *reason*, *tradition*, and *experience*, against the position that there is no sin in those who are justified.

First, the position of absolute sinlessness after justification is contrary to *Scripture* (1 Cor. 1:2; Gal. 5:17), especially all those passages in Paul's writings that insist that the flesh continually lusts against the spirit, and the spirit against the flesh.[16]

Second, to say that there is no sin in believers is contrary to the *experience* of innumerable believers. Almost every believer has experienced some sort of ongoing struggle, having received saving faith, of contending with the hazards that follow saving faith, often with doubts as to whether one even had the faith or not. That is very common to the life of faith. One need not feel alienated or guilty or in despair when one goes through such a "wilderness state," a condition in which having been delivered like Moses crossing the Red Sea, having gone through baptism, having gone through the waters and being born into a renewed life, one then finds oneself wandering in the wilderness still on the way to Canaan.[17]

[13]"On Sin in Believers," B 1:318–19, sec. 1.5; "The Great Privilege of Those That Are Born of God," J V:227–31, sec. 2, italics added.

[14]"On Sin in Believers," B 1:317–19, sec. 1.

[15]Alternatively Wesley lists Scripture, reason, and experience as doctrinal norms, as in "The Repentance of Believers," sec. 1.2, and on other occasions "Scripture, reason, and Christian antiquity," as in his preface to his collected works, vol. 1 (1771).

[16]"On Sin in Believers," B 1:321–25, sec. 3.

[17]"On Sin in Believers," B 1:323, sec. 3.7.

Third, presumed absolute sinlessness after justification is a novel, hence untraditional doctrine, unheard of in the ancient church. It is a new doctrine, and any doctrine that is new and unprecedented could not be a fully apostolic doctrine. All heresies postdate apostolic teaching by pretending to amend this teaching. The prayers of the whole Christian *tradition*, East and West, from the ancient Christian writers through the Reformation, confess that the saints continue to struggle with sin.[18] Wesley applied the Vincentian rule of Christian antiquity, "Whatever doctrine is new must be wrong," since unapostolic, "for the old religion is the only true one: and no doctrine can be right unless it is the same 'which was from the beginning.'"[19] "The perfection I hold is so far from being contrary to the doctrine of our Church, that it is exactly the same which every Clergyman prays for every Sunday: 'Cleanse the thoughts of our hearts by the inspiration of thy Holy Spirit, that we may perfectly love thee, and worthily magnify thy holy name.' I mean neither more nor less than this."[20]

Finally, it is by *reason* that a critique is applied to false premises. Wesley discussed the logical dilemma of the doctrine of complete freedom from sin after justification by showing that it has the logical effect of eliciting hopelessness. If this premise is true, then anyone who feels a sinful desire cannot be a believer. That merely leads to despair, not faith. It elicits a double bind: If I think that any subsequent sin after justification negates my justification (disallowing penitent faith), and then if I feel mixed motives and sinful desires, I am likely to conclude that I have lost my faith.

So in "On Sin in Believers" (as well as in "Original Sin" and the "Earnest Appeal") we find the quadrilateral criteria once again explicitly expressed in Wesley's writings: *Reason* concurs with *Scripture*, *experience*, and *tradition* that after faith one still may sin.[21]

3. The Struggle of Flesh and Spirit

a. Degrees of Faith

The two contrary principles, flesh and spirit, continue to struggle and intermesh, latently or overtly, throughout the life of faith.[22] In even the maturest believer there continues a dormant guerrilla war between flesh and spirit.[23]

Anyone walking after the Spirit still feels inwardly these two contrary principles in tension. The Corinthian believers were described as carnal, even while their faith was growing.[24]

One may have weak faith. There are different degrees of faith.[25] One may have a

[18]"On Sin in Believers," B 1:318 – 24, secs. 1.2 – 4; 3.9.

[19]"On Sin in Believers," B 1:324, sec. 3.9.

[20]"An Answer to Mr. Roland Hill's Tract, Entitled 'Imposture Detected,'" J X:450.

[21]"On Sin in Believers," B 1:324, sec. 3.10.

[22]"On Sin in Believers," B 1:321 – 22, sec. 3.1 – 3.

[23]*CH*, B 7:398 – 406, 460 – 63.

[24]"On Sin in Believers," B 1:321, sec. 3.2.

[25]B 3:175 – 76; 3:491 – 98; 9:111, 164 – 65; *LJW* 1:251; 2:214; 5:173, 200; *JJW* 1:481 – 83; 2:328 – 29; JWO 68 – 69, 356 – 62; cf. B 3:266.

tiny foothold on faith, yet even the foothold is the beginning of saving faith, which is being called to pray that faith might increase in strength.[26]

As Wesley describes the "almost Christian," which we have previously discussed, he is not even one with "little faith." The "almost Christian" lacks entirely the faith that trusts God's righteousness.

One may be an "altogether Christian" and still continue to struggle with a weak or partially blinded faith. Faith may have been born without fully and immediately bearing the joyful fruits it could bear in due time.

Believers are "daily sensible of sin remaining in their heart, pride, self-will, unbelief; and of sin cleaving to all they speak and do, even their best actions and holiest duties. Yet at the same time they 'know that they are of God'; they cannot doubt of it for a moment. They feel his Spirit clearly 'witnessing with their spirit, that they are children of God.' "[27] They have not lost faith just because they experience an ongoing struggle with temptation, a continuing combat between flesh and spirit.[28]

b. How the Spirit Combats Bosom Sins: Fear, Doubt, and Self-Deception

In the preface to the 1740 *Hymns and Sacred Poems*, Wesley poignantly described the ongoing struggle of those who having been "justified freely through faith" may "remain for days, or weeks, or months" in this peace, "and commonly suppose they shall not know war any more, till some of their old enemies, their bosom-sins, or the sin which did most easily beset them (perhaps anger or desire), assault them again, and thrust sore at them.... Then arises fear, that they shall not endure to the end; and often doubt, whether God has not forgotten them, or whether they did not deceive themselves, in thinking their sins were forgiven." These struggles are common among believers justified by grace.

> But it is seldom long before the Lord answers for himself, sending them the Holy Ghost, to comfort them, to bear witness continually with their spirit.... Now they see all the hidden abominations there; the depth of pride, and self, and hell: Yet [knowing they are heirs], their spirit rejoiceth in God their Saviour, even in the midst of this fiery trial, which continually heightens both the strong sense they then have of their inability to help themselves, and the inexpressible hunger they feel after a full renewal in his image.[29]

4. Distinguishing Sin Reigning from Sin Remaining

Every faithful babe in Christ, having been baptized, and having received the new birth, and having begun to walk the way of holiness, remains subject to falling. The believer who shares in God's pardoning holiness remains still on a long road leading

[26]"On Sin in Believers," B 1:321 – 25, sec. 3. In defense of degrees of faith, see "The Almost Christian," *JJW*, May 29, 1738; Minutes, August 2, 1745.

[27]"On Sin in Believers," B 1:323, sec. 3.7.

[28]B 1:235 – 36; 3:105 – 6; *SS* 1:164; 2:362; *CH*, B 7:398 – 406, 460 – 63.

[29]*HSP* (1740), J XIV:327, pref. 11.

toward mature responsiveness to grace.[30] The believer is "saved from sin; yet not entirely. It *remains*, though it does not *reign*."[31]

The adversary "remains indeed where he once reigned, but he remains in chains."[32] The demonic powers are chained up even though they rise up and howl. They pretend to have enduring power but in fact do not. Imagine that an enemy is in chains — and that you know the enemy is in chains — yet is still capable of creating a lot of noise and confusion.[33]

Sin no longer has any overwhelming power over the life of the believer, although its consequences and residual effects continue.[34] When I by sinning harm my neighbor, the consequences of that sin may keep on rippling through the next year. I cannot stop the world. It keeps on going. No one by being pardoned is suddenly exempt from having to struggle with the consequences of past sin. Yet faith teaches me that even though I may feel this ambiguity and conflict in my heart, nonetheless, I am daily in the process of yielding myself up to the pardoning word, and therefore there is no condemnation. Sin no longer has radical power over the life of the believer, though its consequences echo.[35]

5. The False Premise of "Sinless Perfection"

Sin in believers remains a vexing daily challenge to be dealt with, but it does not have abiding power, for its power has been radically undermined by the grace of the Son on the cross. The demonic spirits have been bound up. Wesley disputed the fantasy of a sinless perfection that would imagine itself exempt from all future struggle with temptation and all conflict between flesh and spirit.[36] Resisting the phrase "sinless perfection,"[37] Wesley preferred to speak of "perfect love."[38]

So, is the justified person free from all sin? In principle, yes, because God's gift on the cross is the gift of freedom, and yet what is given sufficiently is received deficiently. Hence the gift does not exempt human freedom from its defining conditions of finitude and time or from the daily struggle between flesh and spirit. As new creatures, we do not leave behind our creatureliness completely but are being restored to our original creation.

The further one walks in the way of holiness, the more deeply one is aware of

[30]"On Sin in Believers," B 1:323 – 25, sec. 3.8 – 10. On the distinction between babes in Christ (who grasp pardon but not holiness) and those mature in Christ (who consecrate the full measure of their redeemed powers to steady responsiveness to grace) see "Christian Perfection," sec. 2.1; "On Patience," sec. 10; *ENNT* on Heb. 5:13 – 14; Letter to John Fletcher, March 22, 1775.

[31]"On Sin in Believers," B 1:327, sec. 4.3.

[32]"On Sin in Believers," B 1:331, sec. 4.11.

[33]"On Sin in Believers," B 1:325 – 32, sec. 4. For further reference to the distinction between remaining and reigning, see also "Salvation by Faith," sec. 2.6; "The Great Privilege of Those That Are Born of God," sec. 2.2; "The Deceitfulness of the Human Heart," sec. 2.5; *JJW*, August 10, 1738.

[34]B 1:233, 245 – 46, 314 – 34, 336 – 47, 435 – 41; 2:165 – 66; 4:157, 212.

[35]"On Sin in Believers," B 1:332 – 34, sec. 5.

[36]"Principles of a Methodist," J VIII:363 – 65, secs. 11 – 13.

[37]EA, B 11:65 – 66, 338 – 41; B 1:318 – 32, 416 – 21; 9:53 – 55, 397 – 98.

[38]"Some Remarks on Mr. Hill's 'Review of All the Doctrines Taught by Mr. John Wesley,'" J X:411; cf. *CH*, B 7:183, 187, 506 – 7, 520 – 21.

one's sin. It is a paradox of sin and grace, that those who turn out to be most keenly aware of their inadequacy are walking, breathing saints. Those least aware of their sin are the most distant from repentance. Repentance continues throughout the Christian life.

B. The Repentance of Believers

In the homily "The Repentance of Believers" (1767), Wesley amends and clarifies and, to some extent, corrects some impressions left in his earliest homilies. The text is Mark 1:15: "Repent ye, and believe the gospel" [Homily #14 (1767), B 1:355 – 53; J #14, V:156 – 70]. Among the most penetrating homilies of Wesley, in my view, are the one above, "On Sin in Believers," and this one, "The Repentance of Believers."

1. In What Manner Sin Cleaves to Believers' Words and Actions

a. The Struggle with Tempers Amid the Body-Soul Interface

Believers remain vulnerable to temptation to inordinate affections and disordered loves not beheld in relation to the love of God.[39] However deeply rooted in faith, ordinary believers still struggle with continuing pride, self-will, love of the world, shame, fear of rejection, evil surmisings, and impure intentions.[40]

Tempers that interfere with the love of neighbor, such as jealously, malice, covetousness, and envy, do not suddenly disappear when one has faith. One continues to be tempted to the idolatrous love of earthly things so as to neglect the love of the neighbor under the embrace of the love of God.[41] It is not uncommon for believers to continue to struggle with idolatry, since believers, too, continue to be tempted to imagine that temporal goods are absolute.

The whole of the spiritual life is a subtle equilibrium that is always susceptible to imbalance. When a child is at the point of learning to walk, he finds it difficult to maintain equilibrium. The problem of learning to walk in faith is likewise a problem of keeping equilibrium. The balance is subtle. Growing recipients of sanctifying grace are constantly tempted to imbalance, fallenness, and "backsliding."[42] This imbalance is endemic to the human situation, characterized as it is with finite freedom and the body-soul relation.

b. The Believer Remains Aware of Omissions and Defects

The backslider, having gotten a certain foothold in faith, slips and falls backward. Sin remains in the heart after conversion even when unrecognized,[43] in the subtle

[39]"The Repentance of Believers," B 1:337 – 38, sec. 1.4 – 5.

[40]"The Repentance of Believers," B 1:337 – 38, sec. 1.3 – 5.

[41]"The Repentance of Believers," B 1:339 – 40, sec. 1.7 – 9.

[42]B 3:210 – 26; 4:517 – 19; *LJW* 7:103, 351; 8:61, 111; *JJW* 5:40, 47, 54, 436; 8:31; *CH*, B 7:284 – 98, 628 – 29.

[43]"The Repentance of Believers," B 1:336, sec. 1.1.

forms of pride, self-will, love of the world, the desire of the eyes, self-indulgence, the pride of life, and the desire for glory.[44] Such temptations may recalcitrantly remain lodged within the context of the justified life.[45]

No self-aware believer could remain wholly oblivious that sin cleaves to his words and actions, as seen in sins of omission, inward defects without number, uncharitable interactions, actions not aiming at the glory of God, and in continuing postconversion evidences of neurotic guilt and helplessness.[46] This struggle of flesh and spirit goes on in the heart, in one's affect and activity, both in sins of commission and omission.

But still in all of these things, believers, insofar as they have faith in God's atoning work, have no condemnation. They still have an advocate with the Father. That is what distinguishes the regenerate life.

2. After Justification There Is a Continuing Congruence between Repentance and Faith

Repentance and faith are needed first to enter the kingdom, and then recurrently to continue and grow in the kingdom.[47] The call of the gospel to "repent and believe" does not subside after its first address. If one enters the Christian community initially by repenting and believing, so does one continue in repenting and believing. Repentance remains a daily concern of the Christian life, which is ever anew being offered the promise that God is not only willing but able "to save from all the sin that still remains in your heart."[48] In going " 'from faith to faith,' when we have a faith to be cleansed from indwelling sin," we are "saved from all that *guilt*, that *desert* of punishment, which we felt before."[49]

The congruence between faith and repentance is rhythmical and dialectical: When repentance says, "Without him, I can do nothing," faith replies, "I can do all things through Christ strengthening me."[50] By repentance we recognize our need; by faith our need is met. In repentance we behold our limitations; in faith we recognize our grace-enabled capabilities.

3. The Cure for Sin after Justification

In receiving justifying grace, we are not immediately thereby made behaviorally whole. If we were, it would be "absurd to expect a farther deliverance from sin" after justification.[51] Hence the paradox: those believers that are only slightly "convinced of the deep corruption in their hearts" tend to have "little concern about

[44]"The Repentance of Believers," B 1:337 – 39, sec. 1.3 – 7.
[45]"The Repentance of Believers," B 1:339 – 42, sec. 1.8 – 10.
[46]"The Repentance of Believers," B 1:341 – 46, sec. 1.11 – 20.
[47]"The Repentance of Believers," B 1:335 – 36, proem 1 – 3; B 1:65, 225, 278, 335 – 52, 477; 2:164 – 67.
[48]"The Repentance of Believers," B 1:347, sec. 2.2.
[49]"The Repentance of Believers," B 1:348, sec. 2.4.
[50]"The Repentance of Believers," B 1:350, sec. 2.5.
[51]"The Repentance of Believers," B 1:350, sec. 3.1.

entire sanctification." A profound sense of our *demerit* is precisely needed before we can understand the full compass of the atoning work of Christ. It is not our native strength but our utter helplessness that best teaches us "truly to live upon Christ by faith, not only as our Priest, but as our King."[52]

Immense harm is done by imagining that the gradual reception of sanctifying grace is indistinguishable from the instantaneous reception of justifying grace, for this "entirely blocks up the way to any farther change."[53] After the reception of justifying grace, the believer hears God speaking with a word of power that not only cleanses but in time evicts sin, whereby the "evil root, the carnal mind, is destroyed; and inbred sin subsists no more." This uprooting occurs again by repentance and faith, but "in a peculiar sense different from that wherein we believed [for] justification," in a deepening faith that at length saves to the uttermost.[54]

These are the crucial themes of this important homily titled "The Repentance of Believers." It corrects some dubious tendencies left unclarified in some of Wesley's thoughts on perfect love.

C. A Call to Backsliders

"A Call to Backsliders" is a homily intended to comfort and help those who may despair over their former sense of assurance. The text is Psalm 77:7–8: "Will the Lord absent himself for ever? And will he be no more entreated? Is his mercy clean gone for ever? And is his promise come utterly to an end for evermore?" (Wesley's translation) [Homily #86 (1778), B 3:210–26; J #86, VI:514–27].

1. Hope for the Despairing

a. The Shipwreck of Faith

There is still hope for those who having "begun to run well" but have "made shipwreck of the faith." But for the "uneasy" who earnestly desire change but think it impossible, the problem is different. They may be closer to salvation who think themselves furthest away.[55] More sinners are destroyed by despair than presumption. Many who once fought in spiritual combat now no longer strive, feeling victory impossible to attain.[56]

Wesley is here concerned with that form of despair among believers who, having experienced faith, enter into an extended period of the wilderness state, who tend to become disconsolate. They find themselves backsliding through a lengthy period of spiritual combat in which they are hardly producing the fruits of faith. Such are not beyond the grace of God.[57]

[52]"The Repentance of Believers," B 1:352, sec. 3.4.
[53]"The Repentance of Believers," B 1:350, sec. 3.1.
[54]"The Repentance of Believers," B 1:347, sec. 2.2.
[55]"A Call to Backsliders," B 3:212, proem 4–5.
[56]"A Call to Backsliders," B 3:211, proem 1–3.
[57]"A Call to Backsliders," B 3:212, proem 4–5.

b. Why Backsliders May Be Drawn to Despair

Backsliders may imagine there is no hope for them, because they find it hard to conceive of being forgiven again, having once been born anew in faith. Having received a full pardon once, they imagine that they cannot ever expect to receive it again. They reason wrongly by analogy from civil governance to eternal governance.[58] But God forgives many times, unlike the manner of civil justice.[59]

At first glance the origin of the backsliders' depression seems too deep to uproot. They may imagine they have so blasphemed the Spirit that there is no hope of further forgiveness (Matt. 12:31 – 32).[60] The blasphemy against the Spirit of which Jesus spoke, however, is the specific act of explicitly abusing the divine name by attributing the Spirit's work to Satan or by directly declaring that Jesus worked by the power of Satan.[61]

2. Overcoming Excessive Scruples

All too scrupulous backsliders may fantasize and mourn that they have committed that "sin that leads to death," as distinguished from sin that "does not lead to death" (1 John 5:16 NIV).[62] The death spoken of in that passage, however, is not eternal death, but the approach to death[63] of "notorious backsliders from high degrees of holiness." Their full redemption awaits the moment of death in order that they might be finally proved by faith meeting death to be ready for eternal life.[64]

They may become scrupulously disturbed by the text in Hebrews: "It is impossible for those who have once been enlightened, who have tasted the heavenly gift, who have shared in the Holy Spirit, who have tasted the goodness of the word of God and the powers of the coming age and who have fallen away, to be brought back to repentance" (Heb. 6:4 – 5 NIV). And, "If we deliberately keep on sinning after we have received the knowledge of the truth, no sacrifice for sins is left" (Heb. 10:26 NIV).[65] The sin involved in these passages, however, is the specific one of openly declaring "that Jesus is a deceiver of the people."[66] There is no scriptural reason for despair unless one is making these specific denials.

Wesley countered these false imaginings with the plain evidences of the evangelical revival: Large numbers of "real apostates" were being restored to the way of holiness, in some cases to a higher level of grace than before. In some this change was occurring in an instant.[67]

---

[58]"A Call to Backsliders," B 3:213, sec. 1.1.

[59]"A Call to Backsliders," B 3:217, sec. 2.1.

[60]"A Call to Backsliders," B 3:215, sec. 1.2; cf. 3:555 – 56; *LJW* 5:224.

[61]"A Call to Backsliders," B 3:223, sec. 2.2 (6).

[62]"A Call to Backsliders," B 3:214, sec. 1.2 (1).

[63]On the distinction between physical and spiritual (eternal, second) death, see B 2:287 – 88; 3:185 – 86; FA, B 11:64, 215, 230, 507 – 8; *SS* 1:117, 157; *CH*, B 7:68 – 69, 86 – 87, 129 – 45, 379, 465.

[64]"A Call to Backsliders," B 3:217 – 19, sec. 2.

[65]"A Call to Backsliders," B 3:214 – 15, sec. 1.2 (2 – 4).

[66]"A Call to Backsliders," B 3:219 – 22, sec. 2.2.

[67]"A Call to Backsliders," B 3:222 – 26, sec. 2.

D. Article 12 on Sin after Justification

1. Article 12

The Twenty-Five Articles of Religion are at the core of constitutional American Methodism, extremely safe against any legislative body to amend. One of these articles speaks specifically to the questions we have been discussing. So we have not only John Wesley's witness, but also the core confessions of the Wesleyan tradition to appeal to.

Wesley chose to retain the sixteenth article of the Anglican Thirty-Nine on "Of Sin after Baptism." It appears virtually unchanged in Wesley's Twenty-Five Articles for American Methodism, but under the title "Of Sin after Justification."

This seemingly minor emendation signals that justification is the primary concern of the teaching of baptism, even when it is approached by way of covenant anticipation in the families of the faithful. This does not signal an avoidance of the importance of baptism but connects baptism firmly with the new life of justification by grace through faith.

a. Not Every Sin Committed after Justification Is a Sin against the Holy Ghost

Article 12 defined sin in believers. One may depart from whatever grace God has given, be it prevenient, justifying, or sanctifying grace, because grace does not suppress free choice. To receive justifying and sanctifying grace does not imply that one ceases to be free, but rather that one becomes free in a new way.

The believer remains subject to temptation and prone to fall though continuing inordinate desire. So at whatever stage one is in the curriculum of unfolding grace, there always remains the possibility of sin. Having walked in faith, one may fall into sin. Any movement toward repentance is possible only by grace, not by one's natural power or initiative.

2. Combating Three Distortions

a. The Contrite Cannot Rightly Be Denied the Sacrament

Article 12 resists several distortions:

- that forgiveness is not offered a second time after having received justifying grace,
- that sin after justification is unpardonable, and
- that all sins are unpardonable sins against the Holy Spirit.[68]

The article stipulates, "The grant of repentance is not to be denied to such as fall into sin after justification."

Sin against the Holy Spirit is that sin so hardened against the hearing of the Word and against one's own conscience that one has decided not to put oneself in

[68]*DSWT* 145–47, 199–200.

a place where one can be pardoned. Forgiveness is being offered on the condition of penitence. Those not truly penitent are not ready to receive this forgiveness. It is not that God's pardoning word on the cross remains unspoken unless we accept it. For it is in principle offered to all. Rather, contrition is the subjective condition of our readiness to receive what is already there, namely, the forgiveness of God. For only "to such as truly repent this forgiveness is being offered."[69] Amendment of life is required to authenticate repentance.

The offer of forgiveness is not to be denied penitents who fall into sin after justification. The church does an injustice when it denies to the contrite the means of grace for their sins after justification or the preaching of forgiveness to the penitent.

b. On Rising Again after Falling

Article 12: "After we have received the Holy Ghost we may depart from grace given and fall into sin and by the grace of God rise again and amend our lives."

The prayer of absolution in the service of Holy Communion calls to mind among worshipers that forgiveness is addressed to all, yet there is a conditional premise that our pardon hinges on conscious readiness to receive it. We do not receive pardon from God without any reference to our repentance and faith.

It is hoped that once pardoned and delivered, the new believer is strengthened and reconfirmed. Each believer must ready himself anew for each time of receiving Holy Communion. Repentance recurs daily.

c. The Claim of Sinlessness

Article 12: "Therefore they are to be condemned who say they can no more sin as long as they live here, or deny the place of forgiveness to such as truly repent."

In intentionally retaining this article of the Anglican tradition, Wesley underscores the points made above in the homilies "On Sin in Believers" (1763), "The Repentance of Believers" (1767), and "A Call to Backsliders" (1778). In Wesley's abridgment of the Anglican Articles in 1784, this principle became constitutionally so fixed as to become virtually unamendable.

The article rejects the exaggeration that those who are justified by grace through faith can no longer sin. The motive is to guarantee to penitent believers access to Holy Communion. It resists the abuse that pardon and Holy Communion be withheld from those penitently justified and reborn into the family of God.

When we take seriously the three homilies discussed above, a brilliant equilibrium is seen in Wesley's teaching. These three stand deliberately as a further clarification of the intent of previous homilies on free grace and the great privilege of those born of God.[70]

---

[69]"The Righteousness of Faith," B 1:215; cf. 229.

[70]For further clarification of Wesley's intent in amending the Thirty-Nine Articles to twenty-five, see *DSWT* 105–11.

Further Reading on Sin and Sanctification

Sin and the Repentance of Believers

Cho, John Chongnahm. "John Wesley's View of Fallen Man." In *Spectrum of Thought*, edited by Michael Peterson, 67 – 77. Wilmore, KY: Francis Asbury, 1982.

Dorr, Donal. "Total Corruption and the Wesleyan Tradition: Prevenient Grace." *Irish Theological Quarterly* 31 (1964): 303 – 17.

Sanctification

Flew, R. Newton. *The Idea of Perfection in Christian Theology*, 313 – 34. Oxford: Oxford University Press, 1934.

Lindström, Harald G. A. *Wesley and Sanctification.* Nashville: Abingdon, 1946.

Oden, Thomas C. *Classic Christianity.* San Francisco: HarperOne, 2003.

Peters, John L. *Christian Perfection and American Methodism.* New York: Abingdon, 1956.

Runyan, Theodore, ed. *Sanctification and Liberation.* Nashville: Abingdon, 1981.

Sangster, W. E. *The Path to Perfection.* London: Hodder and Stoughton, 1943.

Wood, J. A. *Christian Perfection as Taught by John Wesley.* Chicago: Christian Witness, 1885.

CHAPTER 11

History and Eschatology

The dismal condition of the *existing* world must be seen in relation to the promise of the condition in which it will be when God's redemptive work is *finished*.

We will now consider a group of Wesley's homilies that deal with time: time past, time present, the spread of the gospel, and finally, time future. After this we will inquire into divine judgment and the new creation.

These topics cluster around the classic questions of the study of God's purpose in future time (eschatology). Wesley is not here presenting a theoretical speculation, but rather a practical scriptural teaching of the momentous transition from our life in time to our life in eternity. These questions are constantly faced by pastors and church leaders.

A. The General Spread of the Gospel

The first of these sweeping homilies, "The General Spread of the Gospel," takes Isaiah 11:9 as its text: "The earth shall be full of the knowledge of the LORD, as the waters cover the sea" [Homily #63 (1783), B 2:485 – 99; J #63, VI:277 – 88].

The ultimate future destination of individuals is closely related to the teaching of justification by grace through faith that we have discussed above. This looks toward the future justification at the end of history as we know it. There those who are justified by faith are covered in Christ's righteousness. Those who presume to be justified by works are judged by their works.

Those who are justified by faith alone will show in their lives that faith alone works by love that mirrors the image of God in ordinary human life following the new birth. In this way, questions of ethics interweave with end-time destiny, as seen in the final judgment. Between now and then, there is the rest of future time prior to the final judgment. In this time "in between the times," the divine imperative impinges on all human actions. This chapter deals with that future time within still-unfolding human history. What does it call for among people of faith?

Wesley looks toward the actual transformation of society as an implication of evangelical testimony, when "the earth will be filled with the knowledge of the LORD as the waters cover the sea" (Isa. 11:9 NIV).[1]

[1]"The General Spread of the Gospel," B 2:487, sec. 7.

1. The Present Dismal Condition of the World

a. The Spiritual Condition of the Dying World

It is evident from the present wretched condition of history that God's redemptive work is *not yet complete.* A pathetic pall of darkness, ignorance, and misery hovers over the face of the earth.

Amid this unhappy condition, bluntly viewed, some are *tempted* to imagine that the Holy Spirit has withdrawn from it. They assume that as long as human sin is so recalcitrant, nothing is likely to change in any significant way. This invites a deadly cynicism and hopelessness about the possibility of human renewal.[2]

In his portrayal of the bleak picture of the present spiritual condition of the entire world, Wesley does not spare Western "Christendom." Special attention, however, is given to Islam and popular Near Eastern religions.[3]

2. Whether Transformation of the World through the Power of the Gospel Is to Be Expected

a. The Scriptural Promise

In spite of this prevailing hollowness, and precisely through it, God's providential economy is gradually working itself out. God's purposes are in the process of being fulfilled despite all human resistances. There is still a long way to go, but God knows the future. The Spirit still has much work to do *in us.*[4] Meanwhile time is on God's side. However realistic Christian believers may be in examining the disheartening proneness of humanity to sin, they may look with even temperament toward the renewing power of God the Spirit, who promises ultimately to transform this world and *fulfill entirely the work God has begun.*

The hope for the future is not grounded in naturalistic optimism, but unmerited grace.[5] Faith takes it as an elementary premise of revelation that God's grace is working reliably to transform radically the whole human condition, even when this outworking is an enigma when seen from the narrow domain of empirical investigation without the aid of divine revelation.[6] *What we see happening* in history is only the beginning, merely a fragment of a long process, the end of which we do not yet see. But we can *behold with the eyes of faith* the promised end by trusting that the one who meets us on the cross will complete his work in and through the Spirit. A coming world is promised in which the loving knowledge of God is effectively producing uninterrupted holiness and happiness, covering the whole earth.[7]

Unrealistic? Optimistic? Consult the Scripture. It is pessimistic with respect to

---

[2]"The General Spread of the Gospel," B 2:487, sec. 7.

[3]"The General Spread of the Gospel," B 2:486 – 87, secs. 3 – 5.

[4]"The General Spread of the Gospel," B 2:486, sec. 2.

[5]Concerning Wesley's mode of eschatological reasoning, see B 1:169 – 72, 357 – 59, 494 – 95; see also hymns: *CH*, B 7:146 – 61, 716 – 17.

[6]"The General Spread of the Gospel," B 2:489 – 92, secs. 9 – 16.

[7]"The General Spread of the Gospel," B 2:487 – 89, secs. 7 – 9.

natural fallen human willing and the pretense of self-salvation. Optimism is a category of time expectation that projects better conditions to arise in the future out of natural man and man under the law. If so, Wesley is not optimistic, because we can expect no redemption out of either natural or legal man as such. Scripture teaches a hopeful realism that transcends both humanistic optimism and humanistic pessimism. Wesley's teaching holds fast to two paradoxical tendencies: the dismal future of natural man, and the glorious future of evangelical man. This future of reborn life is coming already to those who live under grace.

b. The Awakening

Wesley viewed the evangelical revival as a concrete sign of hope and a model of the general spread of the gospel in world history. This is not the only historic instance of vast Christian awakening, but the one most observable and palpable in the West in the eighteenth century. Other awakenings may be even more clearly viewed in the postapostolic period, the early ascetic period, and in the magisterial Reformation period.

Wesley thought that his contemporaries need only to reflect on how grace is currently working in the revival to open their eyes. In palpable ways, grace is working to prepare hearts for contrition, to bring persons toward repentance and justifying grace, and in due time sanctifying grace. These times show how God the Father is still at work through the saving deed accomplished once for all on the cross by God the Son. Many have come with assurance to say, "Abba, Father," through the atoning work of the Son.

The triune God is imminently active in all phases of this revival: God the Father is welcoming the faithful into the family of God by faith. God the Son is offering his atoning grace to convert individuals, one by one, by persuading them in cumulative numbers to receive divine grace freely, without demeaning or destroying their liberty. This occurs by the power of God the Spirit who is able and willing to convert whole nations and, in due time, the whole world.[8]

c. What God Is Doing in History

God raised up a few young, inconsiderable neophytes at Oxford to witness that "without holiness no one will see the Lord" (Heb. 12:14 NIV).[9] That was in the 1730s. By the 1780s when this homily was written, fifty years later, God was visibly working in the huge evangelical revival on a vast scale.

From Oxford the fire spread across England, Ireland, Scotland, and Germany, and to the Americas. By the 1830s, fifty more years later, Wesley's connection of spiritual formation would lead in the extension of the Great Awakening to the world mission movement. By the 1890s, the Word would spread through the Wesleyan and related charismatic and Pentecostal movements through Scandinavia,

[8]"The General Spread of the Gospel," B 2:489 – 90, secs. 10 – 13.
[9]"The General Spread of the Gospel," B 2:490; 11:115 – 16, secs. 10 – 13.

continental Europe, and on to Russia, Africa, China, and the Pacific Rim.[10] The lives of millions are being touched by what the Holy Spirit is doing.

As hearers are born again from above by the Spirit, so the leaven of renewal is spreading from one to another. The Word is made hearable through preaching the world over.

d. Will the Spread of the Gospel Continue?

Assuming that such a work has begun, what reason do we have to think it will continue? Wesley's simple logical syllogism is gently pressed: If God can redeem a cavalier, unprofitable, class-conscious English gentleman at Oxford, God can work wonders with any sinner; and if so, there is no intrinsic reason why the whole of the human condition cannot be changed. Though there will be impediments along the long road, the purpose of the triune God will not be finally thwarted by human recalcitrance.

Suppose the Scripture promise is wrong. There seems to be so much evidence against it. Wesley argued that it is less reasonable for the community of faith to posit the inevitability of the defeat of God's purpose. The bleak assumption that God has wrought so glorious a work as the patristic and Great Awakening revivals only to let them die away due to human resistance is implausible. Luther had the more dismal prognosis that a particular revival of religion would likely last little more than thirty years. But as Wesley was writing, the evangelical revival had already been proceeding for fifty years and was still going strong.[11]

It is more reasonable to assume that "God will carry on his work in the same manner as he has begun."[12] We are witnessing the spread of experiential knowledge and love of God reaching out to all the world.

On this basis of scriptural and experiential Christianity, Wesley thought we have sufficient reason to look toward a time when all the inhabitants of the earth may be reestablished in universal holiness and happiness, and the dross cleaned away.[13] While critics may dismiss this as folly, Wesley returned to Scripture for the validation of this promise. This is not a form of empirical historical knowledge (although such knowledge already confirms it), but of that which is knowable only by the spiritual senses — the new birth of hearing and seeing enabled by faith.[14]

The gospel intends to be good news of God's saving action within history, and not merely beyond history. This view is today sometimes misnamed as a form of "realized eschatology" (or in another context "realized millennial" teaching). The gospel is promised to spread and lengthen to its full extension. Now we see only a

[10]"The General Spread of the Gospel," B 2:489, sec. 11.

[11]"The General Spread of the Gospel," B 2:492, sec. 16; cf. "On God's Vineyard"; *LJW*, Letter to William Black, November 26, 1786.

[12]"The General Spread of the Gospel," B 2:491 – 93, secs. 14 – 16.

[13]"The General Spread of the Gospel," B 2:493 – 95, secs. 17 – 21; cf. "Scriptural Christianity."

[14]See previous discussion on sense knowledge and the spiritual senses and on faith as the intimation of things hoped for and the evidence of things unseen.

faint dawning of a vast historical process that in God's time will appear illumined in the full light of day.[15]

3. One by One

a. The Spirit Works First One by One and Only Then into Social Processes

The Spirit patiently addresses us one by one, individually breaking down our resistances, nudging the ungodly toward faith. What happens quietly and inwardly in an individual's repentance and faith has consequences for the unseen meaning of world history.

Behold the patient ways of the Spirit. The spread of the gospel occurs one by one to all. Just notice what God is doing in your own heart, and you can then grasp something of what God is in the process of doing everywhere.[16]

This is not an argument for automatic humanistic progress in history or one based on optimism about human competency — ideas entirely foreign to Wesley. Hidden in the premise of this argument is a deeper judgment about the Holy Spirit's sure determination to fulfill the mission of the Son.[17] By this grace, people are invited to experience scriptural Christianity, which intends to execute its commission to spread to all the inhabitants of the world, giving all the opportunity to hear the good news.

b. Imperative Authorization for World Mission: To the Ends of the Earth

A world mission is envisioned in which knowledge of God is spreading to the unhearing nations of the world, even to the "remotest parts" of "Asia, Africa, and America."[18] Even in the mission to the "Mohametans" there is hope. Admittedly Wesley saw even in his century that the Muslim world loomed as a "grand stumbling block," but one that could be softened by acts of faith becoming active love in schools, relief, and medicine. But he warned that change would occur only when the sorry lives of professing Christians are replaced by faith active in love, when "their words will be clothed with divine energy, attended with the demonstration of the Spirit and of power."[19] He hoped that "the holy lives of Christians will be an argument they [Muslims] will not know how to resist."[20]

God is able finally to gather the new Israel "out of all countries" and "cause them to dwell safely."[21] As this is occurring, "all those glorious promises made to the

---

[15]"The General Spread of the Gospel," B 2:492 – 93, sec. 16.
[16]"The General Spread of the Gospel," B 2:490 – 93, secs. 13 – 18.
[17]"The General Spread of the Gospel," B 2:493 – 95, secs. 18 – 20.
[18]"The General Spread of the Gospel," B 2:493, sec. 18.
[19]"The General Spread of the Gospel," B 2:495, sec. 21.
[20]"The General Spread of the Gospel," B 2:496, sec. 22.
[21]"The General Spread of the Gospel," B 2:498, sec. 25; Jer. 32:37 – 41.

Christian Church" are being gradually accomplished. At length "violence shall no more be heard in thy land."[22]

It is not as if we are autonomously building the kingdom of God, but rather that God is working in us and through grace-laden human willing and acting in order to bring about the larger purpose of redeeming the history of sin. God is carrying on the work of providence in the same manner that it was begun and is moving steadily toward the dawn of the latter-day glory.[23]

c. Human Suffering Viewed from the Perspective of Eternity

Those who lack an overarching worldview of meaning in the whole of history are likely to remain especially vexed by the continuing problems of *evil and suffering.*

Scriptural Christianity's end-time perspective on history is the only full and satisfactory answer to the salient objections against the wisdom and goodness of God. Dismal world-bound projections take human recalcitrance more seriously than they take divine grace. Some are tempted to object that God is unjust for overpromising, and that seemingly is validated, because these present conditions of the world are unjust. This gloomy, abstract, and unscriptural reading detaches present history from the future of history. It is abstract because it abstracts salvation history out of real occurring history.

Rather, the justice of God must be viewed from its end. No doubt about what happens in the end: divine judgment. Until that time, we are able to see by our spiritual senses a providential and salvific purpose gradually working to fully repair the broken human condition.[24]

B. On Faith, Hebrews 11:1

This homily titled "On Faith: Hebrews 11:1," returns to the Scripture text of previous homilies on faith: "Faith is ... the evidence of things not seen" (Heb. 11:1) [Homily #132 (1791), B 4:187 – 200; J #122, VII:326 – 35]. It deals with life after death, mystery, and what we know from Scripture about the intermediate state between death and the final judgment.

1. The Soul in Death

a. What Happens after Death?

Ministers of the gospel are often asked questions about what happens immediately after death. These questions arise out of common human concern and are answered clearly in scriptural teaching following the analogy of faith (viewing each part in the light of the whole of Scripture, and the whole in the light of each part).

"What kind of existence shall I then enter upon, when my spirit has launched out of the body? How shall I feel myself ... when the organs of hearing are moulder-

---

[22]"The General Spread of the Gospel," B 2:498 – 99, sec. 26; Isa. 60:18 – 19; 61:11.
[23]"The General Spread of the Gospel," B 2:492 – 93, sec. 16.
[24]"The General Spread of the Gospel," B 2:499, sec. 27.

ing into dust, in what manner shall I *hear*? When my brain is of no further use, what means of *thinking* shall I have?"[25] What shall I be and do after my death? What will the intermediate state between death and the final resurrection be like, when my spirit is out of my body?

Here Wesley is willing to discuss, with cautious exegetical conjectures, the question of the situation of the immortal soul at the time of death.[26] It appears that he is answering questions put to him by many anxious communicants he counseled in his incessant travels and ministry.

b. Much We Are Not Prepared to Know

Wesley speaks personally as a very old man. He poignantly describes himself already as "strangely connected with a little portion of earth, but this only for a while. In a short time, I am to quit this tenement of clay, and remove into another state," which the living know not and the dead cannot tell.[27] "How strange, how incomprehensible, are the means whereby I shall then take knowledge even of the material world!"[28]

Admittedly, there is much of the invisible world of which we can "know nothing, and indeed we need to know nothing."[29] Most of our ideas and impressions remain conjectural, even with the most acute reasoning and widest data, lacking the promises of divine disclosure.

c. A Glorified State beyond Present Human Discernment apart from Grace

It is at least clear that we will go from one existence to another very different one: from life to death, from time to eternity.[30] There are many indications from Scripture that the spirits of the righteous are to be blessed by dwelling with God face-to-face. Transgressors will remain infinitely distanced from the eternal blessedness of God.[31]

To those who ask, "Is heaven a state or a place?" the fitting response is, "There is no opposition between these two.... It is the place wherein God more immediately dwells with those saints who are in a glorified state." "Place" is an extendable metaphor that points to a reality beyond time and space—eternity. Its essential feature is "to see God, to know God, to love God.[32]

We shall then know "both His nature, and His works of creation, of providence, and of redemption. Even in paradise, in the intermediate state between death and

[25]"On Faith, Hebrews 11:1," B 4:189, sec. 2, italics added.

[26]"On Faith, Hebrews 11:1," B 4:188, sec. 1; Letter to William Law, *LJW* 3:359. Letter to Sarah Wesley, April 12, 1788, *LJW* 8:54; cf. *LJW* 3:372; on knowledge of survival after death, see B 2:289–90, 595–97; 4:52–53, 288–89, 299.

[27]"On Faith, Hebrews 11:1," B 4:188, sec. 2; cf. J IV:49ff.; *JJW*, December 15, 1788.

[28]"On Faith, Hebrews 11:1," B 4:189, sec. 3.

[29]Ibid.

[30]"On Faith, Hebrews 11:1," B 4:180, sec. 4.

[31]"On Faith, Hebrews 11:1," B 4:194, sec. 9; B 2:365–72; 3:41–43, 185–88, 196–97; 4:32–34.

[32]Letter to Mary Bishop, April 17, 1776, *LJW* 6:213.

the resurrection, we shall learn more concerning these in an hour than we could in an age during our stay in the body."[33]

2. Faith's Grasp of the Invisible through Revelation and the Spiritual Sense

a. Knowing by Faith

What depths of understanding await us in the end! All that we can know of the future world by natural light is but "one degree better than utter darkness."[34] Only by divine revelation can we know of this coming world, and what we can know requires active faith.[35] "These things we have believed upon the testimony of God.... By this testimony we already know the things that now exist, though not yet seen."[36] All our speculations will pass away.

Meanwhile, in order to know the spiritual world, we must be given a sensory competency of a quite different nature. Faith is that spiritual sense that lays hold of the invisible by trusting in God's revealed Word. "By faith we understand" (Heb. 11:3 NIV), for faith is "being sure of what we hope for and certain of what we do not see" (Heb. 11:1 NIV [1984]).

C. Faith and the Intermediate State

1. In Abraham's Bosom

a. The Spirits of the Righteous

The intermediate state is distinguished from heaven. In the intermediate state — whether Hades or paradise — both the spirits of the righteous and unrighteous dwell, separated by an impassable gulf, awaiting reunion with their bodies,[37] as portrayed in the parable of the rich man and Lazarus.[38] "In paradise the souls of good men rest from their labors and are with Christ from death to the resurrection."[39]

Those with God will experience eternal joy, abiding in "intimate communion" with the Lord, "continually ripening for heaven." They are "inexpressibly happy." These find expression in the biblical picture of dwelling "in Abraham's bosom."[40] Believers "will be perpetually holier and happier, till they are received into 'the kingdom prepared for them.'"[41]

---

[33]Letter to Mary Bishop, April 17, 1776, *LJW* 6:213; B 2:289 – 90; 3:537 – 41; 4:190 – 92, 195 – 97, 211 – 13, 288 – 89; cf. *LJW* 6:26.

[34]"On Faith, Hebrews 11:1," B 4:198, sec. 14.

[35]"On Faith, Hebrews 11:1," B 4:198, secs. 14 – 15.

[36]"On Faith, Hebrews 11:1," B 4:199, sec. 16.

[37]*LJW* 6:214.

[38]"On Faith, Hebrews 11:1," B 4:189, sec. 4; cf. #115 "Dives and Lazarus."

[39]Letter to George Blackall, February 25, 1783, *LJW* 7:168; for his critique of medieval scholastic and Tridentine views of purgation, see B 2:292, 374 – 75, 581.

[40]On the metaphor of Abraham's bosom, see B 2:156; 3:35; 4:7, 33, 116, 190.

[41]"On Faith, Hebrews 11:1," B 4:191, sec. 5; cf. *LJW* 5:299, 306: 6:216, 224: *JJW* 5:195.

The spirits of the righteous will "swiftly increase in knowledge, in holiness, and in happiness, conversing with the wise and holy souls that lived in all ages.... They will forget nothing. To forget is only incident to spirits that are clothed with flesh and blood."[42] Rational arguments for immortality may complement faith's discernment but cannot be a substitute for this divinely revealed wisdom.

b. Incorporeal Spirits Discerned by Faith

God employs incorporeal spirits to accomplish his purposes in the visible world. They converse with other spiritual beings.

They advance in holiness and in the love of God and of humanity. They may be given "astonishing senses" to perceive the depths of the orders of beings, virtues, powers, and dominions that are imperceptible by physical senses.[43]

It is not improbable that righteous spirits of God's messengers (the angelic beings) may move about on the earth doing God's pleasure, ministering to persons on the earth by counteracting wicked spirits and protecting persons from harm.[44]

Faith has eyes that enable the faithful to glimpse something of the spirits of the just made perfect. They intercede in close relation with the living faithful, attending to and caring for their good. They are happy to be "permitted to minister to those whom they have left behind."[45]

Like angelic creatures, the saints in heaven will recognize each other and enjoy communion with the patriarchs, prophets, apostles, and martyrs. They will be able to traverse "the whole universe in the twinkling of an eye, either to execute the divine commands or to contemplate the works of God."[46]

For now, we in the flesh can thank God for the evidences of things unseen, and for the new senses of faith that are being opened in our souls. We are called to give thanks "to God for enlightening us to these things which we would otherwise not know."[47]

D. Signs of the Times

The third of these homilies deals with the momentous transition from time to eternity. It takes as its text Matthew 16:3: "Ye can discern the face of the sky; but can ye not discern the signs of the times?" [Homily #66 (1787), B 2:521 – 33; J #66, VI:304 – 13].

1. The Times and Signs of Which Jesus Spoke

In the time of the coming of the Anointed One, God took our nature to die for

[42]"On Faith, Hebrews 11:1," B 4:192, sec. 6.
[43]"On Faith, Hebrews 11:1," B 4:192, sec. 7.
[44]"On Faith, Hebrews 11:1," B 4:197, secs. 11 – 12.
[45]"On Faith, Hebrews 11:1," B 4:197, sec. 12.
[46]"On Faith, Hebrews 11:1," B 4:196, sec. 11.
[47]"On Faith, Hebrews 11:1," B 4:199, sec. 17.

us. Expected by the prophets and announced by the Baptist, many signs and wonders attest his coming: the blind see, the lame walk, the deaf hear, and the poor have the gospel preached to them.[48]

When our lives are hid in Christ, we participate in his life. The mighty deeds of God become more discernible to us to the extent that we share in his life, death, and resurrection. Those who by faith are given eyes to see rejoice in new life being given: lepers are cleansed, the dead are raised up, the lame throw away their crutches. These were evident to the faithful in the revival. Many such signs were beheld and attested. They anticipate the heavenly blessings.

Yet how unprepared the gathered people are to see the deeper signs of God's latter-day glory. It has long been promised that God would complete his mission to reconcile humanity through the ministry of the Holy Spirit. The kingdom is coming without observation, like a mustard seed growing silently, like a little leaven in the meal that gradually leavens the whole loaf.[49]

2. The Signs of These Times

a. The Great Awakening

During the five decades of evangelical awakenings in England and America in which Wesley lived and taught,[50] such signs were abundantly evident. The spiritually deaf were hearing the whispers of grace; the poor were hearing the gospel preached and its evidences manifested through love. The spiritually blind were coming to see through the eyes of faith in the light of the ministry of the Son. They were and still are being converted by the hundreds of thousands. Former profligates and formal religionists have had their hearts warmed. They are turning to the active life of faith working through love, happy in life, triumphant in death.[51] This can be seen empirically in a vague and external way, but by faith more truly. In this way God is revealing himself in the light of Scripture's promise to those of simple faith. They may see with the eyes of faith far more than the wise and learned.

There are many signs now at hand that point to the emergent completing, sanctifying work of the Spirit.[52] This work is gradual and happens in God's own time. Our petitions are not unheard. The world mission of the church to the ends of the earth is reaching toward a new state of recognition and readiness.[53]

These signs of the times are occurring on the vast scale of the whole of human history, and we are glimpsing only a small part. They have occurred steadily in the history of salvation, but they are more evident today in the evangelical revival,

[48]"The Signs of the Times," B 2:523 – 25, sec. 1.
[49]"The Signs of the Times," B 2:525 – 27, sec. 2.
[50]1735 to 1787 at this time of writing.
[51]"The Signs of the Times," B 2:530, sec. 2.8 – 9.
[52]"The Signs of the Times," B 2:525 – 26, sec. 2.1 – 4.
[53]"The Signs of the Times," B 2:531, sec. 2.10.

even to empirical observation, if we are willing to look. But looking occurs by the spiritual senses.

Fair-minded historians who have studied carefully the social consequences of the Great Awakening have often reported that many positive social effects have been accomplished by initiatives strongly begun or supported by that Awakening, notably the end of slavery; care for poor; the critique of materialistic hedonism; the stress on individual responsibility, thrift, and generous giving; peace; and the relief of world hunger and suffering.

b. Why Hearts Are Hardened

Why then is so much dull human consciousness still so unready to discern these signs? In a culture full of pride, ruled by disorderly passions, habitually loving the creature more than the Creator, it is not surprising that many hearts have become hardened to God's gracious coming.

This adulterous and sinful generation cannot see the signs of these times. The evidences are there for anyone to see, but their eyes are not open.

No matter how radiant the emerging signs, even if they glare in our eyes, our jaded sensibilities may remain closed to them. Lacking spiritual senses, which the new birth enlivens, we miss what is dramatically happening all about us in the history of revelation.[54]

c. Our History and Future History

Our history is being lived out amid the gradual emergence of the advent of the latter-day glory, the completion of the redemptive purpose beyond fallen history.[55] Though incomplete, it shows momentous signs of ever-fuller appearance. Anyone can pray for grace to bring this movement of history toward its fulfillment in eternity. God is fulfilling his promises, and for those who have eyes to see, it is a mighty display of divine power and love throughout the whole earth. The evangelical revival offers a window into final eschatological fulfillment.[56]

d. The Hazards of Time-Bound Speculations on the End

Unlike some interpreters who were calculating a final reckoning on a particular date, Wesley did not speculate on explicit predictions of final judgment.[57] He specifically rejected the particular form of amillennial interpretation that held that "'the new Jerusalem came down from heaven' when Constantine the Great called himself a Christian.... He would have come nearer to the mark if he had said, that was the time when a huge cloud of infernal brimstone and smoke came up from the

[54]"The Signs of the Times," B 2:525–29, sec. 2.1–7.
[55]*LJW* 6:80; B 1:215–16; 2:482; 4:33–34.
[56]*LJW* 1:284.
[57]*LJW* 8:63, 67.

bottomless pit."[58] But he did think that the revival was signaling that the triune God was at work in God's own time to bring his promises into final fulfillment.

Only occasionally, as in the case of Revelation 13, does Wesley speculate on millennial sequences. Following Johann Bengel, he interpreted the beast as the corrupted church, especially as it was corrupted in medieval sacramental teaching, especially in the period following Gregory VII.[59] "When the 'beast' is destroyed, Satan is bound for a millennium, then loosed, to gather his great army with Gog and Magog for the final battle, where, with a great fire from heaven, his force is destroyed. He is finally cast into the lake of fire and brimstone to be tormented day and night."[60] The vision of the end of history is the victory of God.

These are the major themes dealt with in Wesley's thoughts on future time and the transition from here to eternity. The next and final chapter of this second volume inquires into Wesley's teaching on heaven, hell, divine judgment, and the new creation. For Further Reading on Eschatology, see pages 304 – 5.

[58]"The Signs of the Times," B 2:529, sec. 2.7; cf. 3:449 – 50, 470.
[59]*ENNT*; Rev. 13:1 – 12.
[60]*WC* 124; *ENNT* on Rev. 13.

CHAPTER 12

Future Judgment and New Creation

Wesley's most succinct summary of eschatology appeared in his famous "Letter to a Roman Catholic." It begins:

> I believe God forgives all the sins of them that truly repent and unfeignedly believe his holy gospel; and that,
> at the last day, all men shall arise again, everyone with his own body.
> I believe that, as the unjust shall after their resurrection be tormented in hell forever,
> so the just shall enjoy inconceivable happiness in the presence of God to all eternity.[1]

In this chapter we will review four major homilies that convey Wesley's explicit teaching on the future judgment: "The Great Assize," "The Good Steward," "On Hell," and "The New Creation."

A. The Great Assize

This stunning homily, "The Great Assize," has as its text Romans 14:10: "Before the judgment seat of Christ" [Homily #15 (1758), B 1:354–75; J #15, V:171–85].

This is the only sermon Wesley preached in a civil court.[2] An assize was a periodic session of a superior court of law for trial of civil and criminal cases. It brought a demeanor of impressive solemnity wherever it was held.

The Great, or Last, Assize was a metaphoric symbol of the completely real last judgment.[3] However solemn any human court might seem, another is coming that will arouse far greater solemnity: the final day of judgment when all motives will come under divine investigative judgment.[4] Those who understand how inescapable this final judgment will be will find their moral behavior and spiritual sensibility transformed by the stark awareness of it.[5]

---

[1]Letter to a Roman Catholic, JWO 495–96, sec. 10; cf. 1:227–28; cf. B 2:365–72; 3:41–43, 185–88, 196–97; 4:32–34.

[2]February 27, 1758, in Bedford; *JJW* 4:254.

[3]Cf. *LJW* 4:345; 6:79; B 1:147–48, 359–66; 2:292–96; 3:187–88, 400–402; 4:141–43, 319–20.

[4]B 11:316–17, 404–6, 475–76, 487–89; *CH*, B 7:132–33, 146–61, 716–17.

[5]"The Great Assize," B 1:356, proem; cf. B 2:292–96.

1. Circumstances of the General Judgment

a. The Judge

Those present at this judgment are all the human living and the dead of all times. All the just and the unjust are judged. The Judge is God. The premise of the triunity of God underlies this teaching: God the Father is Judge of justice, God the Son is divine Advocate, God the Holy Spirit is the reader of hearts.

Scripture attests certain signs on earth — earthquakes,[6] floods, awesome events — by which the seriousness of the coming judgment is anticipated, accompanied by signs from the heavens: the sun will darken, the stars stop shining, the dead will rise at the last trump, and all will stand before the throne of the Lord who will gather the nations and separate sheep from goats.[7]

The judgment itself is presided over by the Father, the Creator, who is the one incomparably just and merciful Judge. The Advocate is one who has empathically shared our fragile frame, who knows what it means to be tempted yet without sin, who knows what it means to weep, face death, and die. Our Advocate is the incarnate Son who in his flesh suffered the wounds of our transgressions, and because of his obedience unto death was exalted to the right hand of the Father.[8] The all-seeing investigator is God the Spirit who sees into our inmost hearts and motives.

b. The Duration of the Trial

The duration of judgment will be as long as it takes to deal fairly with each and every case. The present time (from creation to consummation) will end. The day of the Lord will begin.

The day of the Lord will commence with the general resurrection, but how long it will continue is not temporally measurable, because for the Lord one day is as a thousand years. So "day" need not be taken as a twenty-four-hour period of time, but an unspecified heavenly interval, perhaps extensive, seeing through the task to be done.

"Some of the ancient Fathers drew the inference that what is commonly called 'the day of judgment' would be indeed a thousand years. And it seems they did not go beyond the truth; nay probably they did not come up to it," for "it may not improbably comprise several thousand years. But God shall reveal this also in its season."[9] The venue of judgment is unspecified except as the great white throne high above the earth.[10]

---

[6]Remembering the Lisbon earthquake of November 1, 1755, cf. "Serious Thoughts Occasioned by the Late Earthquake at Lisbon," 1755. Cf. also B 1:354 – 75.

[7]"The Great Assize," B 1:358 – 59, sec. 1.2 – 3.

[8]"The Great Assize," B 1:359, sec. 2.1; cf. 3:400 – 402.

[9]"The Great Assize, B 1:360, sec. 2.2; cf. B 7:716 – 17.

[10]"The Great Assize," B 1:361, sec. 2.3.

c. The Opening of Books

"It is then 'the dead, small and great,' will 'stand before God; and the books' will be 'opened'—the book of Scripture, to them who were entrusted therewith, the book of conscience to all mankind.... Thou wilt appear without any shelter or covering, without any possibility of disguise, to give a particular account of the manner wherein thou hast employed all thy Lord's goods."[11]

The command of God in Scripture and conscience is the law in this court. The conscience is the refraction of the divine command. No one escapes. No one comes in a mask. The investigation is highly particular and inwardly personal.

d. The Judged

Those to be judged are all who ever have lived, to give account of their words and works, viewed comprehensively over their entire lives. Everything done in darkness will be brought to light: actions, motives, every idle word, every inward working of every human soul.[12]

With consummate fairness, their good and evil deeds will be remembered, and the faithful who trust God's promise are entirely pardoned according to the gospel covenant.[13]

The metaphor portrays each one standing before the Judge and in some way recollecting, witnessing, and beholding the entire history of his or her moral decision making before the cosmic audience. The angelic observers rejoice in the evidences of faith active in love.

2. The Consummation

According to the vision in the Revelation, after the execution of the sentence will come a great and holy conflagration, a consuming fire in the temporal heavens and earth, not as if rendering them nothing or to annihilation. Rather, they will undergo a change "like the formation of glass, after which the fire can have no further power over them."[14] The purpose of the fire is to purify and ready the cosmos for eternal service in the celestial city.[15] Then will come the creation of new heavens and a new earth wherein the righteous shall dwell, and where the Lord will reign eternally.[16]

---

[11]"The Good Steward," B 2:293, sec. 3.2; cf. Letter to the Bishop of Gloucester, B 11:487–88.

[12]"The Great Assize," B 1:362–63, sec. 2.5.

[13]"The Great Assize," B 1:360–63, sec. 2.2–6. J. A. Bengel's commentary on Revelation (1740), translated into English in 1757, had predicted the date for the millennium as 1836. Wesley was in many ways greatly indebted to Bengel and had reproduced Bengel's chronological appendix in his own work. Though Wesley sympathized with some aspects of Montanus, he did not sympathize with its specific individual doctrine of the end time. Wesley hesitated to become entangled in a speculative attempt at apocalyptic chronology. Cf. "The Real Character of Montanus" and "The Wisdom of God's Councils," B 1:350n.; Jer. 31:34; Heb. 8:12.

[14]"The Great Assize," B 1:367, sec. 3.2.

[15]When his nephew Samuel became a Roman Catholic, John Wesley may have been jesting when he wrote that if he has faith, "he may, indeed, roil a few years in purging fire; but he will surely go to heaven at last!" Letter to Charles Wesley Jr., May 2, 1784, *LJW* 7:217.

[16]"The Great Assize," B 1:368, sec. 3.3.

3. The Contemporary Moral Relevance of the Contemplation of Final Judgment

Earthly judges are given by God's providence the fearful requirement to be his ministers, to "execute justice, to defend the injured, and punish the wrong-doer."[17] Every earthly judgment rightly should be executed in humble faith, aware of one's accountability before the final Judge, and following in the way of the one who mixed justice and mercy with incomparable wisdom.

All are called to bear in mind the coming judgment, its universality and inescapability, so as to form prudent present moral judgments.[18] All human judgments are relativized in relation to the one who is incomparably just.

B. The Good Steward

The picture of the investigative judgment portrays the fair process leading up to the final judgment as portrayed in Scripture. The text is the parable of the good steward in Luke 16:2: "Give an account of thy stewardship; for thou mayest be no longer steward" [Homily #51 (1768), B 2:293 – 96; J #51, VI:136 – 49].

1. The Investigative Judgment

a. Accountability for the Soul

At the Great Assize, the soul will then be examined. The Judge of all will inquire, using clear and plain terms anyone can understand. Among these questions:

> How didst thou employ thy *soul*?
>
> I entrusted thee with an immortal spirit, endowed with various powers and faculties, with understanding, imagination, memory, will, affections. I gave thee withal full and express directions how all these were to be employed.
>
> Didst thou employ thy *understanding*, as far as it was capable?
>
> Didst thou employ thy *memory* according to my will?
>
> In treasuring up whatever knowledge thou hadst acquired which might conduce to my glory?
>
> Was thy *imagination* employed, not in painting vain images, much less such as nourish foolish and hurtful desires, but in representing to thee whatever would profit thy soul, and awaken thy pursuit of wisdom and holiness?
>
> Were thy *affections* placed and regulated in such a manner as I appointed in my Word?
>
> Didst thou give me thy heart?
>
> Was I the joy of thy heart, the delight of thy soul, the chief among ten thousand?
>
> Did the whole stream of thy affections flow back to the ocean from whence they came?[19]

[17] "The Great Assize," B 1:371, sec. 4.

[18] "The Great Assize," B 1:372 – 75, sec. 4.3 – 5.

[19] "The Good Steward," B 2:293 – 94.

b. Stewardship of the Body

The examination of lifelong trusteeship of the body will proceed:

The Lord will then inquire, "How didst thou employ thy *body* wherewith I entrusted thee."

I gave thee a *tongue* to praise me therewith.... Didst thou employ it, not in evil-speaking ... but in such as was good, as was necessary or useful, either to thyself or others? Such as always tended, directly or indirectly, to "minister grace to the hearers"?

I gave thee, together with thy other senses those grand avenues of knowledge, *sight*, and *hearing*. Were these employed to those excellent purposes for which they were bestowed?...

I gave thee hands and feet and various *members* wherewith to perform the works which were prepared for thee."[20]

c. Stewardship of Possessions

The examination of the lifelong stewardship of goods and *possessions* will continue:

How didst thou employ the *worldly goods* which I lodged in thy hands?

Didst thou use thy *food* ... to preserve thy body in health, in strength and vigour, a fit instrument for the soul?

Didst thou use *apparel*, not to nourish pride or vanity, much less to tempt others to sin, but conveniently and decently...?

In what manner didst thou employ that comprehensive talent, *money*?... Not squandering.... Not hoarding.... But first supplying thy own reasonable wants, together with those of thy family; then restoring the remainder to me, through the poor, whom I had appointed to receive it; looking upon thyself as only one of that number of poor whose wants were to be supplied out of that part of my substance which I had placed in thy hands for this purpose; leaving thee the right of being supplied first, and the blessedness of giving rather than receiving?...

Didst thou employ whatever was pleasing in thy person or address whatever *advantages* thou hadst by education ... for the promoting of virtue?[21]

d. Stewardship of Time

The examination of the lifelong guardianship of usage of *time* will inquire:[22]

Didst thou employ that inestimable talent of time with wariness and circumspection, as duly weighing the value of every moment, and knowing that all were numbered in eternity?

Above all, wast thou a good steward of my grace, preventing, accompanying, and following thee?

Then "well done, good and faithful servant!... Enter thou into the joy of the Lord!" [or the other dreadful sentence].[23]

---

[20]"The Good Steward," B 2:293–95, sec. 3.3–4.
[21]"The Good Steward," B 2:295, sec. 3.5.
[22]EA, B 11:60–62; cf. B 2:286, 296–97; *LJW* 8:270.
[23]"The Good Steward," B 2:296, sec. 3.6.

2. The Vindication of Divine Mercy

In the investigative judgment, God will vindicate his own justice. His moral perfection will be displayed in the "amazing contexture of divine providence." How? By showing in such a plausible way why he permitted evil that the righteous will rejoice with joy unspeakable when its outcomes are made clear.

This vindication displays the wisdom, power, and mercy of God in their precise conjunction: For each free agent "all the circumstances of their life should be placed in open view, together with all their tempers, and all the desires, thoughts, and intents of their hearts. Otherwise how would it appear out of what a depth of sin and misery the grace of God had delivered them?"[24]

On no other basis is a plausible teaching of evil and suffering (theodicy) possible than that the justice of God is finally made clear through all transient ambiguities.[25] For the atoned-for faithful "it will be abundantly sufficient for them that 'all the transgressions which they had committed shall not be once mentioned unto them' to their disadvantage."[26] Their sins are covered by the righteousness of the Son on the cross.

3. The Separation of the Just and Unjust

A great division will take place: Believers will mercifully receive a sentence of acquittal. "All their good desires, intentions, thoughts, all their holy dispositions, will also be then remembered" along with "their sufferings for the name of Christ."[27]

The wicked who have spurned the unmerited grace offered by God will be fairly judged according to their thoughts, words, deeds, and tempers. This includes all of their affections, desires, motives, circumstances. Upon this they will hear the dreadful sentence pronounced.[28]

There is little fascination with damnation as such; the focus is on God's just and providential purpose. There is minimal talk about the specific conditions of reprobation, but these are well known to private individual conscience.[29] The pronouncements on the last day remain fixed and irrevocable, since it is the last day.

C. Of Hell

The text of the homily "Of Hell" is Mark 9:48: "Their worm dieth not" [Homily #73 (1782), B 3:30 – 44; J #73, V:381 – 91].

Even those who most love God do well to consider what has been revealed in Scripture concerning the final destiny of the unrighteous.[30] Jesus made repeated reference to the consequence of sin as final just punishment.

[24]"The Great Assize," B 1:364 – 65, sec. 2.10.
[25]B 2:398 – 99.
[26]"The Great Assize," B 1:365, sec. 2.11; Ezek. 18:22.
[27]"The Great Assize," B 1:366, sec. 2.12; *CH*, B 7:146 – 61.
[28]"The Great Assize," B 1:366, sec. 2.12.
[29]*LJW* 5:167, 270, 344.
[30]*SS* 1:22; 2:412.

The teaching of hell functions as a constraint on the ungodly and as a means of preserving the faithful from sin.[31] Hence this teaching is as pertinent to believers as unbelievers.[32]

Hell is that final condition "where 'their worm dieth not, and the fire is not quenched'" (Mark 9:48). The biblical teaching is "awful and solemn: suitable to His wisdom and justice," differing widely from the idle tales of pagan myths.[33]

1. What the Ungodly Lose

There is a distinction between what the ungodly *lose* and what they *feel*. They lose God. Hell is fundamentally banishment from the presence of God, hence viewed as an absolute deprivation of the good.[34]

The punishment of loss (*poena damni*) occurs when the soul separates from the body of the ungodly. At the moment of death, the unrighteous experience the loss of all senses of pleasure, all sources of gratification. There is no beauty, no light, no music, no friendship. The only inward senses are feelings of shame and loss. The greatest loss is the loss of God. "Depart from me" (Matt. 25:41 NIV).[35]

2. What the Ungodly Feel: Worm and Fire

a. The Worm of Remorse and the Unquenchable Fire: God's Wrath toward Sin

To the punishment of loss is added the punishment of sense, which is expressed in two arresting metaphors: worm and fire. In death, whether buried or cremated, we face either worm or fire. In either case, the earthly worm dies or the fire goes out. But hell is posited as a place where this desolation does not end, where the worm does not die and the fire is not quenched, because God cannot permit unrepented sin in his presence on the last day.

Anticipative intimations of this worming of conscience in present life are guilt, self-condemnation, shame, and remorse that wounds the spirit and unleashes unholy tempers, and hatred of God out of self-loathing. These already give us some idea of the disaster of total separation from God. The worm is the *inner torment* of a guilty conscience.

b. The Fire

The fire is the *outward torment* of material anguish.[36] This is what the unrighteous feel (*poena sensus*). What is lost? The loss of their finite idolatries. Their gods have clay feet. They burn with frustration over the loss of their gods.

The condition is everlasting. The time of choosing is used up. But the fire of

[31]Letter to William Law, J IX:506–8.
[32]"Of Hell," B 3:31–32, pref. 1–3.
[33]"Of Hell," B 3:33, pref. 4; cf. B 1:366–67.
[34]*JJW* 1:139n.; 5:552; *SS* 1:22; 2:412.
[35]"Of Hell," B 3:34–35, sec. 1.1–4; B 4:58–59.
[36]"Of Hell," B 3:40–41, sec. 3.1–2.

God's holy wrath is not consumed. It continues. There is no company in hell, no respite from pain, no interval of relief, no sabbath rest, only uninterrupted night with uninterrupted misery. The term of the sentence is forever.[37] God's purpose is to put an end to sin.

The fire is not to be viewed merely as symbolic but real, yet not necessarily "real" according to our present limited, finite, physical understanding of the ordinary fire.[38] It is an eternal fire, because the Word of judgment is spoken by the eternal God, unlike our temporal angers and remedies.

c. Why So Horrible?

But why does Scripture speak in such horrible terms? There is a providential motive that hopes until the last breath to draw the person toward saving grace. The Holy Spirit wishes to rouse us to repent and believe, and to abstain from evil in this life. This is the pragmatic argument for hell: sin has consequences. Until the last breath, it is remediable.

Those who come to the divine Judge with contrition and saving faith, trusting in his righteousness in Jesus Christ, receive the benefits of paradise: the society of angels, the spirits of just men made perfect, conversing face-to-face with God, drinking forever of the waters of life, and enjoying forever the glory of God. Such thoughts are meant to inspire hope in God, not despair over our misery.[39]

3. Countering William Law's Speculations against Divine Judgment

In this connection, we introduce a telling letter John Wesley wrote to his former mentor William Law [To William Law, January 6, 1756, *LJW* 3:332 – 70; J IV:466 – 509].

a. Whether God Lacks a Capacity for Anger against Sin

In the later writings of William Law, after 1735, Wesley whiffed the stench of corruption of Enlightenment optimism, which deprived God of any capacity for negation or judgment. Wesley understood all too well why preachers might be tempted to preach such "smooth things." But he did not expect it in William Law. Law's view is explicit that there is no punitive justice in God, no divine anger against sin. Here we have his own portrayal of God as an ambivalent, irresolute divine parent who refuses to punish his children, either in this world or the next.[40]

The rejoinder to such soft-headedness is found in the constant testimony of Scripture that "whom the Lord loveth he chasteneth" (Heb. 12:6) and that "the Lord is ... slow to anger, and plenteous in mercy. He will not always chide: neither will

---

37"Of Hell," B 3:42, sec. 3.3.

38B 4:19 – 23; cf. *LJW* 2:98; *SS* 2:412.

39"Of Hell," B 3:42 – 44, sec. 3.3; J VII:234 – 35, 247 – 55.

40On the divine anger against sin, see *LJW* 3:345 – 48; B 1:359 – 66; 2:292 – 96; 3:187 – 88, 400 – 402; 4:141 – 43, 319 – 20.

he keep his anger for ever" (Ps. 103:8 – 9).[41] "Had God never been angry, He could never have been reconciled," Wesley confessed personally. "I know He was angry with me till I believed in the Son of His love; and yet this is no impeachment to His mercy."[42]

b. The Fantasy of Avoidance of Divine Judgment

The sins under judgment are voluntary. The will must collude at some level with the temptation to flout the divine command. This defect of will applies to our cooperation with social sins, psychological habituations that our willing could have avoided, unjust political collusions, and the default of parenting.

Law's view premises the opposite: that God cannot be angry with our defiance of his command. This implies that God has no capacity for justice. For even our natural conscience calls for just law. God's justice cannot be even weaker than our own natural conscience. If God is without capacity for being offended at persistent sin, then there is no way to posit any final judgment whatever, as does Scripture. Hell is the outcome of willfully and persistently offending God's righteousness in our thoughts, words, and deeds. We have been given many opportunities for repentance.

If God cannot do this one thing (discipline the unjust), God cannot do anything. William Law's tendency to bind up the will of God to exclude rejection of disobedience is itself unjust. It runs counter to the elementary teaching of the omnipotence of God. If God cannot, in a metaphorical sense, be "outraged" over man's disobedience to the divine command, then God is misconceived as less than the one we address in prayer as "Almighty." Any sentence that begins with "God cannot" cannot be a reference to the true God.

Wesley quipped to his former mentor William Law, "No hell, no heaven, no revelation."[43] Law had diminished hell to the general notion that "damnation is only that which springs up within you," having all to do with psychological processes and nothing to do with divine justice.

Wesley spoke with Scripture of an all-too-real hell as eternal separation from the source of all good. Whatever path modern Wesleyans have taken, Wesley himself held fast to the clear preaching of Jesus concerning a real hell more horrible than our worst imaginings. When we come up before the final divine judgment, we will see that the real judgment is far more devastating than our most terrible visualizations.

In his letter to Law, Wesley carefully rehearsed the argument of Peter Browne's *Procedure, Extent and Limits of Human Understanding.*[44] This is in order to establish his case that the chief cause of eternal misery will be eternal exclusion from the beatific vision of God.

---

[41]To William Law, *LJW* 3:345 – 51, sec. 2.3; Prov. 13:24; Heb. 2:6 – 8.

[42]Letter to Mary Bishop, February 7, 1778, *LJW* 6:298.

[43]To William Law, *LJW* 3:370, sec. 2.7.

[44]Peter Browne, *Procedure, Extent, and Limits of Human Understanding.* Cf. B 3:350 – 51.

In order to conceive of final judgment, there must be posited the future general resurrection of the just and the unjust. "The eternity of these punishments is revealed as plainly as words can express" in Scripture. This vision of final judgment would not have been included in the sacred text if it had the purpose merely of challenging us while there is time.[45]

"I have now, Sir, delivered my own soul," concluded Wesley, hoping that Mr. Law would come to his senses and renounce "all the high-flown bombast, all the unintelligible jargon of the Mystics, and come back to the plain religion of the Bible, 'We love him, because he first loved us.'"[46]

D. The New Creation

Wesley's homily "The New Creation" deals with the text of Revelation 21:5: "Behold, I make all things new" [Homily #64 (1785), B 2:500–510; J #64, V:288–96].

The vision of the future in the Revelation of John presents a strange scene, remote from all our familiar sensibilities and natural apprehensions.[47] The text points to a mystery beyond finite knowing. Yet we must try to understand it as much as possible through our spiritual senses, "interpreting Scripture by Scripture, according to the analogy of faith."[48]

1. New Heavens, New Earth

The new heaven and earth are wrongly identified by some with a particular period of human history in which the riches of Constantine were poured upon Christendom ("a miserable way ... of making void the whole counsel of God"). The post-Constantinian premise is too simple. Rather, Scripture refers to the end of this world and the beginning of the eternal age, to "things that will come to pass when this world is no more."[49]

Biblical cosmology envisioned not a single heaven, but heavens, not only the heaven of air (the sky), or a higher heaven of stars (which we can to some degree see), but also a transcendent heaven where God dwells, which will not be changed when the other heavens are renovated.[50]

The new heavens and the new earth are a complete reversal of the whole history of sin. After the general resurrection and final judgment, a new beginning is made, which corresponds with the new creation of the resurrected life of Christian believers.

---

[45]To William Law, *LJW* 3:368–70, sec. 2.7, quoting P. Browne, *Human Understanding*, 351; Letter of February 18, 1756, to Samuel Furly. On hell see *LJW*, B 1:227–28; 2:133; 3:30–44, 168, 263; 4:33, 58–59, 665–68.

[46]To William Law, 2.7, *LJW* 3:370.

[47]"The New Creation," B 2:501, sec. 1.

[48]"The New Creation," B 2:501, sec. 2; see also "Justification by Faith," sec. 2; and "The End of Christ's Coming," 3.5.

[49]"The New Creation," B 2:501–52, sec. 4.

[50]"The New Creation," B 2:502–3, secs. 5–9; *CH*, B 7:161–76; for further reference to heaven, see B 2:289–90, 392; 4:116, 288–89.

2. The General Restoration of Creation

a. An Integrated Condition of Holiness and Happiness

A universal restoration will follow a universal destruction, a new age to succeed this present age.[51] In the new heaven will dwell righteousness, where all will be perfected in "exact order and harmony."[52] This is a picture of the postfallen world, where God will make a new start of a new creation.

The present physical elements are not brought to nothing but rather transformed and divested of their power to destroy:

the air will be refined,
the water unpolluted,
fire will no longer destroy or consume but purify so as to "retain its vivifying power,"
the earth will be made perfect,
where all the elements are being "changed as to their qualities, although not as to their nature."[53]

This transmutation will elicit "a far nobler state of things, such as it has not yet entered into the heart of men to conceive."[54]

The Paradise lost in the fall will be restored. Wesley described this new physical and animal creation as a world of abundant flora and fauna: a myriad of flowers, the wolf indeed lying down with the lamb, all forms of animal creation, having been delivered from the "deplorable effects of Adam's apostasy," abiding together in peace.[55]

Based on scriptural texts, Wesley further conjectured that the lower region of the air will no longer be agitated by hurricanes, tempests, and terrifying meteors.[56] On earth there will be no deserts, weeds, bogs, thorns, poisonous plants, or uncomfortable extremes of temperature. Hopes of the modern ecologist for the future of nature wilt in the presence of Wesley's sweeping descriptions, which simply follow plain sense biblical precedent.

b. Restoration of the Divine Image in Humanity

Perfect love, the restoration of the divine image in humanity within history, is an anticipatory expression of the final restoration beyond history.[57]

The reign of Christ has already begun in the present dispensation. The believer tastes already the actual impartation of the glory to come. Present salvation is the "earnest" of final salvation.[58] Earnest is meant in its anticipatory sense of a down

[51]See also B 2:455 – 50, 500 – 510; 9:108, 370, 407; *CH*, B 7:81, 85, 118 – 23, 251 – 55, 338 – 39, 536 – 37. On the destruction of death, see B 2:482.

[52]"The New Creation," B 2:504, sec. 10; cf. B 4:116.

[53]"The New Creation," B 2:504, sec. 10.

[54]"The New Creation," B 2:503, sec. 7; *LJW* 6:187; on cosmic redemption, see B 2:455 – 50, 500 – 510.

[55]"The New Creation," B 2:509, sec. 17.

[56]"The New Creation," B 2:503, sec. 8; see also "God's Approbation of His Works," 1.10.

[57]B 1:57, 76; 3:175; 2:455 – 50, 500 – 510; *CH*, B 7:118 – 23, 251 – 55, 536 – 37.

[58]"The New Creation," B 2:501, secs. 1 – 4.

payment, such as in our modern term "earnest money." Salvation on earth anticipates the salvation of the whole of nature and history. Resurrected human life, refashioned in the divine image, will become like the angels in swiftness, agility, and strength.[59]

For the resurrected righteous, there will be no more death, sorrow, pain, or sin, but "an intimate, an uninterrupted union with God; a constant communion with the Father and his Son Jesus Christ, through the Spirit; a continual enjoyment of the Three-in-One God, and of all the creatures in him."[60] The redeemed will be restored to "an unmixed state of holiness and happiness far superior to that which Adam enjoyed in paradise."[61]

E. Conclusion

In this chapter, we have explored Wesley's understanding of the meaning of universal history, including the future of personal continuance of the soul after death and the body in the resurrection, and in final judgment and the new creation, a fitting end to this volume on Christ and Salvation.

In the third volume, we will turn to Wesley's practical, pastoral teaching on the church, the ministry, care of souls, the care of the family, the worshiping community, the ministry of Word and sacrament, the unity of the body of Christ, and pastoral leadership. Soul care is especially focused in the care for the neighbor. The "neighbor," in its original Greek, refers to the next one at hand, the one now nearest to you.

Further Reading on Eschatology

Collins, Kenneth. *A Faithful Witness: John Wesley's Homiletical Theology*, 189 – 204. Wilmore, KY: Wesleyan Heritage, 1993.

Cubie, David L. "Eschatology from a Theological and Historical Perspective." In *The Spirit and the New Age*, edited by R. L. Shelton and A. R. G. Deasley, 357 – 414. Anderson, IN: Warner, 1986.

Cushman, Robert Earl. "Salvation for All: John Wesley and Calvinism." In *Methodism*, edited by W. K. Anderson, 103 – 15. New York: Methodist Publishing House, 1947.

Downes, Cyril. "The Eschatological Doctrines of John and Charles Wesley." PhD diss., University of Edinburgh, 1974.

Dunning, H. Ray. *The Second Coming: A Wesleyan Approach to the Doctrine of Last Things*. Kansas City: Beacon Hill, 1995.

Harper, Steve. *John Wesley's Theology Today* Chap. 8, 107ff. Grand Rapids: Zondervan, 1983.

[59]"The New Creation," B 2:509, sec. 17; "The General Deliverance," 1.5.

[60]"The New Creation," B 2:510, sec. 18; "On the Trinity," sec. 17.

[61]"The New Creation," B 2:510, sec. 18; cf. B 2:39 – 40, 475 – 76; "Justification by Faith," 1.4; *LJW* 3:338; 4:98. On the golden chain of pardon, holiness, and heaven, see B 3:149 – 50.

"John Wesley a Premillenarian," *Christian Workers Magazine* 17 (1916): 96–101.

Lindström, Harald. "Sanctification and Final Salvation." In Robert W. Burtner and Robert E. Chiles, *A Compend of Wesley's Theology*, 273ff. Nashville: Abingdon, 1954.

Marino, Bruce. "Through a Glass Darkly: The Eschatological Vision of John Wesley." PhD diss., Drew University, 1994.

Mercer, Jerry. "The Destiny of Man in John Wesley's Eschatology." *WTJ* 2 (1967): 56–65.

Monk, Robert. *John Wesley: His Puritan Heritage*, 122ff. Nashville: Abingdon, 1966.

Rall, Harris F. *Was John Wesley a Premillennialist?* 12–13. Toronto: Methodist Book and Publishing House, 1921.

Strawson, William. "Wesley's Doctrine of the Last Things." *LQHR* 184 (1959): 240–49.

West, Nathaniel. *John Wesley and Premillennialism.* Louisville: Pentecostal Publishing Co., 1894.

Williams, Colin. "Eschatology." In *John Wesley's Theology* Today, 191ff. Nashville: Abingdon, 1960.

Wilson, David D. "The Importance of Hell for John Wesley." *PWHS* 34 (1963): 12–16.

Alphabetical Correlation of the Sermons in the Jackson and Bicentennial Editions

The Bicentennial edition is represented by B. The Jackson edition is represented by J. Sermon numbers are often preceded by the pound sign (#). An asterisk (*) indicates that the homily was wrongly attributed to Mr. Wesley in at least one of its early editions, with the correct author supplied, or has varying titles or numbers in different editions.

The Almost Christian (#2, B 1:131 – 41 = #2, J V:17 – 25) — Acts 26:28

Awake, Thou That Sleepest (#3, B 1:142 – 58 = #3, J V:25 – 36) — Ephesians 5:14

A Call to Backsliders (#86, B 3:201 – 26 = #86, J VI:514 – 27) — Psalm 77:7 – 8

The Case of Reason Impartially Considered (#70, B 2:587 – 600 = #70, J VI:350 – 60) — 1 Corinthians 14:20

The Catholic Spirit (#39, B 2:79 – 96 = #2, J V:492 – 504) — 2 Kings 10:15

*The Cause and Cure of Earthquakes (by Charles Wesley — #129, Jackson ed. only, VII:386 – 99) — Psalm 46:8

The Causes of the Inefficiency of Christianity (#122, B 4:85 – 96 = #122, J VII:281 – 90) — Jeremiah 8:22

A Caution against Bigotry (#38, B 2:61 – 78 = #38, J V:479 – 92) — Mark 9:38 – 39

Christian Perfection (#40, B 2:97 – 124 = #40, J VI:1 – 22) — Philippians 3:12

The Circumcision of the Heart (#17, B 1 398 – 414 = #17, J V:202 – 12) — Romans 2:29

The Cure of Evil Speaking (#49, B 2:251 – 62 = #49, J VI:114 – 24) — Matthew 18:15 – 17

The Danger of Increasing Riches (#131, B 4:177 – 86 = #131, J VII:355 – 62) — Psalm 62:10

The Danger of Riches (#87, B 3:227 – 46 = #87, J VII:1 – 15) — 1 Timothy 6:9

Death and Deliverance (#133, B 4:204 – 14; not in Jackson)

Dives and Lazarus (#115, B 4:4 – 18 = The Rich Man and Lazarus, #112, J VII:244 – 55) — Luke 16:31

The Duty of Constant Communion (#101, B 3:427 – 39 = #101, J VII:147 – 57) — Luke 22:19

The Duty of Reproving Our Neighbor (#65, B 2:511 – 20 = #65, J VI:296 – 304) — Leviticus 19:17

The End of Christ's Coming (#62, B

2:471 – 84 = #62, J VI:267 – 77) — 1 John 3:8

The First Fruits of the Spirit (#8, B 1:233 – 47 = #8, J V:87 – 97) — Romans 8:1

Free Grace (#110, B 3:542 – 63 = #110, J VII:373 – 86) — Romans 8:32

The General Deliverance (#60, B 2:436 – 50 = #60, J VI:241 – 52) — Romans 8:19 – 22

The General Spread of the Gospel (#63, B 2:485 – 99 = #63, J VI:277 – 88) — Isaiah 11:9

God's Approbation of His Works (#56, B 2:387 – 99 = #56, J VI:206 – 15) — Genesis 1:31

God's Love to Fallen Man (#59, B 2:422 – 35 = #59, J VI:231 – 40) — Romans 5:15

The Good Steward (#51, B 2:281 – 99 = #51, J VI:136 – 49) — Luke 16:2

The Great Assize (#15, B 1:354 – 75 = #15, J V:171 – 85) — Romans 14:10

The Great Privilege of Those That Are Born of God (#19, B 1:431 – 43 = #19, J V:223 – 33) — 1 John 3:9

Heavenly Treasure in Earthen Vessels (#129, B 4:161 – 67 = #129, J VII:344 – 48) — 2 Corinthians 4:7

Heaviness through Manifold Temptations (#47, B 2:222 – 35 = #47, J VI:91 – 103) — 1 Peter 1:6

Hell (#73, B 3:30 – 44 = #73, J VI:381 – 91) — Mark 9:48

Human Life a Dream (#124, B 4:108 – 19 = #124, J VII:318 – 25) — Psalm 73:20

The Imperfection of Human Knowledge (#69, B 2:567 – 86 = #69, J VI:337 – 50) — 1 Corinthians 13:9

The Important Question (#84, B 3:181 – 98 = #84, J VI:493 – 505) — Matthew 16:26

In What Sense We Are to Leave the World (#81, B 3:141 – 55 = #81, J VI:464 – 75) — 2 Corinthians 6:17 – 18

An Israelite Indeed (#90, B 3:278 – 89 = #90, J VII:37 – 45) — John 1:47

Justification by Faith (#5, B 1:181 – 99 = #5, J V:53 – 64) — Romans 4:5

The Late Work of God in North America (#113, B 3:594 – 609 = #131, J VII:409 – 29) — Ezekiel 1:16

The Law Established through Faith, 1 (#35, B 2:20 – 32 = #35, J V:447 – 57) — Romans 3:31

The Law Established through Faith, 2 (#36, B 2:33 – 43 = #36, J V:458 – 66) — Romans 3:31

Lord Our Righteousness (#20, B 1:444 – 65 = #20, J V:234 – 46) — Jeremiah 23:6

Marks of the New Birth (#18, B 1:415 – 30 = #18, J V:212 – 23) — John 3:8

The Means of Grace (#16, B 1:376 – 97 = #16, J V:185 – 201) — Malachi 3:7

The Ministerial Office (#121, B 4:72 – 84 = #115, J IV:72 – 84) — Hebrews 5:4

More Excellent Way (#89, B 3:262 – 77 = #89, J VII:26 – 37) — 1 Corinthians 12:31

The Mystery of Iniquity (#61, B 2:451 – 70 = #61, J VI:253 – 67) — 2 Thessalonians 2:7

National Sins and Miseries (#111, B 3:564 – 76 = #111, J VII:400 – 408) — 2 Samuel 24:17

The Nature of Enthusiasm (#37, B 2:44 – 60 = #37, J V:467 – 78) — Acts 26:24

The New Birth (#45, B 2:186 – 201 = #45, J VI:65 – 77) — John 3:7

New Creation (#64, B 2:500 – 510 = #64, J VI:288 – 96) — Revelation 21:5

Of the Church (#74, B 3:45 – 57 = #74, J VI:392 – 401) — Ephesians 4:1 – 6

Of Evil Angels (#72, B 3:16 – 29 = #72, J VI:370 – 80) — Ephesians 6:12

Of Former Times (#102, B 3:440 – 53 = #102, J VII:157 – 66) — Ecclesiastes 7:10

Of Good Angels (#71, B 3:3 – 15 = #71, J VI:361 – 70) — Hebrews 1:14

On Attending the Church Service (#104, B 3:464 – 78 = #104, J VII:174 – 85) — 1 Samuel 2:17

On Charity (#91, B 3:290 – 307 = #91, J VII:45 – 57) — 1 Corinthians 13:1 – 3

On Conscience (#105, B 3:478 – 90 = #105, J VII:186 – 94) — 2 Corinthians 1:12

On Corrupting the Word of God (#137, B 4:244 – 51 = #137, J VII:468 – 73) — 2 Corinthians 2:17

On the Death of Mr. Whitefield (#53, B 2:325 – 48 = #53, #133, J VI:167 – 82) — Numbers 20:10

On the Death of Rev. Mr. John Fletcher (#133, B 3:610 – 29 = #133; J VII:431 – 52, 1785) — Psalm 37:37

On the Deceitfulness of the Human Heart (#128, B 4:149 – 60 = #128, J VII:335 – 43) — Jeremiah 17:9

On the Discoveries of Faith (#117, B 4:28 – 38; #117, J VII:231 – 38) — Hebrews 11:1

On Dissipation (#79, B 3:115 – 25 = #79, J VI:444 – 52) — 1 Corinthians 7:35

On Divine Providence (#67, B 2:534 – 50 = #67, J VI:313 – 25) — Luke 12:7

On Dress (#88, B 3:247 – 61 = #88, J VII:15 – 26) — 1 Peter 3:3 – 4

On the Education of Children (#95, B 3:347 – 60 = #95, J VII:86 – 98) — Proverbs 22:6

On Eternity (#54, B 2:358 – 72 = #54, J VI:189 – 98) — Psalm 90:2

On Faith (#106, B 3:491 – 501 = #106, J VII:195 – 202) — Hebrews 11:6

On Faith (#132, B 4:187 – 200 = #122, J VII:326 – 35) — Hebrews 11:1

On the Fall of Man (#57, B 2:400 – 412 = #57, J VI:215 – 24) — Genesis 3:19

On Family Religion (#94, B 3:333 – 46 = #94, J VII:76 – 86) — Joshua 24:15

On Friendship with the World (#80, B 3:126 – 40 = #80, J VI:452 – 63) — James 4:4

On God's Vineyard (#107, B 3:502 – 17 = #107, J VII:203 – 13) — Isaiah 5:4

*On Grieving the Holy Spirit (by William Tilly — #137, Jackson ed. only, J VII:485 – 92) — Ephesians 4:30

*On the Holy Spirit (by John Gambold — #141, Jackson ed. only, VII:508 – 20) — 2 Corinthians 3:17

On Knowing Christ after the Flesh (#123, B 4:97 – 106 = #123, J VII:291 – 96) — 2 Corinthians 5:16

On Laying the Foundation of the New Chapel (#112, B 3:577 – 93 = #112, J VII:419 – 30) — Numbers 23:23

On Living without God (#130, B 4:168 – 76 = #130, J VII:349 – 54) — Ephesians 2:12

On Love (#149, B 4:378 – 88 = #149, J VII:492 – 99) — 1 Corinthians 13:3

On Mourning for the Dead (#136, B 4:236 – 43 = #136, J VII:463 – 68) — 2 Samuel 12:23

On Obedience to Parents (#96, B 3:361 – 72 = #96, J VII:98 – 108) — Colossians 3:20

On Obedience to Pastors (#97, B 3:373 – 83 = #97, J VII:108 – 16) — Hebrews 13:17

On the Omnipresence of God (#118, B 4:39 – 47 = #118, J VII:238 – 44) — Jeremiah 23:24

On Patience (#83, B 3:169 – 80 = #83, J VI:484 – 92) — James 1:4

On Perfection (#76, B 3:70 – 87 = #76, J VI:411 – 24) — Hebrews 6:1

On Pleasing all Men (#100, B 3:415 – 26 = #100, J VII:139 – 46) — Romans 15:2

On Predestination (#58, B 2:413 – 21 = #VI:225 – 30) — Romans 8:29 – 30

On Redeeming the Time (#93, B 3:322 – 32 = #93, J VII:67 – 75) — Ephesians 5:16

*On the Resurrection of the Dead (by Benjamin Calamy; see appendix B of B 4:528 – 30 = #137, Jackson edition only, VII:474 – 85) — 1 Corinthians 15:35

On Riches (#108, B 3:518 – 28 = #108, J VII:214 – 22) — Matthew 19:24

On Schism (#75, B 3:58 – 69 = #75, J VI:401 – 10) — 1 Corinthians 12:25

On Sin in Believers (#13, B 1:314 – 34 = #13, J V:144 – 56) — 2 Corinthians 5:17

On a Single Eye (#125, B 4:120 – 30 = #125, J VII:297 – 305) — Matthew 6:22 – 23

On Temptation (#82, B 2:156 – 68 = #82, J VI:175 – 84) — 1 Corinthians 10:13

On the Trinity (#55, B 2:373 – 86 = #55, J VI:199 – 206) — 1 John 5:7

On Visiting the Sick (#98, B 3:384 – 98 = #98, J VII:117 – 27) — Matthew 25:36

On the Wedding Garment (#127, B 4:139 – 48 = #127, J VII:311 – 17) — Matthew 22:12

On Working Out Our Own Salvation (#85, B 3:199 – 209 = #85, J VI:506 – 13) — Philippians 2:12 – 13

On Worldly Folly (#126, B 4:131 – 38 = #126, J VII:305 – 11) — Luke 12:20

On Zeal (#92, B 3:308 – 21 = #92, J VII:57 – 67) — Galatians 4:18

Origin, Nature, Property, and Use of Law (#34, B 2:1 – 19; #34, J V:433 – 46) — Romans 7:12

Original Sin (#44, B 2:170 – 85 = #44, J VI:54 – 65) — Genesis 6:5

Prophets and Priests (#121, B 4:72 – 84 = The Ministerial Office, #115, J IV:72 – 84) — Hebrews 5:4

Public Diversions Denounced (#143, B 4:318 – 28 = #143, J VII:500 – 508) — Amos 3:6

Reformation of Manners (#52, B 2:300 – 324 = #52, J VI:149 – 67) — Psalm 94:16

The Repentance of Believers (#14, B 1:335 – 53 = #14, J V:156 – 70) — Mark 1:15

The Reward of Righteousness (#99, B 3:399 – 414 = #99, J VII:127 – 38) — Matthew 25:34

*The Rich Man and Lazarus (#115, see Dives and Lazarus, B 4:4 – 18 = #112, J VII:244 – 55) — Luke 16:31

The Righteousness of Faith (#6, B 1:200 – 216 = #6, J V:65 – 76) — Romans 10:5 – 8

Salvation by Faith (#1, B 1:117 – 30 = #1, J V:7 – 16) — Ephesians 2:8

Satan's Devices (#42, B 2:138 – 52 = #42, J VI:32 – 43) — 2 Corinthians 2:11

Scriptural Christianity (#4, B 1:159 – 80 = #4, J V:37 – 52) — Acts 4:31

The Scripture Way of Salvation (#43, B 2:153 – 69 = #43, J VI:43 – 54) — Ephesians 2:8

Self-Denial (#48, B 2:236 – 59 = #48, J VI:103 – 14) — Luke 9:23

Sermon on the Mount, 1 (#21, B 1:466 – 87 = #21, J V:247 – 61) — Matthew 5:1 – 4

Sermon on the Mount, 2 (#22, B 1:488 – 509 = #22, J V:262 – 77) — Matthew 5:5 – 7

Bicentennial Volume Titles Published to Date

Note: Volume 1 was published in 1984. Subsequently, ten more volumes have been published. As of this date of publication, nineteen Bicentennial volumes remain to be published. They are marked with an asterisk (*). Here we have used the Jackson, Sugden, Telford, Curnock, and other editions to supplement the preferred Bicentennial edition.

1. Sermons 1 – 33
2. Sermons 34 – 70
3. Sermons 71 – 114
4. Sermons 115 – 51
*5. Explanatory Notes upon the New Testament I
*6. Explanatory Notes upon the New Testament II
7. A Collection of Hymns for the Use of the People Called Methodist
*8. Forms of Worship and Prayer
9. The Methodist Societies, History, Nature, and Design
*10. The Methodist Societies: The Conference
11. Appeals to Men of Reason and Religion and Certain Related Open Letters
*12. Doctrinal Writings: Theological Treatises
*13. Doctrinal Writings: The Defense of Christianity
*14. Pastoral and Instructional Writings I
*15. Pastoral and Instructional Writings II
*16. Editorial Work
*17. Natural Philosophy and Medicine
18. Journals and Diaries I
19. Journals and Diaries II
20. Journals and Diaries III
21. Journals and Diaries IV
22. Journals and Diaries V
23. Journals and Diaries VI
24. Journals and Diaries VII
25. Letters I
*26. Letters II
*27. Letters III
*28. Letters III
*29. Letters IV
*30. Letters V
*31. Letters VI
*32. Letters VII
*33. Bibliography of the Publications of John and Charles Wesley Letters VIII
*34. Miscellanea and General Index

Subject Index

G

H

I

Scripture Index

Share Your Thoughts

With the Author: Your comments will be forwarded to the author when you send them to *zauthor@zondervan.com.*

With Zondervan: Submit your review of this book by writing to *zreview@zondervan.com.*

Free Online Resources at

www.zondervan.com

Zondervan AuthorTracker: Be notified whenever your favorite authors publish new books, go on tour, or post an update about what's happening in their lives at www.zondervan.com/authortracker.

Daily Bible Verses and Devotions: Enrich your life with daily Bible verses or devotions that help you start every morning focused on God. Visit www.zondervan.com/newsletters.

Free Email Publications: Sign up for newsletters on Christian living, academic resources, church ministry, fiction, children's resources, and more. Visit www.zondervan.com/newsletters.

Zondervan Bible Search: Find and compare Bible passages in a variety of translations at www.zondervanbiblesearch.com.

Other Benefits: Register to receive online benefits like coupons and special offers, or to participate in research.